Plato's *Euthydemus*

Plato's *Euthydemus*

Analysis of What Is
and
Is Not Philosophy

THOMAS H. CHANCE

UNIVERSITY OF CALIFORNIA PRESS
Berkeley   Los Angeles   Oxford

University of California Press
Berkeley and Los Angeles, California

University of California Press, Ltd.
Oxford, England

© 1992 by
The Regents of the University of California

Library of Congress Cataloging-in-Publication Data

Chance, Thomas.
  Plato's Euthydemus : analysis of what is and is not philosophy
/ Thomas Chance.
      p.   cm.
  Includes bibliographical references.
  ISBN 0-520-07754-7 (alk. paper)
    1. Plato. Euthydemus.   2. Philosophy.   3. Methodology.   4. Logic.
  5. Reasoning. I. Title
  B369.C43 1992
  160—dc20   91-25519
                                                         CIP

Printed in the United States of America
9 8 7 6 5 4 3 2 1

To My Teachers of Greek in Berkeley
Elroy L. Bundy   W. Gerson Rabinowitz

CONTENTS

Acknowledgments   xi

PROLOGUE   1

Obstacles to the Study of Plato's *Euthydemus*   3

On the Literary Form of the Dialogue   13

Socrates' Opening Conversation with Crito   15

Statement of Purpose   17

1   THE FIRST ERISTIC DISPLAY   22

The Protreptic Restrictions and Criterion   22

The Arguments   26
    Are those who learn the wise or the ignorant?
    (E1 and D1)   28
    Do those who learn learn what they know or
    what they do not know? (E2 and D2)   34

Inescapable Questions (Ἄφυκτα Ἐρωτήματα)   40

On the Equivocal Use of Μανθάνειν   47

Conclusion   52

2   SOCRATES' PROTREPTIC MODEL   54

Kleinias' Initiation into the Mysteries of Philosophy   55

Kleinias Begins to Climb the Ladder   65

On Wisdom, the One Good   72

Conclusion   75

3   THE SECOND ERISTIC DISPLAY   78

On Becoming Wise (D3)   81

On the Impossibility of Falsehood (E4 and E5)   86

On Speaking Badly of the Bad (D6)   92

Interlude   95

On the Impossibility of Contradiction (D7)   97

The Refuters Refuted   100
  On whether phrases have sense (D8)   104

Conclusion   107

4   THE PROTREPTIC CONTINUES   110

The Production and Use Criterion   111

The Art of Logic-production   114

Dialectic   118

Socrates' Central Conversation with Crito   122

The Royal Art   124

Conclusion   128

5   THE THIRD ERISTIC DISPLAY   130

Part One   130

Socrates Already Possesses the Sought-after Knowledge
  (E9)   131

Turnabout Is Fair Play   136

Socrates Knows All Things Always (E10)   141

Socrates' One Little Question   154

Transitional Interlude: The Hydra and the Crab   156

Part Two   157

On Family Relationships (D11)   158

The Eristification of Ktesippus   160
  A father is the father of all (K12)   161
  Ktesippus beats his father, the dog (D13)   163
  On the need to possess many goods (E14)   164
  On having gold "in" oneself (D15)   166
  On things capable of sight (E16)   168
  Speaking of the silent and silence of the
    speaking (D17 and E17)   170
  Conclusion   173

Eristic in the Treatment of the Forms (D18)   175

It Is Fitting to Cook the Cook (D19)   183

Socrates Can Sell or Sacrifice His Zeus (D20)   186

Is Heracles Puppax? (D21)   189

Conclusion   189

EPILOGUE   194

The Victory Celebration   194
    The praise   195
    The counsel   198

Socrates' Final Conversation with Crito   199

Conclusion   206

Appendix I. The Rhetorical and Dramatic Divisions of
the *Euthydemus*   211

Appendix II. Catalogue of Eristic Arguments   213

Appendix III. On Μάθησις   215

Notes   219

Select Bibliography   279

ACKNOWLEDGMENTS

The opportunity to study with Elroy Bundy for the last three years of his life marks that period of my own when I made the decisive turn toward the study of things ancient. His death would have left me without a teacher, had I not had the good fortune to read Plato's Greek for more than a decade under the direction of Gerson Rabinowitz, with whom I first read the *Euthydemus* during the winter and spring of 1984. The results of that reading came to form my original manuscript, which I completed by the summer of 1986.

Convinced that my fundamental thesis was correct, but knowing that I had to prove it in greater detail, I began a second reading of the dialogue in 1987 with Kenneth Quandt, who proved to be the perfect interlocutor with whom to share my project. For more than a year we read and discussed the *Euthydemus* in a way that would, I'm sure, please our teachers. Every page of this book has benefited from his forceful and enthusiastic criticism.

For reading and commenting on my manuscript, I want to thank Kenneth Dorter, Mark McPherran, and especially A. A. Long, who supported my project from its inception.

For their friendship along the way, I thank Hayden Ausland, Scott and Nancy Bradbury, Patricia Bulman, Frank DeRose, Charles Taliaferro, and Steven White.

For assisting me at all stages of production, I thank Mary Lamprech of the University of California Press.

Berkeley 1991

PROLOGUE

The *Euthydemus* has attained an unwarranted distinction in Plato's corpus: despite its obvious length, its striking artistic merits, and the broad range of topics that it treats, it has been neglected more than any other important dialogue. Of course, such scholars as Shorey, Friedländer, and Guthrie have not excluded the *Euthydemus* from their general surveys, and most comprehensive studies of Plato do contain at least a short chapter assigned to the dialogue. But it cannot be denied that the *Euthydemus* has failed to inspire much in the way of a response from scholars of Greek philosophy, and in fact we shall look in vain for a single published work in English devoted exclusively to a systematic and coherent interpretation of this strange yet fascinating dialogue.[1] If, for example, we compare the sheer amount of exegetical material that has been compiled on the *Euthydemus* with that on the *Meno*, a work with which it is often compared, then we shall find a remarkable disparity. But when a comparison also reveals that such works as the *Ion, Charmides, Laches,* and *Lysis*, shorter dialogues intentionally limited in philosophical scope, have each received more attention from scholars over the last thirty years than the *Euthydemus* has over the entire history of Platonic interpretation, then it becomes difficult not to wonder at the cause.

To grasp the seriousness of this problem with some concreteness, we need to introduce a few examples. If not the finest, then certainly one of the finest and most thorough studies on Plato's thought to come out of England in this century is I. M. Crombie's two-volume *Examination of Plato's Doctrines*. Yet a search of his work will reveal that he has devoted less than four pages of analysis to this dialogue.[2] Are we to conclude from this fact that the *Euthydemus* doesn't contribute significantly to Plato's doctrines? We may pardon Crombie for passing over the *Euthydemus* because this dialogue doesn't offer anything approaching an unambiguous package of doctrine that can be removed from it and handed over. In this work Plato has chosen to concentrate primarily on conversational procedures, both dialectical and eristical, and not on the results obtained from the exercise of these procedures on a subject matter. So perhaps we should expect to find the dialogue figuring prominently in discussions on method rather than doctrine. Yet it is hardly an exaggeration to say that the *Euthydemus*, far from being the locus for debate on method, has for the most part failed to figure in such discussions at all.[3] And what is stranger still is that this dismissal of the *Euthydemus* has occurred at a time when secondary literature on Platonic method has proliferated at a staggering rate, when numerous studies have traced with much thoroughness and accuracy the most minute developments in the Socratic elenchus, in Socratic induction, in the role of hypothesis and diairesis—in short, in almost all aspects of Plato's method. In fact, if the *Euthydemus* does find its way into scholarly studies, it is usually relegated to something less than a subordinate position, where it can be found cited among the footnotes, providing at best evidence to confirm or to deny this or that view on the development of Plato's method. And here too an example readily comes to mind: no one has written more extensively or carried out his analysis with more refinement and accuracy on the topic of Platonic method than Gregory Vlastos, and yet throughout his long career he has tended to steer clear of any serious engagement with this dialogue.[4] Are we to conclude from this fact that the *Euthydemus* doesn't contribute significantly to Plato's method?

What about Euthydemus himself, for whom this dialogue is titled, and his brother Dionysodorus? How have they fared in the history of philosophical thought? Diels and Kranz do not list them among the sophists in volume two of *Fragmente der Vorsokratiker*.[5] They are absent from one of the largest bibliographies yet compiled on sophistic literature, C. J. Classen's *Sophistic*, although a catalogue of scholarly information has been provided for such impressive figures as Alkidamus, Euenos, Lykophron, Phaleas, and Xeniades.[6] And in volume three of his *History of Greek Philosophy*, W. K. C. Guthrie does not include the pair among "The Men" whom he lists as the sophists.[7] So who are these two clowns, whom the learned world seems inclined to ignore, and yet whose historical existence cannot be denied?[8] In the pages that follow, we shall gain a close familiarity with this two-headed antithesis to the genuine philosopher, as well as with other problems that pertain to the interpretation of this dialogue.

OBSTACLES TO THE STUDY OF PLATO'S *EUTHYDEMUS*

It is unbecoming to indulge at greater length in the easy sport of demonstrating that the *Euthydemus* has been ignored. What can we say then about the much more difficult question of why this is so? One reason for the dialogue's relative obscurity is its persistent ability to resist the efforts of those who must fix its place in the conjectural chronology of Plato's writings before they can feel confident enough to enter upon its analysis. And here again the star example is Gregory Vlastos. He is keenly aware of what importance the dating of this work has for his own vision of the development of Plato's thought. In fact, in order to accommodate the *Euthydemus* to that vision, he has felt the need to open up another category between the early and middle dialogues, which he calls the "transitional," so that he can place the work, as his theory requires, between the *Gorgias* and the *Meno*.[9] Yet it may come as some surprise to those unschooled in the thorny problems of dating Plato's works that, in the nineteenth century, scholars just as responsible and respected as Gregory Vlastos were equally convinced that the dialogue was late, that it had more in common with the *Phaedrus* and *Theaetetus* than with the *Lysis* and *Hippias Major,* and that it could even have been composed after the *Sophist.*[10] And it may come as an even greater surprise that almost a century ago Paul Shorey had already articulated with precision the dilemma that can face anyone who approaches the *Euthydemus* armed with the developmental hypothesis:

> To the partisans of development the dialogue offers a dilemma. Either this mature logic must be assigned to an early work, or a late work may display comic verve of style and engage in a purely dramatic, apparently unsuccessful, Socratic search for the political art.[11]

At present we are not in a position to appreciate at its real value what Shorey has said. But to his remarks we shall return at the proper time, after we have completed our analysis of the dialogue. For now, our immediate task is simply to illustrate that the choice between the apparently irreconcilable opposites "early" and "late" has tended to lead interpreters of this dialogue to embrace one horn of the dilemma and to surrender the other. Last century, for example, Henry Sidgwick was so captivated by the mature logic of the *Euthydemus* that he

willingly accepted the late alternative. Not only did he argue that the
dialogue was composed with the *Sophist,* but he thought that it could
provide the evidence for a reappraisal of the role of the eristic sophist
in that movement; and he concluded that the "eristic" represented a
distinctly different type of sophist, arising from the pupils of Socrates
himself, and found only in the late works when the sophist of the
early dialogues "was gradually shrinking back into the rhetorician out
of which he had expanded."[12] For Sidgwick, the comic verve of the
dialogue presented no difficulty, for he viewed it as perfectly consistent with Plato's urge to present "a caricature of the Megarian Logic."
But in working out his position, he naturally passed over in silence all
the features that have now convinced more recent scholars that the
Euthydemus is unsuccessful, aporetic, and composed before Plato
moved into the middle phase of his development.

   In this century, and especially over the last fifty years, there has
been an increasing tendency for British and American scholars to fix
the position of the *Euthydemus* as "late early" or "early middle." What
this means in practice is that they have now come to place the dialogue
before the *Meno.*[13] We may suspect, however, that this "placing" of the
work is not just a tentative hypothesis but an unquestioned assumption that continues to shape and to control much inquiry into the dialogue, if we direct our attention to the silence that now tends to super-
vene upon its "late" or "mature" features.[14] After a casual nod in the
direction of the dialogue's "rollicking comedy" and "eristic foolery,"
the exponents of the early hypothesis inevitably come to stress the
work's unsuccessful, aporetic qualities. For example, Guthrie finds
"the most advanced piece of Platonic thinking in the dialogue" precisely where Shorey suggested he would find it, in Socrates' abortive
search for the political art.[15] Unable, as he admits, to observe anything
in the *Euthydemus* that "takes us beyond the position of the *Lysis* or
Hippias Major," Guthrie cannot see amid the eristic clowning of the
dialogue what Harold Cherniss has referred to as "the unmistakable
reference to *transcendent ideas* which it contains."[16] In effect, the partisans of the early hypothesis solve the dilemma between "early" and
"late" by denying that the *Euthydemus* exhibits "mature logic," and the
outcome of this choice has been to divert attention away from what
Sidgwick and Shorey understood to be mature, namely, Plato's treatment of eristic.[17] And herein lies the weakness of any case that attempts to establish an early date. For the evidence that can be culled

from Plato's scathing caricature of eristic not only militates against the early hypothesis, but also provides compelling reasons why this dialogue must be mature. In fact, all the evidence of our analysis reinforces the same conclusion, that Gregory Vlastos and all those who follow him in placing this dialogue in an "early" or "transitional" category are probably wrong. For if we put to one side their various attempts to trace the development of Plato's method from dialogue to dialogue and instead concentrate upon what is required for an adequate explanation of the *Euthydemus* itself, then it seems to me at least that it is far more likely that Plato composed the *Euthydemus* with or after the *Meno* rather than before.[18]

What then about the other side of the dating dilemma? Does this mean that the *Euthydemus* is late? We cannot overturn the positions of Crombie, Sidgwick, Edwin Gifford, or anyone else who views this dialogue as contributing to the later, so-called critical, phase of Plato's development.[19] Nor, for that matter, can we deliver a knockdown argument against G. E. L. Owen, who has found a place for the *Euthydemus* right alongside the *Republic*, the centerpiece of Plato's corpus, because if some Diety were suddenly to lift the veil and kindly allow us to glimpse the truth in these matters, then the honor of the correct view might even fall to him.[20] For no one has established with certainty the place of the *Euthydemus* in Plato's dialogues. Otherwise, it would not be, as it has been called, "the goldmine for unitarians."[21] One thing, however, will emerge from these studies with some certainty: it will no longer be sufficient for critics of the *Euthydemus* to find some convenient, out-of-the-way place for this dialogue, where it can function to support this or that view on the development of Plato's method, and, in the process, to continue to live in denial, as it were, preferring to ignore the fact that Plato has chosen to devote no less than half the contents of this work to the articulation of its mature logic.[22]

If the difficulty of dating the *Euthydemus* has worked against freeing it from obscurity, then much the same thing can be said of our inability to produce a historically satisfying account of eristic. For the origin, growth, and decline of this strange technique of argument continue to present historians of philosophy with many unsolved problems. What then is this "ape of the elenchus," as it has been called by Lewis Campbell?[23] That eristic is a post-Parmenidean phenomenon, both beginning and developing sometime between Parmenides' *floruit* and the full presentation of eristic in Plato's *Euthydemus*, is at least universally agreed. Consequently, Zeno is often cited as an important precursor to eristic by those who stress its Eleatic origins; for we can see its germ in that peculiar style of adversary argument which he devised to criticize, invalidate, and ultimately to render null and void all tenets other than his Eleatic ones.[24] Several factors, moreover, combine to make Protagoras, if not the originator of eristic, then certainly a major contributor to the philosophical presuppositions that helped to engender the method; for he neither had nor sought a criterion of truth, he claimed any issue could be debated equally well both *pro* and *contra*, and he was credited with having composed a work titled *The Art of Controversy* (ἡ τέχνη ἐριστικῶν).[25] Also, we should not overlook the role played by Euthydemus himself in these matters, for our historical records indicate that he contributed to the general field of contentious debate by publishing arguments of an eristic type.[26] In this regard, it is also important to note that we possess something like a specimen of eristic in the treatise titled Δισσοὶ Λόγοι, which proves conclusively that such a style of argument did indeed exist before the composition of the *Euthydemus*.[27] And, as we already noted, it has even been argued by Henry Sidgwick that the growth and development of eristic was given no little impetus by the pupils of Socrates himself, and that the *Euthydemus* was, in part, designed by Plato to attack these renegade Socratics, especially Antisthenes, Eucleides, Eubulides, and others who threatened to impugn the true nature of the Master's work.[28]

Further, no history of eristic would be complete that failed to take into account the texts of Isocrates, who repeatedly tried to pin the tag of eristic not only on these Socratics but even on Plato himself, a fact that is of some importance to our study;[29] for it indicates that already at the time of the *Euthydemus* the label "eristic" could function as a convenient term of abuse available to all.[30] Consequently, we are under no necessity to assume that Plato has composed his dialogue to attack any particular eristic or identifiable school of eristic. When, moreover, we continue our search for this art of controversy beyond Plato and Isocrates, we find that in the logical works of Aristotle, eristic is clearly identified with a perverse or sham form of reasoning that was regarded by him nevertheless as significant enough to warrant a special treatise of its own, the *Sophistici Elenchi*.[31] Then, in post-Aristotelian philosophy, eristic continues to appear in Stoic treatises on logic where it was regarded both as a special technique of argument, the mastery of which might be useful training for one who intended to become a serious philosopher, and also as a form of "logic" abused by philosophers in general, and especially by the skeptic Arcesilaus.[32] Finally, once our records begin to show that the Stoics were shifting their emphasis away from logic, eristic simply seems to disappear just as mysteriously as it appeared shortly after Parmenides had completed his work.

The image of eristic, then, that emerges from this unduly condensed account of its rise, use, and status in decline can certainly appear to be something like the following for any unsympathetic critic who might want to comment on the attention and use accorded to it by Plato in the *Euthydemus*. Having arisen from one or more obscure sources as a specious form of reasoning, trivial at best, this pseudo-science of argument is then given such disproportionate attention and scope in the *Euthydemus* as to expose Plato to a charge of wasting his effort on a minor phenomenon in the history of Greek philosophy, a phenomenon whose insignificant place and relative unimportance within that history both Aristotle and the Stoa, later and with much less effort, were easily able to establish.[33] Here, then, is the problem. If we look to our historical records on eristic, it becomes difficult, if not impossible, to find a sufficiently weighty motive that could have inspired Plato to write the *Euthydemus*. But to argue at this point that he has exaggerated the importance of eristic would obviously constitute a *petitio principii*. We must withhold our judgment on Plato's view of it until we have studied the *Euthydemus*, his single most important text for determining what he conceives it to be. And fortunately this study will not require a historical but a philosophical inquiry into what the dialogue itself has to offer.

Before we can undertake this inquiry, however, we must turn to another obstacle that continues to consign the *Euthydemus* to relative obscurity: the fact that we have grown accustomed to encounter its eristic portions in a predominantly Aristotelian context. As we know, it is not uncommon for historians of philosophy to unite two works that have a similar content. Nor is it unusual for them to apply the discoveries of the one composed later in time to the other in order to explain what may be unstated or unclear in the earlier work. But when these discoveries consist of an array of technical terms and classifications that are, to a significant degree, foreign to the spirit and to the letter of the work to be explained, then it is possible to distort or

even to misrepresent the aims of the earlier author. And these remarks are intended to apply with full force to the assimilation of the
eristic content of Plato's *Euthydemus* to the discoveries of Aristotle's *Sophistici Elenchi*.[34]

This process of assimilation was under way even in antiquity. In his
commentary on Aristotle's *Topics,* Alexander of Aphrodisias remarks:

> Plato in his *Euthydemus* and Aristotle in the introduction to his
> treatise on dialectic say that the eristic and sophistic syllogism are
> one and the same.

And the Platonist Albinus assures us:

> We can find the method of sophisms (τὴν τῶν σοφισμάτων
> μέθοδον) technically sketched by Plato in his *Euthydemus,* if we take
> up the text correctly, so that in it are outlined what sophisms
> (σοφίσματα) are in language (παρὰ τὴν φωνήν), what they are in
> things (παρὰ τὰ πράγματα), and what are their solutions (λύσεις).[35]

That Plato doesn't have a syllogism of any type, much less an eristic
one, is of course obvious. Obvious too is the fact that he doesn't have a
method of sophisms, he doesn't make a distinction between fallacies in
language and those in things, and, despite Albinus' claim, he doesn't
present in his *Euthydemus* anything that even approaches a theory of
solutions.[36] And if we were not aware that Albinus and Alexander
lived at a time when it was the custom to produce new and dazzling
blends of Platonic and Aristotelian thought, we might be perplexed
by the easy way in which these two commentators have linked the
Euthydemus to Aristotelian doctrine. So perhaps when modern re-
searchers begin to work on the *Euthydemus* and do not find therein
anything like a clear exposition of Aristotelian doctrine, we could reasonably expect that they would entertain the possibility that Plato
might have had in mind additional, if not wholly different, aims from
what these ancient witnesses have suggested. But, in actuality, the
same urge to assimilate the one to the other persists. For example, in
his commentary on the *Euthydemus,* M. J. Routh was not at all reluctant to use Aristotle's apparatus to explicate the eristic sections, and to
his edition of the work Augustus Winckelmann even added the complete text of the *Sophistici Elenchi*.[37] Hermann Bonitz isolated and catalogued the dialogue's twenty-one eristic arguments, or "sophisms," as
he called them.[38] And Edwin Gifford took over Bonitz's catalogue of

sophisms and rigorously applied the language and classifications of Aristotle to the eristic arguments in his 1905 commentary. For the next thirty-five years, however, there were few direct contributions to the study of the *Euthydemus*.[39] Then a decisive alteration and redirection in Euthydemian studies came in 1941/42 under the aegis of Richard Robinson, who did not directly analyze the dialogue itself but whose now classic book *Plato's Earlier Dialectic* and especially his two articles, "Ambiguity" and "Plato's Consciousness of Fallacy," have exercised and continue to exercise a powerful influence on the study of this work. Before Robinson, scholars had primarily used Aristotle's doctrine of fallacy as a heuristic tool for the clarification of Plato's eristic arguments. But in his two articles Robinson called into question whether Plato could have had any abstract, theoretical consciousness of that doctrine and, hence, whether Plato could have grasped, explained, and so solved the paralogisms in the very arguments that he himself had put in his own dialogue. In response to this attack Plato's defenders have quite naturally answered the question affirmatively. And given the nature of Robinson's challenge and the way it has been met, the nay- and yea-sayers on this topic have generated the kind of controversy that continues to exhibit certain unmistakable affinities to that very eristic quibbling which it is Plato's purpose in the *Euthydemus* to criticize. But to assess the magnitude of Robinson's influence, we need only point to the fact that it is against his views, more than anyone else's, that Rosamond K. Sprague has directed her spirited defense of the *Euthydemus*.[40] Correctly discerning in his analysis a general attack against Plato's logical competence that could have particularly harmful consequences for the *Euthydemus*, Sprague has written several books and articles designed, in part, to rehabilitate Plato's logical abilities. Keeping a lonely vigil beside this dialogue throughout her career, she has persistently maintained that Plato consciously and deliberately employed the use of fallacy as one technique among others in his philosophical argumentation; to this distinguished American scholar, therefore, falls the honor of having kept the *Euthydemus* alive in discourse for the last thirty years. Following in her footsteps, R. S. W. Hawtrey has recently provided a valuable service to the dialogue by unifying in his new commentary the results of research since 1905, even as he continues Sprague's vindication of the *Euthydemus*.

But the noble efforts on the part of those who have sought to increase our appreciation of the *Euthydemus* have done little to disturb the complacency of habit, and for this failure they are themselves partly responsible. For by defending the dialogue within the Aristotelian framework of analysis and, in particular, by continuing to analyze the eristic sections with the aid of the *Sophistici Elenchi,* the defenders of the *Euthydemus* have inadvertently helped to create and are now continuing to maintain the impression that in some lisping fashion Plato was trying to contribute to Aristotle's project before Aristotle himself had done his work.[41] Moreover, this impression has fostered another misconception that has continued to align the *Euthydemus* more closely with Aristotelian doctrine. For there is now an increasing proclivity among scholars to regard the eristic sections as something like a rough handbook on fallacy with a gymnastic function, as if Plato were presenting a collection of logical puzzles or paradoxes whose mechanics the intelligent reader is supposed to work out for himself in order to be better trained for doing philosophy. To show how widespread and influential this view on the nature and function of the eristic sections has become, the words of C. L. Hamblin, a leading authority on the subject of fallacy, will suffice:

> With hindsight we can see the *Euthydemus* as an exercise in Logic, and the absurdities of the sophists as a set of puzzles for the would-be theoretical logician. Aristotle's *Sophistical Refutations* can then be regarded as a first step in constructing the relevant logical theory.[42]

The operative word here is "hindsight." Once interpreters of the *Euthydemus* confine its twenty-one eristic arguments within the Aristotelian context and then carry out their analysis and evaluation of each "sophism" in terms of the Stagirite's doctrine of fallacy, then it can indeed appear with hindsight that Plato was trying to exercise our minds on a set of logical puzzles before he himself had even made "a first step in constructing the relevant logical theory." But why are we so reluctant to entertain the possibility that a philosopher of Plato's stature may have had in mind other, non-Aristotelian aims? For if we cannot find another purpose for Plato's eristic but must continue to assume that his *Euthydemus* consists, in part, of a handbook on fallacy with a gymnastic function, then we will be unable to check the flood of embarrassing and seemingly insurmountable problems that have effectively blocked the sound appreciation of his dialogue. For example, of the twenty-one sophisms catalogued by Bonitz, Plato "solves" only the first two, and, what is more, Richard Robinson has denounced both solutions as evincing a wholly inadequate under-standing of the fallacy of equivocation.[43] And if Plato tried and failed to solve the first two, then we have little reason to expect that he could have done any better at solving the remaining nineteen. It seems im-possible then to avoid the bizarre conclusion that Plato, a wretched logician, made himself the adversary of the sophists without being able to establish clearly what a sophism is.[44] Consequently, anyone who tends to have a low opinion of Plato's logical competence can easily end up in the position of Gilbert Ryle, who has concluded that in the *Euthydemus* Plato, who is himself "not yet a logician," sets forth "a dramatized collection of sophistical elenchi" to which he makes "no positive contribution" in order "to stimulate the young Cleiniases" to finish his work.[45] Now, however wrongheaded this view may be, it nevertheless typifies a certain attitude toward Plato that continues to reinforce the already entrenched orthodoxy concerning the urgent need to apply Aristotelian solutions to the *Euthydemus*. To a significant degree, then, anyone who may sense that there is something crucially important to learn from this dialogue will immediately encounter a style of exegesis that has tended to form an almost impenetrable bar-rier to what this dialogue has to teach.

It would seem, however, that Plato's critical attitude toward writers of handbooks would prove at once the sheer impossibility that he ever intended the eristic sections of the *Euthydemus* to form a rough hand-book on fallacy; and besides, this view contradicts Aristotle's own proud claim to originality in the study of fallacy which, according to him, did not exist at all until he took it up.[46] But mere habit has so managed to shift the burden of proof regarding this untested as-sumption that in Germany Hermann Keulen has gone to no little effort to disprove what has always lacked proof.[47] Rejecting the notion that the *Euthydemus* offers a handbook on fallacy, he makes the first serious attempt to formulate a full-scale analysis of the eristic sections of the *Euthydemus* outside the Aristotelian sphere of influence in gen-eral and the doctrine of fallacy in particular. His path for this new style of exegesis, as he acknowledges, was charted by Paul Shorey, who solved the dating dilemma that he had posed to the developmentalists by arguing that the "*Euthydemus*, like the *Cratylus*, is a repertory of Pla-tonic thoughts that link it to 'earlier' and 'later' dialogues." Beginning from Shorey's hypothesis—that the *Euthydemus* is a serious work that offers to those already initiated in Platonic thought numerous clues that point beyond themselves to other works in the corpus—Keulen demonstrates how Plato consciously allows the brother-pair, in the midst of their comic routine, to stumble quite unconsciously over philosophical issues of the greatest import, the real working out of which Plato has reserved for proper treatment in other dialogues.[48] For the most part, however, Keulen is content to bind the first eristic section and the first half of the third to the *Meno;*[49] he leaves untouched the Socratic portions of the work and treats the central eristic section primarily as a basis for speculating upon the historical origins of eristic. Obviously, then, more can and must be done in the direction initially indicated by Shorey and later traversed, to a degree, by Keulen. Furthermore, it must be admitted that Keulen's analysis labors under a clear disadvantage: he finds the meaning and intelligibility of this dialogue in its relation to other works and not in itself. Consequently, he is vulnerable to attack from anyone who wants to criticize him for explaining the obvious, the *ipsa verba* of the *Euthydemus* itself, by the nonobvious, the other works of the corpus, which are assumed to explain and thus "solve" its meaning. Our task, therefore, must be to show that the eristic arguments perform their own function within the work itself.

If the eristic episodes are not just grist for an Aristotelian analysis, and if they are also something more than a repertory of thoughts or clues that point to other dialogues where disciples of Plato can find his positive solutions, then what is the overall purpose of the eristic argumentation? To this question we can begin to sketch our answer by noting one feature that has remained constant among all who have analyzed the mature logic of this dialogue. No effort has been made to form a synoptic view of the eristic sections in order to prove that Plato has assembled his dramatized collection of twenty-one eristic arguments in a definite order; that these arguments form a unified discourse that is intended to dissuade us from engaging in the verbal acrobatics of eristic; and that in this portion of his work Plato is in fact criticizing the kind of activity found, for example, in Book 8 of the *Topics* rather than just presenting raw material desperately in need of classification under a method of sophisms. At any rate, the time has come to discard all attempts to solve the *Euthydemus* that have ranged outside the sphere of Platonic discourse, because however much the Aristotelian form of exegesis may have assisted us in explaining the text, it has also directed our attention away from considering why

Plato has used this occasion to present the mature logic of the *Eu-thydemus*. We can now attain far more significant gains if we concentrate our analysis upon the dialogue itself.

ON THE LITERARY FORM OF THE DIALOGUE

Although scholars have frequently praised the *Euthydemus* for the sheer perfection of its formal composition, even claiming that it rivals the *Symposium* in this regard, a common sentiment can still be found that persists in seeing the work as somehow outside the mainstream of what constitutes Greek literature.[50] So, in order to break through its apparent foreignness, which has often barred a sympathetic reading of the text, we must address the problem of its literary composition. One way to show how securely this dialogue fits within Greek literary forms would be to isolate and to list the vast array of features from epic, lyric, tragic, and comic genres that it contains. But it is better to take up these small points as we encounter them. Instead, we shall concentrate upon the work's overall literary form and its relation to its content.

Plato begins the *Euthydemus* with a two-part prologue, ends it with a two-part epilogue, and between them constructs five episodes, clearly marked off as such by conversational interludes that function not unlike the choral odes of Greek drama. Altogether then, in its general features, this work exhibits the standard form of an Attic tragedy. But by investing this form with a content, now-playful, now-serious, with the comic antics of the brother-pair predominating, Plato gives clear evidence of loosely modeling his dialogue after that easily recognizable but little appreciated genre known as the satyr play or tragicomedy.[51]

To this dramatic structure so familiar to the theatergoers of his time, Plato also links another structure equally familiar to the partisans of Greek oratory. For he incorporates the five-part episodic framework into a *narratio* that Socrates delivers to his longtime friend and companion Crito. As a result, we must complement our study of the work's dramatic form with an analysis of its rhetorical features as well.[52] Accordingly, in the categories of the ancients themselves, we find that the *Euthydemus* is just a straightforward sample of deliberative oratory by which, in part, Plato hopes to persuade or to exhort his listeners to take *a forward step toward* philosophy, as he conceives it.[53] This exhortative or persuasive aspect of Plato's dialogue has come to be called *protreptic*.[54] Indeed, it is well known that the second episode of the *Euthydemus* contains the first surviving specimen of a protreptic discourse, a new philosophical genre that will play a lengthy and significant role in the remaining history of Greek philosophy. In addition to Plato, Antisthenes and Aristotle are credited with having contributed to the genre, and Hellenistic philosophers are known to have composed numerous protreptic works that were designed to induce young men to pursue philosophy in whatever way the various schools conceived it. Further, it is a matter of historical record that Plato's protreptic is likely to have influenced Aristotle's; that Cicero, in turn, is likely to have used Aristotle's contribution to the genre as the model for his own *Hortensius,* and that eventually St. Augustine marks his first significant turn toward God from the moment he picked up and read Cicero's work. And we know that Clement of Alexandria converted the genre to his Christian purpose, that the Neo-Platonist Iamblichus wrote his Προτρεπτικός with the *Euthydemus* at his side, and that echoes of the genre reached all the way to Boethius.[55] So the influence of protreptic discourse was felt for more than nine hundred years after the composition of the *Euthydemus,* and for this reason alone we must regard Socrates' exhortation to philosophy as a historical and literary document of immense significance.

But owing to the care with which Plato has constructed his protreptic model, that forward step toward philosophy, which he exhorts us to take, turns out to be at the same time *a step away from* what he conceives philosophy not to be; and with this observation we come upon something important. Although the *Euthydemus* is known to contain a protreptic discourse, it is also a fact that more than half of its content is not persuasive at all, but dissuasive. In this way Plato turns the tables on our expectations by presenting the inversion of the protreptic, or its antithesis, the *apotreptic*.[56] As we can gather from this term, Plato's motive for this portion of his dialogue is to turn us away from the pursuit of a strange technique of argument that has come to be called eristic. And here again we must acknowledge an inescapable fact: the mature logic of the *Euthydemus,* that is, its apotreptic, eristic logic, which more than anything else is responsible for engendering that feeling of uneasiness in the reader, has been placed in the text by conscious design. Skillfully lacing the first, third, and fifth episodes of his work with the comic antics of the brother-pair, Plato expresses this dissuasive intention through a tripartite discourse that sets up a downward movement from the humorous and playful to the utterly banal and absurd. In the *Euthydemus* Plato has fused together both a rhetorical and a dramatic structure in such a way as to create a tension between tragedy and comedy, between persuasion and dissuasion. Why he has orchestrated this perfect blend of the serious and the playful will emerge gradually, as we work our way through the text. For now, enough has been said to permit us to make a few brief remarks on the beginning of the dialogue.

SOCRATES' OPENING CONVERSATION WITH CRITO
(271 A 1–272 E 1)

In this dialogue, so important for gaining a thorough conception of eristic activity, the word *eristic* is used only once (272 B 10). Such economy of usage is not accidental and so calls for our attention. Upon inspection, we find that Socrates uses "eristic" as a capping term for the astounding wisdom that he encountered the day before in the Lyceum. Crito too had been present at the debate but was unable to hear anything clearly because of the noisy crowd. So, when meeting Socrates the next day, he asks: "Who was he, Socrates, with whom you were talking yesterday in the Lyceum?" And with this question the dialogue begins.[57] In answer, Socrates informs his friend that he was conversing with Euthydemus, but not only with him; for there was not one but two; Dionysodorus, his brother, also performs a role in their arguments. Though acknowledging that he is unfamiliar with the pair, Crito can at least correctly label them sophists (σοφισταί).[58] But then he goes on to ask, "Where are they from?" and "What's their wisdom (σοφία)?"[59] On their origin, Socrates is somewhat vague; he thinks that he can trace their family line back to somewhere in or around Chios, that they migrated from there to Thurii, and that, since fleeing this colony, they have already been active for many years in nearby regions. But he is not at all vague on their wisdom; it is amazing (θαυμασία). In fact, he tells Crito that the two are absolutely omniscient and, accordingly, have brought into sharper focus for him the true meaning of the word *pancratiast*. For the sophist-pair are not mere athletes of a somatic wisdom like the two Acarnanian brothers, who knew how to fight only with their bodies. Rather, they have perfected the art of warfare entire by becoming the practitioners and professors of an art that combines the ability to teach and to perform hoplite warfare, forensic oratory, and now eristic, their last and most recently accomplished form of combat. Indeed, the brother-pair have at last placed the coping stone (τέλος) atop the edifice of their pancratiastic science by becoming consummate professionals "at fighting in argument and refuting whatever is said, alike whether true or false."[60] Here, then, are the three stages of the *tripartite eristic* (to use Grote's felicitous phrase), that are designed to capture the fact that the brothers have exhausted the three forms of fighting in which one can seek to dominate over all, on the somatic level, on the forensic, and now in the realm of pure controversy, the final form of combat that has crowned the propaedeutic studies of their earlier years. In this brief but revealing summary, Socrates circumscribes the context in which we are to isolate and study the *ars rixandi*.

Now it may not be obvious what connection these contentious athletes and their eristic science have with military and forensic strife. To establish that connection, we should note that as fighters in a sporting event like the pancration, the most brutal of all ancient athletic contests, the brothers are required to bring a kind of savage enthusiasm to their verbal combat.[61] That this same enthusiasm is required in hoplite warfare is of course obvious and needs no elaboration. And if we make a slight adjustment, taking into account the difference in mode of warfare, we can easily see such savagery operating whenever these fighters-in-words enter into the logomachy of the courts. But if a still tighter connection is needed to establish the analogy between the art of controversy and these other forms of strife, then we can find the common feature that ties the brothers' final discipline to the others by noting that all of them demand rigorous training and endless practice in order to perfect a set of routine maneuvers, designed to culminate in an apparently effortless performance of a thoroughly brutal activity in which one individual triumphs and another suffers defeat.[62] One way then to track down this pseudo-science of argument is to follow as closely as possible the routine maneuvers of the brother-pair in their quest to attain victory in verbal combat. This portion of our study will require that we enter into the labyrinth of eristic discourse and analyze, in detail, all twenty-one arguments of the brothers.

In addition to providing Crito with this concise characterization of eristic activity, Socrates states his intention to surrender himself to the warrior-pair in the hope that they can fulfill their promise to teach him this art of wrangling. But this plan seems quite unreasonable to Crito, who immediately expresses the fear that Socrates may be too old to learn. So, countering his friend's anxiety by noting that the brothers too were almost old men before they began to study eristic, Socrates goes on to exhort Crito to join with him and with a contingent of other graybeards in the quest to attain instruction in this new science of argument. Socrates even suggests that they dangle Crito's sons before the elderly athletes as bait in order to guarantee that the brothers will undertake their instruction as well. For his part, Crito is somewhat reluctant to commit himself to such a project, but, to his credit, he is sufficiently aroused by Socrates' exhortation to ask for a more detailed account of what he is to learn. It is in response to this question that Socrates begins to narrate the full story of eristic wisdom (ἐριστικὴ σοφία).[63]

STATEMENT OF PURPOSE

At this point the preferred course of action would be to move directly to Socrates' *narratio* and to begin establishing the preliminaries for our first encounter with eristic. But this direct approach is not possible, for it would disguise the fact that, in addition to presenting an analysis of the *Euthydemus,* I am also conducting, in I trust a respectful way, a polemic against the current trend in Euthydemian criticism. So I do not want to conceal, in eristic fashion, the nature of the challenge I am issuing. The results of my analysis point uniformly to the following observation: the near dismissal of the *Euthydemus* from scholarly discourse constitutes not only striking evidence that both it and its place within Plato's thought as a whole have been misunderstood and misvalued, but implies as well that if it is ever to be restored to its rightful position of value within the corpus, then the obstacles that continue to keep it in relative obscurity—its confinement within an Aristotelian context, our inability to appreciate the crucial significance of eristic, and the grip of the "early" or "transitional" hypothesis— must now be overcome. To achieve this end, I shall present an interpretation of the *Euthydemus* itself and assume that if it is judged to be correct to any appreciable degree, then the obstacles will have to disappear. Although I do not harbor illusions regarding the invincibility of my own analysis, I do believe that it is at least sound enough to clear the way for a more accurate and more adequate understanding of this dialogue. But since the *Euthydemus* is so ambiguous, its irony so thorough and sustained, since it is so susceptible to misinterpretation even on the part of the most well-meaning critic—not to mention how easily it can become the plaything of this or that charlatan and obscurantist—I want to take this opportunity to state in brief compass and without ambiguity how I intend to proceed, the thesis that informs the whole, and the gist of my results.

Along with Harold Cherniss, I cannot believe that Plato "thought with his pen."[64] So I maintain the position throughout that Plato has given us in the *Euthydemus* a faithful report of what he had already thought, and that he has conveyed that thought to us with the utmost care and perfect tact. I treat the *Euthydemus* as it deserves to be treated, as a complete and finished work of art, a whole that makes sense both in terms of itself and in relation to its author's other compositions. And I assume at the outset that the dialogue itself is the *datum* to be explained, that it has its own order which challenges our minds, and that with patient study we can articulate that order without having to resort to Aristotelian solutions.

From the beginning to the end of my analysis, I argue for a single thesis that is so far from being new or revolutionary that expressions of it can be found, without fail, in the literature of our learned tradition. For one fact continues to emerge with unanimity from a survey of scholarship on Plato's *Euthydemus:* eristic appears *similar* to, but is really *different* from, dialectic.[65] Indeed, the similarity is so great that the distinction between the two can and did become blurred in the eyes of many, and so it has been argued that Plato composed his dialogue to distinguish the one from the other. Yet, at the same time, it has also been recognized that Plato has portrayed the differences between the two techniques of argument so sharply that any discerning critic can and should easily see that the two procedures differ from each other by the widest possible margin. Similarly, with one voice commentators agree that although the eristics who use this method may appear to be philosophers to undiscerning observers, still it is obvious that Plato has gone to no little effort to portray them as mountebanks, mere imitators and sophistic frauds, who in reality are false or pseudo-dialecticians.[66] By the agreement of all, then, it can be said that slipping in under the mantle of dialectic as its understudy, eristic is capable of producing the shadow of sameness to, whereas in reality it is altogether different from, dialectic. But what does this *consensus omnium* really mean, if we take it seriously and attempt to apply it consistently and systematically to the *Euthydemus* from beginning to end and in matters large and small? Much of what follows is dedicated to completing just this project. For I maintain that in the *Euthydemus* Plato does not present a simple contrast between eristic and dialectic, but that with some degree of precision, not to say exactness, he actually depicts eristic as *the* antithesis to dialectic, in fact, as *the* very paradigm of otherness. This thesis, however, has never been properly appreciated and cannot, so long as the meaning of this dialogue is controlled by a hypothesis that persists in allowing only its unsuccessful, aporetic features to come to light.[67] But once it is recognized that Plato has used the occasion of the *Euthydemus* to fashion consciously and deliberately the antipode to his own philosophical method, then the overall design of this work becomes visible.

The *Euthydemus* is a dramatized dialogue between Crito and Socrates in which the latter narrates the story of eristic wisdom. In this story Socrates presents primarily, but not exclusively, the methodological features of conversational procedures, both eristical and dialectical, set within an apotreptic and protreptic context. For more than half of its content, the emphasis of his *narratio* is apotreptic; that is, the main burden of its function is to dissuade the reader from exercising a logical procedure that is perverse to the extreme, one which deserves to be ridiculed, but which cannot be swept aside with a casual nod in the direction of historical accidents: the rise of logic-chopping Eleatics or Megarians. For the mere fact that eristic was present in the Greek world during Plato's lifetime is all the evidence we require to give his work an anchor in horizontal history. But the activity itself Plato has resurrected from oblivion by transforming it into his negative paradigm. For once eristic has been severed from its origins in space and time and transfigured into a symbol, it can be operative whenever and wherever genuine philosophical activity veers from the true path and begins to degenerate into its opposite. Unleashing all the forces of his tragic and comic art, his powers of persuasion and dissuasion, his love of irony and satire, and even an impulse to slander and abuse, Plato has created for our inspection that measure of baseness and ugliness in all philosophy, and thereby transformed the brothers into types from which we are to turn.[68] In this work Plato allows philosophers the rare opportunity to laugh at a grotesque caricature of themselves, but with his characteristic intelligence in these matters he also arrests the pain that such a confrontation with our own philosophical ugliness would cause by altering that experience into the ludicrous. In half of its intention, then, the *Euthydemus* is a comedy or, better still, a philosophical satire with a dissuasive aim; it thus demands for its comprehension that the reader interpret its symbols accordingly, or else risk misinterpreting it. And, make no mistake about it, the price we pay for misinterpretation is significant. For failure to attribute to the *Euthydemus* its due weight causes us to operate with a distorted, overly positivistic view of Plato's method that does not take into account the thoroughness with which he analyzed how *not* to think, to speak, and to act.

If the *Euthydemus* were exclusively a presentation of eristic wisdom, then there would be no way to establish its meaning, and any analysis of it would just drift to and fro like a raft on the tides of the Euripus. But it is impossible for Socrates to tell the story of eristic without, at the same time, including the story of his own wisdom, which then serves as the standard of comparison for us. Against that Socratic standard we can see eristic "wisdom" for what it is, a pseudo-wisdom that in reality turns out to be, by an ironical inversion, a real ignorance (ἀμαθία) that can reside deep in the recesses of the philosophical soul.[69] And how are we to conceive of that soul which possesses this ignorance and plies the eristic method? For that we can borrow a device used by Glaucon in the *Republic*. Picture, if you will, Euthydemus and Dionysodorus wearing Gyges' ring with reverse effect.[70] Imagine them turned inside out, losing any inward depth of serious ethical character they might have had, and becoming, as it were, invisible even to themselves. At the same time, regard the pair as a phenomenon of only surface denotation, a flagrantly visible caricature of Plato's own devising. And, suppose that, like marionettes that gambol before the puppeteer's screen, Plato introduces the couple upon his stage to perform a philosophical dance. Then, throughout their pseudo-philosophical routine, Plato portrays them, in the concrete fashion of a comic artist, as a grossly exaggerated phantasm of what the philosopher should not be, or what is other than or different from the philosopher.[71] Finally, to ensure that we can recognize the brother-pair for what they are, the disfigured, inverted image of the philosopher, Plato also provides us with a touchstone against which this two-headed mutation can be measured, the unvarying standard of Socrates himself.

Once it is recognized, then, that Socrates' *narratio* contains not one λόγος but two, that the twofold pair, eristic and dialectic, so qualify each other by their sameness and difference that the one cannot be fully appreciated without the other, and that, in sum, Plato has used the occasion of the *Euthydemus* to combine a brilliantly crafted parody of sophistic antilogy with a remarkably subtle yet forceful exhortation that is designed to persuade all of us to pursue virtue and to love wisdom, then the "early" or "transitional" hypothesis that currently controls and limits most inquiry into this dialogue will be seen for what it is, an ill-chosen, lopsided method that is at variance with the very intention of the work itself. Furthermore, once we have descended into this eristical mode of argumentation and found therein that Plato is in complete control of what he is doing, that he not only allows each eristic argument to perform its own function within the whole, but also subsumes all twenty-one of them into a well-orchestrated, tripartite movement that is intended to illustrate the look of an illogical world diametrically opposed to his own, then our analysis will provide solid comfort for all of those who have become dissatisfied with the spectacle of a Plato who fumbles about in the dark, clumsily trying to discover "the relevant logical theory," that will turn on his lights, as well as our own, and who, frustrated, is content to leave behind a record of his failures in the form of *sophistici elenchi* that, he hopes, young schoolboys will someday be able to solve. We are confident, moreover, that if we complement our detailed analysis of the individual arguments with a sensitive literary treatment, demonstrating that Plato is again in complete control, that by clear techniques and for clear reasons he has presented to us this perfect intermingling of form and content, that, in short, nothing in his dialogue has been left to chance, nothing is a fluke, then the riddle of the *Euthydemus* will be solved, its importance for Plato's thought secured. Finally, I am assuming at the outset that Plato could not portray the antithesis to his own philosophical method and the two-headed antitype to the serious philosopher unless he himself were already in possession of the positive models. I am confident that this assumption is correct, for it is the very essence of the comic to undercut the presentation of a serious archetype.[72]

1

THE FIRST ERISTIC DISPLAY

THE PROTREPTIC RESTRICTIONS AND CRITERION
(272 E 1–275 D 2)

In this chapter it is our primary purpose to analyze the two argument-pairs that constitute an advertisement for eristic wisdom, and then, on the basis of that analysis, to begin establishing those features which characterize the mechanics of eristic argumentation. Before attending to these matters, however, we must first treat certain preliminaries in order to set the stage for our initial encounter with eristic and its two-headed representative. For our point of departure, we begin when Euthydemus and Dionysodorus announce publicly that their former pursuits, military science and forensic oratory, have become mere sidelines, whereas now they claim to possess the ability "to impart virtue (ἀρετὴν παραδοῦναι) best of men and most quickly" (273 D 8–9). Then, not afraid to back up this boast, they go on to assure Socrates that "we are indeed in town for the very purpose of showing and teaching our wisdom, if anyone wants to learn" (274 A 10–B 1).

Given the magnitude of their claim and the easy confidence with which they support it, we might be tempted to disbelieve them. But for now we should resist that temptation, recalling that they have after all won the loyalties of a large gathering of students and for some time have been performing a road show of sorts in which they play the leading roles. Indeed, they have even exhibited the versatility necessary to alter the content of their performance. Formerly, their curriculum consisted of hoplite warfare and courtroom rhetoric, but now, keeping abreast of what excites the young, they are in Athens for the express purpose of marketing eristic (ἐριστικὴν παραδοῦναι), only they disguise this fact by labeling their product virtue, a commodity for which there is always a demand. Aware that it is no simple task to give the full account of human excellence, Socrates quickly seeks to confine their display to a discourse that instills in a youth

22

merely the first urge toward moral virtue. Because the moves by which he transforms his conversation with the brothers into a protreptic discourse are so crucial, we need to examine them in detail:

> Now I'll grant you [said Socrates] that it is a real chore to exhibit this power in full, so tell me this: Can you make a good man only out of someone who has already been persuaded that he should learn from you, or can you also do this for someone who is not yet persuaded, because he doesn't suppose, in general, that virtue can be learned or that you two are its teachers? Come, take this latter student; is it the function of the same art to persuade him that virtue is teachable and that he can learn it best from the two of you, or is it the function of another art?
>
> Of course, Socrates, it is the function of the same art, replied Dionysodorus.
>
> Then can you, best of present-day men, exhort someone to attend to philosophy and virtue?
>
> We think so, Socrates.
>
> Well then, put aside the display of the full account for another occasion and concentrate on this. Persuade this young man here that he should philosophize and attend to virtue, and you will gratify me and the others.
>
> (274 D 6–275 A 7)

The brothers have made a sweeping claim to teach anyone who wants to learn. Socrates now begins to probe this assertion with a disjunctive question that posits two different students. Does your power, he asks, extend to perfecting only "someone *who has already been persuaded* that he should learn from you, or can you also do this for someone *who is not yet persuaded,* because he doesn't suppose, in general, that virtue can be learned or that you two are its teachers?" Both doubts recall two familiar questions: Can virtue be taught, and, if so, who are its teachers? One might even suppose that the unpersuaded student is Socrates himself, if the Socrates of the *Meno* and *Protagoras* can be cited as evidence. Were the *Euthydemus* to engage these two questions, it would perforce begin to retrace topics familiar from those dialogues. But Socrates doesn't steer the discussion in that direction. Before allowing the brothers to respond to his question, he formulates another that shifts the emphasis of the conversation in a crucial way. He drops the distinction between the persuaded and the unpersuaded student in favor of concentrating upon the one *who is not yet persuaded.* Then he causes the question to turn, not on the student, but on whether it is the function of *one and the same art* or of *another* to persuade that individual who still entertains doubts about the teachability of virtue or its instructors. At the very least Socrates is here questioning whether the power to impart virtue involves more than a simple transference or handing over of goodness to anyone who wants to learn. In order to impart excellence, Socrates is suggesting, the successful protreptic master must also have the power to uncover the prior convictions of a student and, in some cases, persuade the skeptical to alter their views. In short, Socrates is forcing the brothers to acknowledge that *persuasion* must play a crucial role in the preliminary stages of virtue-teaching. So once Dionysodorus assures him that the persuasive function is indeed part and parcel of one and the same art, and not a different one, separable from that skill which transfers goodness, Socrates can ask whether they would be best of present-day protreptic masters at this part of teaching virtue as well, that is, at the task of *exhorting* or *persuading* someone to pursue philosophy and excellence.

Behind Socrates' maneuvers, it must be noted, lies a compelling argument. The brothers have already boasted that they are the best at imparting virtue. They have just now admitted to Socrates that their skill includes the persuasive power to alter the convictions of a skeptical student. Therefore, they must also surpass all mankind at this protreptic aspect of virtue-teaching. So when Dionysodorus smugly affirms that they possess this additional power, Socrates can provide the cap to the restrictions that his initial questioning has established. He bids them to put aside the full display of their power for some other occasion and instead to concentrate upon the mere protreptic task of persuading a lad to philosophize and to attend to virtue. But then, in the course of sealing these restrictions upon the brothers' instruction, Socrates also provides them with a touchstone for evaluating the success of their protreptic, Axiochus' son, Kleinias, who just so happens to be seated beside Socrates. Not the result of literary accident, Kleinias' position at Socrates' side has been carefully prepared for by selected details that have already created a charming picture of him. Crito has commented on his fine stature and comely appearance, and Socrates has reported on how he entered the Lyceum followed by a throng of admirers and, in particular, by Ktesippus, who is here singled out for special attention because he will later replace his favorite as the criterion for evaluating eristic.[1] And once inside the gymnasium, we are told, Kleinias observed Socrates sitting alone, advanced straight toward him, and sat down, a vignette that allows us to imagine what is not said, that on numerous occasions Socrates has gradually effaced the boy's shyness through unrehearsed efforts at instruction.[2] It is also certain that as the direct descendent of the older Alcibiades and first cousin of the notorious Alcibiades, Kleinias possesses that outstanding natural talent customarily associated with Athenian nobility.[3] And although still young, he is at least old enough to have reached that critical age when he is ready to be turned or converted to the philosophic life, and yet there is not the slightest indication that he harbors any skeptical doubts about the teachability of virtue. Quite simply, Kleinias represents that ideal student who is ready either to gel beautifully if the protreptic phase of his education is properly handled, or to be corrupted by adverse influences if he is dissuaded from the pursuit of philosophy and virtue.[4]

To sum up then, the brothers began with a general claim to impart virtue but are now required to persuade a specific individual to pursue it. Their student is not the passive recipient of a product (as their formula, to impart virtue, might suggest the mechanical handing over of a thing), but a subject ready to undergo a change that must entail the active pursuit of a goal. In short, Socrates has taken the sophistic boast of the brothers, drawn out certain implications embedded in it, and then restricted their display to the persuasive or protreptic element in their teaching. This maneuver not only establishes the arena for the contest between the brothers and Socrates, between eristic and dialectic; on the dramatic level, it also prepares the way for the descent into the banal, the complete reversal of our expectations, when persuasion gives way to dissuasion, seriousness to play. But here we want to stress just one implication of Socrates' maneuver to confine eristic within the protreptic context, for indirectly it will lurk behind all the antics of the brother-pair.[5] By linking the persuasive or protreptic discourse to virtue-teaching in general, and by restricting the brothers' instruction to that part in particular, Socrates has forced them to display their knowledge of human psychology; for the ability to persuade requires a knowledge of soul.[6] As will become abundantly clear, the *Euthydemus* is designed to portray two "philosophers" unconcerned about the restrictions demanded by the protreptic discourse, unconcerned about how to produce arguments, unconcerned about when, where, and how to use the arguments they have produced, and, most important, unconcerned about what, as protreptic masters, they should be most concerned about, namely, the *soul* of that individual whom they are attempting to exhort in their protreptic discourse. On the comic level, this inattention to soul will help to produce the humorous antics of our two clowns, but philosophically it will generate a host of those disturbing perversions which typify the antithesis to true dialectical discourse.

THE ARGUMENTS (275 D 2–277 C 7)

The first eristic display concentrates upon the philosophical topic of learning, one related to the prologue, taken up again and again throughout the dialogue, and central to Plato's thought as a whole. We must note this fact among our preliminaries because the brothers are going to obscure the entire field of learning by traversing back and forth over now its subjects, now its objects, and then again over the processes that link both subjects and objects.[7] To argue that Dionysodorus and Euthydemus intend to conduct a genuine inquiry into this immensely complicated topic is no doubt impossible. They seem to have chosen it for their first display-piece simply because the learning act is so riddled with ambiguity that it provides an ideal arena within which to exercise their argumentative powers—an exercise in this case consisting of the ambitious undertaking of leading a young interlocutor to the antithesis of a thesis.[8] But at this early juncture we are anticipating too much. Before examining in detail the arguments that the brothers use to contradict and to refute Kleinias, we must first turn to the more immediate task of outlining the eristic model for controversy.

In this first episode both sophists exhibit a pattern of argumentation that will recur in slightly altered form throughout their verbal dueling. We may observe its formal principles for the first time when Euthydemus puts a disjunctive question to Kleinias that ostensibly seeks to discover the subjects of learning: "Which of the two are those who learn (οἱ μανθάνοντες)," Euthydemus asks, "the wise (οἱ σοφοί) or the ignorant (οἱ ἀμαθεῖς)?" At this point we must say "ostensibly" because we do not yet know whether Euthydemus is in fact trying to discover anything. He may be attempting to determine which students have the capacity to learn—the wise or the ignorant—in order to establish whether Kleinias is a member of the group capable of learning and hence a fit subject for instruction. Or perhaps he assumes that by taking Kleinias through his paces on the question "Who learns?" he can teach as he goes along. In fact, the protreptic discourse, requested by Socrates, is an ideal procedure for assisting philosophers in both the teaching and discovery process. We soon learn, however, that this initial question does not seek to discover or to teach anything.[9] Instead, it is a well-calculated device by which Euthydemus offers Kleinias the seeming advantage of selecting his answer from only two possible alternatives. But what the boy cannot grasp at this moment is that his answer, "The wise are those who learn," binds him to a thesis that the sophist immediately attacks. Simply by responding to this disjunctive question, Kleinias becomes the defender of a thesis in an eristic dispute, while Euthydemus becomes the opponent of that thesis.[10] The surprise factor alone proves adequate to account for Euthydemus' easy victory in this opening repartee, without Kleinias' even realizing that he has become the victim of a verbal villain.

Moreover, the boy's answer determines more than just his thesis. It reveals where Euthydemus must drive his line of attack. After Kleinias selects "the wise" for the subject term of the thesis, Euthydemus knows what antithesis he must establish, namely that "The ignorant are those who learn." The other three arguments of this series will exhibit a similar pattern. So, to avoid any confusion regarding which thesis Kleinias is attempting to defend or which antithesis the brothers are seeking to establish in both argument-pairs, it will be necessary to provide a schema that pictures the theses and antitheses as coordinates, so to speak, within which and through which the brothers drag the complex topic of learning. Although this schematic outline may appear somewhat cumbersome and mechanical, we insist upon its use at first in order to help treat a style of argumentation that does not seek to instruct its listeners, but to cloud issues and to stun interlocutors. Finally, we can avoid considerable confusion at the outset of our journey into eristic argumentation if we look forward to the interlude between the first and second episodes where Socrates begins to disentangle Kleinias from the verbal traps of the brothers by offering him a simple lesson in ambiguity (277 E 5–278 B 2). There he explains that *learn* (μανθάνειν), an equivocal term, has two senses: to gather knowledge (τὸ λαμβάνειν ἐπιστήμην) and to understand (τὸ συνιέναι). If we remember that the first meaning of the verb "to

gather knowledge" applies to Euthydemus' first argumentative chain
(E1) and to Dionysodorus' second (D2), whereas the second meaning
"to understand" corresponds to Dionysodorus' first argument (D1)
and to Euthydemus' second (E2), then we can avoid a substantial
amount of confusion that the brothers will generate in these initial
arguments.[11]

Are Those Who Learn the Wise or the Ignorant?

(E1)

> *Trigger question:*   Are those who learn, the wise or the ignorant?
>
> *Thesis:*   The wise are those who learn.
> *Antithesis:*   The ignorant are those who learn.

Then Euthydemus said: Do you call some men teachers or not?
He agreed.
Are they teachers of those who learn in just the same way that
the lyre master and grammar master were teachers of you and of
the other children, and you were learners?
He assented.
Is it the case that, when you were learning (ἐμανθάνετε), you did
not yet know (οὔπω ἠπίστασθε) what you were learning (ταῦτα ἃ
ἐμανθάνετε)?
We didn't know, he said.
Then were you wise (σοφοί), when you didn't know these things
(ταῦτα)?
Of course not, he said.
Then if not wise, ignorant (ἀμαθεῖς)?
Certainly.
Then in learning what you didn't know, you were learning,
when you were ignorant.
The young man nodded.
Therefore, the ignorant learn, Kleinias, and not the wise, as you
suppose.

(276 A 3–B 5)

Euthydemus begins his first attack with a familiar question formula; Socrates, too, frequently asks his interlocutors whether they call
something by some name, in order to secure agreement on the terms

employed and on the reality corresponding to them. By the mere use of this formula, then, the sophist immediately invites us to compare his questioning procedure with that of Socrates.[12] But to grant, as Kleinias does, that he calls some men teachers is also to prepare the way for another admission. There cannot very well be teachers without subjects who are taught. So in his second question Euthydemus moves to establish this necessary link between teachers and students. As yet, however, he has not delivered a knockout punch. At this point he is just beginning to construct the context for his refutation. But observe how, beginning with the subordinating clause in his second question, the sophist slyly shifts the argument into past time, specifies the teachers as lyre master and grammar master, and casts Kleinias and his fellow pupils in the role of learners.[13] Now he can play directly on the past experiences of the boy.

In his third question Euthydemus injects the two activities of knowing and learning into his argument. Here he is treating learning as an activity in which the children *were engaged* while they were under the tutelage of their teachers. Knowing, on the other hand, is something that the boys have *not yet attained*. Still further, the activities of learning and knowing are linked by an unspecified "what" or subject matter, which refers in a vague way to what they *were learning* but *did not yet know*. Importantly, by negating the activity of knowing with the temporal indicator "not yet," Euthydemus establishes that knowing is something different from and occurring later in time than learning, while at the same time he manages to create the appearance that learning can eventually end in knowing; this much, at any rate, is built into the syntax of this third question. But the appearance of future knowledge is an illusion, for the sophist is here treating *learning* and *knowing* as mutually exclusive opposites: that is, he does not allow for a middle ground or continuum between the two. Consequently, learning denotes the *process* of which knowledge is the unattainable *result*. So a subject is either knowing or learning but cannot possibly bridge the gap between the two activities by "coming to know" objects of knowledge.[14]

The full argumentative force behind treating learning and knowing as exclusive antinomies is revealed in the fourth question when Euthydemus begins to concentrate upon "the wise," the subject term of Kleinias' thesis. But now his question does not concern the wise abstracted from a context, but the disposition of Kleinias himself and his fellow students when they *did not yet know* the subject matter of their instruction. In the context thus created, Kleinias cannot acknowledge that he and his schoolmates were "wise" in relation to objects that were as yet unknown. For at that time they were merely learners in the act of gathering knowledge about what was being taught. Consequently, when Kleinias denies, as indeed he must, that they were wise in relation to what they were just beginning to learn, he has unknowingly destroyed the original thesis. So the sophist is now free to establish the contrary thesis. In his fifth question Euthydemus shifts the focus from the wise to the ignorant, the key term of the antithesis. Since Kleinias has just granted that they were *not wise,* Euthydemus simply flips him to the other limb of the disjunct and asks whether they were *ignorant.*[15] And just as the boy destroyed the thesis with his answer to the previous question by denying that they were *wise* in relation to unknown objects, so too now, by affirming that they were *ignorant* in relation to them, he has in effect granted the antithesis of the thesis.

Although it may be tempting to ask why Kleinias grants concessions that so easily overturn his position, we should remember that, within the dramatic frame of the dialogue, it is Plato's intention to portray him as unfamiliar with this agonistic form of questioning, a consideration that alone can account for his apparent failure. Nor is there any reason to wonder why Euthydemus succeeds in bouncing him from one term to another so effortlessly. In the *Symposium,* for example, Diotima corrects Socrates himself for a similar mistake when he too fails to grasp the middle ground between wisdom and ignorance, and she is not trying to deceive him.[16] But in this context the sophist has intentionally laced his argument with ambiguous terms. That *learn* is equivocal cannot be denied, for Socrates himself will soon expose the two senses of the verb operative in this eristic show-piece. And as if this factor were not enough, additional equivocations have been detected in the terms *wise* and *ignorant,* each having two denotations that correspond to the two uses of $\mu\alpha\nu\theta\acute{\alpha}\nu\epsilon\iota\nu$; the strong sense of *wise* (knowledgeable or all-knowing) operative in (E1) is incompatible with the weak sense of *learn,* to gather knowledge, whereas the weak sense of *ignorant* (unlearned or uninformed) is here referring to a subject who is in the very process of gathering knowledge; and this further insight into equivocal terms does indeed help to clarify (E1). But even closer inspection reveals that all key terms of this argument are *never* satisfactorily clarified.[17] We have, rather, a sliding scale of meaning where terms fluctuate back and forth between poles, between strict and loose, between refined and unrefined senses.[18] In this first argument, Kleinias selects "the wise" for the subject term of the thesis. This choice fixes him on one side of that scale. Then, through his line of questioning, Euthydemus topples the thesis by constructing a context in which "wise" can no longer be predicated of those who learn. This maneuver is not accomplished by the use of a single equivocal term or even by a string of equivocal terms, as is usually suggested, but by an entire network of argumentative techniques orchestrated by Euthydemus;[19] for the shift in the meaning of *learning* or, for that matter, of both *wise* and *ignorant* could not be accomplished without the addition of the activity of knowing, the subject matter that the boys were attempting to learn, and the context of Kleinias' primary education. It is for this reason that a study of fallacy directed solely toward individual terms has not provided and cannot provide an adequate account of the eristic sections of the *Euthydemus*. It can be helpful, to be sure, but it is not sufficient. For the application of the Aristotelian treatment of fallacy to the sophistical refutations of Plato's dialogue crowds the fullness of each argument into some minor portion of the whole. Instead, we must picture the entire environment of words if we want to achieve a more satisfying picture of eristic activity.

To bring his refutation to a close, Euthydemus connects the ignorant explicitly with the process of learning. The wise cannot be candidates for those who learn because they already have the objects in question, but the ignorant can, for they are just beginning to gather knowledge about the as-yet-unknown subject matter. For his conclusion Euthydemus emerges from past time into the present in order to state generally and formulaically both the antithesis and the thesis. He even adds a personal touch by addressing Kleinias with the vocative and reminding him that the outcome of this argument is not as he supposes, additions that should alert us to the fact that Euthydemus has not directed his argument toward truth but against Kleinias himself, forcing the boy to knuckle under to his superior argumentative skill.[20]

(D1)

      Thesis: The ignorant are those who learn.
  Antithesis: The wise are those who learn.

And even before the youngster could duly catch his breath, Dionysodorus took over the argument and said: What about when the grammar master was dictating to you, Kleinias, which of the children were learning what was being dictated (τὰ ἀποστοματιζό-μενα), the wise or the ignorant?

The wise, said Kleinias.

Therefore, the wise learn and not the ignorant, and so just now you did not answer Euthydemus correctly.

(276 C 1–7)

When Dionysodorus hears his brother close (E1), he has his cue for action. Seizing the opportunity before Kleinias can fully recover from his first defeat, the sophist launches another attack.[21] Following Euthydemus' lead, he introduces a temporal clause that, given its past general form, again shifts the context of the argument into some indefinite time during Kleinias' primary education; he brings back a teacher, this time selecting the grammar master for closer attention, and again casts Kleinias and his schoolmates in the role of learners. But when Dionysodorus slips the new expression "what was being dictated" into his disjunctive question, we see at once that he has replaced those vague, unspecified "things" of (E1) with considerably more specific objects of learning. At the very least we are to imagine an activity in which a schoolteacher recites letters or even a whole lesson of some sort, and the pupils repeat the letters orally or perhaps write them out in some exercise. What we have here is that entrenching process by which the fundamental elements of knowledge are drilled into the minds of children. Whatever else this activity of dictation may mean, it allows for a shift in the sense of *learn* from its weak (to gather knowledge) to its strong sense (to understand). As long as in (E1) the objects of learning were not specified, and the activity of learning was opposed to knowledge, the term *wise* could easily be held in reserve for subjects who already possessed knowledge, whereas the word *ignorant* could be predicated of those who were in the process of gathering knowledge. But now, since Dionysodorus has subtly dropped the distinction between knowing and learning and has altered the objects of learning into dictated letters or a repeated lesson of some sort, Kleinias can truthfully answer this disjunctive question by "the wise," because, in the context thus created, there was indeed a sense in which the clever among the boys already understood the sub-

ject matter of dictation. Dionysodorus follows up Kleinias' single response "the wise" by stating the conclusion of (D1) in such a way as to
mirror the very language that his brother used to polish off (E1), save,
of course, for transposing the subject terms "the wise" and "the ignorant." Obviously, then, we can see what Dionysodorus' strategy was.
Seizing upon the antithesis of (E1) as if it were a new thesis that
Kleinias was supposed to maintain, the sophist has sought, by only
one well-timed and brilliantly delivered question, to dupe the boy into
reaffirming the original thesis of (E1). Such theatrics cannot help but
create the overall impression that the brothers are performing a well-
rehearsed routine in which their teamwork has reached near perfection. Dionysodorus even imitates his brother by adding a personal reminder with "just now you did not answer Euthydemus correctly."
The stress here on failing to answer correctly once again emphasizes
that Kleinias has not yielded to the self-evidence of truth but to Dionysodorus' verbal superiority.[22]

But suppose that, under the influence of (E1), or even through a
stern resolve to thwart Dionysodorus' line of attack, Kleinias had answered the disjunctive question not by "the wise"—which then provided the sophist with his easy refutation—but by "the ignorant." It is
not difficult to imagine how Dionysodorus would then alter his line of
questioning. He would begin to exploit the possibilities in his new expression, "what was being dictated," in the same way that Euthydemus
will exploit the term *letters* ($\gamma\rho\acute{\alpha}\mu\mu\alpha\tau\alpha$) in his next argument. Then
Dionysodorus' verbal assault would take the shape that it will in (E2),
though of course he would argue his case on the subject-side rather
than the object-side of the dilemma. But at this point it is not Plato's
intention to have Dionysodorus push (D1) so far that it begins to en-
croach upon (E2). Such a move would disrupt the symmetry that the
argument-pairs are designed to exhibit as a unit, and any resistance
on the part of Kleinias would detract from that simplicity of character
which is designed to make this eristical triumph seem so gratuitous.
Instead, by falling naively into this carefully laid verbal trap, Kleinias
spares the sophist the trouble of having to extend the first argument-
pair. Midway through this eristic showpiece, then, we find that the
tables have been turned on Kleinias twice. Both alternatives offered in
the disjunctive question, "the wise" and "the ignorant," have been successfully predicated of those who learn, and both have been rejected.

It can now appear to Kleinias that neither the wise nor the ignorant learn, or both.[23] From the side of the subject, learning can appear to be either impossible or very easy to accomplish.

Do Those Who Learn Learn What They Know or What They Do Not Know?

(E2)

> *Trigger question:* Do those who learn learn what they know (ἃ ἐπίστανται) or what they do not know (ἃ μὴ ἐπίστανται)?
>
> *Thesis:* Those who learn learn what they do not know.
> *Antithesis:* Those who learn learn what they know.

What about this? Euthydemus said. Do you know letters (γράμματα)?

Yes, he said.

All?

He agreed.

Now whenever someone dictates anything, does he dictate letters?

He agreed.

Then does he dictate something that you know, he said, if you know all?

On this point too he agreed.

What about this? he said. Do you learn whatever someone dictates, or does he who doesn't know letters learn (ὁ μὴ ἐπιστάμενος γράμματα)?

No, he said, I learn.

Well then, you learn (μανθάνεις) what you know (ἃ ἐπίστασαι), he said, if you know all your letters.

He agreed.

Therefore, you did not answer correctly, he said.

(277 A 1–B 2)

Euthydemus triggers (E2) with another disjunctive question. This time, however, he shifts the emphasis of the attack from the subjects to the objects of learning. At once we should notice the vagueness of the "what" is learned. In (E1) the objects of learning were "things," and in (D1) they became "what was being dictated." Now in (E2) the sophist offers only a relative pronoun with a suppressed antecedent. We may, therefore, already anticipate that, regardless of which alternative Kleinias selects, Euthydemus will concretize the "what" learners learn with objects of knowledge in such a way as to undermine the boy's thesis. Again, with his answer "Those who learn learn what they do not know" (276 E 9), Kleinias becomes the defender of a thesis that Euthydemus immediately attacks. For his first question he fills in the relative pronoun with letters and asks Kleinias whether he knows them. He can, of course, expect an affirmative answer. All Greek children who have come under the tutelage of a grammar teacher have learned, and so know, their letters. Already, then, Euthydemus' eristic challenge is clearly established. If he can induce Kleinias to admit that, in addition to knowing, he also "learns" his letters, then he has successfully bounced the boy back to the antithesis he wants to establish.

The eristic fondness for brevity is well illustrated by Euthydemus' second question, which concerns the boy's knowledge of letters in a quantitative sense.[24] And when Kleinias affirms to know "all" letters, he has unawares trapped himself within an inclusive body of knowledge. For if there were some letters he did not yet know, then he could still learn something in the looser sense of gathering knowledge, and the distinction between learning and knowing would not be effaced. But, as it is, Euthydemus has succeeded in laying a trap from which the boy will not escape. In his third and fourth questions the sophist continues to construct the context in which Kleinias will learn what he already knows. Bringing back the activity of recitation introduced by his brother in (D1), Euthydemus slips in letters for the objects of dictation and forces Kleinias to admit that he knows that part; after all, it cannot be denied that letters are part of what is recited. Then, in his fifth question, the key one for this refutation, Euthydemus introduces two uses of the pivotal term *learn* into an environment that on this occasion prevents the verb from taking on its weaker sense of "gathering knowledge." For when Kleinias reflects upon his own situation, he must admit that he "learns" in the strong sense of "understands," because the objects of his learning, namely, dictated letters, are already known. On the other hand, when he considers the case of his opposite, "he who doesn't know letters," Kleinias must deny that this individual can learn in any sense at all, for without a knowledge of letters he cannot even begin to come upon the first thing learned. So the very gap between learning and knowing that provided the lever for overthrowing the thesis of (E1) has now been collapsed by the sophist for the purpose of toppling the thesis of (E2). Here too, we should note, Euthydemus has unwittingly stumbled over a real problem, that of the first thing known and its relation to the rest of our body of knowledge. (E2) has come very close to the eristic argument of the *Meno*.[25]

Euthydemus announces his victory with a clear statement of the antithesis: "Well then, *you learn* what *you know*, if you know all your letters." But now the importance of the context cannot be more clearly indicated. For the antithesis of (E2) is expressed with two verbs in the second person singular (ἐπίστασαι and μανθάνεις), whereas the original disjunctive question and thesis statement assumed an air of universality. Again, that the failure in the argumentation is to be found in Kleinias and Kleinias alone, Euthydemus emphasizes in his concluding remark: "Therefore, you did not answer correctly." With the completion of this argument, we see that Kleinias is no longer in need of that grammar master whom Euthydemus and his brother introduced in (E1) and (D1). For now he is no longer a learner (μαθητής), but a knower of letters (ἐπιστήμων γραμμάτων). In fact, if we turn back to (E1), we find that Euthydemus has contradicted his first argument. If we fill in those "things" of (E1), which the boys were attempting to learn, with the concrete letters of (E2), then we can see that Kleinias and his fellow students were in fact "wise" when they were learning letters that they already knew.[26] So after only his second argument, we observe that Euthydemus has remained verbally infallible, but not verbally consistent. This verbal inconsistency, so characteristic of eristic activity, will later provide Socrates with the basis for establishing the verbal fallibility of the brothers.[27]

As should now be clear, (E2) expands and elaborates (D1), only Euthydemus has shifted to the object-side of learning and argued the case more concretely. Yet both arguments are similar in that the sophists have toyed with the strict sense of *learning*, "to understand," in such a way that the verb has become hardly, if at all, distinguishable from *know*. Even the conclusion of (E2) extends what is implicit in (D1). Both "Kleinias" as knower of letters and "he who doesn't know letters" can now be seen for what they are, as concrete realizations of "the wise" and "the ignorant" of (D1). Here, in (E2) and (D1), the brother-pair have joined their argumentative forces and are in agreement.

(D2)

> Thesis: Those who learn learn what they know (ἃ ἐπίστανται).
> Antithesis: Those who learn learn what they do not know (ἃ μὴ ἐπίστανται).
>
> Tell me, isn't learning to be gathering knowledge of what (ἐπιστήμην λαμβάνειν τούτου) one is learning?
> Kleinias agreed.
> And knowing, he said, isn't it to have knowledge already (ἔχειν ἐπιστήμην ἤδη)?
> Yes.
> Then isn't not-knowing not yet to have knowledge (μήπω ἔχειν ἐπιστήμην)?
> He agreed with him.
>
> (277 B 6–C 1)

The conclusion of (E2) triggers the next argument. After assuring Kleinias that he has been utterly deceived by Euthydemus, Dionysodorus reasserts the distinction between learning and knowing that was blurred in (E2). His strategy for achieving this trick is to set forth what might appear to be definitions, but which are really nothing more than verbal paraphrases of those terms that Euthydemus has featured throughout his questioning: first, Kleinias agrees that learning is to be gathering knowledge of what one is learning; then that knowing is to possess knowledge already, whereas not-knowing is not yet to possess knowledge. Significantly, by using an indeterminate object (τούτου) for what is learned, Dionysodorus moves away from the concrete letters of (E2) and returns to the vagueness of the "things" of (E1). The infinitives, linked by the verb *to be*, create an almost abstract atmosphere, far different from the concrete context of (E2). Armed with these new levers, the sophist can set his latest verbal trap:

> Are those who are gathering something (οἱ λαμβάνοντες ὁτιοῦν) those who already have it (οἱ ἔχοντες ἤδη) or those who don't have it (οἵ ἂν μὴ ἔχωσιν)?
> Those who don't have it.

Well then, have you agreed that those who don't know (τοὺς μὴ
ἐπισταμένους) belong to this group, to those who don't have it, and
not to those who do?

He nodded.

Then, do those who learn belong to those who are gathering
something, and not to those who have it?

He granted it.

Therefore, those who do not know (οἱ μὴ ἐπιστάμενοι) learn,
Kleinias, and not those who know (οἱ ἐπιστάμενοι). (277 C 1–C 7)

The key to understanding this fourth argument is to observe how
synonyms and antonyms are used for a contentious purpose. Compare, for example, Dionysodorus' first question with the one that Euthydemus used to trigger (E1). The expression "those who are gathering" is a synonym for Euthydemus' "those who learn (οἱ μανθάνοντες)."
Likewise, "those who already have it" and "those who don't have it"
gloss "the wise (οἱ σοφοί)" and "the ignorant (οἱ ἀμαθεῖς)," respectively. With these "new" terms, Dionysodorus can repeat (E1) in a
fresh way. Consequently, when Kleinias answers this first question
with "those who don't have it," he affirms in effect the view that the
ignorant are those who learn, and thus restates both the antithesis of
(E1) and the thesis of (D1). Now if we fix our attention upon that indefinite "something (ότιοῦν)," which our learners are attempting to
gather but do not yet have, then we may also observe that Kleinias has
both undone the thesis of (D2) and already granted its antithesis. For
"those who don't have it" are uninformed learners in the very process
of gathering knowledge about "something" that they do not yet have,
that is, about *what they do not know.* Contrarily, "those who already have
it" or "the wise" cannot learn *what they know,* as Kleinias himself did in
(E2), for they already "have" the object in question. So once again
Kleinias has fallen into an eristic trap that Dionysodorus has expertly
tailored to fit the specifications of this refutation. Now the sophist is
free to complete his line of questioning as he sees fit. But he does not
polish off (D2) mechanically by a formal statement of the rejected thesis and established antithesis; that would be too easy.

In his second question Dionysodorus continues the course of the
argument on the basis of Kleinias' earlier concessions, asking him
whether he has also agreed that "those who don't know" belong to the
class of "those who don't have it" and so are among those still gathering something. And when Kleinias agrees, it becomes obvious that the

boy has reversed what he just said at 277 A 8. Now "he who doesn't know letters" can in fact come to know them by simply gathering knowledge about what he doesn't know or have. With the introduction of the subject "those who don't know," we can at last match up the synonyms of these argument-pairs with their corresponding antonyms: *the wise* (οἱ σοφοί), *those who already have* (οἱ ἔχοντες ἤδη), *those who know* (οἱ ἐπιστάμενοι), and *those who learn* (οἱ μανθάνοντες), in the sense of "those who already understand" (τὸ συνιέναι) correspond to *the ignorant* (οἱ ἀμαθεῖς), *those who don't have* (οἱ μὴ ἔχοντες), *those who don't know* (οἱ μὴ ἐπιστάμενοι), and *those who learn* (οἱ μανθάνοντες), in the sense of "those who are gathering knowledge" (τὸ λαμβάνειν ἐπιστήμην). Both senses of the verb *learn* fluctuate back and forth between the polar terms on the subject-side of learning. On the object-side, this oscillation is effected by corresponding shifts in the terms used to designate what is learned: *things* (ταῦτα), *what was being dictated* (τὰ ἀποστοματιζόμενα), *letters* (γράμματα), and *something* (ὁτιοῦν).

In his final question Dionysodorus adds nothing significantly new. He merely links the weak sense of *learn* with its synonym "those who are gathering," a connection that he already implied at 277 B 6–7. As we can expect, the sophist caps his conclusion with the vocative address, but let us look more closely at the precise wording of his final statement. Since the two expressions for the subjects, "those who don't know" and "those who know," are synonyms for "the ignorant" and "the wise," the conclusion of (D2) can also read: "Therefore, the ignorant learn, Kleinias, and not the wise."[28] Thus, not only has Dionysodorus ended this argument precisely where his brother did (E1); but he has also reversed the conclusion that he himself established in (D1). So again, just as (E2) contradicted (E1), (D2) has now refuted (D1).[29] Like his brother, then, Dionysodorus is victorious but inconsistent. Obviously (D2) does not adhere as closely to the schema that we have provided as some might like, for Dionysodorus has shifted back to the subject-side of learning and so does not offer an exact statement of the antithesis.[30] But there really is no problem here. Plato's design is simply to have (D2) turn back upon and dovetail with (E1), and thereby to complete the links between the twofold argument-pairs.[31]

Throughout this performance the brothers have operated on the unstated assumption that learning does in fact exist; that is, they have acted as if they answered affirmatively to the bare Eleatic dilemma, whether learning is or is not. On this assumption, they first offered Kleinias two possibilities for its subjects, the wise or the ignorant. Then they reduced both alternatives to absurdity by showing that either answer led not only to a contradiction (that was easy to accomplish), but even to its opposite. In the second argument-pair, they performed a similar operation, only this time toying with the objects of learning, and again demonstrated that either horn of this dilemma could also lead to a contradiction. These contrasting arguments display the final form such antinomies can take, as well as the consummate skill by which they can be delivered. They constitute, in sum, an advertisement for eristic wisdom, and we may well doubt whether Hippias or Gorgias or even Protagoras himself could have staged a performance to surpass this one. The brothers are not to be denied their due kudos. They have successfully demonstrated their ability both to produce and to use arguments for the purpose of punching out a boy. We are presumably to imagine a development in which arguments *pro* and *contra* on the topic of learning have undergone a progressive crystallization until finally, here in the *Euthydemus,* they have achieved their ultimate expression. Certainly the fifth antinomy of the Διςςοὶ Λόγοι (1–10), which features "the wise" and "the ignorant," can be cited as evidence to support the view that such a development was in fact occurring at the close of the fifth century.

INESCAPABLE QUESTIONS (Ἄφυκτα Ἐρωτήματα)

We began this chapter by establishing the protreptic restrictions within which Socrates confined the brothers, the criterion by which we were to judge the effectiveness of their exhortation, and the agonistic model for verbal dueling that trapped the young Kleinias in a web of inescapable questions. Then we passed in review four argumentative sequences that were interrelated by a degree of difficulty and sophistication not usually appreciated by critics of these matters. In fact, these argumentative pairs constitute a specimen of reasoning not unlike, in form at least, any of the hypotheses of the *Parmenides,* a fact that alone should cast doubt upon the need to import an Aristotelian method of sophisms in order to solve the fallacies of the *Euthydemus.* Quite apart from the very real danger that such a method of exegesis may actually obscure Plato's intention, it has unquestionably directed attention away from the clues, within the dialogue itself, that reveal his design. To recover that design, then, we must return to the text and, in particular, to the first eristic scene, to begin constructing a still broader context for evaluating the general features of eristic activity.

We may start by noting what happens immediately after Euthydemus puts his first disjunctive question to Kleinias. While the boy is considering his response, Dionysodorus, with an eager grin of anticipation, leans slightly to his right and, for Socrates' amusement, predicts the final outcome of the first dispute: "Whichever way the young man answers," Dionysodorus assures Socrates, "he will be refuted." At this point Socrates does not know on what basis Dionysodorus can make such a prediction, yet he does see the need to warn Kleinias. As it turns out, he is too late to rescue the boy from the clutches of the brothers, who then proceed to pin him to the ground for the first fall. Then, during the interval between Euthydemus' second trigger question and Kleinias' response, Dionysodorus again seizes the opportunity to inform Socrates that his brother has just released another question not unlike the first. And when Socrates assures him that their first question was a dazzling success, Dionysodorus proudly comes forth with: "All our questions, Socrates, are of this sort, inescapable (ἄφυκτα)." What then does the elder of the two sophists disclose to us about eristic activity by calling their questions *inescapable?*

To begin with the obvious, the inescapable nature of their questions, as Socrates immediately notes, provides the brothers with the basis of esteem that they enjoy from their students.[32] But is Plato trying to tell us something more by allowing the word *inescapable* to slip from the sophist's mouth? We have already seen how Euthydemus' opening question gave Kleinias the seeming advantage of selecting an answer from only two possible alternatives.[33] And we have also observed how Euthydemus undermined that advantage by using the disjunctive question as a weapon in a vicious game of refutation.[34] Furthermore, we are aware that this kind of aggressive behavior in argument is not in itself improper, nor, for that matter, is it infrequent in Plato's dialogues. In the *Gorgias,* for example, where the endless logomachies take on several of the characteristics of a street-fight, we see how competitive the game of questioning and answering can become. But what is so disturbing about this particular case is that Kleinias is not allowed to deliberate carefully and to formulate a position that he then chooses to defend publicly against all comers—a perfectly rational way, many might argue, for an interlocutor to behave in a society where discourse is assumed to profit by the clash of ideas. To the contrary, Euthydemus has here used the disjunctive question as a tactical weapon in order to guarantee that the thesis, which the boy is forced to uphold, can take only one of two possible forms; and thus he has quite literally put the thesis in Kleinias' mouth.[35] And if Euthydemus can continue to saddle his opponents with only one of two alternatives, then he has succeeded in making his eristic challenge considerably easier. First, he need prepare ahead of time only two lines of argument on each particular topic in order to contradict theses or defend antitheses, as the case may be. And second, he can store away the various lines of attack in his memory for recall as weapons in upcoming verbal combats.[36] All that is required for this activity is that the sophist maintain his position as questioner and manipulate the line of questioning in such a way as to keep maneuvering opponents onto topics for which he has an arsenal of prepared refutations.[37] So if eristics can continue to perform this, their own proper work, then there is indeed a sense in which their questions are inescapable, for whichever way an interlocutor responds, he will be refuted. In this manner, then, the brothers can achieve a measure of verbal infallibility. In fact, they can achieve what might be called the ultimate fantasy of eristic sophists, a sustained state of everlasting victory in contentious debate. But regardless of how absurd this delusion will turn out to be, we must not fail to observe that Plato is here treating a serious disease of the soul to which any "philosopher" may succumb.[38]

Now perhaps no feature of this disease is more conspicuous than the willful employment of inescapable questions, and if we are ever going to grasp with some certainty those elusive "rules of eristic" so frequently bandied about in scholarly discourse, we must continue to analyze this questioning procedure at still greater depth. So far the brothers have employed only two inescapables. Yet we have witnessed enough to conclude that, once the victim takes the bait and provides his eristic master with an answer, the remaining questions of each argument have a programmable sequence: inescapable questions are thus preludes to inescapable arguments (ἄφυκτοι λόγοι). But the questioning techniques of the brothers do not function as smoothly in episodes three and five as they have just done, nor should we expect them to do so; after all, this first episode is a display-piece for this kind of thing, and the brothers catch the naive Kleinias by surprise. In fact, in the third episode Socrates launches a direct attack against these unfair questioning procedures, and throughout the fifth episode he continually interjects disruptive miscues into eristic question-dueling. And Ktesippus too will seize upon the eristic argument, grapple with the brothers on their own terms, and derail even further the smooth mechanics of their questioning, so that in the end we come to observe something closer to comic dialogue than to dialectical discourse, something closer to slapstick than to philosophy. But what will become increasingly apparent, as we work our way through the whole dialogue, is that all inescapable questions, together with their equivocal terms and syntactical ambiguities, are but preludes to frozen pieces of reasoning, stored away for future recall and requiring only a set of triggers or cues to set in motion inescapable arguments.[39]

To illustrate this point, then, that only the right trigger or cue is necessary to set in motion a crystallized refutation, we need to analyze some examples from later argumentative chains, one, (E4), which pictures eristic mechanics at their very best, and two others, (E16) and (D21), which arise later in the final episode, after the procedures for standardized question-chains have come somewhat unraveled. For our first example we can begin our analysis at the moment when Socrates reaffirms his own commitment to the moral improvement of Kleinias and urges the brothers to undertake his instruction in a serious and professional manner (282 D–E). At this point Dionysodorus immediately reshapes this appeal into a disjunctive question which he uses to finesse Socrates into defending a thesis, and then launches an attack, (D3), in such a way that the appeal for the boy to become wise turns out to be, through a masterpiece of jugglery, a wish for him no longer to be, or for him to perish (283 B–D). Not seeing the merits of this philosophical joke, however, Ktesippus, Kleinias' lover, then counters Dionysodorus' conclusion with this aggressive and rude taunt:

> O my Thurian guest, if it were not too rude a thing to say, I would say, "May destruction fall upon your head," for what it was that prompted you to accuse me and the others falsely ($\kappa\alpha\tau\alpha\psi\epsilon\acute{\upsilon}\delta\eta$) of such a thing ($\tau o\iota o\hat{\upsilon}\tau o\nu\ \pi\rho\hat{\alpha}\gamma\mu\alpha$), which I find impious even to speak ($\lambda\acute{\epsilon}\gamma\epsilon\iota\nu$), that I could want him to perish.
>
> (283 E 2–6)

When he concluded (D3) with a false accusation, Dionysodorus succeeded in provoking this response from Ktesippus. Now, seizing upon
the young man's words, Euthydemus launches a verbal assault, (E4),
on the topic of falsehood that will lead directly to his next argument,
(E5); then the falsehood problem will continue to appear, in one guise
or another, throughout the third episode. So it is crucially important,
not just for isolating the mechanics of inescapables in general but also
for understanding the entire third episode, to observe how Euthydemus shifts the line of discourse onto a topic for which he and his
brother have a repertoire of stock arguments:

> What? said Euthydemus. In your opinion, is it possible to falsify
> (ψεύδεσθαι)?
> Yes indeed, [Ktesippus] said, unless I am mad.
> Does one do so by speaking something (λέγοντα τὸ πρᾶγμα)
> about the subject under discussion, or by not speaking?
> By speaking, he said.
> Then if one speaks it, he doesn't speak anything other among
> things which are than that which he speaks, does he?
> No, of course not; for how could he? said Ktesippus.
> And that which he speaks is also one distinct thing apart from
> other things which are.
> Yes, of course.
> Then does he who speaks that, speak that which is (τὸ ὂν λέγει)?
> Yes.
> Well then, surely he who speaks what is and things which are
> speaks the truth (τἀληθῆ λέγει); and so, if Dionysodorus speaks
> things which are, he speaks the truth and says nothing false against
> you (οὐδὲν κατὰ σοῦ ψεύδεται).
>
>   (283 E 7–284 A 8)

At this point there is no need to discuss the change in meaning
from "accuse falsely" to "falsify" or even to begin sorting out the numerous equivocations in the polysemantic term "speaking." Such
problems have almost inevitably led critics to adopt some form of the
Aristotelian treatment of fallacy. At this stage our task is simply to isolate the terms in Ktesippus' rebuke that Euthydemus carefully sifts
out, reshapes, and transfers into another context in order to force the
falsehood topic into the debate.[40] In particular, he drops the prefix
(κατά) from the compound verb *accuse falsely* (καταψεύδῃ) and retains
only the absolute infinitive *falsify* (ψεύδεσθαι); he alters "such a thing,"

which referred specifically to Dionysodorus' rude insult, to a vague "something," itself ripe for a twist in meaning, once he fastens upon the act of speaking and begins to explore its ambiguities; and finally, after he shows that, by excessively minute verbal links, "to speak something" can become "to speak that which is," which, in turn, can become "to speak the truth," Euthydemus returns to the term that originally triggered the argument (καταψεύδῃ), restores the prefix κατά (only now it governs σοῦ), and finishes (E4) with: "[he] says nothing false against you." In this example we should marvel first and foremost at the brothers' perfect teamwork. Playing the role of straight man, Dionysodorus provokes Ktesippus' angry response in which Euthydemus seizes upon the trigger and formulates the inescapable question: "In your opinion, is it possible to falsify?" Since the question requires only a yes or no answer, and since the (intuitively correct) answer "yes" may be anticipated, Euthydemus can stand ready to crank out the frozen line of reasoning that has come to form the basis of (E4).

Not all verbal links will be transformed into inescapable questions as smoothly and successfully as the one just discussed. As the dialogue continues, the triggers and cues that connect the various topics will become more and more far-fetched. Yet still, amid the plethora of non-sequitur discourse, we can with certainty isolate the triggers that set in motion all the sophisms. For example, in the latter half of the fifth episode (299 D 1–E 9), Ktesippus reveals that he has mastered at least one technique for derailing eristic procedure, that of hitting upon a bizarre counterexample. In (D15), Dionysodorus fancied that he had gained a refutation by forcing the young man to agree to the absurd notion that it is a good thing to have a talent of gold in the skull. But Ktesippus blocked the sophists' triumph by responding:

> They do say that the happiest and best of the Scythians (Σκυθῶν) are those who have plenty of gold in their own skulls . . . and, what is still more surprising, they both drink out of their own gilded skulls and see down (καθορῶσιν) into them, even as they hold their own head in their hands.
>
> (299 E 3–9)

The Scythians were of course notorious for gilding the skulls of their enemies and using them as drinking cups.[41] Here, by picturing a context in which it is a good thing *for them* to have gold in their skulls,

Ktesippus successfully checks Dionysodorus' refutation. But at the same time he leaves himself open to Euthydemus, who now launches the next attack, (E16). Seizing upon the trigger words "Scythians" and "see down," Euthydemus formulates an inescapable question that turns on the ambiguity, both syntactical and onomastic, found in the phrase "things capable of sight":

> But which of the two? said Euthydemus. Do Scythians (Σκύθαι) and the rest of mankind see (ὁρῶσιν) what is capable of sight (τὰ δυνατὰ ὁρᾶν) or what is incapable?
>
> (300 A 1–2)

Although Euthydemus has managed to pick up "Scythians" and "see" from (D15) and to plug them into the now familiar disjunctive formula, unlike (E4) this argument has a comparatively thin thematic connection to both the preceding and subsequent arguments. The argumentative routine of the brothers has now become disjointed, their teamwork sloppy, their success minimal.

In our third and final example, (D21), Ktesippus provides the trigger with the interjection and explanatory vocative "Puppax, O Heracles." Here Plato brings the fifth and final episode to a close by having Dionysodorus force these two terms into the disjunctive formula and ask (303 A 7–8): "Is Heracles Puppax or Puppax Heracles?" With this concluding inescapable question, we have at last reached the final absurdity. No matter how senseless and inappropriate words may be, they can still be grist for the questioning procedure of eristic, since argumentative form, now completely divorced from any meaningful content, has been honed into a weapon for the purpose of beating interlocutors speechless—a state that Socrates himself refers to as absolute enslavement to eristic wisdom.[42]

To repeat, a careful study of episodes three and five shows that either Socrates or Ktesippus initiates each eristic argument by providing the triggers that allow the brothers to formulate and then release inescapable questions for which they themselves have stockpiled refutations.[43] This point has been demonstrated at such length in order to show that there is Platonic method behind eristic madness, that he is parodying an excessively mechanical form of argumentation that has lost its spontaneity and immediacy, lost its ability to confront living issues and living interlocutors.[44] In the *Euthydemus* Plato has displayed a series of artificial and deliberate arguments on a variety of contemporary topics which have undergone a progressive development and crystallization such that, in the repertoire of verbal villains like Euthydemus and his brother, they can become an arsenal of verbal weapons for the appearance of verbal infallibility. At this early stage of our analysis it is essential to have this overview on all three eristic sections before we encounter any further instances of eristic argumentation. Otherwise, we, too, may become enmeshed in the labyrinthian *homonymia* of the sophist-pair, quibbling over this or that fallacy, even doubting whether Plato is conscious of fallacy at all.

ON THE EQUIVOCAL USE OF MANΘÁNEIN
(277 D 1–278 E 2)

To argue whether in the *Euthydemus* Plato displays a consciousness of ambiguity, in general, or of the mechanics of this or that fallacy, in particular, is still to operate within the framework that Aristotle carved out for the study of syllogistic miscues. Although the *Euthydemus* is certainly an important document in the historical development that finally culminated in the systematic treatment of fallacy, we must remember that Aristotle strove to develop a logic that was consistent with his goal of scientific precision in verbal descriptions. A necessary part of that logic was a branch that waged war against all forms of error in reasoning and, in particular, against ambiguity, which was a literary device operative as early as Homer, but which suffered a perverse twist at the hands of fifth-century sophists, who distorted its power for their own purpose of psychological management.[45] So whereas it is no doubt helpful to analyze the twenty-one sophisms catalogued by Bonitz as specimens of abortive argumentation typical of a primitive age before Aristotelian logic, we must also recognize that such an emphasis can obscure, and in fact has already obscured, the attempt to recover what this dialogue has to offer. To save the *Euthydemus,* then, we must work back to a time prior to Aristotle when, for Plato and his contemporaries, ambiguities in language existed for all. What differed was the motive governing their use or, in the case of unscrupulous individuals, their deliberate abuse. In this first eristic display Plato has pictured for us the abuse of ambiguity. But a fact that never escaped him is that these first two sophisms illustrate considerably more than just the ambiguous use of terms. They contain a host of other perplexities as well, not the least of which are the psychological riddles involved in any account of learning and knowing; and such knots cannot be unraveled simply by making a few verbal distinctions.[46] Thus, not only equivocations but also other fallacies in the Aristotelian sense, which continue to crop up throughout the eristic sections of the *Euthydemus,* are best regarded as an index to just one type of difficulty that Plato inherited from the sophists and sought to solve in the most economical way possible. But the crucial point to remember is that Plato's method for solving them is not to write the treatise *Sophistici Elenchi;* that honor falls to Aristotle.[47]

Turning out attention, then, to where we left the dialogue before our excursus upon inescapable questions, we find ourselves in a position to complete our analysis of the first episode. When Socrates observes that Kleinias is about to sink under the pressure of eristic skirmishing, he wisely interrupts the contest and provides the boy with a general critique of what has just happened (277 D 4–278 C 7).[48] Urging him not to be surprised if the brothers' arguments appear unfamiliar, Socrates likens the entire experience to the performance that attends the chairing of an initiate into Corybantic mysteries.[49] Like those who minister unto such rites, Socrates explains, the brothers are just dancing about, raising a din of intoxicating music, and causing him to lose consciousness of everything but the whirling rhythms of their logic, all to induce him to submit, in Corybantic fashion, to forces outside himself.[50] By calling attention here to the *external* pressure that the brothers have brought to bear upon their young subject, Socrates emphasizes that Kleinias has not been refuted in any genuine sense. Rather, Euthydemus and Dionysodorus have conjured up the phantom of refutation by manipulating the context in which his answers have appeared; in fact, every answer that Kleinias gives to the questions of the first eristic can be shown to be correct, at least insofar as he understood what was being asked and so answered in accordance with his true beliefs; and for that matter, it can also be shown that the noble Kleinias continues to answer correctly and truthfully from his first remark till his last, when Plato finally removes him from center stage (290 D 8); so the boy's apparent failure to uphold the λόγος is just that, apparent. But, as Socrates continues, there is a significant respect in which the brothers are inferior to Corybantic ministers. The two sophists can stir up emotions, disorient, and even render their subject delirious; that is, they can perform the preliminary steps to their eristic mysteries by applying external pressure and bringing about submission. But, unlike their Corybantic counterparts, they are powerless to deliver the final rites, which are intended to cap the ceremony by returning the neophyte to a state of calm and tranquility.[51] In Plato's vivid portrayal, then, the brothers are suddenly transformed into the phony ministers of pseudo-philosophical mysteries, and as such they become the perfect foil for Socrates, who in the next episode will accomplish the initiation in the true sense.[52] But before he undertakes this task, Socrates offers Kleinias a more serious analysis of this sophistic ritual:

> Now then consider what you have heard to be just the preliminaries of their sophistic rites. For first, as Prodicus says, you should learn about correctness in words ($\pi\epsilon\rho\grave{\iota}$ $\grave{o}\nu o\mu\acute{a}\tau\omega\nu$ $\grave{o}\rho\theta\acute{o}\tau\eta\tau os$); and in fact the two foreigners are pointing this out to you, because you did not know that, although we can apply the word *learn* ($\tau\grave{o}$ $\mu a\nu$-$\theta\acute{a}\nu\epsilon\iota\nu$) when someone, beginning with no knowledge about some field, at a later time gathers knowledge ($\lambda a\mu\beta\acute{a}\nu\eta$ $\tau\grave{\eta}\nu$ $\grave{\epsilon}\pi\iota\sigma\tau\acute{\eta}\mu\eta\nu$) about it, we can also apply the same word when, having knowledge already ($\grave{\epsilon}\chi\omega\nu$ $\check{\eta}\delta\eta$ $\tau\grave{\eta}\nu$ $\grave{\epsilon}\pi\iota\sigma\tau\acute{\eta}\mu\eta\nu$), someone uses it to reexamine that same field in action or speech. Although in the latter case we tend to use *understand* ($\sigma\nu\nu\iota\acute{\epsilon}\nu a\iota$) more than *learn*, still there are occasions when we use *learn* as well. And what you failed to detect, as they are pointing out, is that the same word can apply to people in opposing states, to the knower and the not-knower.
>
> (277 E 2–278 A 7)

In this passage Socrates first gives credit to Prodicus for stating a general principle of sophistry, that one is obligated to learn about correctness in words; and we need not suspect that he is being completely ironical; if Kleinias were to possess the power to disentangle near synonyms, he might not have fallen into these verbal traps.[53] Then, in order to provide a concrete illustration of this principle, Socrates goes on to identify the twofold sense of the Greek verb *learn* ($\mu a\nu\theta\acute{a}\nu\epsilon\iota\nu$).[54] But, unlike the brothers, he is not treating the two meanings of this word as mutually exclusive; he is not suggesting that "from the beginning" refers to an absolute fixed point of no knowledge at all, and that "having knowledge already" denotes an understanding so complete as to preclude the need for further inquiry; nor by "subjects in opposing states" does he mean the absolute knower and the absolute not-knower, that is, the wise and the ignorant in their mutually exclusive sense; for that would be to tread across the fallacies of the brothers.

Rather, Socrates is concentrating the whole force of his solution upon the task of articulating that middle realm between the extremes by stipulating for Kleinias *two different occasions* when the word in question is actually used.[55] Ordinarily, he emphasizes, we use the word *learn* to refer to the act of gathering knowledge about some unknown subject matter, although there are occasions when we use it for the critical survey or reexamination of a field that one has already learned. But not without heavy irony is the credit that Socrates attributes to the brothers for providing Kleinias with this lesson in Prodicus' wisdom, as if all along they had been trying to demonstrate a truth about predication, that one and the same word can denote subjects in contrary states.[56] Here, Socrates has just culled the gist of what was contained in their performance and generously credited these two mountebanks with teaching Kleinias this valuable lesson.

Can we detect anything in Socrates' solution to justify the conclusion that Plato is unconscious of the logical fallacy of equivocation? Richard Robinson believed that he could, and in a sense he is correct to complain that "the *Euthydemus,* just because it is so *concrete,* does not settle the question what abstract consciousness Plato had of fallacy."[57] What is more, he could have continued beyond this question to indict the work's concreteness for almost all its shortcomings, its inability to settle questions regarding the principles, procedures, and psychological implications of this eristic technique of argument; for it cannot be denied that Plato has chosen to leave us with an extremely concrete display of the subject matter under investigation. But what has proven to be a source of irritation to Robinson—the dialogue's concreteness— is precisely what makes the *Euthydemus* such a singular philosophical work. In fact, it is this very concreteness that reveals Plato's consciousness of another type of ambiguity, whereby an author uses the characters of his own devising to direct the audience to what is unstated or unconscious in the speakers. In this form of representation the author can appeal to an audience "through" his characters and not just "in" their language.[58] So at a level beyond the mere *ipsa verba* of this scene, we find that Plato could not have provided a better illustration of the equivocal nature of the learning act than he has already done through the action of the dialogue itself.[59] Socrates, who has himself learned and so understands the correct use of words, is now in the very process of extending that knowledge to the task of instructing Kleinias, who is just beginning to learn, that is, to gather knowledge about correctness in words; and in the fourth episode the boy will bridge the gap between gathering knowledge and understanding when he sets out on his own to apply his new knowledge to another subject.[60] In contrast, the brothers, who have recently dropped military science and forensic oratory in favor of eristic, have just demonstrated how to misapply their newly acquired "knowledge" by punching out a boy in argument; and this too, even as Plato transforms them into the perfect vehicle for illustrating how the deliberate abuse of equivocation can mislead our thinking. It is in this fashion, then, by having the dialogue itself instantiate its own meaning concretely, that Plato demonstrates beyond question that he is in complete control of what he is doing.

After disambiguating the equivocal μανθάνειν for Kleinias, Socrates goes on to purge the harmful aspect of the boy's experience by calling the brothers' performance "play," a form of verbal sport in which his apparent defeat need not have serious consequences. But we should note with care why he can call eristic activity a mere game:

> I can use the word *play* (παιδιάν) for this reason: if someone should learn many or even all such tricks, he would be no closer to knowing how things are (τὰ πράγματα . . . πῇ ἔχει), but he could play with people by tripping them up and overturning them through differing over words (διὰ τὴν τῶν ὀνομάτων διαφοράν).
>
> (278 B 3–7)

Socrates grants that by *differing over words* eristics can trip up and overturn their opponents in verbal controversy.[61] In fact, they can have a jolly good time of it playing in this way, but such eristic sport should not be confused with the serious business of pursuing the truth; and here Socrates has, with precision, put his finger upon the limitations that apply to all logical-linguistic analysis. Mongering in paradoxes, toying with language games in a historical and philological vacuum, and even the study of logic itself are but preliminaries to serious philosophical activity and should never be allowed to usurp the whole of that activity. For these propaedeutic disciplines can never pass outside the realm of language and logic to a knowledge of how things really are. They can, of course, provide tools for inquiring into the nature of things—Socrates, too, will play on the ambiguity of terms—but, as Plato has just demonstrated, such studies can also provide the savage weapons of verbal violence if they are "learned" by unscrupulous individuals who then pervert their use for prestige and profit.

CONCLUSION

In the opening pages of this chapter we said that Kleinias was the criterion by which we were to judge the effectiveness of the protreptic discourse. He was that ideal student ready to gel beautifully if the protreptic phase of his education were properly handled; for neither self-satisfied nor complacent, he was tenuously balanced or equipoised, as it were, between the poles wisdom and ignorance, ready to be urged forward or knocked backward, depending upon how the next stage of his learning was handled. As luck would have it, the brothers arrived in Athens, accompanied by their clique, at precisely the right moment for undertaking the next phase of his instruction. Through some verbal jugglery of his own, Socrates used a series of questions to finesse the brothers into restricting the expression of their wisdom to the protreptic aspect of virtue-teaching, and then provided Axiochus' son as the subject of that instruction. But against the youngster, the eristic model for verbal interchange became gratuitous, and instead of producing different arguments and using them differently in order to fit their instruction to the protreptic context, the sophist-pair performed a masterpiece of legerdemain by juggling mere words in a polished routine that turned disturbingly comic within its context. For in this first episode they have ravaged the activity of learning, that very activity by which human excellence can be imparted, first from the side of the subject, and then from that of the object. They were aided in this destructive enterprise by the fact that the whole field of learning is freighted with ambiguities on which they could capitalize for the purpose of giving a free exhibition of their stunning power to contradict any interlocutor—provided, of course, that they could also determine their victim's thesis beforehand through the skillful employment of inescapable questions. Within the protreptic context, however, the very success of this playful triumph has utterly undone serious instruction in virtue by revealing with all manner of dramatic clarity the comic inversion of the brothers' original boast, that is, their unique ability *to betray virtue* (ἀρετὴν παραδοῦναι) best of men and most quickly.

These four refutations, which together constitute an eristic show-piece, are in reality, as Socrates notes for our benefit, merely a playful anatreptic, analogous to pulling a chair out from under someone who is about to sit down, a move rendered the more perverse because their victim, Kleinias, has been portrayed as the kind of lad least deserving of such treatment. Finally, to appreciate this first episode properly, we should remember that although Plato has spent no little effort in dramatizing this masterpiece of eristic argumentation, unparalleled for its refinement and conciseness, he also wants us to see that this first eristic display has more in common with dance routines, ball games, and bogus initiation rites than with serious pedagogy—that, in truth, it is nothing more than play, a form of verbal sport that cannot perform a serious role in the business of virtue-teaching.[62] For that serious performance, we must now turn to the next chapter and examine how Socrates, the true protreptic master, guides the discourse.

2

SOCRATES' PROTREPTIC MODEL

Instead of fulfilling their promise to deliver a protreptic discourse, the brothers merely played with Kleinias by giving a display-piece that was antithetical to the serious instruction required by the occasion. To ensure that serious instruction, Socrates himself now offers to guide the pair in what he conceives to be the proper way to conduct the protreptic address. Consequently, the Socratic guidance of the discourse gains an additional significance: not only will he do the serious business of the dialogue by guiding Kleinias to philosophy, but also he will present the brother-pair with a paradigm that they themselves can imitate. Accordingly, both Kleinias and the brothers become the subjects to whom Socrates delivers his remarks, and this fact greatly increases the structural complexity of the *Euthydemus;* for it reveals that this protreptic model, while whole and complete in itself, is also a partial element or exemplum in the broader dialogue between Socrates and the brothers. In fact, on two occasions, both before and after he converses with Kleinias, Socrates meticulously designates this broader aspect of his protreptic by addressing Euthydemus and his brother with the vocative.[1] Add to this observation that Socrates both begins the first episode and ends the second with vocative addresses to Crito, and we can also see that the outer frame of the dialogue, the conversation between Socrates and Crito, is still intact.[2] And inasmuch as we have isolated these strands to the structure of the dialogue, we must now guard against the tendency to detach the first episode from the second and to seek some positive doctrine in the latter without having to account for its relation to the former; after all, both episodes qualify each other in important respects by their sameness and difference.[3] At any rate, it should be clear by now that the five-part episodic structure, so striking to the casual reader, is actually a formal device that Plato has used to give shape to the events of Socrates' narration, and that this dialogue is in reality a series of interconnected and interpenetrating conversations. To such considerations regarding the work's overall artistic integrity I shall return, after we have traced the entire pattern of thought in Plato's *Euthydemus*. For the present enough has been said to warn the reader against the danger of treating Socrates' protreptic in isolation from its wider context.

How then are we to receive this second episode? For that, we need to examine the remarks that Socrates himself gives us in order to guide our understanding. Before he begins, he informs the brothers that he will dare to speak *extemporaneously*, and he follows up this clue with another (confirmed again after the exhortation) that he may appear to do so *amateurishly*.[4] Both clues should be sufficient warning against scrutinizing his line of thought for what it was never intended to have, namely, that precision in argument which he attributes not to himself but to the brothers.[5] But we should not conclude from these remarks that Plato is unable to achieve the kind of tightfisted precision that will appear later in the protreptic genre. Rather, in the *Euthydemus* Plato is under an artistic constraint to prolong the exhortation to such an extent that when Kleinias finally begins to take the reins of the discourse in the fourth episode, we do not feel any breach in the verisimilitude that this work must strive to attain.[6] In fact, it is precisely all these features, the extemporaneous, unprofessional, unduly long, and untechnical nature of this protreptic model, that Plato has consciously and deliberately used, not just to attain verisimilitude, but to provide the sharpest possible contrast to the presentation of that newfangled antilogical reasoning of the brothers. To determine the success or failure of Socrates' paradigm, we need only consider how it affects its immediate audience. If Socrates succeeds in exhorting Kleinias to pursue philosophy and so provides an adequate model for Euthydemus and Dionysodorus to imitate, then he will have achieved what he is setting out to accomplish. In this chapter, too, we shall continue to concentrate on the methodological features of conversational discourse, on the hypothesis that this model exhortation is not only a self-contained unit directed to Kleinias in particular but also, and more broadly, an integral part of the whole, illustrating proper dialectical correctives to the destructive elenchus displayed by the brothers.[7]

KLEINIAS' INITIATION INTO THE MYSTERIES OF PHILOSOPHY (278 E 3–280 B 5)

Where to begin inquiry, how to proceed from that beginning, and to what end philosophical inquiry should advance are questions that always concerned Plato. He has already assured us that Socrates will tackle the *how* question through the guidance of the discourse. But what are we to say about the *beginning* and *end* of this protreptic model? For that we need to turn to the first question put to Kleinias: "Do all of us want to fare well (ἆρά γε πάντες ἄνθρωποι βουλόμεθα εὖ πράττειν)?" Here Socrates has submitted an inescapable question in the true sense of that expression, for to respond negatively is ridiculous and senseless.[8] Unlike the question that Euthydemus used to trigger the first eristic, this one neither embarrasses nor confuses Kleinias. It does not turn him into the defender of a thesis or entangle him in a verbal dispute. Rather, by answering affirmatively he becomes a participant in a cooperative inquiry with Socrates, who has just established with his question a first principle in a twofold sense: first, he has provided a firm basis of support, a secure and incontestable principle from which Kleinias can begin his upward journey; and second, he has projected the end of that journey, the ultimate goal toward which not only Kleinias but all of us strive. What, by contrast, does this first principle tell us about eristic procedure?[9] To answer this question, let us return briefly to the circumstances surrounding the beginning of the first episode (275 C 5–D 4). Feigning perplexity at the start of his narration in mock imitation of the poets (for to recollect a wisdom so immense is no slight task),[10] Socrates invokes the Muses and Memory to assist him in his effort and then here are his words: "Euthydemus began from here somewhere (ἐνθένδε ποθέν)." The phrase "from here somewhere" refers to the source of that beginning. It points to the *where* or *from what basis* the sophist began. But by the very vagueness of the expression Socrates is suggesting that Euthydemus is without a secure, sound beginning.[11] Similarly, eristic is without an end or goal toward which its inquiry advances, for it does not "advance" in any ordinary sense of that word—it just bounces back and forth between antinomous poles. As a result, the brothers have neither a beginning nor an end to their protreptic because they do not start from established principles or advance toward agreed-upon conclusions. So, to overcome the arbitrary and accidental beginning of eristic, Socrates must adopt for the occasion the literary device of invoking the Muses and Memory.[12]

From the first principle of his protreptic, Socrates initiates the next stage of their journey by asking Kleinias whether they can achieve what is now admitted to be their universal aim by acquiring many goods (πολλὰ ἀγαθά). Socrates even suggests that the answer to this question is simpler than the first, though here we may suspect a touch of irony.[13] At any rate, he does not leave this question untested but begins immediately to probe what Kleinias understands by good things. To approach this problem, Socrates offers a list that ranks goods conveniently into four types. First, all agree that to be wealthy is a good. Then, from wealth, the star instance of an exterior good, Socrates puts forth two somatic goods, health and beauty, only to cap this second class by adding the general clause, "to be supplied adequately in body with the rest." From the goods of the body he moves to items that are acknowledged to be "good" by citizens of a polis, such as family connections, political powers, and honors. For his fourth and final type he lists goods of the soul, to be temperate, just, and courageous, qualities that we can immediately identify as three of the four cardinal virtues. Although, as Socrates admits, someone may dispute the enrollment of this fourth type among the goods (arguing, say, that we do not practice justice as a good but as a necessity, because the law requires it), Kleinias does not hesitate to include these psychic goods in the fourfold list.[14] That this classification is loose and not rigid is indicated by the casual way in which Socrates introduces the items. He does not use a regular term for classifying (τιθέναι) until he questions Kleinias on the status of psychic goods. In fact, it is not at all clear what Socrates is up to, for now he just simply selects Wisdom (Σοφία) for special consideration. His focus here on wisdom should not seem completely accidental, for this virtue can be found in ethical discussions in fifth-century literature, and in our text the term has been prominent ever since Crito first introduced it. In fact, the noun σοφία has already turned up eleven times before it is personified in this passage,[15] and, as the dialogue progresses, wisdom will continue to increase in importance until at the end we observe that all the strife and combat of the *Euthydemus* has been in some sense for its attainment.[16] But here we should resist the temptation to regard it as the fourth member of the cardinal virtues, for Socrates does not make such a connection. He simply asks Kleinias whether he ranks wisdom among the goods. To the question of *where* in the chorus of goods wisdom is to be ranked, we shall soon return. But for the present Socrates does not press its significance. Once Kleinias agrees that they have exhausted the possibilities for ranking goods, he simply shifts to the next phase of his protreptic λόγος:

Then upon recollection (ἀναμνησθείς) I said: Yes, indeed, we
are likely to leave out the greatest good of all.
What is this? he said.
Good fortune (εὐτυχίαν), Kleinias. Everybody, even the un-
sophisticated (οἱ φαῦλοι), say that it is the greatest of goods.
True, he said.

(279 C 4–8)

Whereas Plato carefully constructs the context so as to allow his
case for the importance of wisdom to build gradually, we can find no
antecedent remarks in the *Euthydemus* that have adequately prepared
us for this reference to good fortune; its sudden prominence appears
accidental, uncaused. Why Socrates has suddenly capped wisdom with
this new item we shall see later, after we have examined the movement of thought in this section, but for now we must state the obvious.
Prompted by a recollection, Socrates has hastily submitted good fortune as a candidate for classification in order to ward off any embarrassment that may occur through his failure to include what all take to
be not just a good, but the greatest good. Where, then, in the chorus
of goods are we to rank good fortune? To be candid, we have not been
instructed on what to do with the term.[17] That it represents some kind
of threat to a philosophical protreptic, we may gather from Socrates'
remark that "even the unsophisticated" embrace it as the greatest
good.[18] Moreover, translators usually render the term by "good luck"
or "good fortune," implying thereby that it refers to a favorable coin-
cidence of circumstances that do not depend on the subject who acts.[19]
As such, we may be tempted to classify it among exterior goods, regarding it as some abstract *cause* or even as some divine agent beyond
human control. Or perhaps the term is not to be divorced from its
root, τύχη; accordingly, it would refer to that "chance" or "pure luck"
which can often be discovered operating in human affairs.[20] What
would then make fortune good or favorable is whether the events of
which it is alleged to be the cause turn out "well (εὖ)" for someone.[21]
This subjective response reveals that good fortune can also be regarded as the *result* of events caused by chance. At the very least we
misinterpret Socrates' strategy if we do not see that by introducing
good fortune he is also introducing a whole cluster of problems that
directly influence his protreptic. Consequently, we can anticipate that
Socrates will seek to remove whatever challenge good fortune may
represent:

Then I had a second thought (μετανοήσας) and said: We have almost turned out ridiculous before our guests, son of Axiochus.

Why? he said.

Because, after we classified good fortune in our former list, we began just now to speak about it again.

What is that?

Certainly it is ridiculous to add a second time what has already been classified and so to repeat ourselves.

How do you mean this? he said.

Surely, I said, wisdom is good fortune (ἡ σοφία . . . εὐτυχία ἐστίν). Even a child could recognize this—and he expressed wonder (καὶ ὃς ἐθαύμασεν); he was still so young and innocent.

(279 C 9–D 8)

Just as unexpected as Socrates' *recollection* of good fortune is his sudden *reconsideration* of its role among the goods. Although again it may be difficult to determine what he is planning to do, we can be sure that both mental events refer to psychological acts in which eristic cannot indulge. Once an eristic argument is set in motion, the rigid form of its line of questioning does not permit the freedom to recall outside points of interest or to reformulate positions in light of second thoughts. Such flexibility, however, is necessary for a dialectician, who seeks to meet the contingencies of all occasions. So here, by implication, Socrates is criticizing the inflexibility of eristic, a point that verges on open indictment once we observe that even the criticism he aims at himself and Kleinias for saying the same thing twice is also directed at Euthydemus for twisting questions around the same topic.[22] But if Socrates' strategy is still difficult to determine, perhaps we should consider what has been stirring in the mind of his young interlocutor ever since wisdom was first enshrined among the goods. Prior to Socrates' recollection, Kleinias had either affirmed or denied the questions that were asked. But at 279 C 5, Socrates dropped the questioning procedure in favor of simply recalling the likelihood of omitting the greatest good. This statement prompted Kleinias for the first time in the dialogue to ask a question of his own. He followed up this question with a second when Socrates reported on the folly that they almost incurred before their guests. He asked a third when it was further suggested that good fortune had already been entered among the goods, and he even put a fourth when Socrates remarked on the ridiculousness of repeating their earlier remarks. Assured, then, by these four questions that Kleinias is indeed following the tracks of the λόγος, Socrates abruptly stuns him by remarking: "Surely wisdom is good fortune." Now although this seemingly strange claim will soon be modified, our attention at this point should be directed to the boy's immediate reaction: he experiences wonder (καὶ ὃς ἐθαύμασεν). Obviously, then, Socrates' reminiscence and second thoughts do not just guide us from one line of reasoning to another; they also signal two additional moves in a series of dialectical strategies designed to awaken Kleinias' spirit of inquiry. And the wonder experienced here by Kleinias is our first unambiguous indicator that Socrates has indeed awakened that spirit.[23] Throughout this episode and into the fourth, Socrates will orchestrate other conversational techniques, the cumulative effect of which will be to stimulate Kleinias' philosophical awareness to such a degree that he will confidently seize the reins of the discourse on his own. But for the present Socrates must continue to introduce him into the mysteries of philosophy.

Having successfully evoked wonder in his young interlocutor, Socrates begins anew to guide him through another catalogue. This time, however, he shifts from goods to arts and uses them as exempla in a series of questions designed to approach wisdom from yet another direction:

> Once I became aware of his amazement, I said: Don't you know, Kleinias, that for success (εὐπραγίαν) in flute music, flute players are most fortunate (εὐτυχέστατοι)?
> He agreed.
> And also in the reading and writing of letters, grammar teachers? Certainly.
> What about the perils of the sea, surely you don't suppose that any individuals are more fortunate, as a general rule, than wise (σοφῶν) pilots?
> Of course not.
> What about when on campaign, with whom would you more gladly partake in the vicissitudes of chance, with a wise or an ignorant (ἀμαθοῦς) general?
> With a wise one.
> What about when you are sick, with whom would you gladly risk danger, with a wise or an ignorant doctor?
> With a wise one.
> Is that because you suppose you would act with greater good

fortune, if you should act with a wise partner rather than with an ignorant one?

He assented.

(279 D 8–280 A 5)

For his first two moves Socrates returns to those activities which Euthydemus had introduced, music and grammar.[24] Taking up first the flute player and then the grammar master, Socrates carefully inserts both into a context where he can qualify them with an adjectival form derived from "good fortune." Here the words "most fortunate" modify the two artisans, who achieve success through the proper application of their skill in fields where the criteria for correct action are usually so clear that luck or chance, whether good or bad, has little room to operate. With these two *exempla*, then, Socrates has constructed the context in such a way that good fortune cannot be antithetical to or even compete with wisdom, since both music and grammar seek by art to overcome the unforeseen. So in its new environment good fortune cannot be a *cause* of goods but must be a *result* achieved by an intelligent person's judicious use of the goods at his disposal. For his third question Socrates shifts to the art of sailing, where the unpredictability of chance has considerably more power to influence action than it does in music and grammar; hence, he adds the qualification "as a general rule."[25] To deny, however, as Kleinias does, that any individuals are "more fortunate" than pilots is to affirm that they too are "most fortunate." So Socrates' third example just confirms the same conclusion as the first two, that concerning success in sailing, professional pilots are most fortunate. But in this question he makes a significant addition by bringing back "the wise" to designate what kind of pilots he has in mind. For the reintroduction of this expression is an unambiguous sign that Socrates is beginning to connect his elenchus to that of the brothers. To continue that connection, he introduces two more arts, strategics and medicine, but, importantly, in his fourth and fifth questions he shifts to verbs in the second person singular so that, just as Euthydemus did in (E2), he can address Kleinias directly.[26] Further, to balance "the wise," he brings back "the ignorant," and when it is observed that Socrates puts both questions disjunctively, we cannot fail to see that he is here linking up this phase of his protreptic to the first argument-pair, (E1) and (D1). Now, however, Kleinias is not selecting one of two answers in some abstract, artificially constructed context, but choosing with whom he himself would more gladly risk dangers when on campaign or sick: with the wise or the ignorant practitioner of an art. Here the boy's choice neither saddles him with a thesis nor entangles him in a verbal dispute, but establishes instead his own preference, set in the realm of his own experience. For his final question in this series Socrates seeks to determine whether, in turn, Kleinias bases his preference for "the wise" on a more general preference for the wise over the ignorant because the skilled practitioner of any craft can guarantee a greater degree of good fortune than the nonprofessional. And when for the third straight time Kleinias expresses his preference for "the wise," Socrates leaps from the observation of individual cases to a general statement regarding not the wise man, but the nature of wisdom itself, as if an act of insight had suddenly discerned the universal and disengaged it in a generalization: [27]

> Wisdom therefore in every case causes (ποιεῖ) us to experience good fortune (εὐτυχεῖν). For wisdom could never err (ἁμαρτάνοι), but must (ἀνάγκη) act correctly (ὀρθῶς πράττειν) and hit the mark (τυγχάνειν); for otherwise, it would no longer be wisdom.
>
> (280 A 6–8)

Stating the conclusion first, that wisdom in every case causes men to experience good fortune, Socrates then presents the reasoning upon which it is based: Wisdom could never err, but must act correctly and hit the mark, for otherwise (if it had erred), it would no longer be wisdom.[28] Here the use of the verb τυγχάνειν, translated by "hit the mark," is significant, for, positioned as it is beside the notion of "correct action (ὀρθῶς πράττειν)," it has been divested of any trace of randomness that might be retained in its root. So both verbs serve quite well to link wisdom to good fortune. Finally, then, we are in a position to see what was obvious even to a child. Wisdom is good fortune in the sense that it *causes* good fortune, which in turn becomes the *result* of a prudent choice of means on the part of a skilled agent or wise man, who has correctly hit the target of ethical action because he is acting under the influence of wisdom. To contrast "acting correctly" and "hitting the mark," Socrates has submitted "error," which is here incompatible with wisdom.[29] For if an agent fails to attain his end, then another force must be guiding that action. Socrates does not here elaborate on what that force is or who the agent may be, although antecedent and subsequent actions clearly suggest that ignorance and the ignorant are the culprits.[30] In fact, even before Kleinias is granted the opportunity to respond to the argument, there is a dramatic break in the narrative where Plato allows us to imagine that the boy resisted Socrates' conclusion on the infallibility of wisdom so that the two had to follow out another line of thought that eventually reached a conclusion acceptable to both:[31]

> The two of us agreed finally (I do not know how) that our main point was the following: When wisdom is present, with whomsoever it is present, there is no additional need for good fortune. And once we both accepted this conclusion, I began again to question him about the status of our earlier agreements.[32]
>
> (280 B 1–5)

Although Plato denies us access to the arguments that finally undermined the position of good fortune among the goods, we can nevertheless determine Socrates' strategy for introducing it. Temporarily throwing the young man off track by initiating an abrupt transition away from wisdom, the main topic under consideration, to another item, good fortune, originally championed by the many and the unsophisticated, Socrates has caused good fortune to reappear in other forms in the context of skilled professionals and their arts until he has not only checked any threat it might pose to the success of his protreptic, but has also used it as foil for elevating wisdom to its place of primary significance.

Now anyone who has thus far followed Socrates' protreptic without losing sight of its connection with the first episode might want to ask: "With whom, Kleinias, would you more gladly undergo the dangers of the protreptic, with the wise protreptic master or the ignorant?" Such a question, as a point of dramatic completeness, begs to be asked by those who remain aware that the brothers and Socrates, eristic and dialectic, are in a competitive struggle for the allegiance of Greek youth; and it would not be difficult for us to predict which of the two Kleinias would prefer. So, too, as a point of dramatic completeness, we must comment further on the significance of the return of "the wise" and "the ignorant" in Socrates' questioning. At the moment of his first eristic challenge (275 D 5–6), Kleinias dimly intuited that Euthydemus' trigger question, "Who learns?" confronted him with a real dilemma, with a real problem about human values. Consequently, he there experienced genuine embarrassment and confusion. But his choice, "the wise," was crucially significant because it revealed at least his original inclination toward what he wanted to be. And Socrates has now made the ground for that choice a matter of conscious awareness by guiding him through a series of questions that have uncovered the basis of that preference in the fact that, if he were wise, he would have a greater likelihood of attaining happiness. So never having viewed the alternatives "wise" and "ignorant" as mere linguistic items positioned at the end of antinomous poles, Kleinias has gradually come to see that wisdom and ignorance are real goals to pursue or avoid. As someone who is genuinely engaged in the activity of learning and aspiring to be successful and happy, Kleinias now knows why he should prefer to be wise rather than ignorant.

It is possible that an unsympathetic critic may be lulled by the very simplicity and concreteness of this charming little scene into undervaluing what has here been accomplished. Plato has dramatized a casual encounter between two members of the same polis in which Socrates tested Kleinias' attitude toward generally accepted opinions; with the results thus attained, he began confidently from the boy's own convictions to guide him along a path of thought that has eventually led both of them back to their first point of departure, only to arrive there with a fresh understanding. With complete justification, then, we can say that Plato has here presented the very *locus* of the pedagogical experience.[33] But even more remarkable is the fact that he has also designed this scene to imitate a dance step. Presenting these introductory rites to his philosophical mysteries almost as if they were a prelude to a choral song, Plato has used Socrates as a vehicle to orchestrate a pattern of thought that could rival one of Pindar's prooimia.[34] Once having passed in review a list of conventional items that led to and were foils for wisdom, the object of primary focus, Socrates introduced good fortune, again as a foil, and again to concentrate still more attention on wisdom. After this ascent from particular goods to the abstract qualities of wisdom and good fortune, he turned back to concrete sciences and imparted a gnome on the wise man, which, in turn, he capped with the gnome on wisdom itself. Finally, having allowed us to imagine another movement of the same type, Socrates signaled the end to this phase of his philosophical dance by dismissing good fortune and returning to a reconsideration of the hypothesized goods. That Plato should imitate such a movement in the *Euthydemus* may at first seem surprising. But this surprise disappears altogether when we recall that Socrates has already compared the brothers to good dancers (276 D 5–6), has likened Euthydemus in particular to an instructor relaying signals to his chorus (276 B 6–7), and has described the entire eristic performance as dancing preparatory to initiation (277 D 6–E 2). Clearly, then, it has been Plato's intention all along to picture Socrates, in direct contrast to the brothers, as the true leader of the philosophic chorus, initiating the lad into the mysteries of dialectical thought by helping him to determine where in the chorus Wisdom is to be ranked: τὴν δὲ Σοφίαν ποῦ χοροῦ τάξομεν; (279 C 1).

KLEINIAS BEGINS TO CLIMB THE LADDER
(280 B 5–281 D 2)

Socrates and Kleinias have progressed through a cooperative inquiry in which they were able to conclude that the presence of wisdom eliminated any additional need for good fortune. But this conclusion, as important as it may be, has come at the end of a digression that was forced upon them by Socrates' recollection and second thoughts. So now Socrates proposes to pick up the thread of the λόγος by returning to their original beginning. But in reformulating this second point of departure, he makes a significant addition to their first principle (280 B 5–6): "We concurred, I said, that we would be happy (εὐδαιμονεῖν) and fare well (εὖ πράττειν) if we should have many goods." Although Socrates makes this statement as if it were already agreed upon, there is no trace of the verb εὐδαιμονεῖν in his earlier remarks.[35] So what permits him to say this? From the inception of this protreptic, we assumed that εὖ πράττειν could be translated by its passive sense, "to fare well," but there was room for doubt; the word also has the active sense, "to succeed." In this second beginning, Socrates makes it clear that we are indeed to view "faring well" and "happiness" as (near) synonyms.[36] So with happiness unequivocally established as the target at which we all aim, Socrates now begins to test the hypothesis upon which it was first said to depend, the possession of many goods. But instead of doing so by cataloguing more good items, he shifts to another procedure of argument, the technique of positing a series of hypotheses in order to investigate what higher principles govern the presence of these goods. The first hypothesis concentrates on benefit, the second on use:

Now would we be happy through the presence of these goods, if they should fail to benefit us or if they should benefit us (ὠφελοῖ)?

If they should benefit us, he said.

Then would they do so, if they should merely exist for us, but we should fail to use (μῆ χρώμεθα) them?

(280 B 7–C 1)

Kleinias readily accepts the first hypothesis, that we would be happy through the presence of goods, only if they should benefit us; but before he is allowed to agree to the second, that benefit from goods would depend, in turn, on the condition that we use them, Socrates reformulates the problem in a considerably more concrete way. Submitting two examples, food and drink, he asks whether we would benefit from them if we should fail to eat or drink. When Kleinias gives the required denial, Socrates could move directly to the next higher hypothesis. But instead he probes the importance of use and benefit in greater detail:

> What about all our craftsmen? If they were to have all the implements suitable to the performance of their end (ἔργον), but should fail to use them, would they succeed (εὖ πράττοιεν) simply on account of their acquisition (κτῆσιν), because they had acquired everything that a craftsman is obligated to acquire (δεῖ κεκτῆσθαι)? For example, a carpenter, if he were to equip himself with the appropriate tools and enough wood, but should fail to build, is there any way he would benefit from his acquisitions?
>
> In no way, he said.
>
> What if someone were to acquire money and all the goods of which we were just now speaking, but fail to use them, would he be happy (εὐδαιμονοῖ) because of the acquisition of these goods?
>
> Certainly not, Socrates.
>
> Then apparently, I said, he who is going to be happy not only should acquire (δεῖ κεκτῆσθαι) the goods of our list, but also should use them, or else no benefit accrues from his acquisitions.
>
> You're right.
>
> Then, Kleinias, have we finally arrived at a sufficient (ἱκανόν) criterion for making someone happy, that is, both the acquisition of goods and their use?
>
> I think so.

(280 C 3–E 3)

Examining benefit and use in the context of craftsmen who have equipped themselves with those exterior goods necessary for both the activity and final product of their craft, Socrates has considerably refined our sense of those goods which were formerly said merely to exist or to be present with us; for craftsmen do not just acquire goods; they carefully select those goods which are suitable for the end of their function.[37] To capture this refinement, Socrates introduces another key notion of his protreptic, the act of acquisition ($\kappa\tau\tilde{\eta}\sigma\iota\varsigma$). Then, even on the assumption that craftsmen have acquired all those goods which they must have for their particular work, he asks Kleinias whether they "would succeed" without the use of their goods. In this, the protreptic's final use of $\varepsilon\tilde{\upsilon}\ \pi\rho\acute{\alpha}\tau\tau\varepsilon\iota\nu$, we observe the conflation of several shades of meaning that have come to cluster around this compact term. Here, we have translated it by "would succeed," though earlier we rendered it as "faring well." The present translation seems justified because between the two formulations of his first principle, Socrates allowed the notion of success to surface twice, once when he slipped in the noun success ($\varepsilon\tilde{\upsilon}\pi\rho\alpha\gamma\acute{\iota}\alpha\nu$: 279 E 1) and then again when he proved that wisdom must act correctly ($\acute{o}\rho\theta\tilde{\omega}\varsigma\ \pi\rho\acute{\alpha}\tau\tau\varepsilon\iota\nu$: 280 A 8). So here, with his final use of $\varepsilon\tilde{\upsilon}\ \pi\rho\acute{\alpha}\tau\tau\varepsilon\iota\nu$, we are in just the right position to feel the tension that pervades its active and passive sense. Craftsmen could not "fare well" and "be happy" unless they were "to succeed" with the materials and instruments they have acquired. Earlier we demonstrated how Socrates could restrict the role of good fortune in his protreptic, even as he was expanding the significance of wisdom. Here, by manipulating two senses of $\varepsilon\tilde{\upsilon}\ \pi\rho\acute{\alpha}\tau\tau\varepsilon\iota\nu$, he has exploited this ambiguous word in order to bridge the gap between the process and the result, between our action and the happiness that we seek to attain from it.[38] So at last a point that some have had difficulty accepting is now clear: Socrates, too, can juggle ambiguous terms and even equivocate if he determines the situation warrants it. But the end for which he employs this dialectical technique is not ambiguous. Needless to say, he is not driven by an anatreptic urge to refute Kleinias, nor is he attempting to disentangle and to clarify closely related concepts for his young interlocutor, though obviously this is a result of his effort; nothing prevents linguistic analysis from being a valuable technique on occasion. Rather, Socrates has his mind's eye focused on a single task, the protreptic goal of exhorting a young man to turn toward wisdom and virtue. This is the work at which he must succeed if he is going to earn the victory palm in his contest with the brothers.

Kleinias is not allowed to answer the question "Would they succeed?" Instead, Socrates reformulates the problem by applying benefit and use to a specific case. From among craftsmen he selects the carpenter for primary attention, identifies his acquisitions as tools and lumber, and concretizes use with building. Then, to the question whether a carpenter would benefit from the goods he has acquired if he did not work wood, Kleinias gives an emphatic denial. From this example Socrates leaps to a quite general hypothesis, asking whether anyone *would be happy* through acquiring goods, even on the condition that he should acquire those previously listed but should not use them;[39] and here, too, we see the protreptic master at work, for in this question Socrates has again captured the passive sense of εὖ πράττειν by shifting back to its (near) synonym "would be happy."[40] When Kleinias again gives the required denial, Socrates can finally connect benefit and use once and for all. However refined our concept of acquisition may be, goods in themselves cannot guarantee benefit. They may be *necessary* for benefit, but they can never be *sufficient* (ἱκανόν). Benefit requires use. At last Socrates is ready to submit a formula that may have some claim to adequacy. He asks whether both the acquisition of goods and their use are sufficient for the end of producing the happy man. At this point Kleinias is willing to acquiesce.

So far we have used hypotheses like steps on a ladder in order to ascend to a formula that we are hoping will ensure our happiness. But this formula, too, is going to be inadequate, since one of its key ingredients, the *use of goods,* is still in need of qualification. That further analysis is now provided by Socrates, who posits yet another hypothesis that once again expands the parameters of his argument:

> But which of the two? I said, if someone uses them correctly (ὀρθῶς) or incorrectly?
> Correctly.
> You're right, I said. For if someone uses anything incorrectly (μὴ ὀρθῶς), this act produces more harm than if he were to leave it alone; the former is bad, whereas the latter is neither good nor bad. Don't you agree?
> He assented.
> What about this? In the production and use of lumber, isn't that which perfects correct use (ὀρθῶς χρῆσθαι) nothing other than the knowledge of building (ἐπιστήμη ἡ τεκτονική)?
> Certainly, he said.
> And further, I suppose, in the production of equipment, that which ensures correctness (τὸ ὀρθῶς) is knowledge (ἐπιστήμη).
> He agreed.
> Then, I said, regarding the use of what we were at first calling

goods, wealth, health, and beauty, is it knowledge that guides (ἡγουμένη) the correct use of all such goods (τὸ ὀρθῶς πᾶσι τοῖς τοιούτοις χρῆσθαι) and corrects (κατορθοῦσα) our action, or something else?

It is knowledge, he said.

(280 E 3–281 B 2)

The addition upon which Socrates now focuses is that of *correct* use, and here we observe the evaluative terms *good* and *bad* in uses that look suspiciously unlike anything we have encountered so far.[41] For the first time the words do not refer to things but to the use of things. Although Kleinias accepts the addition of correctness without hesitation, Socrates does not go on, as one might expect, to assign "good" to correct use. He does state without ambiguity that misuse is bad, even worse than leaving things alone (at least the nonuse of things can cut a middle path between good and bad); but, without elaborating further on this moral or nonmoral realm, Socrates continues to lead Kleinias upward by focusing his attention on the need for correctness. Returning to his last example, he asks Kleinias whether in carpentry that which can perfect correct use is anything other than the knowledge that pertains to building. When Kleinias agrees to the sovereignty of knowledge in this case, Socrates moves to a statement that is noteworthy for what it lacks. The problem under examination is still that of perfecting carpentry, but Socrates has dropped out both use and carpentry in order to leave the addition of correctness emphatically positioned beside knowledge. And his motive for doing so becomes readily apparent in his final question. Expanding the materials to be used beyond carpentry to include, once again, the original list of goods, Socrates makes a graceful leap to a more general notion of knowledge by asking whether the correct use of all such goods is perfected by knowledge, since it both regulates or guides action and corrects errors when, for example, the unforeseen conspires to drive actions off their course. When for the third straight time Kleinias expresses his preference for knowledge, Socrates has all the distinctions he needs to complete this upward phase of his protreptic λόγος:

In every acquisition (κτήσει) and action (πράξει), then, it is presumably knowledge (ἐπιστήμη) that offers to men not only good fortune (εὐτυχίαν), but also success (εὐπραγίαν).

(281 B 2–4)

Here Socrates has not only sublated both the hypothesized goods and their use into his concepts of acquisition and action, but also, by bringing back good fortune and success, he has unmistakably linked this conclusion to his earlier one on wisdom. And although seeming to have forgotten the addition of correctness, in reality Socrates need not include it, for "correct" use has been taken up by Knowledge, which is finally beginning to appear something like the power that is sufficient for leading us to happiness.

At this point we might anticipate that Socrates would continue to extend his analysis even further by beginning to probe the connection between knowledge and happiness, but instead he reverses his line of argument and begins to lead Kleinias back down the ladder which they have just ascended. Removing the intellectual component that is responsible for good fortune and success, he asks the boy whether benefit can accrue from acquisitions if there is no longer a guiding and correcting force for action (ἄνευ φρονήσεως καὶ σοφίας). On this hypothesis, he asks Kleinias to consider the problem in the following way:

> If someone should act less (πράττων), would he err less (ἐξαμαρτάνοι), and if he should err less, would he fail less badly (κακῶς πράττοι), and if he should fare less badly (κακῶς πράττων), would he be less miserable (ἄθλιος)?
>
> Certainly, he said.
>
> Now would someone more likely do less, if he were poor or wealthy?
>
> Poor, he said.
>
> If he were weak or strong?
>
> Weak.
>
> If he were held in honor or out of honor?
>
> Out of honor.
>
> If he were brave and temperate, or if he were a coward?
>
> A coward . . .
>
> On all such examples (πάντα τὰ τοιαῦτα) we agreed with each other.
>
> (281 B 8–D 2)

This first question, threefold and tightly condensed, requires un-packing.[42] In the first limb Socrates introduces action and error, which is also a way of bringing back use and misuse. In the second he links error to failure by joining it to the active sense of κακῶς πράττειν, here translated by "fail badly." In the third he slides to the passive sense of κακῶς πράττειν, to fare badly, and then connects this meaning to misery, ending with that poor wretch who has had the misfortune of attaining the opposite of what is agreed to be the goal of our striving. Thus, Socrates' threefold hypothetical question reverses the connections that he already established among "correct use," "success," "faring well," and "happiness." The brothers are not the only ones who can juggle synonyms and their corresponding antonyms. But just as in his earlier line of argumentation Socrates demonstrated that knowledge and wisdom caused benefit by joining together the positive qualities of the column, so too now he has shown that their absence vitiates benefit, by connecting the negative qualities "misuse," "failure," "faring badly," and "misery."

Having shown what advantages can result from doing less if one should be so unlucky as to act without the guiding and correcting force of reason, Socrates now attempts to determine under what circumstances an individual would more likely do less. In these questions, too, he continues the descent by extending the inquiry all the way back to the hypothesized goods, even repeating, with his first four examples, the original order of his list. Beginning with the exterior good wealth, he passes to the bodily excellence of strength, then to the political honor of holding office in the polis, and finally to the virtues of the soul. But, importantly, these "goods" are now conjoined to what are customarily regarded as their opposites and are no longer designated as either good or bad. In fact, the questions have lost their evaluative content altogether. Socrates is here emphasizing their quantitative aspect by examining under what conditions an agent does less. In this context it doesn't matter whether the agent possesses a characteristic that is conventionally labeled good or the reverse. Even courage and temperance, popularly conceived, are neither good nor bad, whenever one evaluates them apart from what causes their goodness or badness. What is significant here is simply the conditions under which someone would do less. In every instance Kleinias agrees that the advantage of doing less falls to that agent who has acquired what is conventionally considered to be the undesirable characteristic. Socrates uses a summary formula to break off his line of questioning, without providing any final cap to the reasoning, although the general conclusion is clear enough. Since an agent who acts without a guiding and correcting force (whether that force be knowledge, wisdom, prudence, or reason)[43] would be less miserable the less he should attempt to do, it is to his benefit to do less because the absence of the intellectual component guarantees error, error leads to failure, failure to faring badly, and faring badly renders one miserable, the very opposite of what we all desire.

ON WISDOM, THE ONE GOOD (281 D 2–282 D 3)

In sum, Kleinias, it is likely that for all those things which we at first said were good, our argument doesn't prove this, that they are, in their nature, good in themselves (καθ᾽ αὐτὰ πέφυκεν), but apparently our account is as follows: if ignorance (ἀμαθία) guides them, they are greater evils than their opposites to the extent that they have more power to serve that evil ruling element; but if prudent wisdom (φρόνησίς τε καὶ σοφία) guides them, they are greater goods, although in themselves neither of them is of any value (οὐδενὸς ἄξια).

Apparently, he said, it seems to be as you say.

What then follows from what has been said? Is it that none of these other things is either good or bad, but of these two (τούτοιν δὲ δυοῖν ὄντοιν), wisdom is good, and ignorance bad?

He agreed.

(281 D 2–E 5)

Returning again to what he has twice before referred to as goods (280 D 2 and 281 A 7), Socrates now tells Kleinias that the argument is probably not about those things at all, whether they are in their own nature good by themselves. For we assign value to things depending upon whether the commanding faculty leads to their correct or incorrect use. Here Socrates chooses ignorance and prudent wisdom to represent those two forces under whose leadership what were formerly styled goods become greater or lesser goods or even evils, relative to their capacity to serve either ruling element. By themselves, however, both those former goods and their opposites are neutral or without value. Socrates does not hesitate to follow out the final implications of his argument. In view of his most recent discoveries, he can now assign the value terms *good* and *bad*. Of other things, no one of them is good or bad absolutely, for they can achieve only comparative goodness or badness; but of these two ruling forces, wisdom is good and ignorance bad. In this sentence construction, it should not go undetected that this is the only use of the dual in Socrates' protreptic model. He employs it here to draw special attention to the fact that he has at last hit upon a real and true antinomous pair, wisdom and ignorance.

So with the two value predicates, good and bad, properly tethered to their subjects by the reasoning power of the λόγος, Socrates has finally come to where he may now seem to have been steering the protreptic ever since he posited his first hypothesis.[44] Then, the attainment of what was acknowledged to be our universal goal in life was said to depend upon the possession of many goods. From that hypothesis Socrates began to examine those goods, in which process he effected the shift and reduction from the many to the one, from a plurality of goods to *one* good, and not to just any good, but to *the* one good, wisdom, which is not a possession in the conventional sense of the term but is somehow or other "present with" an individual. Once again, then, Socrates has reinforced for Kleinias the need to learn about correctness in words. Like the word *learn,* good is equivocal. It has strict and loose, refined and unrefined senses. It can apply to wealth, to health or beauty, sometimes to the possession of political power and honor, and also to powers of soul such as courage and temperance. What is more, those very things that we call good can from time to time be called "bad," whenever human ignorance, usurping control over the ruling element, gains the opportunity to misuse our acquisitions. But strictly speaking, as the argument now indicates, the correct use of the term *good* comes into being when we restrict its application to wisdom.

Now it only remains for Socrates to show Kleinias that their joint inquiry has not produced playful arguments without serious intent, but conclusions that actually compel him to choose a certain course of action. Since knowledge offers good fortune, success, and, ultimately, happiness by being the guiding and correcting force that not only causes benefit to accrue from use but also guarantees that the use of possessions turns out to be correct, the moral imperative seems obvious: Acquire knowledge. Yet Socrates does not voice this commandment. Instead, he exhorts everyone (and not just Kleinias) to prepare himself to be as wise as possible. But this exhortation (it cannot fail to do so) also gives rise to another problem. Wisdom is not a commodity like money that can be handed over or inherited from father to son. So how can one acquire wisdom and then incorporate it into one's

soul? Here Socrates merely suggests that it can be shared (μεταδιδόναι) from one party to another and that Kleinias can without
shame serve another for any decent service in order to become wise.[45]
But then Socrates immediately undercuts this suggestion by positing
yet another higher hypothesis still in need of consideration: if wisdom
is teachable and does not turn up automatically. For not just *sharing,*
but all these terms, *handing over* (παραδοῦναι), *being present* (παρ-
εῖναι), *acquiring* (κεκτῆσθαι), and *inheriting* (παραλαμβάνειν), assume in some sense that wisdom is teachable, and so long as this possibility remains untested the sovereignty of wisdom can still be
questioned. Yet Kleinias accepts this final hypothesis without resistance, thereby relieving Socrates from the need to pursue the kind of
discussion that Plato reserves for the *Meno*[46]; for the question of the
teachability of wisdom would inevitably force Socrates to examine the
question "What is wisdom?" and that indeed would require a lengthy
investigation. But with this problem aside, Socrates can now advance
Kleinias to the critical moment of decision:

> So now . . . wouldn't you affirm that one must philosophize (φιλ-
> οσοφεῖν) and don't you yourself have in mind (νῷ) to do just that?
> Certainly, Socrates, he said, to the full extent of my ability.
> (281 D 1–3)

Presenting the choice to Kleinias on two levels, on the general necessity of pursuing wisdom and on the particular question of whether he
himself is going to do so, Socrates has skillfully positioned wisdom,
the object of love and learning, squarely before the young man's mind
(νῷ). Aware that there is much of which he is still ignorant, yet wise
enough to know that he still needs to learn, Kleinias passes from
thought to action without a hitch and chooses to do philosophy.

For his part, Socrates is aware that he has failed to analyze wisdom
with thoroughness and that even what analysis he has provided is still
in need of greater refinement. So he turns to the brothers at the end
of his protreptic and invites them to improve upon his model by overcoming its defects; for, as he admits, it was the work of a layman who
spoke with difficulty and at too great length (282 D 6–7). Either re-
fine the paradigm, he suggests, by repeating it with professional skill
(τέχνῃ), or complete the unpacking of wisdom by examining whether
Kleinias should identify and acquire each several form of knowledge
or one, the possession of which guarantees happiness. But without ad-

vancing to these considerations himself, Socrates can legitimately bring his efforts to a close. After having guided Kleinias far enough to allow him to opt for the pursuit of wisdom to the best of his ability, Socrates has not only completed this serious phase of the dialogue, but he has also provided the brothers with a protreptic specimen that has proved successful. Given the limitations that he himself and the brothers applied to their task at its inception, Socrates can take some pleasure in his small victory.

CONCLUSION

Before we analyze the remaining three episodes, in which the complexity of the *Euthydemus* increases dramatically, and while the contrast between the first two episodes is still in its sharpest and simplest form, it will be useful to take stock of some important points that we have already gained. Kleinias has reached that critical time in his life when he is equipoised between wisdom and ignorance, ready to be turned. Wielding their two-edged sword of paradox, the brothers turned him, all right. They flipped him on his back in a gratuitous, albeit astonishing, display in which they completed two twofold refutations through the skillful manipulation of bogus antinomies. By contrast, Socrates began in a methodologically sound way to repair the damage done by the brothers. He first gained acceptance to an inescapable question, that all of us want to fare well, a universal and incontestable principle, the rejection of which is ridiculous and senseless. Having secured this ultimate ground for his protreptic, Socrates then initiated Kleinias into the mysteries of philosophy by guiding him through a complex orchestration of dialectical techniques. First, he tested the boy's attitude toward conventional goods, in the course of which he made wisdom the object of primary focus. Then, by a series of hypotheses in which a number of relevant concepts were posited and examined, Socrates helped the youth to ascend to that region where for the first time both "good" and its converse, "bad," were linked to correct and incorrect use. Here, Socrates concentrated Kleinias' attention on the intellectual component in correct use until once again wisdom, now personified as Knowledge, appeared. From this height, where he might have investigated the relationship between knowledge and happiness, Socrates chose instead to reverse his line of argument and to lead the boy back down the same path whence they came. In his cross-questioning, Socrates worked between anti-nomous poles in order to set up degrees of value within the realm of opposites. In this particular case he constructed a real antinomy be-tween wisdom and ignorance, the one, the only true good, the other, the only true evil, whereas all other so-called goods and evils gained value by the degree to which they were guided by wisdom and igno-rance respectively. Having thus established his exhortation within this domain of value, Socrates then had a clear basis for his protreptic ap-peal, a clear reason on the basis of which he could persuade Kleinias to turn toward wisdom and away from ignorance. For wisdom is not only the one good, the cause of the goodness in other things; but it has also become the most immediate target at which Kleinias can now aim in his quest to attain happiness, on the hypothesis, of course, that it is teachable. But the answer to this vexed question is both "yes" and "no." Wisdom cannot be handed over mechanically and quickly to anyone who consents to pay the price, as the brothers have advertised. But if teaching is causing reminiscence of the really real, prompted by proper questioning in the process of which the student is turned, re-oriented, and then impelled toward wisdom, as we have just observed, then the teaching of virtue and knowledge can indeed take place. But a word of caution here. We should not allow the remarkable success of this episode to seduce us into imagining that Kleinias has made per-manent advances toward wisdom; that cannot happen in so short a period of time. He has taken only the first step toward the goal, and for now Socrates is satisfied with merely redirecting him away from conventional goods toward the one good.

Finally, let us return for a moment to Euthydemus' original ques-tion: "Who learns, the wise or the ignorant?" After having worked our way through Socrates' protreptic, we now find ourselves in a position to specify the proper answer with some confidence; it is Kleinias. With his first commitment to philosophize to the best of his ability, Kleinias has himself become the concrete climax to the first eristic enigma. And what are we to suppose is the object of his learning? Something the young man both knows and doesn't know: Wisdom. Those who learn in the strict sense are philosophers (οἱ φιλόσοφοι), because their love (φιλία) impels them toward wisdom (σοφία).[47] Yet lovers of wisdom can represent a broad spectrum of individuals who are at various stages along that path. At one end, Plato has presented Kleinias, who has just now chosen to pursue wisdom. At the other, we find Socrates, the protreptic master himself, who is capable of instilling that love of wisdom in another. But the subject of that instruction cannot be, in the words of the brothers, "anyone who agrees to answer." He must be a *fitting soul*, Kleinias of Athens, son of Axiochus, grandson of the elder Alcibiades.[48] Socrates and Kleinias, teacher and student, are the two real poles in this protreptic enterprise, bound together by their joint project, the positive pursuit of wisdom. Here, then, in direct contrast to the playful game of eristic, Plato has demonstrated that the serious study, which can rightly be called philosophy, is dialectic because it possesses the power to convert the soul to the philosophic life.[49] It is as if the eye of Kleinias' soul has undergone the initial phase of the philosophical conversion, which is also, by implication, a rejection of the bogus dualism of the brother-pair, a turning away from the horizontal antinomies of contentious debaters in favor of a veritable, vertical antinomy between wisdom and ignorance, neither of which is truly attainable in this life, although both do exist as objective *termini*, or outer guides, for our reorientation.

3

THE SECOND ERISTIC DISPLAY

It has become fashionable to assert that the six "sophisms" of this episode mark a significant "advance" in the dialogue because, "more important than the first two," they produce results that are "much more serious from a philosophical point of view."[1] For, as it is argued, since "the Eleatic logic which is at the bottom of the majority of fallacies in this present scene is inextricably tied to a metaphysics which denies becoming," Plato has "to expose these arguments" before he can "provide a satisfactory basis for the theory of Forms."[2] Now these assertions, while they are not wholly off the mark, are likely to distort Plato's intention at the very beginning of this episode. For though it is not inconceivable that Euthydemus and his brother are indeed a grotesque caricature of Parmenides and Zeno (and thus the *Euthydemus* presents, in part, a withering parody of Eleatic formalism), such polemical considerations, however important they may be for the history of Greek philosophy, reside in the distant background and should not blind us to Plato's more immediate objectives. In fact, in order to appreciate that distant past at sómething like its real value, we must first examine with some thoroughness those very problems which continue to challenge Plato as he constructs the second eristic display, the subject matter for this, our third chapter.

First of all, Plato must continue to dramatize his antithesis to the genuine philosopher by filling out his comic antitype with dramatic completeness. Clearly, this concern is a literary restraint that forces him to advance the action of his dialogue, but we have yet to determine the direction of that advance. Strictly speaking, it is not accurate to say that the brothers as character types develop within the context of the dialogue; at any rate, they do not develop in the way Kleinias and Ktesippus do. Rather, their characterization, like that of Socrates, does not undergo change but is as it were filled out; accordingly, both Socrates and the brothers remain throughout the dialogue those fixed poles under the influence of which the two young men, Kleinias and Ktesippus, do advance and change. We have already dealt extensively with Kleinias' advance under the guiding influences of both eristic and dialectic, and we shall complete his character portrayal in the next chapter. But for the present we must continue to follow the course of the dialogue itself, and so now we shift our emphasis to Ktesippus in order to concentrate upon how he reacts to his first encounter with eristic. Socrates, too, continues to be center stage, for on two occasions he is forced to break his silence and enter directly into this eristic universe of discourse, first in order to curb the mounting hostility between Ktesippus and the brothers (285 A 2) and then to counter the young man's defeat by turning the tables on the brothers themselves (286 B 7). Like the first two episodes, this third one is both a self-contained unit of dramatic action and a single part in a much larger unity that projects beyond itself by initiating the first critical moment or stage in the eristification process of Ktesippus. Although Plato does not complete this process until more than halfway through the fifth and final episode, we can at this point reveal the principle that he will use to effect this conversion: with no little subtlety and artistic finesse, Plato will gradually shape Ktesippus' character into a likeness of the eristic masters themselves.[3]

Moreover, fused with the artistic restraints that continue to limit Plato's choices is the philosophical motive that governs the two remaining eristic sections. To be sure, beneath the surface structure of the dramatic action Plato is examining views that have filtered down from giants like Parmenides and Protagoras. But more important to an understanding of the *Euthydemus*, these views are "now" in the verbal repertoire of contemporary philosophers, who are unacquainted with the convictions that motivated their predecessors. As representatives of this "new" type of philosophical experience, Plato has presented for our inspection Euthydemus and his brother, who have contracted an extreme philosophical disorder that has caused them to lose all orientation toward the Good. Without that standard or measure, then, the brothers just drift to and fro on the tides of the Euripus, supremely confident that they alone have intuited the truth, that nothing is secure in words or things.[4] So when Plato portrays the elder of the two sophists initiating the action of the second eristic by shifting abruptly from problems of learning and knowing to those of being and becoming, he is in fact offering a quite concrete picture of a disputant who has jumbled up our universe of discourse by dragging epistemological and metaphysical difficulties into a protreptic discourse where they do not belong. Neither canvassing the goods of our ethical life nor establishing hypotheses to test and ultimately to account for those goods, Dionysodorus just differs over terms in the language game of eristic sport.[5] So, to put the matter precisely, Plato does not allow the brothers to advance philosophical issues at all. Instead, he pictures them criss-crossing, seemingly at random, back and forth across the disparate fields of philosophical inquiry (and increasingly so, especially as the dramatic action of the fifth episode advances) without any concern for proper philosophical method. What remains constant in their argumentation (and this is the crucial point) is the operation of a single methodological principle: *the conversion of any interlocutor's responses to logic in order to extract from them the means for refutation.*[6]

In the first chapter we concentrated upon this principle and demonstrated certain paradigmatic features of its operation. We showed how the brothers injected the topic of learning into the debate, finessed Kleinias into theses on both its subjects and objects, and then concluded their performance by demonstrating that this topic could generate theses either horns of which eventually led to contradictions. In the six eristic arguments of this section the brothers continue to employ their method, but they dispense with the illusion of offering two genuine alternatives in their inescapable questions; for one of the two possibilities is obviously counterintuitive or contrary to what any reasonable person would believe. Here their strategy is simply to grant the seemingly stronger argument to their opponents and then, through nothing more than a display of their argumentative powers, to contradict and ultimately to refute those positions which have come to appeal to common sense. This aspect or movement of eristic wisdom will continue to roll on until the very act of contradiction itself becomes the battleground for eristic sport. But the apparent triumph of Dionysodorus on this topic will have the very real effect of ushering in a still deeper and more penetrating level of complexity. Indeed, it is at this crucial juncture that Socrates first confronts the brothers directly; for the first time, that is, the two poles, dialectic and eristic, begin to contend with each other in earnest. In the pursuit of our analysis of the *Euthydemus,* we shall continue to trace the movements of this episode, beginning at the beginning and following the path of the λόγος as it unfolds.

ON BECOMING WISE (D3) (283 B 4–D 8)

Tell me, Socrates and you others, who claim that you want this young man to become wise (σοφὸν γενέσθαι), are you playing (παίζετε) when you say this, or do you truly desire it and are you serious (σπουδάζετε)?

(283 B 4–7)

By beginning (D3) with an inescapable question that incorporates the antithesis between play and seriousness already introduced by Socrates at 278 C, Dionysodorus at once demonstrates his omnivorous appetite for digesting any content that comes his way. It is immediately evident that he is here not presenting two real options. Aware that Socrates has repeatedly stressed his serious commitment to Kleinias' welfare, Dionysodorus can easily anticipate which of the two disjuncts Socrates will affirm. Moreover, certain as he is of the thesis his opponents will accept, the sophist is also immediately aware of his eristic challenge. He must demonstrate a sense in which Socrates and the others are playing when they wish Kleinias to become wise; that is, he must discover how to swing his adversaries back to the other side of this dilemma. Socrates, on the other hand, is open and in fact must be open to the possibility that Dionysodorus is asking for real information; the brothers could have taken his protreptic appeal playfully, when in fact he intended it seriously; and this possibility could explain why they acted as they did in the first eristic.[7] So, to eliminate any further misunderstanding on his position, Socrates vows never to deny that he wants Kleinias to become wise. But he soon discovers that this vow, rather than clarifying his stance, has the effect of making him the target of Dionysodorus' next attack:

What then is your claim? he said. Do you want him to become wise (σοφὸν γενέσθαι)?
Yes indeed.
And now (νῦν), he said, is Kleinias wise or not (σοφός ἐστιν ἢ οὔ)?
He says not yet; he is not a boaster, I added.

But you want him to become wise (γενέσθαι αὐτὸν σοφόν), he
said, and not to be ignorant (ἀμαθῆ δὲ μὴ εἶναι)?
We agreed.
Therefore, who he is not, you want him to become, and who he
is now (ὃς δ' ἔστιν νῦν), no longer to be (μηκέτι εἶναι).
When I heard that, I was disturbed (ἐθορυβήθην).

(283 C 5–D 4)

In the first eristic display the subjects of learning were frozen at two
extremes, and there existed no process by which learners could
bridge the gap between ignorance and wisdom through coming to
know objects of knowledge. In (D3) Dionysodorus introduces that notion of process (γενέσθαι) for the first time, only to use it for his next
refutation. To begin the argument, he asks Socrates to affirm a clear
and unambiguous statement of the thesis that he has vowed never to
deny.[8] If, then, there is no possible confusion on what Socrates wants
Kleinias to become, still the sophist asks: "And now (νῦν), is Kleinias
wise or not?" To this question Dionysodorus can anticipate the answer
"not wise," for Socrates has repeatedly said that he wants Kleinias to
become wise, and, in fact, to become wise was the goal of his protreptic. Furthermore, even to affirm this question, as Socrates indicates,
would be the mark of a boaster. So why does the sophist even bother
to ask this question? At this point strategic considerations prevail.
With his second question Dionysodorus has not only anchored both
the boy and the argument to the present moment (νῦν); he has also
managed quite unobtrusively to slip the verb *to be* (ἔστιν) into his line
of questioning. Having thus established the context to his liking,
Dionysodorus can begin to counter what Socrates wants Kleinias to
become.

Moreover, if we attend to this second question from Socrates' point
of view, we can see that the sophist has actually presented his opponent with a real problem. Socrates is aware that this "now" introduced
by Dionysodorus captures something ambivalent about Kleinias' immediate condition; it expresses the tension that pervades the boy's
existence. At the present moment Kleinias is in part wise and in part
ignorant, but "now" fortunately, after the success of the protreptic, he
is at least on a trajectory toward wisdom. "Now" he has the target
within his sight, but he has "not yet" attained the end. Mere mortals,
in fact, cannot fully attain the wisdom that has just been articulated by
Socrates, for it exists as the goal or terminus for our reorientation. All

of this, however, is of no interest to Dionysodorus. The sophist has hypostatized this "now" into a linguistic entity that he can manipulated like any other counter in a game of refutation. In fact, he has turned it into an absolute fixed point from which, as we shall see, any change will necessarily entail deadly ramifications. In his third question Dionysodorus alters the expressions "wise" and "not wise" to "wise" and "ignorant," and here perhaps it may appear that he again plans to juggle these two terms. But the dichotomy between "wise" and "ignorant" is not the lever that will overturn the thesis. Rather, at this point Dionysodorus' primary strategy is simply to position the linguistic item *not to be* (μὴ εἶναι) at the very end of its colon where it can effectively balance its contrasting term *to become* (γενέσθαι). And we should not be surprised by Socrates' ready agreement to this question; insofar as it is possible, he wants Kleinias *to become* wise and *not to be* ignorant. But the sophist's next move requires the reader to exercise extreme caution.

Momentarily delaying his fourth question, Dionysodorus reformulates the third into a statement that swallows up the predicates "wise" and "ignorant" into relative clauses, a move that creates considerable ambiguity. For it is now unclear whether these two clauses modify the subjects or continue to perform the role of predicates. Assisting this move, crucial to the outcome of the refutation, is a trick first noticed by Gifford: ὅς (who) has here replaced οἷος (what kind), thereby disguising the fact that the clauses are properly the predicates of the verbs.[9] Complementing this syntactic ambiguity is the related problem of whether in turn the two infinitives *to be* (εἶναι) and *to become* (γενέσθαι) now stand absolutely or link subjects to predicates. And to complicate matters still further, Dionysodorus has expanded his expression "not to be" into "no longer to be (μηκέτι εἶναι)," thereby adding a temporal indicator that can oppose the fixed point established by "now."[10] For our purpose, we should direct special attention to the second half of Dionysodorus' statement: "You want him . . . who [he] *is* now, no longer *to be* (ὃς δ' ἔστι νῦν, μηκέτι εἶναι)." Here the verb *to be* (ἔστι and εἶναι) can carry two senses: (1) to be (ignorant) and (2) to be (simply). Hence the sentence can be translated: "You want him, who is now (ignorant), no longer to be (ignorant)" or "You want him, who is now (simply exists), no longer to be (simply to exist)." At this critical moment it is impossible to determine with certainty which sense of the verb *to be* is operative, since Dionysodorus is still in the process of shifting from the first to the second meaning, a task that is not completed until his next question.

But significantly, with his remark "When I heard that, I was disturbed," Socrates distances himself from Kleinias' partisans. To understand his reaction, we need to pay particularly close attention to the context; for those who translate ἐθορυβήθην by "I was thrown into confusion" may be in danger of misinterpreting the subtlety of this crucial transition. One might assume that if Socrates were not confused but fully conscious of the fallacy employed in (D3), he would intervene and analyze equivocal εἶναι the same way he earlier analyzed μανθάνειν; the fact that he doesn't move to solve the fallacy could then be construed as evidence for Platonic confusion on the several senses of being. But Socrates' behavior becomes intelligible if we regard his earlier solution to the problem of learning as *the* paradigm for a type of analysis. In fact, it became the permanent model for equivocation, after Aristotle anchored its form in his logical treatise (*Sophistici Elenchi* 4.165 B 30–34). Had Plato wanted to do so, he could have had Socrates disambiguate (D3) as well, though of course this mere possibility doesn't mean that this or any other solution would be equally satisfying to all; but he could do it.[11] Here in the context of the *Euthydemus*, however, it suits Plato's immediate purpose to hint indirectly at the source of the problem by picturing Socrates' disturbance at the very moment when Dionysodorus is beginning to swing the argument back to the other side of the disjunct, and then to withdraw him from the debate altogether. After all, Plato need not repeat his method of solution, since he has already illustrated it effectively. Besides, he now intends to develop Ktesippus' role in the debate; and for that he must remove Socrates from the stage. But in the immediate context of (D3), Socrates becomes disturbed the instant he hears Dionysodorus scramble both the syntax and the terms of the sentence, because he believes he has just reached an unambiguous understanding with him on the importance of their protreptic enterprise. He thus anticipates a serious exhortation from the sophist and not more wordplay. But now Dionysodorus seizes upon the opportunity provided by this subtle break in the flow of the argument to deliver the *coup de grâce:*

> Taking advantage of my condition, he grabbed hold of the conversation and said: Then am I to understand that, since you want him who now is no longer to be, you want him, presumably, to per-

ish (ἀπολωλέναι)? And yet, how valuable would such men be, as friends and lovers, who would be so eager for their beloved to perish utterly!

(283 D 4–8)

In several limbs of this argument Dionysodorus has introduced a form of the verb *to be*. Now, in his fourth and final question, we see the eristic purpose behind these and other moves. With no little argumentative finesse he smoothly and deliberately slips in the qualifier "presumably," in order to prolong, ever so slightly, the introduction of the capping term *to perish*, which then suddenly and unambiguously illuminates the intended meaning behind "no longer to be." For at this moment he completes the radical shift from ethics to physics, from the verb *to be* and its use with the ethical predicates "wise" and "ignorant," to a term that signals the annihilation or nonexistence of a physical body. In a comic context such a radical shift in fields would trigger the laughter of the audience; but here, in the arena of the protreptic, it once again prevents the discourse from attaining the ethical seriousness that Socrates has all along hoped to reach.

Dionysodorus does not finish with an emphatic announcement of his opponents' defeat.[12] He does not remind Socrates of his vow never to deny what he had affirmed, nor does he state what is by now obvious, that Socrates and the others must have been playing when they wanted Kleinias to become wise. For he has his gaze fixed on an achievement that far transcends such minor accomplishments. Generalizing about the value of such men, as friends and lovers, who want their favorite to perish, Dionysodorus implies that the partisans of Kleinias want his destruction, an implication with devastating consequences. For he has thereby succeeded in implying that the goal of Socrates' protreptic, *to become wise*, together with its stirring exhortation, *to strive to be as wise as possible*, is not only impossible, but even if possible, undesirable, since any attempt to attain wisdom must entail the destruction of the subject who undergoes change.[13] And so with this astounding argument Dionysodorus has miraculously wiped out the constructive work of Socrates' protreptic and thus cleared the way for eristic play to roll on.[14]

Before turning to the next phase of this sport, we can benefit appreciably by recalling the substance of several important remarks from the first chapter. When we analyze (D3), it should be incumbent upon us to remember that this sophism cannot be adequately accounted for by simply isolating two senses of the verb *to be,* the existential and the predicative, or even by exposing the trick of having "who" stand for "what sort." Onomastic and syntactic ambiguity, *secundum quid,* in fact the entire Aristotelian apparatus for treating fallacies, can isolate only one feature of the numerous difficulties that this dialogue presents for our close scrutiny. More broadly, in each eristic argument Plato has combined a host of well-orchestrated terms, philosophical themes, and artistic motives that not only unify antecedent action and assume their own proper place in the totality, but also continue to initiate the subsequent movements of the dialogue. Indeed, the brilliance of Plato's *Euthydemus* can be marred and disfigured, if we persist in crowding the fullness of each eristic argument into some minor portion of the whole.

ON THE IMPOSSIBILITY OF FALSEHOOD
(E4 AND E5) (283 E 1–284 C 8)

Leaping beyond Dionysodorus' general remark on the value of those who wish for the destruction of their beloved, Ktesippus interprets this conclusion to apply directly to himself. Righteously indignant, he calls down just retribution upon the head of this foreigner who has impiously insinuated a false accusation into his relationship with Kleinias.[15] To the facts of that relationship he has special access, and he knows personally that he does not want his favorite to perish. Even the vague suggestion that he does, far from being the punch line to a philosophical joke of some merit, is to him an impious utterance that demands a retraction. In contrast, the brothers are in no position whatever to know how the relationship really holds between the two young lovers. Yet the elder of the two sophists, by exercising nothing more than his verbal power, has driven a wedge through that relationship and has momentarily cast doubt upon Ktesippus' passionate attachment to his love object.[16] Dionysodorus has committed the crime, and Ktesippus has launched the indictment.

The two arguments (E4) and (E5), which Euthydemus now uses to defend the false accusation of his brother, take the form of a general defense of the impossibility of falsehood.[17] We have already outlined in some detail (*supra* pp. 43–45) how Euthydemus enticed Ktesippus into advocating the positive thesis, that falsehood is real.[18] So now let us concentrate on how Euthydemus, too, abruptly shifts and jumbles up the field of discourse for his eristic purpose. Even a cursory glance at the texts of the Attic orators will prove that the trigger, *to accuse falsely* (καταψεύδεσθαι), is a common forensic term. In forensic disputes, questions of truth and falsity, intentional deception, misrepresentation of facts, false accusations, and the like are everyday matters, as is obvious to anyone who observes courtroom behavior. It is in this clearly defined, legalistic way that Ktesippus has indicted Dionysodorus for asserting a false accusation. But now Euthydemus abstracts the trigger from its duly constituted environment and converts it into the key item of a philosophical thesis that impugns, not the possibility of a false accusation, but the possibility of falsehood in general.[19] This shift from a forensic to a philosophical context proves decisive for advancing the dramatic action, for now Ktesippus, like Kleinias earlier, falls unawares into an eristic trap, and so the game continues.[20]

In his first move to attack the thesis Euthydemus induces Ktesippus to agree that falsehood, if it occurs, occurs in "speaking something (λέγοντα τὸ πρᾶγμα)." Now the obviousness of this move may not seem significant; truth and falsity are, of course, conditions of language. But in the expression "speaking something," Euthydemus has slipped into the argument two crucial elements for his refutation: both the notion of speaking and the object or subject matter that is spoken of.[21] The activity of speaking is important because it provides the linkage for his next three questions. But with each query he submits a different term for the object of speech; and we can easily follow his ruse. After passing from Ktesippus' remark "falsely accusing such a thing (τοιοῦτον πρᾶγμα)" to speaking "something (τὸ πρᾶγμα)," Euthydemus shifts to speaking "it (αὐτό)" and then to speaking "that (ἐκεῖνο)," and finally to speaking "that which is (τὸ ὄν)."[22] Add the fact that what a speaker speaks is both separate (χωρίς) and distinct (ἕν), and we can see how tightly the sophist is forming the connection between word and object, between speaking and what is spoken of.

When Ktesippus answers affirmatively to this final question, "Then does he who speaks that (ἐκεῖνο), speak that which is (τὸ ὄν)?" Euthydemus moves in for the climax. Concluding now, not in the form of a question, but with a summary statement,[23] he just asserts that he who speaks what is (τὸ ὄν) and things which are (τὰ ὄντα) speaks the truth. Here, too, the sophist has pulled off this hoax by subtly manipulating the verb *to be*. Just as Dionysodorus shifted from the predicative to the existential sense of εἶναι in (D3), Euthydemus has now slid from the factual to the veridical sense, and, exploiting the logical connection between fact and truth embedded in the Greek verb εἶναι, he has concluded that anyone who speaks things which are speaks the truth.[24] Then, before Ktesippus can respond, he completes this piece of legerdemain by capping the general conclusion concretely: "And so, if Dionysodorus speaks things which are, he speaks the truth and says nothing false against you." Having thus led his opponent astray by each minute step in the questioning chain, Euthydemus has momentarily pulled the chair out from under Ktesippus, whose apparent fall, we may suppose, triggered no small laughter on the part of the eristic clique.

But knowing that Dionysodorus has spoken falsely about his love for Kleinias, Ktesippus returns to the immediate context and claims: "Yes, Euthydemus, but he who says this (ὁ ταῦτα λέγων) does not speak things which are (οὐ τὰ ὄντα λέγει)." He thus accepts the general form of Euthydemus' conclusion (if A, then B), but contradicts its particular application (but not A, therefore not B). In denying the correspondence, then, between Dionysodorus' words (ταῦτα λεγόμενα) and that to which they refer (τὰ ὄντα), Ktesippus has successfully avoided defeat; but he has yet to escape from the clutches of Euthydemus, who now attacks him with the next argument, (E5):

> Then Euthydemus said: But isn't it the case that things which are not (τὰ μὴ ὄντα) are not (οὐκ ἔστιν)?
> They are not.
> Then doesn't it follow that things which are not are existing nowhere (οὐδαμοῦ . . . ὄντα ἐστίν)?
> Nowhere.
> Then regarding these things, things which are not, is there anyway someone, anyone at all, could perform (πράξειεν) an act so as to make (ποιήσειεν) things which are nowhere actually exist?
> Not in my opinion, said Ktesippus.
>
> (284 B 3–8)

Ktesippus has agreed to the general notion that to speak things which are is to speak the truth, but he has denied that Dionysodorus spoke things which are. Now Euthydemus goes one step further and attempts to prove that merely to speak is to speak things which are. Shifting radically from veridical claims to propositions based in the Parmenidean disjunction between being and not-being (a slippery move, but transparent in Greek because he negates the attributive participle ὄντα with generalizing μή), Euthydemus attacks Ktesippus with two questions that are immediately striking for their abstractness: he asks whether things which are not (1) *are not* and (2) *are existing nowhere*.[25] Here the language unmistakably suggests that the sophist is now dredging the philosophical graveyard for those unutterable and unthinkable items along the path that Parmenides bade us not to follow. For his part, Ktesippus gives the required answers to both questions so that Euthydemus can slide to a third. Introducing the notions of performance (πρᾶξις) and making (ποίησις), he asks whether anyone "could perform an act so as to make things which are nowhere actually exist."[26] When Ktesippus offers up his third straight denial, Euthydemus has established all the preliminaries he needs for constructing his refutation.

> What about our rhetoricians, whenever they speak (λέγωσιν) before the people (ἐν τῷ δήμῳ), aren't they performing (πράττουσι)?
> Yes of course they are performing, he said.
> Well then, if they perform, do they also make (ποιοῦσι)?
> Yes.
> Then is speaking (τὸ λέγειν) both to perform and to make (πράττειν τε καὶ ποιεῖν)?
> He agreed.
> Then, he said, no one speaks things which are not (τά γε μὴ ὄντ'), for in speaking he would at that moment make something. And you have admitted that no one can make that which is not (τὸ μὴ ὄν)—and so according to your own argument no one speaks falsely (οὐδεὶς ψευδῆ λέγει), but if Dionysodorus speaks, he speaks the truth and things which are (τἀληθῆ τε καὶ τὰ ὄντα λέγει).
> (284 B 8–C 6)

Shifting to a concrete case of speaking, Euthydemus counters the "nowhere" of his earlier question by submitting a locus before the people. For performers of speech acts, he offers rhetoricians, those members of the polis who are perhaps most notorious for false speaking. But his focus here is on the simple act of *performance*. Once Ktesippus agrees that those who speak before the people do in fact perform, Euthydemus draws out another implication in speech acts; those who speak are also makers or producers of speech. From here he goes on to force Ktesippus to agree that to speak is both to perform and to make—a necessary conclusion, especially given that the articular infinitive (τὸ λέγειν) indicates *prima facie* that an activity, performed and produced, is under observation. With Ktesippus' agreement to this point, Euthydemus has all he needs to round off (E5). Things which are not cannot be spoken, since the mere act of speaking is to perform and hence to make or to produce linguistic facts (τὰ ὄντα). And Ktesippus has agreed, as Euthydemus reminds him, that "no one can make that which is not" into something which actually exists. Then, linking the attempt to speak "things which are not" to "false speaking," Euthydemus concludes that "no one speaks falsely," as if this were the necessary outcome of Ktesippus' own argument.[27] Finally, applying this conclusion to the particular case, Euthydemus "proves" that his brother need not strive to speak things which are, but merely speak, and then abracadabra: Dionysodorus is not only acquitted of false speaking; he has also spoken what is true and real.

Again granting the argument's general validity but denying its particular application, Ktesippus responds directly to the point at issue: "Yes indeed, Euthydemus, that is, in a sense he speaks things which are (τὰ ὄντα μὲν τρόπον τινὰ λέγει), yet he does not, of course, speak how they really hold (οὐ μέντοι ὥς γε ἔχει)." Ktesippus is willing to grant that in a sense—in fact in the sense just outlined by Euthydemus—Dionysodorus speaks things which are. His verbal utterances do of course exist in that they are spoken words, performed and made by a speaker. But the mere act of speaking does not guarantee that the sophist has spoken how the facts really hold.[28] For Ktesippus can argue that, since Dionysodorus has failed to utter speech (τὰ λεγόμενα) that pictures or corresponds to the true state of affairs (τὰ ὄντα), his words are simply false. By calling them false, however, he would not mean, as Euthydemus has tried to suggest, that Dionysodorus' remarks are absolutely nonexistent. Ktesippus need not be suggesting that the sophist has made the absurd attempt to utter the unutterable "things which are not." Falsehoods can have a quasi-existence at least in the sense that they are other than or different from truly articulated states of affairs. Even though in standard Greek idiom the real and the true are often conjoined, this union need not hold in every particular case of speaking, especially since in (E4) and (E5) Euthydemus has intentionally distorted language in order to make a blatantly false accusation appear to be a true statement of the facts. Once again, then, Ktesippus has warded off defeat when he appeared to be on the very brink of refutation.

At this point one might have the vague feeling that Euthydemus is guilty of a self-contradictory attempt to refute Ktesippus' opinion on the real reality of falsehood by demonstrating, of all things, that it is a false opinion. At any rate, after five disputes we can clearly isolate one feature of eristic arguments, namely their susceptibility to suffer what they dish out. For example, were the general conclusions of (E4) and (E5) really sound, then Ktesippus could pull the chair out from under Euthydemus by arguing that he too spoke the truth and things which are when he indicted Dionysodorus for an impious falsehood; and he will complete such argumentative reversals later in his *aristeia* (298 B 4–300 D 9). But at this early stage of his eristification, Ktesippus is still too passionately attached to the content of the discourse to see such contradictory implications.

As for the brothers, if we can resist the natural urge to hold them in contempt, we can gain a new appreciation for what they are trying to accomplish. In particular, we should marvel at how skillfully Euthydemus has disguised the fact that he was all along providing a defense of his brother's action. In (E4) he gave us no clue that he was even disputing about a past event until he suddenly sprang his brother's name and finished with "he says nothing false against you." Similarly, in (E5), only after he concluded generally that no one speaks falsely and then alluded to the particular case of his brother, did it become apparent that Euthydemus was again seeking to clear Dionysodorus from Ktesippus' indictment. Clearly, then, it has been the brothers' strategy from the beginning to maneuver Ktesippus into the stronger position and to make him the champion of truth and right. Consequently, if he should prove unable to defend this naturally superior position against these various acts of subterfuge, then his defeat would seem to reflect his own lack of verbal skill, a deficiency for which he himself may be held responsible. Correspondingly, if the brothers should demonstrate that their weaker arguments can defeat the stronger, then they would produce a stunning example of their superior verbal skill. After suffering several such defeats, Ktesippus is supposed to conclude that he must at any price acquire eristic, that powerful instrument for ensuring success in all forms of argument. In this sense, then, it can be said that the brothers are producing an advertisement for their eristic wisdom which is designed to persuade potential customers to take the first step toward virtue as they conceive it. But what is the real nature of virtue in this context? It can be nothing more than excellence in the art of controversy, a kind of verbal knack that corresponds to the true method of dialectic in much the same way as popular rhetoric does to genuine philosophy.[29]

ON SPEAKING BADLY OF THE BAD
(D6) (284 C 9–285 A 1)

Ktesippus has successfully blocked Euthydemus' line of attack, but at the same time he has provided another trigger for the next dispute. Seizing upon ὡς (a notoriously ambiguous word in Greek) and the verb ἔχειν, Dionysodorus asks: "What do you mean (πῶς λέγεις), Ktesippus, are there individuals who speak things, how they hold (τὰ πράγματα ὡς ἔχει)?" To consider "how things hold" may lead one to examine in what sense or way things exist. In fact, Dionysodorus' question "what do you mean" reveals that he must first establish how things hold with Ktesippus, that is, establish the truth content of his discourse before he can anchor him to a position.[30] If the sophist seriously intended to examine "how things hold," he might open up the possibility of establishing degrees, or at least differences, in the reality of things and language. If he and Ktesippus were to continue to establish such distinctions, the exclusive antinomies between true and false, real and unreal, even the intentional obfuscation in words and their referents—the now familiar tricks of the brothers—would have to give way. But having no intention of allowing such an inquiry to take place, Dionysodorus moves quickly to entice his adversary into affirming that there do in fact exist individuals who speak how things hold. And Ktesippus, who is still angry about the falsehood concerning his relationship with Kleinias, not only agrees to this, but also adds significantly that those who do so are good men and truth-tellers, a clear reference to the way in which the sophist himself should speak about things. But this additional qualification contributes more to the controversy than Ktesippus had intended. For now Dionysodorus has all he needs to launch the next attack:

> What about this? he said. Do good things hold well (ἔχει εὖ), and bad things hold badly (κακῶς)?
> He agreed.
> And do you agree that good men speak how things hold (ὡς ἔχει τὰ πράγματα)?

I agree.

Therefore (ἄρα), he said, good men speak badly (λέγουσιν κα-κῶς) of bad things (τὰ κακά), Ktesippus, if they speak how they hold (ὡς ἔχει).

(284 D 2–7)

In his first question Dionysodorus toys with the verb *hold* (ἔχει) and its use with the adverbs *well* (εὖ) and *badly* (κακῶς), a Greek idiom that translates into English as the verb *to be* with its predicate. So the sophist is asking, in effect, whether good things *are good* and bad things *are bad*. To this obvious tautology Ktesippus readily assents. But schooled as we have been by (D3), we should note that Dionysodorus has cleverly positioned "badly" at the end of its colon, already suggesting that he intends to twist this item for his refutation. As yet unaware of any trick, however, Ktesippus affirms not only this question, but also the next, when Dionysodorus asks him whether good men speak how things hold. Now the sophist has his opponent right where he wants him. With his inference (indicated by ἄρα), Dionysodorus swings the adverb "badly" from its use with "hold" to its use with "speak," where it now translates "good men speak badly." With this simple move, then, he equivocates on two senses of κακῶς λέγειν: to speak *critically* and to speak *poorly*.[31] Thus, it is his strategy to reduce Ktesippus to absurdity by forcing him to accept the unacceptable conclusion that good men speak badly—that is, they are *poor* speakers—because they are required to speak of bad things, how they are. But quick to see through this trick, Ktesippus immediately closes for a counterattack. Acknowledging a particular case in which good men do indeed speak badly, namely when they "criticize" bad men, he quite unambiguously cautions Dionysodorus about the possibility that good men may speak "badly" of him. Here, in this brilliant display of his own talent for verbal controversy, Ktesippus applies the pivotal expression of the argument, "speaking badly," to the sophist himself and thereby points out yet another aspect of the falsehood problem: intentional falsehoods, such as those employed by Dionysodorus and his brother, involve the stigma of moral censure whenever they are detected.

Quickly rallying to his brother's defense (as indeed he must or else risk losing the argument), Euthydemus contributes to the badinage by reworking the old sophistic trick of confounding the seriousness of one's opponent by ridicule.[32] Ktesippus has emphatically expressed his serious commitment to the debate by the personal nature of his reply. Euthydemus now mocks that seriousness by playfully extending the equivocal formula "speaking badly of the bad" to "speaking mightily of the mighty" and "hotly of the hot (τοὺς θερμοὺς θερμῶς)." In this way he not only averts his brother's defeat but also makes Ktesippus' acceptance of the formula appear absurd. But Ktesippus counters this trick by using the sophist's final words as a trigger for another display of his ingenuity. Converting the expression "hotly of the hot" into its opposite, "coldly of the cold (τοὺς ψυχροὺς ψυχρῶς)," he accurately criticizes the sophist-pair for the frigidity of their discourse and character.[33] The brothers are now in trouble and they know it. So, taking Ktesippus' remark as if it applied personally to himself, Dionysodorus emphatically denounces him for indulging in verbal abuse (λοιδορῇ). And it would, of course, be undignified for eristic masters like Euthydemus and his brother to respond to abuse!

We have come full circle. Ktesippus entered the repartee by reproaching Dionysodorus for uttering a false accusation, a charge that Euthydemus attempted to refute. Dionysodorus has just launched a charge of his own against Ktesippus who, in turn, must move quickly to defend himself. Now regardless of how inappropriate it is for Dionysodorus to indict another for abuse, still we must acknowledge that he has here taught us something about eristic: any form of play, and especially the play of eristic dueling, can easily degenerate into an unfriendly form of competition. Consequently, every eristic worth his salt must have a way to parry all such hostile counterattacks. So, by indicting Ktesippus on the forensic commonplace that an aggressive young man, when fired by anger, is likely to abuse his elders, Dionysodorus has shown how he can give his indictment, if not truth, at least plausibility in this context.[34] But apart from the excesses of Ktesippus' character that have established the likelihood of Dionysodorus' charge of abuse, we can also see that the young man possesses outstanding philosophical qualities as well. In three successive arguments he has demonstrated his skill at controversy, the quickness of his intelligence, and his ability to hit upon important qualifications at the core of the falsehood problem. Even in his abuse, and in his claim to esteem Dionysodorus and to warn him as a comrade, Ktesippus has shown how firmly he is committed to facts, to people, and to truth-telling, especially where his relationship with Kleinias is concerned. But now, at the close of (D6), he is reduced to defending himself, laboring to distinguish that abuse with which he is charged from what he fancies he is actually doing, attempting to admonish and to persuade Dionysodorus not to assert so rudely that he wishes Kleinias to perish. And how do things hold with the brothers? For the most part, they have emerged from this round of controversy unscathed.

INTERLUDE (285 A 2–D 6)

In the first episode the brothers contradicted and refuted Kleinias in a stunning advertisement for their wisdom. Now, in another exhibition, after guiding Ktesippus through three eristic disputes, they have finally reached an impasse. At this crucial juncture Socrates intervenes and in fact must intervene to prevent a further disintegration of the conversation.[35] He begins by playing with Ktesippus, coaxing him to accept what the foreigners have to say and *not to differ over a mere word.*[36] Then, illustrating this advice by himself equivocating on the offending term, Socrates reinterprets "perish" to mean the removal of undesirable moral qualities and thus successfully counters Dionysodorus' earlier shift in the context by transferring this key concept from physics back to ethics. Next, recalling the original boast of the brothers, that they possess the power to make a man good, Socrates continues to redirect Ktesippus away from a debate about mere words to an inquiry into the reality of moral transformation.[37] Finally, he closes by generously offering to become Dionysodorus' interlocutor, thereby himself risking whatever else the sophist may conjure up.[38] Here, then, Socrates has provided much-needed refreshment. He has seemingly put the discourse back on track and even offered hope that he may join with Dionysodorus in a serious discussion.

But the direct confrontation between eristic and dialectic is not forthcoming. Ktesippus is not about to give up his role in the controversy. Still upset by the charge of abuse, he begins to justify his behavior by insisting that he is not angry (though of course we know he is),[39] but simply contradicting what in his opinion Dionysodorus speaks falsely. Then he urges the sophist "not to call contradiction (τὸ ἀντιλέγειν) abuse; for abuse (τὸ λοιδορεῖσθαι) is something different" (285 D 4–6). Here Ktesippus has uncovered a significant problem.

Abuse and contradiction can be near synonyms, and what is contradiction to one person can easily be abuse to another.[40] What is needed at this point to prevent misunderstanding and so save the discussion is a clear statement of the intentions of the speakers. Thus Ktesippus is quite right to begin by distinguishing between these two words. But no sooner does he utter the word *contradiction* than he finds himself embroiled in another controversy. For undaunted as ever, Dionysodorus leaps upon the trigger word and releases the inescapable question: "Do you, Ktesippus, he said, make arguments (ποιῇ τοὺς λόγους) on the assumption that contradiction is real (ὡς ὄντος τοῦ ἀντιλέγειν)?"[41]

Before turning to the dispute itself, we can profit by noting how Dionysodorus succeeds in continuing the game of eristic controversy. Like the expression *accuse falsely* (καταψεύδεσθαι), the trigger word *contradiction* (τὸ ἀντιλέγειν) is at home in a forensic environment. In fact, the noun ἀντιλογία frequently means a trial at which one party is expected to deny or to gainsay the accusations of the other. It is in this sense, then, that Ktesippus has just "contradicted" Dionysodorus. In fact, a close look at his actual language shows how carefully Ktesippus has restricted the entire context of his response; he says: "I am not angry, but just contradicting in *reference* to what *in my judgment* he speaks falsely *in reference to me*" (285 D 3–4).[42] But now, directing his attack against the word ἀντιλέγειν, Dionysodorus shifts the context from the sphere of forensic debate to that of philosophical controversy, and then moves to entice Ktesippus into defending the intuitively superior position.[43]

Finally, in order to observe the unity of this episode, we must remember that the contradiction over Kleinias stands behind the action of this episode. Ktesippus wants him to become wise and not to be ignorant. Dionysodorus, on the other hand, has argued that Ktesippus wants him to be destroyed. They have disputed over the same state of affairs to such a degree that both have leveled charges against each other. Now here, where a contradiction has emerged over Kleinias, where neither disputant has said the same thing, but both have spoken differently on the same topic, Dionysodorus injects into the debate an argument designed to disprove what in reality is going on at the very moment.[44] The contradiction over Kleinias (serious for Ktesippus, playful for Dionysodorus) has culminated in a dispute about the very principle of contradiction itself. And so eristic play rolls on.

ON THE IMPOSSIBILITY OF CONTRADICTION
(D7) (285 D 7–286 B 6)

That the brothers are completely at variance with the obvious facts of reality is a problem that certainly does not disturb them. This discrepancy between the real and the apparent, which they themselves have engendered, continues to promote the very existence of their activity. At the very least, it guarantees opposition which allows them to trick opponents into advocating theses which they can attack. With Kleinias and Ktesippus, all the two sophists did was contradict and attempt to produce refutations. Now, by denying the very possibility of what they have done, Dionysodorus may seem to have undermined their former accomplishments. But more precisely he has finally and unambiguously revealed that formerly they only appeared to contradict and to produce refutations, whereas in reality they have merely sought to display their eristical powers.[45]

In this present dispute it would be inaccurate to say that Dionysodorus entices his opponent into advocating the positive thesis, for Ktesippus aggressively and emphatically embraces the possibility of contradiction. He even asks whether the sophist will himself affirm the negative thesis, that contradiction is impossible (285 E 1–2). But rather than take the bait, Dionysodorus taunts the young man with his inability to demonstrate that a contradiction has ever taken place between two interlocutors. For his part, Ktesippus does not miss the opportunity to offer himself as someone who can demonstrate the reality of contradiction by himself contradicting Dionysodorus. So Dionysodorus, taking him up on this boast, issues the challenge: "Am I to understand that you could uphold an account of this (ὑπόσχοις ἂν τούτου λόγον)?" When Ktesippus affirms his willingness to do just that, both parties in the dispute (and not just the sophists) are privy to each other's intentions for the first time. Ktesippus is consciously attempting to uphold a thesis against the questioning of an attacker, and the goal of this dispute is to win. But before Dionysodorus moves to the argument proper, he tests his opponent with two preliminary questions (285 E9–286 A 3): he asks whether there are λόγοι that correspond to things which are, and whether each particular λόγος that so corresponds states "how" or "that" a thing is, a point that, Dionysodorus reminds Ktesippus, has already been proved.[46] Not seeing how an assent to these two questions can render contradiction impos-

sible, Ktesippus agrees.[47] The verbal assault itself is a clever parody of
an argument that seeks to defeat an opponent's thesis by appearing to
exhaust all possible conditions under which it can hold:

> (1) Would we contradict (ἀντιλέγοιμεν), he said, if we should both
> speak an account of the same thing (τοῦ αὐτοῦ πράγματος
> λόγον), or in such a case wouldn't we obviously say the same
> things (ταὐτά)?
> He went along.

(286 A 4–7)

In this first question Dionysodorus presents a set of conditions
under which we do not contradict. If both speakers should speak the
same account of the same thing, then to be sure there would be no
contradiction. They would both speak one and the same (ὁμός) account (λόγος) and thus would attain *agreement* (ὁμολογία). But obviously this sense of agreement turns on what Ktesippus has granted
to Dionysodorus: that a single λόγος corresponds to each thing.
When, however, two speakers should reach this kind of agreement,
an agreement in the strictest possible sense, they would quite literally
use the *same words* (ταὐτὰ λεγόμενα), thereby creating the picture of
talking machines that just mimic each other (cf. 298 D 1–6). But
needless to say, inasmuch as eristic is an adversarial form of argumentation from its very inception, it cannot attain significant agreement in
this or any other sense.

> (2) Or, when neither of us speaks an account of a thing, he said, at
> that time would we contradict, or under these circumstances
> would neither of us even mention the thing at all?
> On this point too he agreed.

(286 A 7–B 3)

After toying with the notion of strict sameness in language, Dionysodorus now flips the attack to the other side of the dilemma and
proposes a case in which neither speaker speaks an account of the
thing. Under these conditions there can be no contradiction, for neither of the two would even mention the object about which they might
contradict each other. Contradiction requires at the very least that
one person *speak* (λέγειν / *dicere*) *against* (ἀντί / *contra*) another. But in
this instance both interlocutors are so far from speaking against each
other as not even to speak. Here Dionysodorus has again articulated

something that is true and simple. Silence cannot possibly generate verbal contradiction.[48] Yet here too we see the joke that is being played on eristic. As an adversarial form of questioning eristic cannot allow itself to be silenced. In fact, in eristic controversy, silence betokens defeat.

> (3) Well then, whenever I speak an account of a thing, and you speak an account of some other thing, at that time do we contradict, or do I speak about the thing, and you don't speak at all, and how could he who doesn't speak (ὁ μὴ λέγων) contradict a speaker (ἀντιλέγοι τῷ λέγοντι)?
>
> (286 B 3–6)

By bouncing the argument back and forth between the poles of strict sameness and difference, Dionysodorus has eliminated two ways that contradiction can occur. Now, in his third and final move, he cunningly seeks to discover contradiction between the extremes. Positing a case in which both of them speak, but each speaks a different account of two different things, Dionysodorus asks: "at that time do we contradict?" But not waiting for a response, he goes on to explain in the form of a question why in fact they do not contradict. Characterizing the case thus imagined as one in which he speaks about his topic but Ktesippus doesn't "speak at all" [about it], Dionysodorus concludes rhetorically: "And how could a nonspeaker contradict a speaker?" In the end, then, Dionysodorus' sojourn into the middle between extremes describes a situation in which one person speaks and the other does not. And here, too, there is no contradiction.

Contradiction requires at the very least both sameness and difference. It requires that two *different* speakers perform the *same* act of speaking, but in *different* words about the *same* topic. By juggling several senses of sameness and difference, Dionysodorus has created the illusion that contradiction is impossible, and this too when it is clear to all that both Dionysodorus and Ktesippus have been engaged for some time in a heated and abusive contradiction over Kleinias. Furthermore, it should be obvious that in speaking against the possibility of contradiction Dionysodorus is in fact refuted the moment he meets a stubborn opponent who does not allow himself to be silenced; for the opposition itself is all the proof necessary for the continued possibility of contradiction.[49] But Ktesippus, not aware that a simple yet obstinate denial to Dionysodorus' final question again proves the reality of contradiction, suffers the one thing he cannot afford to suffer in an eristic dispute. He is reduced to silence, to a nonspeaker (ὁ μὴ λέγων). So once again eristic play rolls on, and the question naturally arises, can these two verbal machines be made to stop? Enter Socrates.

THE REFUTERS REFUTED (286 B 7–288 A 7)

Ktesippus' defeat hastens the return of Socrates, who immediately identifies this argument as a fossil buried in the graveyard of philosophy before the time of Protagoras.[50] Aware of its anatreptic power to refute others, he also claims that the λόγος refutes itself, the truth of which he anticipates learning from Dionysodorus. To begin his inquiry, he moves to establish that (D7), the argument that the sophist has used to reject the possibility of contradiction, is a mere corollary to the falsehood topic; he asks: "Are you saying that false speech is impossible? For this is the meaning of your argument, isn't it? Either a speaker speaks the truth or doesn't speak? [Dionysodorus] agreed" (286 C 6–9). Here, we must not underestimate the importance of the sophist's agreement. With just this first question Socrates has uncovered a position that Dionysodorus wants to support.[51] In effect, Socrates has maneuvered him into arguing that a speaker speaks the truth, or simply does not speak. A nonspeaker may perhaps make "noise," as is the case when someone beats a bronze pot, but all λόγοι that are λόγοι are true.[52] In fact, they must all be positive λόγοι; for in a λόγος, no one can even say "how" or "that" a thing is not (ὡς οὐκ ἔστι).[53] It is this eristic stance toward the unreality of negative statements that Socrates now proceeds to parody in his cross-questioning by eliciting from Dionysodorus a string of "is not" implications that are tied to the falsehood topic (286 D 1–10); they are, in due order, the impossibility of opining falsely (δοξάζειν ψευδῆ), of false opinion (ψευδὴς δόξα), of ignorance (ἀμαθία), and of ignorant individuals (ἀμαθεῖς ἄνθρωποι). Any λόγος on one of these problems could have provided the locus for (D7). The fact that they have not, and that, instead, the impossibility of contradiction rose to prominence, furnishes additional evidence—were additional evidence still needed—that eristic is not driven by the wheel of logical necessity, but by accident. The immediate cause of (D7) is simply the trigger word *contradiction*, and by having Ktesippus innocently release it and Dionysodorus eagerly pounce upon it, Plato confirms that (D7) is only a paradigm or model dispute likely to arise during the course of an eristic debate when experts in contentious argument, oblivious to proper philosophical method, just drift back and forth between the beginnings and ends of argument.

To cap his line of questioning, Socrates cannot resist injecting into the debate a disjunctive question that seeks to discover whether the sophist is playful or serious:

> Are you just arguing for the sake of argument, Dionysodorus, in order to state a paradox, or truly in your opinion is no one ignorant?[54]
>
> Well, it's up to you to refute the position, he said.
>
> (286 D 11–E 1)

Socrates wants to know whether Dionysodorus is willing to commit himself to the seemingly outlandish position that no individual is ignorant,[55] or is he simply arguing theses, indulging as it were in philosophical sport. But this apparently reasonable question turns out to be powerless to disturb the sophist's universe of discourse. For what continues to safeguard the possibility of this eristic activity, and in particular what allows Dionysodorus to challenge Socrates on this very topic, is the entire *epideictic context* that permits eristics to argue merely for the sake of argument.[56] This context not only sanctions but even assists in constructing a linguistic environment in which the participants can contradict each other without themselves being committed to the truth content of their own words.[57] It ensures that conventional politeness will govern the behavior of the speakers, and it even permits Dionysodorus to call a foul when Ktesippus threatens to shatter that politeness with moral censure. But to the dismay of Socrates, this context can also prevent the discussion from attaining the ethical seriousness that is characteristic of true protreptic debate. In fact, in eristic controversy lack of commitment to the truth and the absence of ethical seriousness can actually aid the debaters by creating that much-needed distance from the subject matter that allows them to concentrate on the mechanics of their argumentative style and on the overall grace of their performance. And here we arrive at an important observation: for Plato, philosophy can degenerate into its antithesis whenever the interlocutors in a philosophical discussion begin *to argue merely for the sake of argument,* that is, whenever they turn philosophy into play, into an epideictic activity designed merely to produce an exhibition of their argumentative powers.[58]

What is more, as Socrates continues to discover, even to suggest that the brothers are indulging in argument for the sake of argument is an improper comment on argumentative procedures and provokes an immediate and caustic challenge from Dionysodorus: "Well, it's up to you to refute the position."[59] So Socrates takes up the challenge and presses harder: "And is refutation possible, according to your argument, if no one speaks falsely?" Even the eristic elenchus itself, as Socrates is now suggesting, advances on the ground that false speaking is possible, and so it too must assume that there exists a class of entities, real in some sense, that falsely attempt to assert what is not.[60] Dionysodorus is now in trouble, and his brother comes to the rescue. Refutation is impossible (οὐκ ἔστιν), Euthydemus admits, and therefore Dionysodorus did not just now bid what is impossible; for how could anyone bid what is not (286 E 4–7)? Finally, Socrates has had enough. He must confess that he simply cannot understand and so fix in his mind these "wise (σοφά)" and "well-established (εὖ ἔχοντα)" positions.[61] But their arguments do hold together well enough for him to see one more implication of the falsehood topic. So, gathering together the results of his cross-questioning (286 D 1–10), he asks: "If it is impossible to speak falsely, to opine falsely, and to be ignorant, then must it also follow that it is impossible to err in action" (287 A 1–3)? When Dionysodorus smugly accepts this consequence as well, Socrates can at last advance his version of the inescapable question:

> Now here finally, I said, is my clownish question. If we do not fall into error either when we act or when we speak or when we think, if this is so, then, in the name of Zeus, of what have you come here to teach? Or didn't you boast just now (ἄρτι) to impart virtue best of men to anyone who is willing to learn?
>
> (287 A 6–B 1)

The final "is not" implication of the falsehood λόγος, the impossibility of error, as Socrates is just now hastening to point out, undermines any claim on the part of the brothers to teach virtue because it eliminates the need for any science of ethics. If we do not err in thought, speech, and action, then the sophists are without both subjects and subject matter to teach.[62] So Socrates' clownish question is in reality inescapable, if, indeed, the brothers will grant that any questions, save their own of course, can be inescapable.[63] Instruction in virtue, then, the field that offers the two foreigners a legitimate excuse for being in Athens, and in particular for mixing with young men in the wrestling facility, has now been so devalued as not to be *the* field of inquiry at all, but simply one on the same level as others, valuable only insofar as it can offer topics for eristic sport. In other words, for eristic all propositions, even ethical ones, are of equal value or, still worse, are of no value at all unless they can be converted into weapons for verbal combat.

But the full impact of Socrates' inescapable question does not strike its target. Instead of answering, Dionysodorus brushes aside his former boast to impart virtue and launches into a polemic of his own. Treating Socrates as if he were some obtuse late learner, Dionysodorus chastises him in the form of a question by asking whether he has become such an old Kronos that he now passes time recollecting (ἀναμιμνῄσκῃ) what was said at first (τὸ πρῶτον), but "cannot cope with what is being said at the present moment (ἐν τῷ παρόντι)." The sudden appearance here of this slam at anamnesis, rolling so cavalierly off Dionysodorus' tongue, should provoke laughter from those who can marvel at the hilarious way in which Plato is spoofing on his own teaching. But apart from the playfulness of this passage, we must note that in any form of cross-questioning, and especially in eristic dueling, where consistency in reasoning is not required, someone is likely to say: "Doesn't what you say *now* contradict what you said *before?*"[64] Prepared for this type of objection, Dionysodorus has just now illustrated how an eristical dodge can ward off the consistency requirement for argument. But what would happen if these two sophists should be allowed to parry all such objections in this manner, and Socrates, on the other hand, should be powerless to recall earlier claims and contrast them to what is now being said? Does this mean that eristic and its two-headed representative are indeed unstoppable? Not necessarily; but we can now see that Socrates' clownish yet inescapable question is unable to penetrate the bombast of this sophist, once he has gained dominance over the universe of discourse. For that penetration Socrates will have to destroy eristic in a far more dramatic and devastating fashion.

In his haste to escape from Socrates' elenchus, Dionysodorus has left another opening for attack. Using his ability to discern (near) synonyms, Socrates asks the sophist what sense the phrase (τὸ ῥῆμα), "cannot cope," can possibly have (νοεῖ), if not the unacceptable "cannot refute." Cornered again, Dionysodorus immediately intuits his task: he must regain control of the line of questioning without having to answer his opponent. So, resorting to yet another dodge, he grasps for a trigger in order to wrestle away the role of questioner from Socrates and then issues the eristic demand to answer. But now the falseness of eristic diplomacy cannot be more transparent. For at last Socrates challenges him directly by asking on what principle he chooses to answer or not to answer, if, indeed, he does so on any principle, save the recognition, of course, that in this particular case an answer guarantees defeat. Out of options and desperate, Dionysodorus responds with another insult backed by commands, making it clear that he is going to force Socrates, in accordance with no principle, to become the respondent for his next attack. Caught in the jaws of necessity (ἀνάγκη), Socrates invites Dionysodorus to take command of the λόγος.

On Whether Phrases Have Sense (D8) (287 D 7–E 4)

Is it by virtue of being alive (ψυχὴν ἔχοντα) that things which have sense sense (νοεῖ τὰ νοοῦντα) or can lifeless things (τὰ ἄψυχα) sense?

Things which are alive.

Then do you know, he said, any phrase (τι ῥῆμα) that is alive (ψυχήν)?

No indeed I do not.

Then why did you ask me just now (ἄρτι) what sense my phrase had (ὅτι μοι νοοῖ τὸ ῥῆμα)?

Why else, I said, than because I erred through my stupidity (διὰ τὴν βλακείαν), or did I not err but speak correctly, when I said that phrases have sense?

(287 D 7–E 4)

Earlier, at 287 C 1, Socrates used νοεῖ to cap λέγεις and in so doing shifted from something like "what *are* you *saying*" to "what *sense does* this phrase *have*." In that context he was referring to the sense or meaning of the sophist's expression "cannot cope" with the argument; and there he was suggesting that it might be just a synonym for "cannot refute." But now, under pressure from Socrates' elenchus, Dionysodorus has been forced to search for a trigger word and generate an inescapable question. Seizing upon νοεῖν to form the substantive "things which have sense (τὰ νοοῦντα)," he begins the sortie by asking whether they "sense (νοεῖ)" by virtue of being alive (ψυχὴν ἔχοντα) or can lifeless things (τὰ ἄψυχα) sense. In this context, "things which have sense" quite naturally refers to living creatures (τὰ ζῷα); accordingly, the equivocal νοεῖ must shift from the "sense" of a phrase to the "sense" of sentient beings. In short, with just his first question the sophist has perverted "meaning" and "signification," not to mention the activity of soul, for his combative purpose.[65]

But Socrates continues to play his role in the game and affirms the obviously correct alternative that things which have sense are alive. With his second question Dionysodorus returns to the place from which he drew νοεῖ, snatches up another item, ῥῆμα, and then attacks his opponent by asking whether he knows "any phrase that is alive." And here too Socrates gives the obviously correct answer, that he knows no such phrase. To conclude, Dionysodorus links "the phrase" with the now incompatible "sense" and asks rhetorically how Socrates could ever be so foolish as to ask "just now what sense his phrase had." Arguing, therefore, that a phrase, since it is lifeless (ἄψυχον), cannot possibly have any "sense," Dionysodorus has apparently created the illusion that by persistently returning to the topic of refutation Socrates has all along been trying to raise, quite literally, a dead issue. Finally, the sophist applies one more brilliant stroke of eristic subterfuge. At 287 A 9, Socrates referred to the fact that the brothers had "just now (ἄρτι)" claimed to impart virtue. But Dionysodorus caused that claim to appear to have been said at first (τὸ πρῶτον), and then proceeded to rebuke Socrates for his inability to cope with the immediate argument (ἐν τῷ παρόντι). Now, at the close of (D8), he cleverly slips into his final question the temporal indicator "just now," fancying that he has thereby illustrated to perfection the eristic demand to cope with what is being said at the present moment. To all appearances, then, Dionysodorus has slipped from Socrates' grasp and produced a knockdown argument.

At this critical moment in the second eristic Socrates initiates the wiliest counterattack yet witnessed in the *Euthydemus*. Just as the expert in the pancration hedges from his position in order to upset the balance of an overly aggressive adversary and thus gain leverage for a fall, so too Socrates appears to lose an argument in order to win *the* argument and counters Dionysodorus' quibble on νοεῖν with a devastating takedown. The sophist committed a tactical error when he finished (D8) with a question rather than a statement of victory. For unlike Ktesippus, Socrates is not silenced but is more than willing to respond and even to offer the reason for his folly: "I erred through my stupidity, or did I not err but speak correctly, when I said that phrases have sense?" When Socrates pinpoints the source of his mistake in stupidity, there is more in his response than self-depreciation. Earlier Dionysodorus not only denied the existence of ignorance and of ignorant individuals, but also challenged Socrates to refute him on this very point (286 E 1). Now, casting himself in the role of an ignoramus, and submitting ignorance as the cause of his incorrect speech, Socrates gladly admits to his error. But he also offers another possibility: "Or did I not err but speak correctly, when I said that phrases have sense?" On this possibility he was correct from the beginning. So finally Socrates has the sophist right where he wants him and, accordingly, releases the inescapable question:

> What is it going to be? Are you saying that I'm wrong or not? For if I didn't make a mistake, you will not refute me for all your wisdom, nor are you coping with this argument. But if I was wrong, then not even so are you speaking correctly when you allege that error is impossible. And I'm not addressing these remarks to what you said a year ago.
>
> (287 E 4–288 A 2)

Zeno had supplied eristic sophistry with one of its chief weapons, the *reductio ad absurdum,* which refutes an opponent's position by asserting that it involves a dilemma, either horn of which leads to a contradiction. The brothers have already made ample use of this procedure earlier against the young Kleinias; and so it is only fitting that Socrates now turns this tactical weapon back upon them. To pin Dionysodorus to a position, he uses the alternative question to determine whether an error was committed, a question that appeals to the simple fact of error. As the bare Eleatic dilemma must indicate, either an error was committed or it was not committed (ἔστιν ἢ οὔκ ἔστιν), and if it was, then it was an error of false speech, ruled out of existence as early as (E4). With this move, then, Socrates has firmly and finally anchored the sophist. Either answer to Socrates' disjunctive question involves Dionysodorus in a defeat, for, unlike the dichotomies of the brothers, this one is real. If Socrates erred, then the error is complete and absolute. If not, then it is nonexistent. Here there is no middle ground, no degrees of erring, no *tertium quid*. If the first horn of the dilemma holds, that is, if Socrates did not err, then Dionysodorus will not refute him in (D8), the final outcome of which has yet to be decided; and for good measure, Socrates reminds him that he cannot cope with this argument. But if the other horn proves true, if Socrates did err, then the sophist speaks falsely when he alleges that error is impossible. Whichever way Dionysodorus answers, he will be refuted.[66] Finally, Socrates caps this real refutation by pointing out that he has overcome the defect of his clownish question. He is now speaking directly to the point at issue and not to some remarks recollected from a year ago. But immediately upon pinning his opponent to the mat, Socrates is most circumspect not to make the defeat personal. It is the λόγος itself, he insists, that has been wrestled to the ground and remains right where he left it. In addition to its anatreptic power to known down others, the falsehood topic possesses an inherent weakness of its own that causes it to collapse and suffer defeat as an unwilling victim, the truth of which, as he predicted (286 C 5–6), he has learned from Dionysodorus himself; and not even the art of eristic, in spite of its precision in argument (ἀκρίβειαν λόγων), has invented the means for overcoming this defect.[67] The brothers have suffered a humiliating loss, as the main piece of their wisdom, the falsehood topic, has collapsed, and one might even suppose that they could not muster enough cheek to reappear after such a debacle. But the comic impulse of this dialogue will allow them, like a two-headed jack-in-the-box, to pop up again, unperturbed by their defeat and ready for the fifth and final episode.

CONCLUSION

Until this very moment when both error and truth are finally and unambiguously revealed, the brothers in an anatreptic frenzy have used arguments as weapons for knocking down others, as if they were pulling chairs out from under unsuspecting victims. Now the λόγος itself has become the instrument of their own destruction, and here, more than anywhere else, we catch a glimpse of Plato manipulating the strings of his two marionettes in order to assure us of the order behind eristic disorder. For what on the philosophical level is a stunning example of an inescapable refutation is also a perfect illustration of a perennial feature of all comic action: comic inversion.[68] Just as the comic playwright presents, for example, a robber robbed or a mugger mugged, so too Plato has presented the refuters refuted, and thus he unites both a philosophical and comic theme for a stunning conclusion to this third episode. But here, as elsewhere, when his satiric wit becomes most manifest, Plato undercuts the playful intention of his work by adding a disconcerting element. For when Socrates does not understate his position the way he did with his clownish question but assures the brothers that beyond doubt this refutation is both inescapable and directed immediately to the point at issue, he also succeeds in rousing Ktesippus from his silence. And this impulsive young man, though himself not yet able to refute the eristic-pair but fully capable of seeing the finality with which they have been crushed in argument, now seizes upon the opportunity to direct some cheerful words of abuse against these two foreign mountebanks.[69] The specter of abuse (λοιδορία), lurking just beneath the surface of the work ever since Ktesippus entered the fray, has now become a real threat, and Socrates must move quickly to soothe him before eristic play does indeed become serious.[70]

The reader should no longer have a vague feeling that eristic is a self-contradictory method, susceptible to suffering what it dishes out. After Euthydemus and his brother have spoken falsely, opined falsely, displayed their ignorance, deliberately misrepresented the facts, and erred in thought, speech, and action, we can see how much Plato is telling us about what is not philosophical method and who are not philosophers. By portraying the brothers shifting radically from problems of learning and knowing to those of being and becoming, leaping gracelessly from truth claims to metaphysical propositions about being and nonbeing, punning inappropriately on ambiguous terms, dodging questions, forcing responses, and contradicting—in short, by portraying all the numerous antics of the brother-pair— Plato has demonstrated with extreme bluntness certain unmistakable characteristics that are designed to stigmatize a technique of argumentation that is diametrically opposed to his own.[71] Linked to these philosophical themes are the dramatic symbols of the work, which have by now taken definite shape. Socrates is the teacher and protector of youth, the possessor and user of the protreptic method, one and serious like philosophy itself. Opposing him are the brothers, fakirs and corruptors of youth, possessors and users of a negative, self-destructive elenchus by which they turn philosophy into a playful, epideictic activity. Clearly identified as the chorus leaders of the ignorant, the brothers now appear to be just as dissuasive as their arguments, whereas Socrates not only can persuade us to turn toward wisdom but is beginning to appear, insofar as it is possible, to be the wise man himself. Through the mere interplay of its dramatic symbols, then, the *Euthydemus* has helped to clarify the real nature of philosophical activity by revealing what we are to pursue and what to avoid.

4
THE PROTREPTIC CONTINUES

To counter the total collapse of the pseudo-science of eristic, and this too on the topic of falsehood wherein our two controversialists have imagined themselves to be invulnerable, Plato now swings the action of his work in the opposite direction and begins to construct the opposing movement or fourth episode of the *Euthydemus*. His vehicle for this transition is of course Socrates, who must first check the ever-increasing hostility engendered by Ktesippus and the brothers and then reassemble the various threads of his protreptic in order to continue his exhortation. So, breaking off the eristic λόγος for the third time, Socrates deflects the abusive tone of the debate by playfully calming down the emotionally charged Ktesippus.[1] Reminding him, as he did Kleinias, that he is unfamiliar with the astonishing power of their wisdom, Socrates goes on to note that the brothers have not yet revealed themselves seriously. Rather, as he says, the two are imitating Proteus, the master wizard himself, in a conscious act of beguilement.[2] Like Proteus, then, who passes through various manifestations but is nothing substantial, the brothers have passed from one argument to another without any system or order, without any serious attempt to display their protreptic wisdom. So Socrates recommends to Ktesippus that they take Menelaus as their model and wrestle the pair to the ground until they can force something serious out of them.[3] "For whenever they begin to show their serious side," Socrates suggests, "something altogether splendid will appear in them" (288 C 3–4).

Now if the steadfastness of a second-rate warrior like Menelaus is all that is needed to bring eristic under control, then this fact should give us pause for thought. Is Plato trying to suggest that if we but tussle with these two wizards long enough, we will discover some deep-knowing wisdom hidden in their λόγος? Quite to the contrary! By having Socrates make an impassioned appeal for the brothers to come out from behind their comic masks, as it were, and to reveal their serious nature, Plato continues his unrelenting ridicule of the perennial tricks of all philosophasters. Behind their acts of sorcery, their ambiguity in the use of words, their incomprehensible talk, their willful obscurantism and intentional fallacies, and especially behind their pedantry, which creates an illusory air of importance all to befool those eager to learn, Plato gives us a timeless portrayal of the concealment or hiddenness that informs all bogus esotericism.[4] Presenting themselves before us as men "all-wise" in discourse, Euthydemus and Dionysodorus are actively engaged in the profitable business of creating the appearance that they possess in readiness a "wisdom" that they can bring forth at any moment they choose. But by constantly appealing to them to quit playing and to be serious, Socrates continues to unmask the truth, that the brother-pair are in reality a kind of two-headed monstrosity or philosophical mutation from the tradition, without any real knowledge at all. But in the *Euthydemus* it is not enough for Socrates merely to expose the false and the fallacious. He must also guide Kleinias along the path that rises far above the foolery of eristic and leads upward toward the acquisition of real knowledge. So now, in this our fourth chapter, we propose to continue our analysis of the authentic wisdom of Socrates, who has conducted and will continue to conduct, insofar as it is possible, an open and honest display of his protreptic power.

THE PRODUCTION AND USE CRITERION
(288 D 5–289 C 6)

The last time we saw Kleinias in action Socrates had directed him away from conventional goods and persuaded him of the need to pursue wisdom. Yet he did not plume himself on his success, for he fully realized that he had completed only part of his task. Most notably inadequate was his failure to provide Kleinias with any concrete determination of the nature of the wisdom to be attained. So, turning to the unfinished business of his protreptic, Socrates begins by recollecting for Kleinias their final point of agreement, that one must philosophize: φιλοσοφητέον. How then does this beginning compare with the beginning of the second eristic? When Socrates turned the λόγος back over to the brothers for their second try at exhortation, he suggested two options (282 D 4–E 6): that they repeat his paradigm by demonstrating its conclusion more rigorously, or that they themselves

provide the full determination of the science (or sciences) to be acquired by examining, in due order, what it is. But his expectations for
success were dashed when the brothers simply marshaled an ill-
assorted heap of arguments that proved to be so disruptive that in the
end he had to confront the pair and cauterize the various heads of
their falsehood topic. By contrast, Socrates' protreptic model now exhibits both direction in its movements and arrangement in its parts;
if for some reason it should be interrupted, say, by an eristic intrusion into speech, Socrates can resume it from the point at which it
breaks off.[5]

Once Kleinias reaffirms his commitment to philosophize, Socrates
begins to determine with greater precision what philosophy is by defining it as the *acquisition of knowledge:* ἡ δέ γε φιλοσοφία κτῆσις ἐπιστήμης. But where does he suddenly find this definition? As our
analysis indicated, the moral imperative of the first protreptic seemed
to be: Acquire knowledge (282 A 5–6). But instead of stating it in that
way, Socrates exhorted Kleinias to become as wise as possible and then
proceeded to show that this exhortation required him to love wisdom.
So, having instilled that love of wisdom in the young man in the first
protreptic, Socrates can now project for him where his love is to end,
that is, in the acquisition of knowledge.[6] Philosophy is thus both the
love of knowledge and its attainment, a process that seeks to discover
itself. But as his next question indicates, philosophy is not just any
knowledge, but one that continually renders benefit to its possessor.
So he now joins with Kleinias in a search for the knowledge that can
guarantee benefit.

Earlier Socrates merely listed goods, arranging them loosely in a
chorus, and among the first to be mentioned was wealth (279 A 7). To
link his present inquiry to that one, he now introduces gold, the sign
of wealth par excellence, and asks whether the knowledge of how to
acquire gold would prove beneficial. Here Kleinias qualifies and must
qualify his response with "perhaps," for he cannot determine whether
knowledge is guiding its use. So Socrates moves to dispel that doubt.
From 288 E 4 to 289 A 3, he neatly summarizes the first protreptic
by recalling the substance of their earlier elenchus (ἐξηλέγξαμεν),
namely, that without the knowledge of how to use gold its acquisition
can prove more harmful than good. Then Socrates asks his young interlocutor whether he can recall that conclusion; and of course
Kleinias remembers what he has learned and now understands. Sig-

nificantly, while Socrates here ties his second exhortation to the first, he also redirects its orientation. For although he mentions gold as something to be acquired, the overall context reveals that his emphasis is not on gold but on mining, the science responsible for its systematic production. And just as gold is found to be inadequate without knowledge to guide its use, so, too, must be the science that produces it. In fact, his remaining examples, the scientific knowledge of how to transform rocks into gold, the art of finance, even medicine and the science of attaining immortality, cannot be the goal of their search because all possess the same shortcomings as the products they manufacture; and thus they are incomplete without, and really subordinate to, the science or sciences that possess the knowledge of correct use. So finally a hierarchy has emerged (as it did when wisdom emerged from the many goods to be the one good), in which the science that uses is superior to the one that produces, and only the one that combines both production and use can possibly satisfy the criterion that has now come into view:

> Therefore, my handsome boy, I said, we need the kind of knowledge (ἐπιστήμης) in which there coalesces at one and the same time both production (τὸ ποιεῖν) and the knowledge of how to use (τὸ ἐπίστασθαι χρῆσθαι) what is produced.
>
> (289 B 4–6)

Having stated the conditions of this formula, Socrates immediately demonstrates its power to reject three candidates from the field of music (289 B 7–C 6): lyre production, harp playing, and flute production. They fail to meet the criterion because production and use are separated and divided in regard to the same subject matter; for simple observation can tell us that the production of musical instruments and their correct use differ widely from each other.[7]

For the most part, then, it may seem that we have witnessed only a negative inquiry, that Socrates' elenchus has proved to be just an *ars nesciendi*. But this judgement would disguise how far we have come, how far up the ladder, so to speak, we have climbed in our search for the master science. For at the same time that Socrates has demonstrated the inability of conventional goods and the sciences that produce them to meet the production and use criterion, he has also advanced the inquiry. By passing in review and rejecting a number of candidates, he has demonstrated that the knowledge to be attained is one that both produces goods and continually renders them beneficial through correct use. Moreover, he has presented Kleinias with a model for how to produce defining criteria and how to use them in particular cases; in short, he has produced a paradigm of the process of dialectical inquiry. So how do these positive characteristics of their search affect the young boy? We shall see momentarily, for Socrates is now about to provide the final springboard that will launch Kleinias into action.

THE ART OF LOGIC-PRODUCTION (289 C 6–290 A 6)

But in the name of the gods, I said, if we were to learn ($\mu\acute{\alpha}\theta οι\mu εν$) the art of producing speech ($\lambda ογοποιικ\grave{η}ν\ τ\acute{ε}χνην$), is this the one we should acquire for being happy?

I don't think so, said Kleinias, as he took hold of the conversation ($\acute{υ}πολαβ\acute{ω}ν$).

What evidence ($τεκμηρί\acute{ω}$) do you use ($χρ\^{η}$), I said?

I can observe, he said, that some speech writers ($\lambda ογοποιο\acute{υ}ς$) don't know how to use their own compositions which they themselves have produced, just as makers of musical instruments do not know how to use their own lyres. But as in music, so here too there are others who can use what those writers have produced, although they themselves are incapable of producing speech. So clearly the art of producing speech is different from the art of using it.

You seem to me, I said, to state adequate evidence ($\acute{ι}καν\grave{ο}ν$ $τεκμ\acute{η}ριον$) that this art of speech writing ($α\~{υ}τη\ \acute{η}\ τ\^{ω}ν\ \lambda ογοποι\^{ω}ν$ $τ\acute{ε}χνη$) is not the one which somebody should acquire for being happy. And yet I thought that here somewhere ($\grave{ε}νταῦθά\ που$) there would appear that science which we have all along been searching for ($ζητο\~{υ}μεν$).

(289 C 6–E 1)

Since Socrates prefaces his introduction of the logic-art by calling upon the gods, we may assume that he is about to offer a serious candidate. So when Kleinias quickly rejects it, and Socrates encourages him by asking on what basis he can do so, we should certainly reflect upon what is happening. In these two lines a radical transformation has taken place. Not only has Kleinias indicated that he is about to don his philosophical wings by taking hold of the $\lambda\acute{ο}γος$, but also Socrates has shown him how to do so by asking him to produce evidence for the rejection of the logic-art.[8] How far then can Socrates guide his young initiate into the realm of speculative philosophy?

Trusting in his observation, Kleinias fastens upon the producers of speech in his everyday experience, those speech writers who equip others with forensic argument but do not themselves speak before the courts. He sees that these familiar practitioners of the art do not combine production and use, and so gives, as Socrates observes, adequate evidence for the rejection of "this art ($α\ddot{υ}τη$ $\dot{η}$ $τέχνη$)" as the one capable of bridging the gap between production and use. But it is not outside the realm of possibility that he could here ask Socrates what he means by "If we were to learn ($μάθοιμεν$) the art of producing speech." He could recall that the twofold sense of $μανθάνειν$ has already been detected, and then go on to ask Socrates whether by "learn" he means "begin to gather knowledge" about producing speech, or "to understand" it in the full sense, whereby he could exercise his knowledge so as to guarantee its correct use. But such a response would require him to realize that he may misunderstand the question that Socrates is asking. Here, when our attention is likely to be focused on Kleinias at the very moment he is engaged in applying the production and use criterion, we may not observe that he has also missed the full implications of Socrates' question by again passing over the equivocal nature of the learning act.[9] Had Socrates chosen to do so, he could have tripped up the boy on this equivocal use of $μάθοιμεν$ or at least used the occasion to repeat his earlier lesson on ambiguity by returning to what it might mean to learn the logic-art. But Socrates doesn't do this, for Kleinias has neither answered incorrectly nor used evidence incorrectly. So rather than contradict him at this crucial stage in his philosophical development by calling attention to his partial grasp of the question, Socrates takes Kleinias' answer in the way that he intends it, and then continues the inquiry.

It is significant that Socrates has chosen this occasion to reveal, for the first time in the dialogue, that he and Kleinias have been conducting an *inquiry* ($ζητοῦμεν$).[10] Here the verb $ζητεῖν$ discloses that for a long time (in fact ever since Socrates posited "faring well" as the end of human longing) they have been searching for the answer to the riddle of our existence, for the one science that can end the quest and make us happy. We have now reached a juncture where it might perhaps appear. For Kleinias has not given a necessary reason why both conditions cannot merge into another art of logic-production, even though this science would not be the rhetorical art as it is conventionally practiced. That Socrates does indeed envision such a science of argument-production is hinted at by his comment "And yet I thought that *here somewhere* there would appear that science which we have all along been searching for." [11] With these words, Socrates is at least suggesting that the mere term λογοποιική should not deter us from searching for the science in question somewhere in this general area. He has already illustrated for Ktesippus the importance of "not differing over a word," when he reinterpreted *perish* to mean the removal of moral depravity (285 A–B). And although the word λογοποιική may appear to indicate a science that only "produces" argument (at any rate, the termination -ποιική may suggest this), still nothing prevents Socrates from having in mind another science in which the arguments themselves, if they are produced correctly by a speaker, necessitate correct use. Of crucial importance is not the mere word λογοποιική, but the meaning or reality to which it refers.

But Socrates here faces a considerably more difficult task than may generally be recognized or appreciated. For the sought-after science is not just the end of the search, but also the very process or method of inquiry that seeks to discover itself; it is both the means and the end, the process and the result. What Socrates cannot do is simply hand it over in the way the brothers claim to hand over virtue, without in part betraying its nature. Even if he wanted to, Socrates cannot do Kleinias' thinking for him, nor can he present him with some ready-made positive result. Rather he must stimulate the youth to inquire for himself so that when, or if, the science does emerge, it will do so as a direct result of Kleinias' own exercise of intelligence. In the process of awakening that capacity, moreover, Socrates has not used a one-dimensional, negative elenchus, but a multifaceted technique of argument by which he has assisted Kleinias to mount up from an original axiom to the art of logic-production, here posited as that concrete determination for the hypothesized "wisdom" of their search. Kleinias meanwhile has successfully followed his protreptic guide up each step until he has now tested and rejected the candidate that Socrates proposed. So with Kleinias both producing and using argument correctly, Socrates must now exhibit the flexibility to conduct the inquiry in another way, without gainsaying him at this moment of his highest achievement. Soon we shall consider how he does this, but first we must call attention to a subtle change that is about to take place. From the beginning, it has been made perfectly clear that the protreptic enterprise calls for the most profound seriousness on the part of its participants, and so far, in contrast to the playfulness of the brothers, Socrates has maintained that attitude. But as he draws ever closer to attaining his goal, Socrates demonstrates how the demands of the protreptic now require him to express that seriousness in another way. In fact, as Kleinias goes about his task more seriously, Socrates becomes more playful:

> Whenever I associate with them, I mean the producers of speech (οἱ λογοποιοί), they seem to me, Kleinias, to be superwise and their art itself something inspired and lofty. And indeed there is nothing surprising in this. For it is a branch of the wizard's art (τῆς τῶν ἐπῳδῶν τέχνης μόριον), and only slightly inferior to it. For the science of wizards enchants vipers, spiders, scorpions, and other savage beasts and diseases, whereas the art of speech writers is the enchantment and consolation of jurymen, assemblymen, and other crowds. Or do you see the matter differently? I said.
>
> No, but it seems to me, he said, to be as you say.
>
> (289 E 1–290 A 6)

Putting to one side his cryptic remark that the goal of their search is "here somewhere," Socrates now prepares to deal specifically with what Kleinias has said. Confessing that his own association with these producers of argument has led him to conclude that they are superwise, and that their science is inspired and lofty, Socrates seems almost ready to deliver a panegyric on the logic-art; and we can see the serious side to his words if we assume that these speech writers have learned, and so fully understand, their science. But when he begins to account for the amazing power of this science by referring to it as a branch of the wizard's art, the ironical twist in his analysis immediately surfaces, revealing that his apparent praise is really a foil for a more generalized polemic against forensic oratory.[12] And it is possible to view this attack as "absolutely superfluous."[13] Since Kleinias has produced evidence and received consent from Socrates, it might seem appropriate for them to turn to another science. But if one seriously entertains this view, the complexity of this charming scene will be lost, for Socrates is doing considerably more than launching polemics. Foremost in his mind is a pedagogical motive. From the hypothetical method by which he has guided Kleinias thus far, Socrates now shifts to another procedure, logical division or diairesis, and prepares to exercise it on the logic-art in order to facilitate their search. He makes speech-production an inferior division of the science of wizardry and links both of them by their common power to enchant their respective audiences, whether they be a variety of beasts and diseases or merely jurymen and crowds.[14] But here we must note that this is not a rigid dichotomy in which both sides of the bifurcation are equally extended; nor is it designed to supply an exact representation of the real relations that obtain between both sciences. On the contrary, Socrates is putting forth only a playful, half-serious use of diairesis by which he hopes to induce Kleinias to recognize that similarities and differences exist between both arts and that, in particular, they share the same end, enchantment.[15] In short, Socrates is here using logical division as a heuristic tool for Kleinias' instruction, the full import of which (whether superfluous or otherwise) cannot be determined until we see its impact on Kleinias.

DIALECTIC (290 A 7–D 8)

Whither then, said I, can we still turn? To what science?

I'm at a loss, he said.

Eureka, I said, I think I've found it (ηὑρηκέναι).

What? said Kleinias.

The art of the general (στρατηγική) seems to me, I said, to be the one more than any other which someone should acquire for attaining happiness.

I don't think so.

Why? I said.

This art is a science of hunting men (θηρευτική).

What of it? I said.

Nothing in the science of hunting itself, he said, goes beyond hunting down (θηρεῦσαι) and capturing (χειρώσασθαι). But when they capture whatever it is they hunt, they are unable to use it, so game hunters and anglers impart their catch to cooks (ὀψοποιοῖς), just as geometricians and astronomers and calculators—since they too are hunters, for they are not engaged in producing figures and proofs, but in discovering realities (τὰ ὄντα ἀνευρίσκουσιν)—and inasmuch as they do not know how to use them, but only to hunt them down (θηρεῦσαι), they—at least, however many of them are not entirely senseless—hand over their discoveries to dialecticians (διαλεκτικοῖς) to employ them to the full (καταχρῆσθαι).

Very good, I said, my fairest and wisest Kleinias. Is that so?
It most certainly is.

(290 A 7—C 9)

For his transition from the art of logic-production to consideration
of the next candidate, Socrates employs a highly charged rhetorical
formula: "Whither do I turn? To what . . . ?"[16] Like a professional
orator, who stirs the emotions of the crowd by feigning perplexity
before he moves to the body of his speech, Socrates confesses his
impasse. When Kleinias joins him and honestly admits his own perplexity, Socrates has his cue for action. But no longer expressing himself in a hypothetical construction, Socrates simply claims to have
made a discovery and then submits the science of generalship as the
final object of their search. But we shouldn't fancy that Socrates is serious. Here he is using the art of the general as a red herring, dragging it across the path of the λόγος in order to determine whether he
can lead Kleinias astray. So how does the boy respond to this playful
attempt at solution? Just as Socrates subsumed the art of speech-
production under a more extensive genus by making it a branch of
the science of wizards, so too Kleinias follows Socrates' lead and, with
complete seriousness, performs a similar operation on the art of the
general; he immediately subsumes it under the more extensive genus,
the science of hunting, and then proceeds with a diairetical analysis of
his own in order to give, once again, adequate evidence for rejecting
this candidate on the basis of its inability to meet both conditions of
the formula.[17] Kleinias has come a long way. His first philosophical
moment came when he experienced wonder at Socrates' tantalizing
identification of wisdom with good fortune (279 D 6—7). Now, no
sooner does the protreptic master produce an analytical tool than
Kleinias uses it to continue the series with such speed and skill that
before long he will shatter the verisimilitude of Socrates' narration.[18]

To begin with, Kleinias establishes the limitations that encompass
every branch of hunting, namely that no part of it extends beyond the
mere act of "tracking down" and "capturing." Then, for examples, he
divides the practitioners of this art into land-based and sea-based
hunters, who can successfully hunt down and capture their quarry
but who also prove incapable of using their acquisitions; so they turn
them over to cooks, who become the master users of these products.[19]
Now, had he wanted to, Kleinias could have advanced to the immedi-

ate application of his distinctions to the art of the general for the
rejection of Socrates' candidate. But he resists the impulse to apply his
method mechanically, and instead, with seemingly parenthetical remarks, as if the thought had just occurred to him, he expands the focus
of his analysis by shifting from these recognizable hunters to geometricians, astronomers, and calculators, a move that requires him to
assure Socrates that these practitioners of the mathematical sciences
are also hunters. To accompany this shift, he submits a different expression for what they do: they "discover" or, perhaps even better,
"recover" realities (τὰ ὄντα ἀνευρίσκουσιν).[20] In its current environment, ἀνευρίσκουσιν obviously covers both the notion of hunting
down and capturing, but the emphasis here is not on actually taking
the quarry in hand (χειρώσασθαι); for, as Kleinias tells us, mathematical hunters know only how "to hunt down (θηρεῦσαι)." At this
point he drops the concrete language of actually grasping the sought-
after prey. So it becomes relevant to ask what mathematicians actually
do seek to discover, if they do not literally grasp their prey. The answer to this question turns on the highly ambiguous term *realities* or
things which are (τὰ ὄντα).

At this point the emphasis that was formerly placed on production
has now shifted to the act of discovery.[21] Of course, mathematicians
produce figures and proofs by the aid of which they attempt to grasp
their objects, just as actual hunters produce any number of instruments by which they seek to capture their prey. But Kleinias' point is
that mathematical hunters do not just produce diagrams, any more
than sea-based hunters merely produce the instruments of fishing; as
hunters, both seek not *to produce* (except incidentally), but *to hunt down*
and *to capture* the proper objects of their investigations.[22] For example,
mathematicians can articulate the principles of calculation, hunt
down the laws of moving bodies in space, or even capture the rules of
earthly measurement; and in the performance of these functions,
they can produce and use diagrams as the means for recovering their
quarry, those elusive "things which are." But what Kleinias wants to
stress is that the objects of mathematics are *not produced*, but *are there*,
existing, whether we are or not, just as is the quarry that game hunters and anglers track down.[23] But the limitation on the mathematicians' power comes into play the moment they try to complete the use
of their discoveries, for this endeavor must entail that they employ
them outside the field of their due expertise. And so, as Kleinias judiciously observes, however many of them are not entirely senseless

hand over their discoveries to dialecticians (διαλεκτικοῖς), who thereby become the master users and overseers of the mathematical sciences.[24]

Some trouble has been occasioned by καταχρῆσθαι.[25] Although the concept of use (τὸ χρῆσθαι) has been featured throughout the dialogue, this is the first occurrence of the term with the prefix κατά. Here the word means the *complete* use of mathematical discoveries, which may require a different use from that envisioned by their discoverers. For example, the dialectical science will test the validity of mathematical discoveries by examining their consequences along the chain of their deductions in order, finally, to give a satisfactory account of those entities. What is more, since dialectic is a synoptic science, it will be able to employ the discoveries of mathematics in other fields and ultimately for the correct moral purpose.[26] To be accurate, however, Kleinias does not mention dialectic, only dialecticians. Throughout his analysis, he does not focus on sciences (except for that of hunting), but on those individuals who practice their arts. In fact, Kleinias does not present dialectic in such a way that a casual reader can complete its content by merely deciphering this indirect communication. From Kleinias' account alone, we cannot recover the full concept of dialectic as the science standing above mathematics. However, because its essential features are known to us from other sources, and not in the form of indirect communication but in very direct instruction, we can at least identify the authoritative background of the boy's remarks.[27] Put more simply, here in the *Euthydemus* it is Plato's purpose to show that Kleinias has the truth of ὄντα latent in his soul and that in a flash of insight he can recall that truth. But this would have been impossible, had not Socrates guided him along this upward path, in due order, through the skillful employment of his protreptic science.[28] It is as if Socrates has gently awakened Kleinias from his adolescent slumbers and caused his soul to rise to some Olympian vantage point where, for a brief moment, he has enjoyed the vision of things beyond this realm.[29] But the philosophical development of the youth does not end here:

> And generals, he said, act in the same way. Whenever they hunt down a city or an army camp, they hand it over to politicians—for they themselves do not know how to use what they have captured— just as, I surmise, quail hunters impart their quarry to quail-keepers. So if, he said, we require that science which, at the same time that it produces or captures (θηρευσαμένη) what it acquires,

will also know how to use it, and if this is the one that will make us supremely happy, then, he said, we must search for (ζητητέον) another candidate in place of the art of the general.

(290 C 9–D 8)

Returning now to the point at which he digressed upon the mathematical sciences, Kleinias applies his distinctions to the art of the general. Noting that, as hunters, generals turn their spoils over to politicians, because they lack the knowledge of the using science, he firmly and confidently rejects Socrates' proposed solution to their search.[30] In his final remarks, moreover, he culls the gist from his negative elenchus by adding his own discovery to the criterion. In addition to production and use, Kleinias now recognizes that the sought-after science must have the power to hunt down and capture those realities which we ourselves do not produce, but which exist and so can be used. At this point he turns the λόγος back over to Socrates with the rejoinder that if they still want to discover the science in question, they must continue their search: ζητητέον.[31]

In his analysis, Kleinias does not consider the possibility that the generals who turn over cities to politicians are themselves very likely to be politicians; that nothing prevents a speech writer from occasionally defending himself in a court of law or a duck hunter from being the cook in his own restaurant. Such blendings of functions do not occur to him because he is so engrossed in trying to distinguish these activities from one another. Moreover, for Kleinias neither the art of logic-production nor dialectic and political science can be the answer to the riddle, because he is unable to pass beyond treating the former as a producing and the latter two as using sciences. In his mind, production and use have become an unbridgeable antinomy, preventing him from seeing that the combination he wants is just beneath the surface of his own words. The possibility of acquiring a master science in which a single individual speaks, thinks, and acts correctly has not yet become a conscious vision of the boy.

SOCRATES' CENTRAL CONVERSATION WITH CRITO
(290 E 1–292 E 7)

We have now arrived at another turning point decisive for the work's formal structure, where Crito interrupts Socrates' narration in order to express his incredulity. This interruption may perhaps come as something of a surprise to many readers who, absorbed in Socrates' story line, may have forgotten that the occasion of this work is the conversation between Socrates and his friend. In fact, not since the opening conversation, when he asked Socrates to explain the nature of eristic wisdom (272 D 5–6), has Crito spoken directly in the work, and the last time his name was even mentioned was some time ago, during the interlude between the second and third episodes.[32] Since then Socrates has been wholly preoccupied with his narration. Not only has he recollected the multitudinous details of the second eristic, but he has also continued to draw together numerous protreptic threads of his own; he has continued to provide the brothers with a protreptic model, continued to guide Kleinias to the very frontier of the intelligible region, and just now even prompted the boy to offer a tantalizing vision of the dialectical science. But in the course of achieving these and other goals, Socrates has finally goaded Crito back into the immediate discussion.

Crito's interruption provides the dialogue with a sobering skepticism, almost as if Kleinias' venture into speculative philosophy has so transcended the limits of the common man's belief that it demanded a discontinuation. But to his question, whether Kleinias did in fact say such things (290 E 1–2), no simple answer can be given. In one sense, he didn't. Socrates did, and now this imagined uncertainty regarding authorship has the simple purpose of reminding us that we have been and still are totally dependent upon Socrates' recollection of what transpired the day before.[33] But in another sense, Kleinias deserves the credit for what he has said, and the proof of it is the degree of verisimilitude sustained by the story right up until this moment. But now that our attention has been turned to Crito, we can see that his skepticism is designed to reveal that he has fundamentally misunderstood the whole nature of the learning process that Socrates has just orchestrated. If Kleinias said what Socrates reported, then in Crito's opinion he has no further need for a teacher; his very speech would be an irrefutable sign that he has already attained all the education he needs; in fact, it would be the result or product of that education. Crito cannot recognize that he has just witnessed Kleinias bridge the gap between learning and knowing by "coming to know" through a cooperative process in which Socrates induced the lad to hunt down and to capture realities that are not part of his everyday conscious awareness and that will lose their tether to conscious moorings and submerge once again into forgetfulness, unless he receives continued support from a skilled questioner over a long period of time. In short, not recognizing that Socrates can trigger the recollection process best of men and most quickly, Crito has failed to see that Kleinias is, in part, responsible for his answers, but that his progress is only temporary.

The problem regarding the authorship of Kleinias' remarks, unimportant anyway now that Socrates is conversing with Crito, is quickly solved. After excluding Ktesippus and the brothers as possible sources, Socrates satisfies Crito's curiosity with the suggestion that the answerer was "one of the higher powers."[34] But to his credit, Crito wants to know about the final result of their search.[35] And although Socrates can no more hand over the end product of the inquiry to him than he could to Kleinias, he does use Crito's newfound interest as a trigger for drawing him into the investigation, even as he drives the analysis still further, away from Kleinias and the protreptic proper, away from the local question of the way to achieve individual happiness, to the broader question regarding the science itself, and ultimately to a consideration of the nature of kingship.

THE ROYAL ART (291 B 1–292 E 7)

Resuming his narration, Socrates announces to Crito that, like boys in pursuit of crested larks, he and Kleinias failed to capture their quarry.[36] Forgoing the lengthy account of their hunt, he tells Crito that they arrived at the kingly science and began to examine it to determine whether they had finally reached their goal. Yet when they fancied themselves to be at the end ($\dot{\epsilon}\pi\grave{\iota}$ $\tau\acute{\epsilon}\lambda\epsilon\iota$), they tumbled into a labyrinth, as it were, and suddenly reappeared at the beginning ($\dot{\epsilon}\nu$ $\dot{\alpha}\rho\chi\hat{\eta}$), as far away as ever from the object of their search.[37] Now this announcement of failure is important because Socrates doesn't view the beginning and end of inquiry as arbitrary points on a horizontal line.[38] Starting from a secure foundation, our universal longing for happiness, he has guided Kleinias along an upward path all the way to the royal art now posited as the terminus of their search. But just when they were about to grasp the elusive quarry, the protreptic master seems to have slipped somehow and to have led his initiate into a regress argument that transported them back to the beginning. Even Crito is eager to know how this failure came about. And fortunately, like Theseus, Socrates has returned from the labyrinth to recall the

tale.[39] Beginning with what he and Kleinias assumed to be their conclusion, Socrates gives this portrait of the science of kingship:

> To this science, both the art of the general and the rest granted
> the power to control their products (τῶν ἔργων) which they had
> crafted, on the ground that it alone knew how to use them (μόνη
> ἐπισταμένη χρῆσθαι). So clearly it seemed to us that this was the
> science we were searching for, that it was the cause of correct action
> (ἡ αἰτία τοῦ ὀρθῶς πράττειν) in our city, and, as Aeschylus puts it in
> his iambic line, that it sits alone (μόνη) at the stern of the polis, pi-
> loting and controlling all things so as to render them useful
> (χρήσιμα ποιεῖν).
>
> (291 C 7–D 3)

In the first phase of his protreptic, Socrates reduced the many
goods to the one good, wisdom, because it proved to be the force that
could guide the use of conventional goods. Now he has narrowed the
field of sciences to the one science, the science of sciences, which oc-
cupies a favored position atop the others as *the* using science because it
can provide the backing for the rest by ruling and guiding their products. Yet even in this idealized picture we can foresee where the kingly
art is in danger of running aground. As a using science, it depends
upon its subordinate arts for its products, but to meet the agreed-
upon formula, it must also produce. So the enthronement of the royal
science is threatened the moment Socrates and Crito renew the search
for what it produces. To assist his interlocutor at the start, Socrates
brings forth two examples: the science of medicine, which produces
health; and that of agriculture, Crito's own occupation, which produces sustenance from the earth.[40] So what, by analogy, Socrates asks,
does the royal art produce? Crito has no answer. So, changing his
strategy, Socrates returns to what he and Kleinias had agreed upon
(292 A 7–B 2): if any science was to be the solution, it must be beneficial and impart something good; and further, it was agreed that only
knowledge was good. Then, using these previous points of agreement
as a means of controlling his analysis of the kingly science, Socrates
immediately rules out its conventional ends such as making citizens
wealthy, free, and without party strife, because even these "products
(ἔργα)" are reduced to the status of neutrals if the political art doesn't
also produce citizens who know how to use such gifts beneficially; for
the science in question must do two things: it must share its knowledge and thus make its citizens wise.[41] And so, Socrates asks, does the

royal art make its citizens wise and good (292 C 4–5)? Is this its product (τὸ ἔργον), the production of wise and good citizens?[42] Crito can see nothing to prevent it, but Socrates continues to challenge him with more questions:

> But does it make all of them wise and good at all things? And is this the science which imparts each and every art, including shoemaking, and carpentry, and all the rest?
> I don't think so, Socrates.
>
> (292 C 7–10)

While not seeing anything to prevent kingship from making its citizens wise and good, Crito can easily see that it is not a science of imparting all knowledge (e.g. shoemaking and carpentry). So Socrates continues (292 D 1): "Well, what knowledge does it impart? And for what shall we use it?" The answer to the first question has already been worked out; since kingship must be the cause of something good and beneficial (and not merely the producer of neutral products), the art must "impart" or "share" itself (294 D 1–4). But to the second question Socrates responds by asking yet another (292 D 5–6): "Are you satisfied, Crito, if we say that it is that by which we shall make others good?" Is the instrumental value or "use" of the royal art to be found in "producing" wise and good citizens? For his part, Crito accepts this solution, but then Socrates asks (292 D 8–9): "And at what will they be good and useful? Or again are we to say that they will make others good, who in turn will make others good?" At this point the λόγος turns back upon itself because, having devalued what are customarily called the products of the political art, Socrates and Crito find themselves unable to stop the regress by specifying "at what" the citizens of the polis will be good and useful.[43] In the face of this difficulty, Plato takes command of his dialogue. To close the fourth episode and to effect a transition, he has Crito remark: "Yes indeed, Socrates, you and Kleinias apparently found yourselves in quite a predicament (ἀπορίαν)."[44]

Even if it is granted that the royal science knows how to use, we find ourselves in trouble the moment we try to determine what it produces; for this horn of the dilemma turns us back to the first-order sciences and their tangible products. But if we search for its "product (ἔργον)" in concrete "goods" like health and food, or in activities like medicine and agriculture that are supposed to produce them, then every candidate will prove inadequate; for kingship does not have a "product" in this sense but the function (ἔργον) of making its citizens wise and good.[45] Hence, to search for its product among first-order sciences, as if it were itself a first-order science, will always prove futile; for the royal art is not one science among many but one over many, sitting alone (μόνη) at the stern of the polis. If, however, we try to follow out the other horn of the dilemma and to establish some higher principle in accordance with which the political art determines what is good, better, and best, then this demand will require us to seek, if we are going to discover any real standard at all, a standard that is beyond "this" universe of discourse; an immanent standard, which varies according to fashion, would not be much of a standard.[46] So rather than advance the inquiry in that direction, in which he would have to unfold, as Shorey says, "the entire teaching of the *Republic* and the *Politicus*,"[47] Plato chooses to have Socrates admit their failure and then guide Kleinias safely back to the beginning.

Although Plato has exercised great skill in constructing this *regressus in infinitum,* he has nevertheless permitted us to observe at least by implication that the art of kingship does not enable all citizens to do all particular skills, such as cutting leather or working wood, because it is a science of universal scope and application that enables each to do well everything that is undertaken. It is not one among many sciences of doing the good thing but the one science of doing the one good. Accordingly, "faring well" or "happiness," the original goal of our longing, can be the gift handed over by the royal art if it performs its one good of making others good. As such, it can be the cause of correct action (ἡ αἰτία τοῦ ὀρθῶς πράττειν) in the polis by making cobblers good at shoemaking and kings good at ruling. But perhaps no one has stated this implied conclusion of the *Euthydemus* with greater precision than Paul Shorey:

> On the assumption that "making others good," as the function of the political art, bears a double sense, and means, with reference to the multitude, making them good through habit, discipline, and instinctive conformity to models set them from above, while for the elite it means the training up of a succession of philosophic statesmen to maintain and perpetuate the ideally best social organism and education—within these limits the *Republic* may be held to provide a sufficient answer to the problem of the tentative dialogues as resumed in the *Euthydemus.*[48]

CONCLUSION

The *Euthydemus* itself does not present a line of argument that builds up to and completely elucidates this science of sciences, but this fact does not indicate immaturity. For the sought-after knowledge also contains the art of suppression and even the art of silence, if the context requires it.[49] And yet, if we retrace our steps and gather together a few threads which we have already established, we can at least sketch the general area wherein the answer is to be found. When the brothers claimed to impart virtue, Socrates referred to this power as a science (ἐπιστήμη), for the possession of which (κτῆμα) they were more blessed than the Great King himself (273 D 5–274 A 7). Then, when the pair assured him that their science of virtue included the protreptic skill (and hence political function) of "making a man good," Socrates asked them to exhort Kleinias to pursue philosophy and virtue (274 D 7–275 A 7). But as their protreptic advanced, Socrates came to understand that the two were in fact arguing a position that was diametrically opposed to the teaching of virtue and wisdom; for if they were correct in maintaining that error was impossible, then there was no longer any need for them to impart excellence (287 A 1–4). And so Socrates undermined their claim to teach virtue by asking this clownish yet inescapable question:

> If we do not fall into error either when we *act* or when we *speak* or when we *think*, if this is so, then, in the name of Zeus, of what have you come here to teach? Or didn't you boast just now to impart virtue best of men to anyone who is willing to learn?
>
> (287 A 6–B 1)

If we now examine this question again in our present context, we can see that the answer to the riddle of the *Euthydemus* consists in having acquired, in the true sense, that knowledge which the brothers originally claimed for themselves and for which Socrates called them "blessed."[50] If an individual should "learn" and so fully "understand" this art (αὕτη ἡ τέχνη), the art of virtue, so as to guarantee correctness in *thought, speech,* and *action,* then he would acquire the sought-after knowledge; for this science is not only incompatible with error and the very antithesis to ignorance itself, the cause of error, but it is also beneficial and good.[51] Moreover, if the possessor and user of this master science were to sit at the helm, guiding and controlling all things so as to render them useful, in his *speech* he would exercise the philosophical rhetoric of persuading citizens, and not a bastard science of beguiling jurymen and crowds; in his *thought* he would exercise the synoptic faculty of tracking down and articulating the truth of ὄντα, and not the pseudo-science of eristic, which delights in differing over terms; and finally, in his *action* he would establish and maintain the just political order by making the souls of citizens wise and good, and he would not above all hunt down and capture the citizenry and then fatten them up with a view toward the marketplace or the banquet table. In short, this blessed ruler would acquire the knowledge that in Plato's view can truly be called philosophy: ἡ δέ γε φιλοσοφία κτῆσις ἐπιστήμης. Although he reserves the full articulation of this conception for other dialogues, nevertheless in the *Euthydemus* Plato has roughly adumbrated this science for those who wish to contemplate it.[52]

Finally, we must note again that the dialogue instantiates itself by portraying its own solution concretely. Every character of this work thinks, speaks, and acts; each is a producer and user of λόγοι. So whoever does so correctly can be said to have acquired the science in question, and from the beginning the underlying assumption has been that the possessor, producer, and user of that art in the full sense is Socrates himself. Why, then, a skeptical critic may ask, does he fail to guide his young initiate out of this maze of argument? As the architect of this labyrinth, Socrates knows that there is only one escape: to make a vertical leap up and out.[53] And yet, at the same time, he does not underestimate the difficulty and the danger of such a move. Not wanting to risk losing Kleinias, the way Daedalus did Icarus, by having him take flight too soon, before he has matured, Socrates is satisfied with just completing his appointed task: through the correct employment of his protreptic wisdom, he has successfully completed the first step toward "making Kleinias good." By contrast, the architects of that inescapable maze in which all its victims perish are the brothers themselves. With nothing real outside their minds to serve as the objects of their contemplation, they have turned to the exploration of the infinite minutiae of language and attained therein all the satisfaction they crave through the playful manipulation of mere words. That deadly prison without doors is the eristic mind itself.[54]

5

THE THIRD ERISTIC DISPLAY

Much of the material in the fifth and final episode of the *Euthydemus* may not be familiar even to the faithful. Those who are usually devoted to Plato's every word may have shied away from the descent we are about to undertake and preferred instead to take refuge in the more uplifting and familiar texts of the master. Although it is easy to sympathize with these loyal disciples, still it should be added by way of encouragement that Plato himself did not shirk from encountering, face to face, the ridiculousness that can come to reside within philosophy itself. For he recognized that a philosopher must consider both what philosophical method is and what it is not, or else risk losing sight of the positive side of that equation, which cannot exist in a vacuum completely isolated from its opposite. So without surrendering either pole or divorcing one from the other, Plato has united the pair, dialectic and eristic, in this singular dialogue in such a way as to hold the two together by a tension. And our minds, by working their way back and forth between the limits, can become better equipped to distinguish the valid from the fallacious, the true from its distortion. In this, our fifth and final chapter, we propose to continue our line-by-line analysis of the remaining evidence for this playful antipode to serious philosophical method so that, with this project completed, we can begin to form something like a final judgment on this pseudo-science of argument.

PART ONE (293 B 1–297 B 8)

Although Kleinias participated in the search for the supreme art, he is not the fitting interlocutor for the complete investigation. So Socrates issues an impassioned cry to the brother-pair, invoking them as if they were the divine Dioscuri, to rescue himself and Kleinias from the third wave of the argument. Here, for the final time, he importunes them to reveal their serious side by demonstrating what that knowledge is which can guarantee the smooth course of an honorable life. But now, when the amateurs should step aside and the serious philosopher should come to the aid of the λόγος, now when Socrates would engage the brother-pair Glaucon and Adeimantus for the full account, Plato, the master craftsman of this dialogue, demonstrates the fine art of sinking in philosophy by having Euthydemus, the philosopher-comedian himself, answer Socrates' prayer.

SOCRATES ALREADY POSSESSES THE SOUGHT-AFTER KNOWLEDGE (E9) (293 B 1–E 1)

Shall I teach (διδάξω) you this knowledge, Socrates, about which you two have been so long perplexed, or shall I prove (ἐπιδείξω) that you have it (ἔχοντα)?

(293 B 1–2)

Can we discern in this trigger question a change that is something of a novelty for eristic, at least insofar as we have come to know it from our dialogue? In the eight arguments that we have encountered thus far, the brothers have attempted to refute their opponents through the instrumentality of a negative, purely destructive elenchus. But now Euthydemus appears to be on the verge of either teaching or proving something constructive. Are we to conclude that eristic possesses the flexibility to argue *pro* as well as *contra*? And what are we to make of this dichotomy between "teaching" and "proving?" Is it real?[1] Significantly, Socrates does not straightway opt for either alternative. Instead, he expresses genuine surprise at Euthydemus' boast: "My blessed man, is this in your power?" Here, with the honorific "blessed" (μακάριε), Socrates indicates what it means for Euthydemus to be able to dissolve his and Kleinias' long-standing aporia. Euthydemus couldn't very well make good on this promise to impart the science in question unless he himself had already acquired it; and for that, as Socrates has remarked (274 A 6–7), he would be more "blessed" than the Great King is for his empire. But if Euthydemus is going to teach the knowledge in question, that means Socrates would have to learn what he doesn't know, and learning is suffering, especially when it has to occur at the feet of an eristic master.[2] So Socrates wisely decides in favor of the latter alternative, which is after all, as he says, "easier" for a late learner like himself. Before turning to the argument, we should reflect upon what it means to prove that Socrates already possesses the sought-after knowledge.[3] In the terms of this dialogue, it can only mean that he is going "to learn what he already knows or understands."[4] With just this first disjunctive question, then, implying as it does the already familiar dichotomies of the first eristic, we find Euthydemus criss-crossing back and forth over the subject matter of his philosophy, weaving the fabric of his discourse with the warp and woof of his eristic science.[5]

> Come then, answer me, he said. Is there something you know?
> Certainly, I said, many things ($\pi o \lambda \lambda \dot{\alpha}$), but they are small ($\sigma \mu \iota \kappa \rho \dot{\alpha}$).
> Enough, he said. Do you believe that it is possible for anything not to be that very thing which it happens to be?
> No, by Zeus, I do not.
> Then do you, he said, know something ($\tau \iota$)?
> Yes I do.
> Then are you a knower, if you know?
> Certainly, of just that thing.
> It makes no difference. But doesn't necessity ($\dot{\alpha} \nu \dot{\alpha} \gamma \kappa \eta$) compel you to know all things ($\pi \dot{\alpha} \nu \tau \alpha$), if you are a knower?
> (293 B 7–C 4)

We have already passed in review more than half the content of this dialogue, and yet Euthydemus and Socrates have not confronted each other one-on-one. Earlier the sophist leveled two remarks at him (286 E 4–7), but there he was just trying to rescue Dionysodorus from an impending refutation.[6] Thus far, then, Socrates has only grappled in argument with the older and weaker of his two antipodes. So now, beginning in that tight-fisted manner of the eristician, Euthydemus engages him for the first time by asking whether there is something he knows; and to our surprise, Socrates, who has gained such notoriety in the history of philosophy for claiming *not* to know, acknowledges that he does indeed know many things. But no sooner does he meet this requirement than he undercuts it by limiting his knowledge to the small.[7] "Enough," responds Euthydemus, who chooses to ignore the qualification. For his second question the sophist leaps to a metaprinciple that appears to govern the immediate context in some way and asks: "Do you believe that it is possible for anything not to be that very thing which it happens to be?" At this rarified level of abstraction, it is natural for Socrates to assume that the "thing" in question is what he just affirmed to know; as such it is not about to change its nature so as to be other than it is; after all, even the most trivial object of knowledge must be constant and invariable. So Socrates can deny with some emphasis that the thing in question can ever fail to conform to the principle. Next, creating the illusion of meticulously abiding by the strict procedures of his method, Euthydemus descends from this principle to repeat the substance of his first question: "Then do you know something?" Again, Socrates repeats his affirmation without hesitation. But then, from the fact that Socrates knows something, Euthydemus tries to establish that Socrates is a knower without qualification, and again, given the compactness of the reasoning, Socrates might easily answer "yes," assuming all along that the object of knowledge is still carried over in thought into this fourth question. But now, as if he were aware of some trick, Socrates scrupulously avoids any possible confusion by filling in the elided object: "Certainly, [I'm a knower] of just that thing," he replied. "It makes no difference," Euthydemus quips, again brushing aside the qualification. Now, on the condition that Socrates is a knower, Euthydemus springs to the next stage of the argument, asking him whether he is under the grip of necessity to know all things, as if somehow or other this were the unavoidable conclusion from the mere fact that Socrates has admitted to be a knower of something. But here Euthydemus does not receive the affirmation he wants, for Socrates not only denies the necessity of the conclusion but also gives a very good reason why it cannot hold:

> No, by Zeus, I said, for there are many other things I don't know.
> Then if there is something you don't know, you are not a knower.
> Yes, my friend, of just that thing, I said.
> Are you then any the less not a knower (οὐκ ἐπιστήμων)? And yet just now (ἄρτι) you claimed to be a knower (ἐπιστήμων). And so you turn out to be the very person who you are, and then again you are not that person, in the same respect and at the same time (κατὰ ταὐτὰ ἅμα).

> (293 C 5–D 1)

Socrates emphatically denies his omniscience on the quite reasonable ground that there are many other things he doesn't know. But this response, however sound it may be, simply allows Euthydemus to swing him to the other horn of the dilemma, from "knowing" to "not-knowing."[8] He concludes: "Then if there is something you don't know, you are not a knower." Undisturbed, Socrates repeats his qualification by reasserting the suppressed object: "Yes, my friend, [I'm not a knower] of just that thing." This time, however, Euthydemus doesn't even bother to dismiss the addition; he merely interjects rhetorically: "Are you then any the less not a knower?" and continues: "And yet just now you claimed to be a knower."[9] Finally, invoking his certain and indubitable principle, the very impossibility of one and the same thing not being what it is, Euthydemus substitutes Socrates himself for the "thing" in question and then concludes that his opponent is guilty of a grotesque violation of the "law of contradiction" by foolishly asserting at one and the same time the contrary predicates, knowing and not-knowing, of one and the same subject.[10] With these final remarks, we can now see clearly what the sophist's strategy has been. At first, he wanted Socrates to agree to know something, and then he intended to slide from this one thing to all things, without having to pass through the middle.[11] Socrates, however, blocked this acrobatic leap from one to all by limiting what he knew to the particular thing in question. He thus forced Euthydemus to retreat from the conclusion that he had hoped to establish and instead to seek to gain his goal indirectly by proving Socrates' omniscience through the sheer absurdity of denying it. Socrates, however, allows Euthydemus to reveal only the contradiction, for he himself draws out all the implications that according to Euthydemian logic must follow:

> Well done, Euthydemus, I said. As the saying goes, you've scored a point. How then do I know that knowledge which we were searching for? Obviously, in the sense that it is impossible for the same thing to be and not to be: If I know one thing, I know all; for I cannot be a knower and a not-knower at the same time. And since I know all things, I also possess that knowledge. Is that the way you state your proof, and is this your clever solution?
>
> (293 D 2–8)

Here Socrates points to the eristic sense in which he knows all things: since it is impossible for the same thing to be and not to be, if Socrates knows one thing, he knows all; and since he has admitted to know one thing, he knows all things: If P, then Q. P, therefore Q. Thus, Socrates possesses the science of their inquiry. But after completing the argument for Euthydemus, Socrates continues: "Is that the way you state your proof, and is this your clever solution?" Euthydemus, of course, doesn't even stoop to respond to this question, and why should he? It was Socrates, after all, who had requested his help in the search for the knowledge in question, and, to his credit, the sophist has spun out a most elegant and economical proof to a problem that has proved to be most difficult and complicated. Had Socrates acquired the good sense to yield to the rigorous validity and crystalline purity of his Euthydemian logic, then, presto, the long-standing aporia would have been dissolved. But in a wholly irresponsible fashion Socrates deflected the line of argument from its appointed end by an irrelevant addition, thus forcing Euthydemus to prove his case indirectly. Then, to make matters still worse—if this is possible—Socrates has now advanced so far in his ignorance of argument as not only to articulate the sense in which he has already acquired the science, but also to state the very principle, the violation of which has caused him to uphold the untenable position of being both a knower and a not-knower. In an eristic universe of discourse, to suffer a refutation is bad enough, but when a disputant pulls the chair out from under himself, without even having to procure an adversary to do the trick for him, the event becomes the unpardonable sin of self-refutation, the ultimate eristic disgrace and the clearest possible sign of *ignoratio elenchi*. Euthydemus is incredulous. All he can do is exclaim: "Out of your own mouth, Socrates, you refute yourself."

Of what does this clever solution really consist? Even if it should be granted that Euthydemus has solved the aporia by showing "that" Socrates has acquired the knowledge in question, he still has not demonstrated "what" the science is—that is, what its real content is—without which, of course, it is of no value. Consequently, this solution is empty and banal; the whole thing is really a spoof on the sophist himself for his inability to prove what, in fact, Socrates has. But what gives to (E9) the full impact of its banality is the particularly significant place that it has come to occupy in the overall orchestration of Plato's design. By positioning this utterly absurd solution to this most serious philosophical problem just after Socrates and Kleinias have struggled in vain to capture the quarry, Plato has managed to create the broadest possible gulf between the true philosopher and the false, between the true method and its double, which clings to it as vice does to excellence. With this rapid descent from the Olympian heights of the Socratic

search for the supreme science into this great cloaca of eristic discourse, we begin anew, for the third and final time, to follow the λόγος
of the brother-sophists, whithersoever it goes.

TURNABOUT IS FAIR PLAY (293 E 2–295 A 9)

To suffer an eristic refutation doesn't disturb Socrates. He has simply
articulated what appears to be Euthydemus' position and then asked
the sophist whether he has done so correctly. He has not refuted himself, but examined the λόγος. In fact, this very command "refute
yourself (ἐξέλεγχε σαυτόν)," if properly conceived, may be construed
as the Socratic maxim par excellence, the one way he found to know
himself. This form of self-refutation is the continual cross-examination of λόγοι so as to bring one's thought, speech, and action into conformity with those arguments which can withstand the test. What to
Euthydemus is an embarrassing, argumentative disgrace is to Socrates
the *sine qua non* of a life worth living. It is difficult to imagine how
Plato could more sharply delineate the two conceptions of the
elenchus.

But now, consistent with his notion of proper method, Socrates
takes over the role of questioner and begins to test whether this argument, too, will collapse from within.[12] If, in the abstract, one examines
the knowing subject in relation to what is known, then three logically
exhaustive possibilities turn up (293 E 5–294 A 3): a subject knows
either nothing (οὐδέν), or some things and not others (τὰ μὲν . . . τὰ
δέ), or all things (πάντα). Euthydemus has just cranked out a frozen
piece of chicanery to prove that knowledge of one thing necessarily
forces Socrates into the unqualified universal position. So now, taking
the brothers themselves as the test case, Socrates seeks to discover
where they stand amid this logical trinity. Beginning with the middle,
that contradictory realm in which he finds himself, Socrates asks the
pair whether they are partial knowers, a question that prompts from
Dionysodorus an immediate denial. So Socrates moves to the extremes, to the poles outside the realm in which he experiences the opposing tensions of life and takes up first the possibility that the two
know nothing. "On the contrary," Dionysodorus retorts, thereby leaving Socrates no alternative except to swing to the other limit, to the
knowledge of all things. And once Dionysodorus humbly affirms their

knowledge of all things, he and his brother have thus avoided Socrates' fate, but must now endure their own: a *universal omniscience* both caused by and conditional upon their knowledge of a single thing.[13] Moreover, in the same breath in which he claims omniscience, Dionysodorus goes on to add an unparalleled act of eristic generosity by assuring Socrates that he, too, knows all things, if he knows one thing. But as Socrates immediately intuits, if the brother-pair are themselves omniscient and can extend all knowledge to another, then they should be able to extend omniscience to all humanity. So when Socrates inquires whether this is in fact the case, Dionysodorus at last comes forth with his truly democratic, truly eristic thesis (294 A 10):

Πάντες, ἦ δ' ὅς, πάντα ἐπίστανται, εἴπερ καὶ ἕν.

All men know all things, he said, if they know just one thing.[14]

Not so very long ago Socrates fell into an aporia because he was unable to track down, much less capture, the science that could put an end to his and Kleinias' search. Now, courtesy of the eristic-duo, not only he himself but all humanity have become the possessors and users of this sought-after science. Finally, Socrates exclaims derisively, the brothers have come out from behind their comic masks to show us their serious side. But not allowing this feigned elation to distract him from cross-examining the λόγος, he continues to take the brothers themselves as the test case and asks them whether their omniscience extends all the way to shoemaking and carpentry (294 B 3−4). Now these two examples, we can be sure, have not turned up by chance. Plato has Socrates use them in order to recall that very part of the dialogue where the Socratic inquiry began to fall into serious difficulty; for the supreme science was supposed to make its citizens wise and good, but carpentry and shoemaking were too particular and too trivial for it to impart to all the citizens (292 C 4−9). So the questions naturally arose, what knowledge does kingship impart, and for what shall we use it? In trying to answer these questions, Socrates eventually slipped into the regress. But now, miraculously, the brothers have overcome that temporary setback. They have just used their eristic science not only to make the citizens wise and good, but to make all of them absolutely wise and good at absolutely everything.

It should be clear by now that the *Euthydemus* presents, in part, a consciously and deliberately crafted vision in which standard valuations have been turned upside down, a kind of superinverted world in which appearance has come to dominate reality. In their latest manifestation our two sorcerers stand before us as the answer to the regress. They themselves solve the enigma by becoming its solution. As the possessors of all knowledge they have not only acquired the science that is responsible for happiness and correct action in the polis, but they have also demonstrated their ability to impart it to all the citizens. For just a brief moment then Plato allows us to imagine the two-headed philosopher-comedian at the helm, piloting the ship of state and rendering all things good and useful. And yet, behind this distorted image, in part grotesque, in part amusing, we can also see that everything the brothers appear to be is contradicted by what they are; that their pretentious boast to know all things just masks the fact that they know nothing of any real value; and that, in reality, they are driven by that all-too-sophistic urge to become the masters and shakers of the universe by implanting a bogus image of their own wisdom in other minds.

Before resuming our line-by-line analysis, we should pause briefly to consider the serious paradigm against which Dionysodorus' thesis, "all men know all things, if they know just one thing," takes on force and meaning. The sophist doesn't specify the content of this "one"; for him, any indiscriminate particular will complete the trick.[15] For Socrates, however, the one he wants isn't just any old object of knowledge. As Friedländer has noted: "Does it not have a meaning for Plato's Socrates quite different from what Dionysodorus intends—if we think of the '*Idea* of the Good,' which confers both the power of knowing to the thinker and the reality of being to the objects of cognizance (*Republic* 508 E)?"[16] Anyone who has acquired the knowledge of this one thing, the Good, would then possess both the knowledge of the relative value of all things and the standard by which to make citizens wise and good. It is "here somewhere" that the *regressus in infinitum* is completely and finally solved, even as the possibility of its existence and attainment renders this latest piece of eristic buffoonery meaningful.[17]

Once Dionysodorus affirms that he knows both carpentry and shoemaking, Socrates proceeds to an even greater degree of particularity, asking the pair whether they are able to stitch gut, as if this were some distinct art of the superordinate science of cobblery. Unwavering, Dionysodorus asserts: "Yes, by Zeus, and to sew leather as well."

Shut out on the topic of crafts, Socrates passes to questions that have become proverbially unanswerable, such as the number of stars and grains of sand; theory cannot approach problems of this type, for they can be solved only by counting, which, of course, is impossible in these two cases. But Dionysodorus now shows his impatience with this line of questioning by responding: "Don't you think that we would agree?" Poor Socrates! He just can't seem to grasp that for eristic the mere act of saying makes it so.

Enter Ktesippus. What prompts him to engage the pair at just this moment?[18] The last time he was on the stage, he belligerently maligned the Thurian visitors for their driveling. On that occasion Socrates immediately defused the potentially hostile situation by advising him to take Menelaus as his model and to wrestle the brothers to the ground as if they were Proteus, the Egyptian wizard. Now Ktesippus translates that advice into action when he enters the fifth episode by demanding that the brothers produce some evidence for their pretentious boast to know all things. But what has prompted him to call for evidence? Here, too, we can observe Plato's strategy, if we reflect back upon the fourth episode where Socrates asked Kleinias to produce evidence for the rejection of the art of logic-production (289 D 1). To illustrate how carefully Ktesippus was attending to that discussion (as well as to everything else), Plato now has him bring forth the evidentiary criterion against Dionysodorus. But we must note the change in our young man's demeanor. Gone is his moral indignation.[19] Ktesippus has accepted the parameters of this science of how to do things with words and is now working from within to combat his adversaries. Yet he undercuts his call for evidence, reasonable by most standards, as soon as he requests each sophist to submit as proof of his omniscience the number of teeth the other has.[20] But dodging this question by submitting one of his own, Dionysodorus asks: "Aren't you satisfied to hear that we know all things?" Now apparently, not only does saying dominate the facts, but hearing what is said is supposed to suffice for verification. But Ktesippus will have none of this. He again undercuts his call for evidence by offering to pry open their mouths to verify their knowledge claims by counting.[21] Fortunately, this one example is all we need to grasp the gist. Socrates spares us Ktesippus' further requests for evidence by noting that he did not cease until he had asked whether the brothers' knowledge extended all the way to "the most shameful things."

In the immediate context of this argument, Ktesippus' demand for
evidence is of critical importance, and not just because it exposes that
undesirable element in omniscience, even if it were attainable—that
the knowledge of all things, claimed so humbly by the brothers, would
have to include knowledge of what no decent human being would
choose to know. But also, by having Ktesippus call attention to the
gross materiality of teeth and other such niceties, Plato suddenly transforms him, even as he calls for evidence, into that familiar Aristophanic
type who deflates the abstract thought of the boastful by applying it to
the common and vulgar. And how do the brothers react to this new
challenge? They immediately recognize that they are being mocked,
and they don't appreciate it. Our two jokers don't like to be the butt of
jokes; they can laugh at others, not at themselves. When Ktesippus
turns comedian, they counter by becoming serious and refuse to allow
him to count their teeth. But this obstinacy, as Socrates observes,
causes them to appear like wild boars driven to impale themselves on
the spear (294 D 6–7). Ktesippus has followed Socrates' advice all
right; he has wrestled the pair to the ground. But in demonstrating
his ability to fight just as dirtily as the eristics themselves, he has also
exhibited that tendency toward argumentative excess that will soon be
given full exposure. Plato has designed this little scene, so telling for
the development of Ktesippus' character, to form a bridge between
his role in the third episode and his final encounter with eristic. For
the present, then, we can conclude that Ktesippus has successfully
passed from *righteous indignation* to *acceptance of the game of eristic controversy,* but at what price?

Drawn on by his incredulity at what has just taken place, Socrates is
now compelled to reenter the debate and ask Dionysodorus whether
he knows how to dance. "Certainly," comes the reply. Then Socrates
caps this line of inquiry by asking whether he also knows how to do
somersaults through knives and to whirl about on a hoop. "There is
nothing that we do not know," the sophist retorts. So, having run the
gamut from crafts and uncountables all the way to mere stunts that
are so unbecoming that no one should choose to do them, Socrates
finds himself completely shut out on the level of content.[22] Shifting to
the problem of temporal universality, he continues the elenchus by
asking: "Do you know all things only now or always?" "Always," comes
the reply. Then Socrates specifies this temporal aspect more carefully:
"And when you were children and as soon as you were born, did you

know all things?" This question, which pushes all their eristic buttons at once, causes both of them to answer "yes" at the same moment.[23]

The brothers' claim to everlasting omniscience has finally proved too much for the group. Socrates and the others cannot help but express disbelief. Then, in the true spirit of eristic controversy, Euthydemus quickly turns this situation to his advantage by offering to dissolve the seeming paradox; and the sophist can gain much by doing so. The incredulity of the group, which he himself engendered, has created the need for him to demonstrate that his claim is only apparently paradoxical; it is a matter of indifference to Euthydemus and his brother whether they refute an obviously true thesis or beguile an opponent into accepting an utterly absurd falsehood, so long as they remain the masters of the λόγος. So, regaining the role of questioner, Euthydemus offers to prove that even Socrates himself agrees to these marvels, provided, of course, that he is willing to answer.[24] For his part, Socrates is jubilant. He is aware that he knows many small things, but that what he wants to know is a science that is truly great. Euthydemus, on the other hand, has just promised to prove that he has already acquired the desired object and in fact has always known it. So there can only be one possibility. The fact that he has acquired the science in question must have escaped his detection up until this very moment. All he has to do is submit to the eristic elenchus, and this master of the science of questioning and answering will cause him to recollect the sought-after knowledge of which, at present, he is unconscious. This eristic proof for his everlasting omniscience will continue, after numerous digressions, until Socrates himself terminates the first half of the fifth episode by making a conscious choice to flee from the clutches of the eristic duo.

SOCRATES KNOWS ALL THINGS ALWAYS
(E10) (295 A 10–296 D 4)

Answer (ἀποκρίνου), [Euthydemus] said.
Ask (ἐρώτα), and I will answer
Are you, Socrates, he said, a knower of something or not?
I am.
Then do you know with that by which (τούτῳ ᾧ) you are a knower or by something else (ἄλλῳ τῳ)?
With that by which I am a knower. For I assume you mean the soul (τὴν ψυχήν). Or don't you mean this?

Aren't you ashamed, Socrates? he said. When you are asked a
question, do you counter with a question?

(295 A 10–B 6)

All the components of this magnificent satire, this grand inversion
of dialectic, are in place once the first two lines establish the roles of
the speakers. Euthydemus will be the questioner (ὁ ἐρωτῶν), Socrates
the responder (ὁ ἀποκρινόμενος), and eristic, that technique of argument which can purge the conceit of knowledge from a boastful interlocutor, is about to become the instrument by which Euthydemus will
demonstrate that Socrates, despite his persistent failure to respond
correctly, not only knows all things but knows them always. What is
Socrates to do when the very person who is exercising the eristic art is
precisely the one most in need of undergoing the purifying benefits
of the elenchus?

Euthydemus' first question reveals the link between (E9) and (E10):
neither argument can get off the ground unless Socrates is a knower
of something. Then, for the second stage of (E10), the sophist asks:
"Do you know with that *by which* you are a knower or *by something
else*?" As he did in (E9), Euthydemus has dropped the object of knowledge and retained the knower, but he has also added a crucial new
element, the "by which" we know. But what is the nature of this "by
which"? Is it the "instrument" by which we know, so that the "by something else" refers to something other than that instrument? To say the
least, Euthydemus' question is open to interpretation because he does
not specify the character of the "by which"; consequently, the "something else" must remain equally obscure. Even by eristic standards this
question is not up to par.[25] But Socrates does have a partial grasp of
his meaning and so opts for the first alternative, the "by which" he
knows, and then adds: "For I assume you mean the soul (τὴν ψυχήν).
Or don't you mean this?" Euthydemus' question, then, which has directed Socrates' attention to the instrument by which he knows, has
caused him to recollect the soul, but when he asks the sophist whether
this is what he means, whether he is in fact inquiring about the soul,
Euthydemus immediately quashes the counterquestion by implicating
him in the shameful act of asking the questioner a question.[26] No
sooner does the eristic hear that dreaded word "soul" than he accuses
Socrates of a procedural miscue, as if his only objection were to the
inappropriateness of the question itself and not to the content.

Here a critic unsympathetic to eristic might want to say: "Euthydemus is a fine one to talk about shame." But if we remember to attend to the sophist's perspective, we can see the basis of his objection. Euthydemus has just established that he is the questioner and Socrates the answerer, yet after only the second question Socrates has failed miserably to perform his role in the game. In the sophist's view, then, this failure is just another example of ignorance of argument, for which Socrates, if he had any sense of (eristic) shame at all, should blush or fall silent.[27] But it is worth noting why Euthydemus takes refuge behind a procedural foul at precisely this moment. Our analysis of the second eristic has shown that the brothers fall back upon the "procedures" or "rules" of argument whenever they perceive some real threat to their position as masters of the game.[28] Therefore, we can conclude that this flight behind rules is just another eristical dodge employed *ad hoc* in order to avoid that awful word *soul*, which causes dread and anger in all eristics.[29] But not ashamed of his counter-question, Socrates even goes on to ask the master eristician for instruction on how he is supposed to behave in argument, an unexpected turn of events that interrupts the second stage of (E10) and ushers in a brief excursus on the proper method of questioning and answering:

Fine, I said, but what should I do? For I'll do as you bid. When I don't know what you are asking, do you bid me to answer anyway and not to question you in return?

Yes I do, he said, for I'm sure you understand (ὑπολαμβάνεις) what I'm saying in some sense, don't you?

Yes I do.

Well then, respond to the sense in which you understand it.

But what if you put your question, intending it in one way (ἄλλη διανοούμενος), and I take it in another (ἄλλη ὑπολάβω) and then I respond to this: are you satisfied if I don't respond to the point at issue?

Yes I am, he said, but, I suspect, you're not.

Well then, by god, I'm just not going to respond, until I inquire.

You're not going to respond, he said, to what you understand on each occasion (ἀεὶ ὑπολαμβάνῃς), because you continually talk drivel (φλυαρεῖς) and are more antiquated (ἀρχαιότερος) than is called for.

(295 B 7–C 11)

From the beginning, it has been the brothers' strategy to construct an artificial environment of words such that nothing can refer outside or penetrate within the context of their own devising. But just now Socrates has released the soul within that narrow enclosure, and so Euthydemus had to react quickly to contain the damage. But the trick he has used for this purpose, the suppression of the counterquestion, reveals something quite perverse about eristic. It is normal to think of dogmatists as people who have answers to the perplexing questions of existence, and it may be correct to do so. But here Plato is examining another side of dogmatism, caused not by having the answers, but by possessing the questions. Through controlling what can and cannot be asked, our two tyrants of discourse try to determine what answers are possible just as dogmatically as any despot who demands the party line from his followers.

If questioning the questioner is *verboten,* what is Socrates to do? For he swears that he'll do as he is told. Euthydemus instructs him to answer to what he understands to be the sense of each question. In effect, the sophist actually wants Socrates to respond on the basis of only a partial grasp of his questions; that is, he wants Socrates to be between the poles of ignorance and knowledge, without a full grasp of the real import of what is being asked. Otherwise, Euthydemus couldn't engineer and so exploit that "misunderstanding" between their minds which allows him to manufacture refutations. On the other hand, Socrates views his counterquestion as a way of minimizing the gap between his mind and the other. Assuming that he is supposed to follow in the tracks of the λόγος that the questioner is establishing, he wants to be certain of the "way (ἄλλῃ)" Euthydemus intends his questioning, so that he can respond on the basis of that understanding. Such clarity, on the procedural level at least, can produce satisfactory answers that are directed to the point at issue. But when Euthydemus frankly acknowledges that he is satisfied with miscommunication, Socrates for the first time in this dialogue digs in his heels and refuses to answer until he is permitted to inquire. But, as is to be expected, our wizard of wrangling has the antidote for recalcitrance: verbal abuse. Poor Socrates! In his folly he keeps on debating how the ceremony of questioning and answering is to be conducted. He just can't seem to grasp that the eristic masters have themselves already established the "way" and, what is more, the eristic clique is present with its rowdy voice to enforce that method. Not the method but the display of the method is under review, and by his ex-egetical remarks on procedures Socrates continues to produce, as Eu-thydemus so delicately puts it, the endless twaddle of an old duffer.[30]

Momentarily we shall consider why Socrates must knuckle under to this latest demand to answer in accord with what he understands on each occasion. But first we should try to imagine what would happen to philosophy if its practitioners, either deliberately through guile or inadvertently through lack of ability, should repeatedly send other minds down a path that is different from the one they travel. What, in short, would philosophy resemble, if misunderstanding were to be-come a central feature of the systematic application of its method? The brothers have already given us a vivid picture of such an illogical world, but from this moment on the whole situation is irrevocably al-tered. For Euthydemus has finally instructed those "other minds" on the eristic rule that governs the answers of the responder; hence, So-crates and Ktesippus can now take full advantage of it for their own purposes. By way of anticipating the results, Plato will allow misun-derstanding to increase to such a degree, especially in the answering antics of Ktesippus, that eristic will finally attain its τέλος in comic log-omachy. In this way Plato reduces eristic quite literally to absurdity by revealing it as a star instance of the ridiculous (τὸ γελοῖον), a species of the ugly (τὸ αἰσχρόν).

> I noticed he was angry with me for poking holes in his argumen-tation, because he wanted to trap me in a net of words and then hunt me down. Then I recollected that Connus too became angry with me every time I refused to yield to him, and thereafter he paid less attention to me on the assumption that I was ignorant. And so, since I had intended to study with him, I thought I should yield, lest he might consider me retarded and so not accept me as a pupil. So I said: Well, if you think I should act in this way, Euthydemus, then I must do so. For there is no doubt, I'm sure, that you know how to discourse better than I do, since my art of conversation is that of the ordinary man.
>
> (295 D 1–E 3)

Socrates' psychological penetration into Euthydemus' anger and frustration, coupled with his own recollection of Connus, turns this event into a deeply significant scene.[31] If we now conceive of Socrates' encounter with Euthydemus as a relationship between a teacher and a would-be student, then we can uncover yet another dimension to this fantastic inversion of dialectic. Socrates is the ignorant student, who has come to learn what he doesn't know from the wise master, who has already acquired knowledge of eristic. In his examination to determine whether this would-be pupil is a fit subject for instruction, Euthydemus has asked a question that Socrates couldn't fully understand. But instead of being overjoyed when his student requests more information on the real meaning of his question, Euthydemus angrily berates him for driveling and being too old to learn. This harsh instruction then causes Socrates to recollect similarly unpleasant treatment from Connus, another stern teacher, who became angry with him for refusing to submit to his musical expertise; as a result, Connus paid less attention to him, on the ground that he was ignorant. Such, it seems, is the timeless plight of those who want to learn; from teacher to teacher the exasperated student gropes.

But the bizarre picture of Connus attempting to instruct someone as notoriously unmusical as Socrates should not divert our attention from the significant way in which music and eristic differ. Teachers of music can usually determine without difficulty who is musical and who is not, even before their pupils reach adolescence, so clear are the criteria for establishing, at the beginning at least, what are the proper moves in the science of music. From this fact we can observe both the wisdom of exposing Kleinias and the other children to a music teacher at the same time they learn their letters (276 A 5), and the sheer folly of an old gaffer like Socrates still trying to learn music at his advanced age (272 C). By contrast, no such exact standards exist in the art of stand-up controversy, although when it suits their purpose, the brothers try to cling to the illusion that the rules are clear even when it is obvious that they are making them up as they go along. Thus, Socrates' recollection is a superb way of establishing the incongruity between the appropriate anger felt by an expert, who teaches a quite concrete science of how to perform a specific task, and the wholly unjustified anger of a philosophaster, who must have his way in argument as if he too possessed an exact science of how to question and how to answer. But even more importantly, there is a significant respect in which both cases are not incongruous. If Socrates fails to keep pace with the way these moderns are doing philosophy, then he may, in fact, face the frightening prospect of being expelled from school. And irony aside, this is a serious threat. For whether the boys are learning the new music of Connus or the new *ars rixandi* of these neoterics, Socrates must be present to shield unsuspecting youth from being stalked by these paid hunters of the attractive sons of wealthy Athenian parents.[32] So, brushing aside Euthydemus' insults and cheerfully yielding to the demand to answer on the basis of his partial understanding, Socrates urges Euthydemus to renew the λόγος:

> So ask (ἐρώτα) again from the beginning.
> Then answer (ἀποκρίνου) again, he said: Do you know by something (τῳ) what you know or not?
> Yes, I said, by the soul (τῇ γε ψυχῇ).
> Again he has answered more (προσαποκρίνεται) than is asked. For I'm not asking by what (ὅτῳ), but whether you know by something (τῳ).
> I answered with more than was called for under the influence of my poor education. So please excuse me. For now I'll answer simply that I know by something what I know.
>
> (295 E 3–296 A 5)

The transition from the excursus back to the second stage of (E10) is effected by the reassignment of roles: Euthydemus will question, Socrates will answer. In his new beginning the sophist tries to overcome the inadequacy of his earlier question by asking one which calls for a simple yes or no answer, or so he thinks. But to his surprise, his muddleheaded student, though this time without asking a question, replies with the substance of his earlier remark: "Yes, by the soul." Again, with only a partial grasp of his teacher's question, and foolishly answering to what he assumes to be the point at issue, Socrates has dared to give the question a content, a meaning, a reality. In fact, he has dared to give it the very same meaning that prompted the excursus in the first place. So we may suspect that Euthydemus should have shown more care in his selection of students, and that he must now qualify his original boast, "to teach anyone who is willing to learn," by excluding dim-witted boobies like Socrates. But most careful not to reveal that he is offended by the hideous word *soul*, Euthydemus again objects on a procedural level, although this time he censures the miscue of "answering more than is asked"; for, as he goes on to explain: "I'm not asking *by what*, but if you know *by something*." Now it is not enough for Socrates to respond in accord with what he understands on each occasion; he must also guard against answering *more* than is asked. But what, pray tell, constitutes "more"? In this case, the answer is obvious. The soul, the very entity that allows us to bridge the eristic antinomy between learning and knowing, between ignorance and wisdom, is again forced out of (E10) by this concept albino who cannot permit the "by which" to assume a content. Otherwise, he might have to treat his interlocutor as a living, breathing human being and not as an object that he can capture in a net of words and beat senseless with the λόγος. But for his part, Socrates graciously complies with this latest demand of his stern taskmaster.

> [Do you know, he said] by this same thing always (τῷ αὐτῷ τούτῳ γ' ἀεί), or are there times when by this (ὅτε τούτῳ), and other times by something else (ὅτε ἑτέρῳ)?
>
> Always, whenever I know (ὅταν ἐπίστωμαι), by this.
>
> Won't you please, he said, put a halt to your superfluous speech (παραφθεγγόμενος)?
>
> But I'm afraid this word *always* may cause us to stumble.
>
> Certainly not us, he said, but if anyone, you. So continue to answer. Do you know always by this?
>
> Always, I said, since I'm required to remove (ἀφελεῖν) the "whenever."
>
> Very well then, you know always by this (ἀεὶ μὲν τούτῳ ἐπίστασαι), and since you always know (ἀεὶ δ' ἐπιστάμενος), do you know . . .
>
> (296 A 5–B 4)

The third stage of (E10) is a graphic example of deviousness. With his opening disjunctive question, Euthydemus attempts to create the illusion that he is continuing in his meticulous manner to probe the character of the instrument by which we know. Having forced Socrates to agree to know "by something," he now appears to be asking whether that something is one, self-same instrument, or two or more instruments; that is, whether there is or is not an identity to that instrument on every occasion of our knowing. Since Socrates has already admitted that he knows "by the soul," it would seem that he must select the first alternative. But it has not escaped his attention that Euthydemus has also injected the temporal indicator "always" into the question. And so, after several disruptions the sophist has finally returned to the key item that originally provided the occasion for this dispute (294 E 6–11).

Earlier Socrates had asked the brothers: "Do you know all things only now (νῦν) or always (ἀεί)?" When Dionysodorus affirmed "always," Socrates removed any ambiguity surrounding this term by submitting two occasions that must be covered: the moment of birth, and when they were children. He thus made it perfectly clear that by "always" he intended an unqualified reference to time in direct contrast to that single moment expressed by "now." Consequently, if Euthydemus is going to attain the thesis of (E10), he must prove that Socrates' omniscience holds for this sense of "always," for absolutely all times. But when the sophist injects the term "always" into this combination of words, he slyly alters the sense of the earlier antithesis; he replaces "now," which Socrates used to oppose "always," with ὅτε, which signifies, not *one* discrete moment in time, but *now* one occasion, and *now* another;[33] and instead of using "always" to refer to all times, he so constructs the context that here the word must refer to "each and every occasion" of our knowing. Why he has done so will become clear momentarily, but for now we must see that, in the mind of the sophist at least, his question is perfectly set for the simple, unadorned answer, "always by this."

This sample of eristic legerdemain is most instructive for revealing a feature of Euthydemus' method. He is fully aware that he is not going to trick Socrates into admitting baldly, "I always know." So he tries to slide indirectly to this goal by leading his opponent to agree first to "[I know] always by this." To this end, he takes the term ἀεί, which has at least two lexical meanings, and, without specifying which meaning he intends (for that would prevent him from exploiting the equivocation), he cleverly juxtaposes ἀεί alongside other terms, which then force it to assume the meaning he wants through its relation to those other terms. But Socrates immediately detects this attempt at beguilement and so comes back with the rib-tickler: "Always, whenever I know, by this." With this response, not only does he quite literally separate the items Euthydemus wants to unite, but he also specifies without ambiguity that "always" covers each and every occasion of his acts of knowing. Thus, denied the simple, unqualified answer "always by this," Euthydemus must again resort to complaining about the sheer inappropriateness of Socrates' superfluous speech.

With the introduction of the word παραφθεγγόμενος, we confront the kind of difficulty that will continue to challenge anyone who tries to convey the sense of this dialogue into another language. For example, a recent translator has rendered the Greek thus: "I must ask you again, he said, not to qualify your answers."[34] Supported in this rendering by no less of an authority than Liddell-Scott-Jones, he has not *translated* παραφθεγγόμενος, but *interpreted* it. To Socrates, the "whenever I know" is indeed a qualification, but only misunderstanding of this passage could lead anyone to fancy that Euthydemus would grant the exalted status of a "qualification" to his opponent's superfluous speech. To him, Socrates has just introduced a fortuitous and incidental remark that has no bearing on the question at hand. But what to him is just misdirected noise is to Socrates a crucial distinction without which the argument cannot assume force and meaning. Here the two forms of speech, eristic and dialectic, diverge in a most illuminating way. Euthydemus asked a question, intending it in one way, and Socrates took it in another and answered to what he understood to be the point at issue: the result, a misunderstanding that is both a gag on the sophist and a *sine qua non* of the argument.

The divergence continues. Socrates defends his qualification by expressing the fear that "this word *always* may cause us to stumble." But this piece of Socratic nonsense forces Euthydemus to correct him: "Certainly not us, but if anyone, you." Poor Socrates! He is still assuming that they are conducting a joint dialectical inquiry (κοινὴ σκέψις) into the truth of a question that concerns both of them equally. So Euthydemus must remind the nincompoop that if he doesn't learn how to perform his role in the elenchus pretty soon, he'll self-destruct again. Then, as he did before, the sophist reshapes the failed question into one that demands a simple "yes" answer: "Do you know always by this?" "Always," responds Socrates, eager to obey, and then he goes on to announce that he is removing the offending word "whenever."[35] So at last Euthydemus can state the conclusion that he wants in this unadorned way: "You know always by this (ἀεὶ μὲν τούτῳ ἐπίστασαι)."[36] But in the very process of shifting to the fourth stage of (E10), this slippery snake finally reveals why he has been toying with the word "always." Prefacing his trigger question with a subordinate clause (ἀεὶ δ' ἐπιστάμενος), from which he has subtracted the instrument of knowing (τούτῳ), Euthydemus smoothly links "always" and "knowing" without any intervening qualifications. By shifting from "always by this" to "always knowing," Euthydemus has shrewdly drifted to the unqualified reference to time everlasting that he needs in order to attain the first half of his thesis. The game continues:

Very well then, you know always by this, and since you always know, do you know some things with this by which (τὰ μὲν τούτῳ) you know and some things by something else (τὰ δ᾽ ἄλλῳ), or all things by this (τούτῳ πάντα)?

All (ἅπαντα), at least what I know (ἅ γ᾽ ἐπίσταμαι), I said, by this (τούτῳ).

Here it comes again, he said, the same superfluous remark (παράφθεγμα).

Well then, I said, I'll remove (ἀφαιρῶ) the "at least what I know."

Nay, he said, don't subtract a single thing. I make no request of you. Just answer me: Could you know all (ἅπαντα) if you didn't know all things (πάντα)?

That would be monstrous, I said.

Well then, go ahead now and add (προστίθει) what you want, he said, for you admit to know all (ἐπίστασθαι ἅπαντα).

Apparently, I said, since the "what I know" has no force (οὐδεμίαν δύναμιν), and I know all things (πάντα δὲ ἐπίσταμαι).

(296 B 3–C 7)

The fourth stage of (E10) begins by mirroring the trickery of the third. Creating the illusion that he is asking whether there is one or more than one instrument involved in every act of knowing objects, Euthydemus appears to have set a question that demands the answer: "All things by this." But Socrates breaks up this combination by adding the qualification "at least what I know," another hilarious joke on the sophist that illuminates at the same time an essential ingredient of the argument. Exasperated, all Euthydemus can do is complain: "Here it comes again, the same superfluous remark." These three qualifications, "the soul," "whenever I know," and "at least what I know," each recollected by Socrates as a result of Euthydemus' cross-questioning, each a significantly different response to what he assumes to be the point at issue, have introduced the unexpected into the rigid line of eristic questioning, and each, in turn, has been quashed by Euthydemus, and in fact must be quashed by him if he is to advance along the narrow chain of his deductions.[37] To the sophist, each addition is just the same old addition, the same old superfluous noise that prevents him from proving Socrates' everlasting omniscience.

So to please his interlocutor, Socrates generously offers to withdraw this qualification too, but Euthydemus doesn't require him to cooperate; the way he deals with contentious babble is to ignore it. Instead, for the third time he reformulates his unsuccessful question into one that demands a simple "yes" answer. This time sequestering both the instrument of knowing and the addition "at least what I know," he asks: "Could you know all (ἄπαντα) if you didn't know all things (πάντα)?" Here, it is possible that by "all" Euthydemus means "everything together" and by "all things" everything separately, so that in effect he is arguing that Socrates, who has just admitted to knowing the whole (ἄπαντα), must also know the parts (πάντα);[38] but it is also possible that the sophist is merely making a distinction without a difference. At any rate, what is important to him at this moment is simply to place a question that guarantees an affirmative answer. Since Socrates has already used "all" to cap "all things" without any discernible difference in meaning at 296 B 5, Euthydemus can confidently use both terms to form an (empty) hypothetical question that will achieved the unqualified "yes."[39] Once Socrates gives him that simple affirmation, Euthydemus has the agreement he wants to the fourth stage of the argument. So he triumphantly badgers his opponent with the taunt, "Go ahead now and add what you want," because Socrates is at the moment powerless to derail the conclusion with his qualifications; for, as Euthydemus adds by way of emphasis, "You admit to know all."[40] Euthydemus' hypothetical question, then, turns out to be just another device which he has used, on this occasion, to join the act of knowing to its objects without any intervening additions, just as above he used a similar trick to link "always" and "knowing."[41]

Socrates humbly accepts the likelihood of his omniscience and then goes on to explain how the sophist has pulled off this hoax. Through his control over the questioning, Euthydemus can determine which answers have force and which do not. Here, by ignoring the qualification "what I know," while attributing full force and meaning to the mere words "I know all things," the sophist has "apparently" attained the second half of the thesis he wants to establish.[42]

Before continuing, we must note another feature of (E10) that demonstrates the precision with which Plato has depicted this inversion of his own method. Socrates regularly allows his interlocutors to add to or subtract from their positions before he begins the cross-examination of the λόγος, and he even permits them to shift positions in midstream, provided they do so openly. Here, in (E10), Euthydemus has grossly perverted this dialectical courtesy by suppressing qualifications until he attains the conclusion he needs, and then, after it no longer matters, he rudely invites Socrates to add whatever he wants; and this too, while it is patently clear to us that he himself has surreptitiously subtracted the "by which" we know from stages three and four of the argument.[43] This champion of the art of controversy has perfected the ability to wipe out distinctions that need to be made, and to unite kinds that should be kept apart.[44]

In the fifth and final stage of (E10), Euthydemus has two objectives: First (296 C 8–10) he must confirm the "truth" of what Socrates is imagined to have stated in stages three and four, namely that he "always knows" and "knows all things";[45] and then (296 C 10–D 4) he must combine these two admissions in order to "prove" that, out of his own mouth, Socrates has agreed to the astonishing thesis that "he knows all things always." That the sophist is able to do so is probably not as interesting at this point as the quasi-religious ecstasy that he experiences in the act of pronouncing this triumph.[46] Returning to the two examples that Socrates introduced, childhood and birth (294 E 9), Euthydemus adds to this list both the moment of Socrates' conception and the generation of heaven and earth as instances that are covered by his everlasting omniscience. Presto, the incredulity of Euthydemus' opponents is dissipated, the paradox dissolved. But there is a catch. Socrates will remain omniscient only so long as this tyrannical father of the λόγος permits it: ἂν ἐγὼ βούλωμαι.[47]

It would be hasty to assume that if Socrates and therefore the rest of humanity know all things always, they would no longer require Euthydemus as their teacher, and he, in turn, would be without anything to teach. For that judgment would severely underestimate the power of this sham-science. In fact, it would be to repeat something like the kind of mistake that Crito made when interpreting Kleinias' progress under Socrates' questioning. Profundity such as Euthydemus has just demonstrated is constantly in danger of being forgotten, and so we will always need an eristician to exercise his science of questioning and answering so as to prompt our recollection of this fairest argument. In spite of recent research and the analysis here presented, there will still be those who persist in reading the *Euthydemus* as earlier than the *Meno*.[48] For them, Plato's teaching on reminiscence cannot provide the deeper background for (E9) and (E10). Without it, however, we may only wonder what account they may offer for these pages of Plato's text. At any rate, inasmuch as there is no conclusive proof that the

Euthydemus antedates the *Meno* in such a way that nothing in the latter can be presupposed in the former, we have felt justified in scrupulously avoiding the attempt to control the meaning of this portion of the dialogue by clinging to a hypothesis that precludes, at the outset, the possibility of discovering what in fact we have found to be there. In this way the philosophical burlesque has been elucidated, and Plato's purpose made evident. Using the theory of recollection as the serious model from which this eristic travesty could deviate, Plato has shown how his very own teaching, which is designed to make us dogged workers and committed seekers after truth,[49] can be warped by a philosophical mutant into an eristic λόγος that can, in turn, obliterate all the benefits made possible by *anamnesis*.

SOCRATES' ONE LITTLE QUESTION (296 D 5–297 B 8)

Socrates is willing to accept his everlasting omniscience, but first he wants the brothers to explain how he can claim to know a proposition of this type: that good men are unjust (ὡς οἱ ἀγαθοὶ ἄνδρες ἄδικοί εἰσιν). "Do I know this, or do I not?" he asks Euthydemus. Since the sophist has just proved Socrates to be omniscient, he must embrace the positive horn of the dilemma: "Of course you know it," he replies. But when Socrates asks him to specify what it is that he knows, Euthydemus is in serious trouble. Not with a partial grasp of Socrates' question but with a full understanding of the threat it poses to his argument, he doesn't respond to the point at issue, but by sleight of hand tries to weasel out of the trap by slipping "not" into his reply, an addition that converts the statement into something which can be known: that good men are *not* unjust (ὅτι οὐκ ἄδικοί εἰσιν οἱ ἀγαθοί). But this "eristic addition" is precisely what Euthydemus claimed the Socratic qualifications to be, merely "misdirected noise." For his part, Socrates accepts the addition as if it did express real content (a content, in fact, the truth of which he claims to have known for a long time) and, in conscious imitation of one of Euthydemus' testy remarks, replies: "But that is not what I'm asking; rather where did I learn that good men are unjust?"[50] The tables are now being turned on Euthydemus, and so his enantiomorph comes to the rescue. "Nowhere (οὐδαμοῦ)," quips Dionysodorus. Thereupon Socrates immediately shifts to the other side of the dilemma and concludes: "Therefore, I do not know this." Into this eristic line of argument, Socrates has sneaked the very real probem of how, when, or where we "learn" and so come to "know" a falsehood. When Dionysodorus hears the problem so formulated, he slips into a familiar groove and just responds in accordance with his eristic training; there can be no place or time or way Socrates could have learned "that which exists nowhere."[51] In the present context, however, his apparently correct answer has the real effect of destroying (E9) and (E10); for, as Euthydemus informs his brother, Socrates is now both a knower and a not-knower. There is only one genuine response for an eristic who has thus ruined an argument: Dionysodorus blushes.[52] But not satisfied with this end to the inquiry, Socrates returns to Euthydemus and continues to press the questioning: "What do you mean, Euthydemus, don't you think your brother, who knows all things, speaks correctly?" Since Dionysodorus is omniscient, he can't very well speak falsely. So perhaps he is speaking the truth when he claims that this falsehood exists "nowhere"; at any rate, Socrates is more than willing to take up the problem with Euthydemus. Now it seems that Dionysodorus' defeat is about to bring down Euthydemus too.[53] Socrates has not only divided but is about to conquer the pair. The situation calls for immediate and desperate action. So, seizing upon the trigger word *brother,* Dionysodorus makes an unconscionable leap to an inescapable question that prefigures the quibbles on family relationships.[54] But when Socrates objects to this gross disruption of his conversation with Euthydemus, Dionysodorus takes refuge in the "rules" of argument and automatically indicts Socrates for "flight ($\phi\varepsilon\acute{v}\gamma\varepsilon\iota\varsigma$)," an unacceptable failure to perform his role as answerer.[55]

Here any falsehood would have proved adequate for the trick. So why has Socrates submitted this one? Is the statement "Good men are unjust" false simply because the "good" men whom we encounter in our experience are not unjust? No doubt there would be radical opposition to this claim. So maybe Socrates is trying to suggest something more complicated. Perhaps he doesn't want to learn that good men are unjust. Is he instead implying that the terms *good* and *unjust* are incompatible predicates? Have they combined in a false statement because their forms, goodness and injustice, do not blend or mix in some way?[56] What, in short, is wrong with saying: "Good men are unjust?" Socrates really wants instruction on this problem, but he is not about to receive it in an eristic context.[57] At this point it suits Plato's purpose to submit a false statement that obviously refers to something and conveys meaning to its hearers, as is evidenced by the fact that Euthydemus immediately intuits the danger that it presents to his argument. To an eristic, a falsehood certainly can "refer" to something and have "meaning" if it threatens to destroy his argument.[58] But now, rather than bicker again with Dionysodorus over questioning procedures, Socrates moves into the realm of myth in order to gain some distance from the immediacy of his entanglement with these two monsters.

TRANSITIONAL INTERLUDE: THE HYDRA AND THE CRAB (297 B 9–D 2)

Dionysodorus' charge of flight points to a breach in the eristic demand that the answerer respond to the questioner. Failure to answer can in itself be construed as a defeat in eristic controversy, or so the sophist assumes. But not worried about such things, Socrates justifies his retreat by introducing a mythical exemplum that qualifies the action of the dialogue in a particularly apt way. Granting that he is weaker than either of the two eristics, Socrates frankly acknowledges the reasonableness of flight; after all, he is just following the precedent of Heracles, who refused to fight against two. But as he unfolds this well-known tale, we suddenly find ourselves out of eristic pettifoggery and into an elaborate simile that directs our attention to the second labor of Heracles.

In the myth, Eurystheus, king of Argos, commanded Heracles to kill the Hydra because she was causing the disappearance of unsuspecting travelers who drew too near her unfathomable swamp. This female demon, the portentous offspring of the god-hated Typhon and Echidna, had a doglike body, innumerable heads, poisonous blood, and such venomous breath that a single whiff could kill. So, careful not to inhale the fetid odor, Heracles tried to bash in her various heads, only to discover that for every head he bashed, two more would spontaneously spring up. To make matters worse, Hera conjured up support for the Hydra in the form of a Crab, which challenged Heracles by nipping at him with six pairs of jaws. Caught in this dilemma, Heracles hailed his chariot driver and nephew Iolaus to come to his aid. Setting a corner of the marsh on fire, Iolaus heated tree limbs in the blaze and seared the roots of the Hydra's severed heads to check their proliferation and stop the flow of their deadly blood.[59]

In unfolding these details, Socrates characterizes the Hydra as a "she-sophist (σοφιστρίᾳ)," a label that immediately strikes us as straining the limits of literary allusion.[60] When, moreover, he continues to inform us that the heads of the Hydra are heads of argument (λόγου),[61] and that the Crab, another sophist (σοφιστῇ), annoyed Heracles by "arguing (λέγων)" against him on the left (see 271 B 7), then we are forced to recognize that Socrates has here passed beyond the realm of mere image and story into a fantastic conceit that compels us to identify the Hydra and the Crab with Euthydemus and his brother.

From the beginning of the dialogue, Socrates has been under the command of his daimon to protect the guileless Kleinias from being devoured by the forces of corruption. But in carrying out this labor, he has been drawn into direct combat with Euthydemus. And just when he finally succeeded in getting a firm hold on this slippery eristician by pressing him on the problem of falsehood, Dionysodorus sidled up to him in order to deflect the argument. Now, when Socrates would like to summon support in this deadly combat, he must pause and reflect: "But if my Iolaus should come, he would do more harm than good." Yet this remark, a reference to Ktesippus who will soon come to the aid of the λόγος, has not always been seen for what it is.[62] In fact, in the recent failure to see Ktesippus as Socrates' Iolaus, we can trace a pattern of misinterpretation that uncovers a persistent inability to appreciate the role of Ktesippus in his upcoming logomachy. For Socrates' remark foreshadows what in fact "his" Iolaus is going to do, once he has been transfigured into the distorted image of a helper;[63] he will lop off the heads of the eristic dilemmas and then cauterize them with his own firebrands in a boyish attempt to check the logorrhea of this slimy watersnake and spineless crustacean. At any rate, we can safely conclude that Plato has here juxtaposed the incongruous acts of clawing and arguing, of chopping off the heads of a she-demon and refuting the fallacious arguments of paradox-vendors, in order to portray eristic as a violent, sophistic intrusion into speech that erupts from subterranean swamps to pollute the atmosphere of our philosophic discourse.

PART TWO (297 D 3–303 A 9)

The first part of this episode has managed to attain some coherence because Euthydemus presided over most of the questioning and the problems of omniscience and its acquisition remained the central topic. But now every semblance of coherence begins to dissipate, as eristic sinks to a new level of haphazardness. Yet here too, behind the apparent randomness of all the action, the skillful hand of Plato does not fail to preserve the structural pattern of his work. By linking together increasing absurdity with increasing profundity in such a way that as eristic becomes more comical, its perversity becomes more threatening, Plato continues to present for our inspection a pure image of what philosophical method should not be. But in order to bring this final part of the fifth episode into the light of conceptual clarity, we must now push our descent even deeper into this seemingly inextricable maze of argument. And so we extend our apologies to the reader at the outset for the infinite minutiae that we are about to encounter. But the only way to track down and capture our quarry is to engage the enemy more closely with our painstaking line-by-line analysis.

ON FAMILY RELATIONSHIPS (D11) (297 D 3–298 B 3)

In the transition from the mythic exemplum to the inescapable question, we again observe that vast gulf between the two techniques of argument. Indulging in that freedom and leisure of the true philosopher to range in all regions of discourse, Socrates has just distanced himself from the immediacy of combat through an imaginary flight of fancy that consciously employed language that did not mean what it said. But his small-minded adversary, intent upon the mere *ipsa verba*, has clasped in his various jaws four items from Socrates' tale (Iolaus, Heracles, nephew, and "mine," converting it to "yours") and now returns to the attack with that persistent and tyrannical demand to answer:[64]

> Now that you have sung this aria, said Dionysodorus, answer. Was Iolaus any more Heracles' nephew than yours?
>
> (297 D 3–5)

Ridiculous on the face of it, this disjunctive question anticipates the obviously correct answer: "Heracles'." Yet Socrates goes on to add to this response, "mine in no way whatsoever," and thereby eliminates the possibility of a *tertium quid;*[65] for in this case his family history proves decisive: "My brother Patrocles," Socrates says, "was not his father." So to the attack again, Dionysodorus asks: "Is Patrocles yours?"[66] Unable to answer this question without a qualification, Socrates notes that Patrocles is his by the *same* mother (ὁμομήτριος), but *not* by the *same* father (οὐ μέντοι ὁμοπάτριος);[67] that is, Patrocles is qualifiedly his by virtue of the fact that they share the same mother. Then, thrilled by this response, as if he suddenly had his opponent in the jaws of some necessity, Dionysodorus immediately snaps: "Therefore, he is your brother and is not your brother."[68] But with like quickness, Socrates repeats the sense in which he is not his brother: "Not by the same father"; that is, Patrocles is qualifiedly not his by virtue of the fact that they have different fathers. Then, undisturbed, Socrates continues to unfold more details of his family tree, still responding to the sophist as if he were seeking real information: "Chaeredemus was his [Patrocles'] father, and Sophroniscus mine." Recovering from his temporary setback, Dionysodorus now tries to operate on the two fathers by asking: "Is Chaeredemus different from a father (ἕτερος . . . τοῦ πατρός)?"[69] But Socrates instantly qualifies: "[Different] from my [father]"; that is, Chaeredemus is qualifiedly not a father by virtue of the fact that he is a different father from Sophroniscus. Cut off again, Dionysodorus must retreat.

Thus far we have observed the Crab creep up, now here, now there, trying desperately to secure a position from which to launch his attack. But Socrates has successfully warded off each sally by qualifying his answers. So, forced to alter his strategy, Dionysodorus now places a disjunctive question that may at first appear to contain a non sequitur:

> Was Chaeredemus a father, though different from (ἕτερος) a father, or are you the same (ὁ αὐτός) as a stone?
>
> (298 A 2–3)

To philosophers engaged in real discourse the second limb of this question is not an apparent, but a true non sequitur. But in eristic discourse it performs a genuine function by providing Dionysodorus with the opportunity to balance "different from" with "same as" and eventually to wring an unqualified sense of "is not" out of the equivocal ἕτερος. For an obvious reason Socrates doesn't respond to the first limb; he has already admitted that Chaeredemus is both a father and different from his father. So, responding only to the second, he counters the strict sense of sameness, which has him be identical to a stone, by voicing his fear that under the influence of this sophist he may soon appear to be as dull and stupid as a stone.[70] But still he admits, in all truthfulness, that he is not the same as a stone. Shifting from sameness to difference, Dionysodorus renews the attack: "Then are you different from a stone?" Again, Socrates replies truthfully: "Of course [I'm] different (ἕτερος)." Finally, then, Dionysodorus has snared his victim, for he has at last forced Socrates to use ἕτερος in the unqualified sense of absolutely "is not" a stone. From here Plato allows this clown of his own devising to carry out a satiric version of (eristic) epagoge against Socrates himself. First, he supports the conclusion he wants with two parallel cases (298 A 6–9):

Socrates is different from a stone; therefore, he is not (a stone).

Socrates is different from gold; therefore, he is not (gold).

Dionysodorus then submits the third and crucial case:

Chaeredemus is different from a father; therefore, he is not (a father).

In this final instance, ἕτερος should not mean "different from" in the unqualified sense of "is not" a father, but simply "another" father, who is different from the father Sophroniscus; after all, the gentlemen are two different fathers. But by putting his final exemplum alongside the other two, Dionysodorus has created the illusion that all three cases are parallel, thus inducing Socrates to respond: "Apparently, he is not a father."[71] Then, incapable of resisting the opportunity to add another reason why Chaeredemus is not a father, Euthydemus remarks: "Yes, obviously, for if Chaeredemus is a father, then the situation is reversed; Sophroniscus, since he is different from a father, is not a father and so you, Socrates, are unfathered (ἀπά-τωρ)."[72] To the rudeness of this *reductio ad absurdum*—hilarious if it were delivered on the comic stage—Socrates does not respond, thereby creating a vacuum so that Ktesippus, that distorted image of the helper, can now come to the aid of the λόγος.

THE ERISTIFICATION OF KTESIPPUS (298 B 4–300 D 9)

The six arguments that Ktesippus is about to help orchestrate have inspired almost no scholarly comment beyond perfunctory characterizations such as "zany" or "absurd." There seems to be a general reluctance to state what authorial intention may be governing this part of the dialogue. But we must do better, if only to provide a ventilation of the problems. Broadly speaking, this section is a magnificent farce on what in sophistical literature came to be called knockdown arguments.[73] Yet within the dialogue as a whole, it is only the third and final phase of a movement that is designed to transform Ktesippus into an eristic warrior. In his first confrontation with the brothers he learned that there was nothing to be gained from directing his attention toward how things really are (283 E–284 E); from Dionysodorus, in particular, he learned that he must uphold the λόγος against the attacker, that he must always be prepared to contradict his opponent, and that, above all, he must never be reduced to silence (285 D–286 B); and from the close of the third episode he was able to glean that he could utter all manner of senseless babble and even be soundly refuted, and still not suffer any serious consequences for such behavior (288 A–B). Then, in his last encounter with the pair, he learned that it was pointless to try to force them to meet a criterion of evidence, since the simple act of "saying" makes it so and merely "hearing" what is said suffices for verification (294 C–D). Now, therefore, having been schooled in these eristic preliminaries, Ktesippus can step down into the ring and confidently engage his adversaries in this mock battle of eristic giants. Let the games begin.

A Father Is the Father of All (K12) (298 B 4–D 6)

And then, having taking over the argument (ἐκδεξάμενος), Ktesippus said: Doesn't your father in turn undergo this same experience? Is he different from (ἕτερος) my father?

(298 B 4–5)

In these opening remarks we see the changing of the guard. By depicting Ktesippus taking over the eristic λόγος from Euthydemus, Plato alerts us that a transition is under way, that the initiate is about to enter upon the higher mysteries of eristic, and that this foreign wisdom will soon find a new avatar in Athens.[74] Now, not as answerer but as questioner, Ktesippus closes upon his adversary.[75] The very wording of his first question unmistakably recalls a mode of argument used earlier in this episode when Socrates turned the eristic λόγος back upon the brothers themselves in order to determine whether they too would suffer self-refutation.[76] In that context, however, he wanted above all to test the consequences of (E9) for his inquiry into the supreme science. But here Ktesippus wants to test not the λόγος, but Euthydemus himself, and in his first two questions he reveals his plan of attack. Having learned that an eristic argument can knock itself down even as it knocks down others, Ktesippus is preparing to launch a counterattack by arguing: since Euthydemus' father is different from Ktesippus' father, he is not a father; *ergo,* Euthydemus is unfathered.[77] In just his initial words, then, the young man shows that he has a remarkable talent for assimilating argumentative techniques and for converting them into weapons for verbal combat.

But immediately recognizing the force of this attack, Euthydemus deflects its threat by denying any difference between their two fathers. Whereupon Ktesippus flips him, in eristic fashion, to the other side of the antinomy and asks whether their two fathers are the same (ὁ αὐτός), an absurdity that the sophist easily accepts. Then, revealing that he, too, has become dizzy with disjunctive madness, Ktesippus asks: "Is he my father only or [is he the father] of others as well?"[78] But without so much as the slightest twinge of conscience Euthydemus responds "Of others" and then proceeds to justify his answer in the form of a question:

> Or do you suppose that the same man who is a father is not a father?
> I certainly did think so, replied Ktesippus.
> But then do you suppose, he said, that what is gold is not gold or what is man is not man?
> Perhaps, Euthydemus, you are not sewing like with like, as the saying goes.
>
> (298 C 2–6)

Clinging to his own version of the law of noncontradiction as if it were some principle of argumentative salvation, Euthydemus is steadfastly maintaining that a father is a father, just as gold is gold and a human being, a human being; for a father cannot be a father of one and not a father of others; there cannot be a partial father anymore than there can be a partial brother or a partial knower; a thing either is what it is or is not: *Non datur tertium.* But far from overwhelmed by the sheer logical force of this indubitable principle, Ktesippus immediately exposes the fallacy of unlike cases with a reference to the proverb "not sewing like to like," and then continues to attack Euthydemus on his own level.[79] Earlier the sophist had used his law of noncontradiction to argue that a knower of something is a knower of all. Now Ktesippus shows that if Euthydemus wants to remain consistent with that lemma, he must also argue that a father of someone is the father of all, and a mother, the mother of all.[80] And again, without feeling the worm of conscience, Euthydemus agrees.[81] Having thus goaded his opponent into accepting the extreme position, Ktesippus now proceeds to remind him of what absolute parenthood entails: (1) his mother is the mother of sea urchins; (2) he is the brother of baitfish, puppies, and piglets; and (3) his father is a dog.[82] And yet each time he does so, the sophist reminds his quick-witted disciple that the same conclusion applies to himself as well.[83] Although not, in the strict sense, having attained an eristical refutation in this argument (for how can he reduce Euthydemus to absurdity when the sophist embraces it so willingly?), Ktesippus has at least wrestled his opponent to a draw.

Ktesippus Beats His Father, the Dog (D13) (298 D 7–299 A 5)

Inspired by the weighty conclusion of (K12), Dionysodorus promptly snatches away the role of questioner and prepares to exact, in another way, the same absurd agreement from his adversary. After fastidiously establishing that Ktesippus possesses a dog, that his dog has a litter of puppies, and that his dog is their father, he spins out an admirable specimen of Dionysodorian logic; in a tight, almost syllogistic way he passes from (1) the dog is yours, to (2) the dog is a father and yours, and finally to (3) the combination of "yours" and "father" in the conclusion: "The dog is your father and so you are the brother of puppies." In fact, the charm of (D13) even cast its spell on Aristotle, who incorporated it into his *Sophistici Elenchi* (24.179 A 34–35), and subsequently this sophism has passed into logic handbooks as a permanent model by which Aristotelians illustrate what they call the fallacy of accident.[84]

But once Dionysodorus has attained this conclusion, he knows that his adversary has a ready response. Ktesippus can mimic Euthydemus (298 D 3–6) and counterattack with: "So is yours and so are you." To prevent him from reversing the argument in this fashion, Dionysodorus maintains his position as questioner and closes with the eristic version of that one little question (μικρόν), which turns out to be the banner one for (D13). He asks: "Do you beat this dog of yours?" Touché! Dionysodorus is now about to convict Ktesippus of father-beating, perhaps the star instance of impiety.[85] Yet, far from being indignant at what this question implies, Ktesippus even advances into the trap knowingly and with a laugh.[86] Undisturbed by the falseness of this conclusion (for he has learned that eristic conclusions are not binding), he just shrugs it off with a jab at Dionysodorus for how many goods their father, the father of puppies, has enjoyed from the wisdom of his wise sons.[87]

On the Need to Possess Many Goods (E14) (299 A 6–C 7)

Taking Ktesippus' concluding remark as if it affirmed the desirability of possessing "many goods (πόλλ' ἀγαθά)," Euthydemus now challenges him with a seeming paradox: "But neither does he need many goods, Ktesippus, nor do you." But instead of affirming the need to acquire many goods, as the sophist hopes he will, Ktesippus exhibits that mechanical urge to seize the role of questioner by trying first to entice his opponent into committing himself on the topic. For his part, Euthydemus gladly accepts the paradoxical thesis that no one has need of many goods, but then cleverly moves to regain the guardianship of the λόγος by attacking Ktesippus as if he were in fact bound to the commonsense thesis:

> Tell me, Ktesippus, whether you deem it good for a sick man to drink a drug whenever he needs it, or does it not seem good to you? Or whenever a man goes into war, do you deem it better for him to go with arms rather than without?
> Yes I do.
>
> (299 A 9–B 4)

With his "yes" answer, Ktesippus is now committed to two seemingly reasonable positions:

1. It is good for a sick man to drink a drug, whenever he needs it; and
2. It is good for a man to have weapons, whenever he goes into war.

Now, with a single question Euthydemus attempts to reduce the first to absurdity:

> Since you have agreed that it is good for a man to drink a drug, whenever he needs it, shouldn't he drink as much as possible (ὡς πλεῖστον) of this good, and will it turn out well in this case, if someone crushes and mixes into the drug a wagonload of hellebore?
>
> (299 B 5–8)

From the "many" goods Euthydemus has selected one, the act of drinking a drug whenever a man needs it. Then, expanding "this good" into the unreasonable act of drinking "as much of it as possible," Euthydemus has apparently refuted his adversary by causing his position to appear ludicrous. But Ktesippus at once conjures up a scenario in which the massive consumption of hellebore proves plausible, namely if the drinker is as large as the statue at Delphi. Presto! Euthydemus' unreasonable case becomes reasonable, and the young man successfully lops off the first head of this λόγος. So the sophist shifts to the other, but this time he shows more caution in the formulation of his attack:

> Then, since it is good to have weapons in war, he said, should a soldier have as many spears and shields as possible (ὡς πλεῖστα), since it is good?
>
> Most definitely, replied Ktesippus. Or don't you think so, Euthydemus, but do you suppose that he should have one shield and one spear?
>
> (299 C 1–5)

Although still trying to swing his opponent to the outermost edge by injecting the unlimited qualifier "as many as possible" into the "good" act of carrying weapons, Euthydemus wisely keeps in his pocket the extreme case by which he hopes to cause the excessively armed soldier to appear ridiculous. In this way he forces his opponent to agree without, at the same time, giving him any place from which to launch a counterattack, or so he thinks. But in a move reminiscent of Socrates' at 295 B 4–5, Ktesippus not only agrees, but retaliates by asking the questioner a question in such a way as to dangle before Euthydemus what is precisely the "reasonable" position that underlies this attack, namely that a soldier has need of only one shield and one spear. Then, when the younger and generally more astute of the sophists takes the bait and answers affirmatively, Ktesippus immediately crushes him by submitting another bizarre counterexample, the monsters Geryon and Briareus, who are famous for their many-handed combat. Presto! Euthydemus' reasonable case becomes unreasonable, and Ktesippus decapitates the other head of the λόγος.

By creating two contexts, one medical, the other military, in which due measure is far exceeded, Euthydemus has sought to produce the illusion that Ktesippus is foolishly committed to the position of excess while picturing himself as the noble defender of the καιρός.[88] To this end, he has used the *consensus omnium* on the desirability of possessing "many goods" as foil for an (eristic) defense of the principle that "nothing in excess" is good for man. But careful not to violate the principle, Ktesippus has outsophisticated the sophist by altering the standard to which it applies. Rejecting "man" as the measure, he has submitted the statue at Delphi, and Geryon and Briareus, standards that have correspondingly altered what is and is not excess.[89] By thus reshaping each context in such a way that it could be a "good thing" to drink a wagonload of hellebore and to carry a vast amount of weapons, Ktesippus has not only rallied support for both positions but even managed to bathe them in "eristic" plausibility. Then, as if it were not enough just to defeat his opponent, he gives proof of his ever-increasing skill in eristic debate by slipping in a parting shot at the pair reminiscent of the one Dionysodorus delivered against him at 283 D 6–8. Mocking Euthydemus and his comrade for failing in this argument to exercise their mastery of hoplite warfare (that realm in which they should have been least likely to err), Ktesippus leaves no doubt with this playful banter that he is well on his way to becoming an affable and cheerful professor of eristic.

On Having Gold "in" Oneself (D15) (299 C 8–E 9)

After Euthydemus proved unable to dodge either of his adversary's counterattacks, he complied with the eristic rule that governs such ignorance of argument and fell silent.[90] Coming to the defense of his brother's topic, Dionysodorus continues to question Ktesippus on the desirability of possessing many goods.[91] With machinelike precision, he induces his opponent to agree: (1) that it is a good thing to have gold; (2) that he ought to have good things always and everywhere (πανταχοῦ);[92] and finally (3) that gold is a good thing. Now obviously there is no profit to be gained from drinking too much (good) medicine or bearing too many (good) weapons, but gold may appear to be something different. It can be acquired and stored away seemingly without limit and so provide a defense against the vicissitudes of fortune. In short, one might want to possess as much of it as possible always and everywhere. Taking advantage of this commonsense view of the role of wealth in the happy life, Dionysodorus now appears ready to knock down Ktesippus:

> Then shouldn't a man have it always and everywhere, and as much as possible *in* oneself (ἐν ἑαυτῷ)? And would he be most happy, if he should have three talents of gold *in* (ἐν) his belly, a tallent *in* (ἐν) his skull and a stater *in* (ἐν) each eye socket?
>
> (299 D 6–E 3)

The Greek ἐν ἑαυτῷ, rendered into English by "in oneself," is one of those expressions guaranteed to torment translators of this dialogue. For here ἐν really carries the sense of "under one's control or power." But it is impossible to use this translation because this first use of ἐν turns out to be foil for the second, when Dionysodorus uses the same word in a different sense. And unfortunately for the translator, the whole force of this argument requires the use of the same English word to cover both meanings of the Greek. If we translate its first use by "under one's power" and the second by "in" the belly, then we lose the sameness. But if we compromise and translate ἐν ἑαυτῷ by "in oneself," then the very awkwardness of the English calls attention to the equivocation too soon in the process of thought and so weakens the force of the joke. In the original language, however, the argument works to perfection. For the instant the Greek ear picks up the word "belly," Dionysodorus' strategy becomes clear, the equivocation manifest, and the joke funny. For at that moment we find the sophist trying to reduce his opponent to absurdity by altering gold, the quintessential exterior good, into an interior good by putting it, quite literally, *in* the belly, *in* the skull, and *in* each eye socket. Should we call (D15) an eristical refutation or a joke? We capture Plato's meaning, I think, when we experience the due tension between the two, without surrendering either.[93] Both are revealed in the process of transition, when the single word, working in consort with other elements of the argument, exhibits its power to pass from one of its meanings to another. To all appearances, then, Dionysodorus seems to have pulled off the refutation which just escaped his brother.[94]

But the wily Ktesippus has not been caught unawares.[95] Having listened intently to both questions in order to be able to recollect, as soon as possible, any answer that will ward off the impending refutation, Ktesippus brings forth the topical exemplum of the Scythians, who are superlatively happy if they should be so fortunate as to gild the heads of their enemy and so have much gold in "their own" skulls. But unlike the brothers, he cannot allow his trick to remain hidden. Acknowledging that he is just toying with "their own" in the same way Dionysodorus did with "yours," Ktesippus exposes the fallacy even as he employs it consciously for his own contentious purpose.[96] Then, continuing to play on the notion of the interior several times over, he adds: the Scythians drink *out of* their own gilded skulls, they see down *inside* them, even as they hold their own skull *in* their hands. In sum, the Scythians have gold *everywhere* (πανταχοῦ).[97] Both (E14) and (D15) cast significant light on the development of Ktesippus' character. They indicate that he has made no effort to grasp the truth content of Socrates' protreptic, since he doesn't reject the need to acquire many goods for the happy life (281 D–E); and, in particular, he accepts gold without dispute as a good (288 E). But inasmuch as he has come to learn that all value in this language game is linked to victory, why should he direct his attention toward truth? His confrontation with eristic has taught him that to attain verbal victory he need attend to only those aspects of argument that he can convert into verbal weapons and then apply for the purpose of knocking down the opposition.

On Things Capable of Sight (E16) (300 A 1–A 8)

From Ktesippus' startling finish to (D15), Euthydemus seizes upon two items for his next argument: "the Scythians" and "to see down (καθορᾶν)." Expanding the former into a universal subject "the rest of men" and dropping the prefix κατά from the latter in order to obtain "see" and "sight" from the bare infinitive (ὁρᾶν), Euthydemus returns to the attack: "Do Scythians and the rest of men see (ὁρῶσιν) what is capable of sight (τὰ δυνατὰ ὁρᾶν) or what is incapable (τὰ ἀδύνατα)?" Familiar now with the vacuum in which inescapable questions function, we must at once bring to light the ambiguous elements of this disjunction:

1. What is capable of sight can mean:
   a. things which can see; or
   b. things which can be seen.

> 2. What is incapable of sight can mean:
>   c. things which cannot see; or
>   d. things which cannot be seen.

With his emphatic response "Obviously what is capable of sight (τὰ δυνατὰ δήπου)," Ktesippus indicates that he is eager to defend the first limb of this dilemma. Consequently, for Euthydemus the game will consist at least in contradicting him on this position and, if possible, establishing a sense in which the other limb can hold. So certain of his eristic challenge, Euthydemus begins the sortie by asking Ktesippus whether he, too, sees what is capable of sight; and, of course, he must agree. Next, submitting their own apparel for the objects of Ktesippus' vision, Euthydemus asks: "Then, do you see our cloaks (ὁρᾷς οὖν τὰ ἡμέτερα ἱμάτια)?" And again Ktesippus must answer "yes," for these objects are obviously an instance of (1b), things which can be seen. Thus far, then, Euthydemus has orchestrated an eristic paradigm of near syllogistic perfection.

Satisfied with having established the preliminaries to (E16), the sophist now closes upon his adversary: "Then, are these capable of sight (δυνατὰ οὖν ὁρᾶν ἐστὶν ταῦτα)?"[98] Here, by explicitly linking together "cloaks" and "capable of sight," Euthydemus fancies that he has at last set a trap from which there is no escape. For his opponent cannot answer "no," because then he could immediately flip him to the second limb of the disjunct and conclude: "Therefore, you see things incapable of sight," since the cloaks of the brothers are an instance of (2c), things which cannot see. So, to avoid this consequence, Ktesippus must answer affirmatively, which he does with "Quite clearly (ὑπερφυῶς)." Then Euthydemus promptly comes back with "But what? (τί δέ)," demanding thereby that Ktesippus tell him "what" their cloaks can see quite clearly.[99] By thus creating a context in which the equivocal "things capable of sight" must assume the active sense of (1a), things which can see, Euthydemus imagines that he has now duped his opponent into defending the "obviously" untenable position that their cloaks do possess the active power of sight and so can see. But Ktesippus is far too experienced in this game of controversy to be punched out by this middling trick. Knowing that any response to the sophist's question will decapitate the λόγος, he answers:

> [They see] Nothing (Μηδέν). But perhaps you don't fancy that they are capable of sight; you're so amusing. But I think, Euthy-

demus, though not sleeping, you've just nodded off, and if it is possible for what speaks to say nothing, you're doing that, too.

(300 A 5–8)

Having carefully guarded himself with each of his replies by making expert use of eristic brevity, Ktesippus has lain in ambush, waiting for his opponent to slip up and provide an opening for a counterattack. Now, when Euthydemus finally presents that opportunity, the young rogue gives a quasi-existence to the dreaded "that which is not" by hypostatizing "nothing" as an object of vision for the brothers' cloaks and thus again crushes Euthydemus in argument. But not content with merely conjuring up a scenario that derails the refutation, Ktesippus continues to press the counterattack by mocking Euthydemus on the ground that he has foolishly come to hold the second limb of the disjunct, that their cloaks are incapable of sight.[100] In fact, the sophist's overall performance in argument has become so amateurish that the young man even feels called upon to explain his elder's failure: (1) though not sleeping, Euthydemus has nodded off; and (2) though speaking, he has said nothing. Here, with his keensighted analysis of error, Ktesippus not only pricks the sophist for what cannot exist in this illogical universe of discourse, namely false speech caused by ignorance; he also cracks one of the best jokes of the dialogue.[101] By calling attention to the fact that the eristic master is both sleeping and not-sleeping and speaking and not-speaking at the same time and in the same respect, Ktesippus consciously and deliberately fingers Euthydemus himself for a gross violation of the Euthydemian law of noncontradiction.

Speaking of the Silent and Silence of the Speaking (D17 and E17) (300 B 1–D 2)

Ktesippus finished (E16) by poking fun at Euthydemus for speaking but saying nothing. Reshaping this remark into an antinomy between speaking and silence, Dionysodorus now generates a twofold argument-pair designed by Plato to provide a fitting climax to the eristification of Ktesippus:

What? Am I to understand, said Dionysodorus, that there can be speaking (λέγειν) of what is silent (σιγῶντα)?
In no way at all, said Ktesippus.

Then can there not even be silence (σιγᾶν) of what speaks (λέγοντα)?
Still less, he said.

(300 B 1–3)

Owing to Dionysodorus' willful exploitation of syntactical ambiguity in both trigger questions, which allows "what is silent" and "what speaks" to denote either the accusative subjects or objects of their respective infinitives, we must reformulate this attack so as to make unambiguously clear what is at issue:

(D17) Speaking of the silent can mean:
   a. Is it possible for what is silent (σιγῶντα) to speak (λέγειν)?
   or
   b. Is it possible to speak (λέγειν) of what is silent (σιγῶντα)?

(E17) Silence of the speaking can mean:
   c. Is it possible for what speaks (λέγοντα) to be silent (σιγᾶν)? or
   d. Is it possible to be silent (σιγᾶν) on what speaks (λέγοντα)?

When Ktesippus hears Dionysodorus formulate his two questions, he understands both in their usual senses; that is, he takes "what is silent" and "what speaks" for the accusative subjects of their respective infinitives. So with his two denials he firmly rejects the possibility of (a) and (c). Consequently, the strategy of the brothers will be for Dionysodorus to lead the attack and for Euthydemus to follow him with a sortie of his own in such a way as to conjure up arguments that dupe Ktesippus into affirming first (b) and then (d), which are, of course, the same as (a) and (c) in *word,* but different in *meaning.*

For his part in the dispute Dionysodorus tries to topple his adversary through the skillful placement of a single question:

But whenever you speak of rocks and wood and iron, aren't you speaking of what is silent (σιγῶντα λέγεις)?
Certainly not, [Ktesippus] said; at least not if I'm visiting a blacksmith's shop, where they say iron shouts out and speaks most loudly, whenever someone handles it.

(300 B 3–6)

Here, by picturing a context in which Ktesippus himself performs the act of speaking, and rocks, wood, and iron are the "silent" objects of

his speech, Dionysodorus appears to have flipped his opponent from
(a) to (b) and thus delivered a knockdown argument. But Ktesippus is
not Kleinias, and we have come a long way since the sophist punched
out the boy with just one question (276 C). Countering Dionysodorus'
query by conjuring up a context in which iron is not silent, but can be
idiomatically said to speak, Ktesippus quite effectively chops off the
first head of this λόγος.[102] So having crushed Dionysodorus on this
one, he calls for the defense of the other (τὸ ἕτερον), a challenge that
Euthydemus immediately accepts:[103]

> Whenever you are silent, said Euthydemus, aren't you silent on
> all things?
> I am.
> Surely then you are silent on things which speak (τὰ λέγοντα
> σιγᾷς), if they are to be included among all things.
>
> (300 C 2–4)

Whereas Dionysodorus introduced Ktesippus as the subject who
"speaks of what is silent," Euthydemus now transforms him into the
subject who is "silent on all things." Then, when Ktesippus answers
affirmatively to this move, Euthydemus brings forth "things which
speak" as objects that form part of all things. The conclusion, therefore, appears unavoidable: Ktesippus is silent on what speaks. So it
seems that Euthydemus has flipped his opponent from (c) to (d) and
thus attained the eristic triumph that escaped his brother. But then
Ktesippus takes over the role of questioner:

> But what about this? said Ktesippus. Aren't all things silent?
> Of course not, said Euthydemus.
> Well then, my good man, do all things speak?
> Yes, certainly, at least those which speak.
> But I'm not asking that, he said, but do all things speak or are
> they silent?
> Neither and both, Dionysodorus blurted out.
>
> (300 C 4–D 1)

To complete his trick, Euthydemus had to make "things which speak"
a part of all things. Immediately discerning the weakness of this ploy,
Ktesippus counterattacks: "Aren't all things silent?" If so, then this
fact would necessarily exclude "things which speak" from inclusion
among all things. Fully aware that if he answers affirmatively his conclusion will be overturned, Euthydemus tries to preserve his apparent

victory by denying that all things are silent. Accordingly, Ktesippus flips him to the other horn: "Well then, my good man, do all things speak?" If all things speak, then there cannot exist a subject, including Ktesippus himself, who is silent on all things. So in a desperate attempt to escape this trap, Euthydemus is forced to qualify his answer by limiting the "all" to "at least" those things which speak, implying, of course, that there are other things among the "all" which do not speak.[104] Induced, therefore, to give the correct answer in spite of all his efforts to avoid it, Euthydemus has committed the *peccatum originale* of eristic. He has slipped out of this exclusive antinomy between speaking and silence only to find himself in the middle, in that contradictory realm of "is" and "is not," where some things speak and others don't, where some are silent and some aren't. With his opponent pinned and wriggling, as it were, in the realm between opposites, Ktesippus mercilessly applies the finishing touch. In language that unmistakably recalls one of Euthydemus' remarks (296 A 1–2) and Socrates' parody of it (297 A 1), Ktesippus denounces Euthydemus for a violation of the rules: "But I'm not asking that, he said, but do all things speak or are they silent?" It can be only one or the other, and whichever way Euthydemus answers, he will be refuted.[105]

Blurting out, "Neither and both," Dionysodorus tries to prevent his brother's defeat by responding to all four possibilities at once. But with this answer he, too, violates proper eristic procedure and so goes down to defeat. Ktesippus is exalted in victory. Crushing both Euthydemus and Dionysodorus on both limbs of this argument-pair, he has successfully reversed the defeat of his favorite, Kleinias, who is now called back for a curtain call. But perhaps most disturbing of all in this finale is Ktesippus' eerie outburst of laughter, for it signals that Plato is at last bringing to a close his portrait of the eristic as a young man. And the precision with which he has completed this conversion cannot be more aptly demonstrated than by Ktesippus' use of ἀπό-λωλε (300 D 5), that very trigger word which first impelled him into the debate (see 283 D 6). Now, with good-natured eristic laughter, he, too, can playfully tell Dionysodorus that he has "perished."[106]

Conclusion

In this sequence of six arguments, we finally observe the full flowering of the eristic pseudo-science. Gone for good is whatever advantage the brothers might have gained from the concealment of their conten-

tious purpose. Euthydemus and Dionysodorus have done everything
in their power to trap Ktesippus, and he in turn has done everything he
could to avoid being trapped, while delivering as many counter-
punches as possible. Adopting the argumentative style of his opponents and concentrating his attention upon their mere words, Ktesippus has taken his rightful position alongside his likes in order to bring
this comic logomachy to its fulfillment. In Plato's imaginative portrayal, then, eristic and the ridiculous have become one and the same.
Yet, behind this grand satire, we cannot fail to discern our author's
deeper seriousness. Almost as if he were conducting a controlled ex-
periment in which he planted a noble seed in a shallow and worn-out
soil, Plato placed Ktesippus in an eristic context at the beginning of
the third episode. For their part, the brothers wasted no time in seeking to eradicate his love of truth and correspondingly his contempt
for falsehood. Then they gradually began to channel his other philosophical qualities, especially the keenness of his memory and the
quickness of his wit, toward the illiberality and pettiness of eristic accuracy and away from the truly liberal discipline of philosophy.[107]
Meanwhile, on his own Ktesippus began to gather knowledge about
eristic, and, through the course of the action itself, he has successfully
come to an understanding of it. Especially significant in this regard
are those scenes in which he did not participate, but during which he
had the opportunity to absorb what the brothers had to teach. In a
word, what Ktesippus has learned from the day's proceedings is the
ability to collect a large number of argumentative techniques, which
he has picked up indiscriminately from Socrates and the brothers,
and then to harness them behind a single purpose, the attainment of
verbal victory at any cost. Now finally, at the end of his participation in
the dialogue, expressions of that learning, like heads from the Hydra,
are virtually exploding from his mind. And Plato has left no doubt as
to the stages of this conversion: from the third episode to the fifth,
Ktesippus has passed from *righteous indignation* at falsehood to a *general acceptance* of the rules of the game, and finally to a *warm embrace* of
the very spirit of eristic itself.

In Plato's vision, eristic compasses a broad spectrum of individuals
who have attained varying degrees of proficiency along that path. At
one end, he has presented the brother-pair, the extreme caricature of
the type; at the other, Ktesippus, who in the course of the dialogue
itself has left no doubt that he is destined to become a full professor of
eristic.[108] Although Socrates advised him to take Menelaus as his

model, he has ended up by imitating the brothers themselves. So to no one's surprise, his "educators" have proven to be the immediate cause of his corruption. They have taught him how to do things with words as quickly and skillfully as Socrates taught Kleinias how to hunt down and capture realities. Here, then, in contrast to the first eristic episode, where we found that comic sense in which the brothers betrayed virtue best of men and most quickly, we have now come upon the tragic sense in which they actually live up to their boast of imparting it. It is as if the eye of Ktesippus' soul has undergone the initial phases of the eristic conversion, which is, by implication, a rejection of the true dualism of Socrates, a turning away from the veritable, vertical antinomies that guide our reorientation, in favor of a turn toward the horizontal antinomies of contentious debaters, who have the cheek to imagine that they alone have attained the truth, that nothing is secure in word or object.

Although Plato realizes that the full analysis of this eristic conversion requires nothing less than a complete pathology of the young philosophical soul, here in the *Euthydemus* he is satisfied with merely projecting upon an objective canvas a concrete representation of it.[109] We can, I think, safely conclude that Plato has used Ktesippus as a dramatic symbol to illustrate how eristic discourse intoxicated Athenian youth, who then delighted like puppies in pulling about and tearing with words all who approached them.[110] In the bittersweet *aristeia* of this aggressive young man, already given to hubris before his encounter with eristic, we confront that disturbing, disconcerting element which bestows upon the *Euthydemus* the seriousness of tragedy. Through the role of Ktesippus, Plato has granted us privileged access into how this foreign wisdom assisted the other manifestations of sophistry in demoralizing the sons of the marathon-fighters, a privilege we might not have had. Later philosophers would have obliterated this pseudo-technique of argument beyond recognition, after they had incorporated it into their own logical treatises, had it not been for the wisdom of Plato, who has preserved it for us by transfiguring it into his negative paradigm.

ERISTIC IN THE TREATMENT OF THE FORMS
(D18) (300 E 1–301 C 5)

Although silent, Socrates has spoken. By remaining speechless throughout the exhibition in which Ktesippus demonstrated his potential for becoming the best of the eristics, Socrates not only affirms the philosopher's need for silence in certain contexts (see *Phaedrus* 276 A); he also voices the loudest possible protest against what has just taken place. But when Ktesippus emphatically announced that Dionysodorus had "perished," Kleinias, pleased by his friend's histrionics, could not restrain his giddy laughter. And so, as one might expect, the return of Kleinias brings with it the return of Socrates, who cannot remain indifferent when this boy's welfare is at stake. Apparently on the verge of launching another protreptic to probe what Kleinias finds so funny about these puzzles, Socrates asks: "Why are you laughing, Kleinias, at what is so serious and beautiful?" Immediately intuiting that to permit the boy to respond to this question would be to forgo a singular opportunity, Dionysodorus commandeers the trigger word *beautiful* and quickly initiates an argument that turns out to be one of the most fascinating disputes of the dialogue:

> What are you saying, Socrates? said Dionysodorus. Have you ever seen anything beautiful (καλὸν πρᾶγμα)?
>
> Yes I have, Dionysodorus, I said, many (πολλά).
>
> Are they different from the beautiful (ἕτερα ὄντα τοῦ καλοῦ) or the same as the beautiful (ταὐτὰ τῷ καλῷ)?
>
> Then in desperate trouble (ἀπορίας), I wavered and thought I had rightly earned my suffering for having opened my mouth. Nevertheless I said they are different from (ἕτερα) the beautiful itself (αὐτοῦ γε τοῦ καλοῦ), yet some beauty (κάλλος) is present with (πάρεστιν) each of them.
>
> If then, he said, an ox turns up beside you (παραγένηται), are you an ox, and because I'm now present with you (πάρειμι), are you Dionysodorus?
>
> Hush, I said.

(300 E 3–301 A 7)

Had we not already reviewed seventeen eristic arguments, we might suppose that when Dionysodorus asks Socrates whether he has ever observed anything beautiful, he is seeking to discover real information about his interlocutor's everyday life. Experience, however, teaches us otherwise. For as soon as Socrates admits to having seen a plurality of such beauties, Dionysodorus instantly releases the inescapable question: "Are they different from the beautiful or the same as the beautiful?" Taking Socrates' response "many" as if it were affirming the claim "many things are beautiful," Dionysodorus is now launching an attack designed to undermine the possibility of predicating "beautiful" of these many instances of beauty. His chief stratagem for this trick is the antinomy between sameness and difference.[111] Taking advantage of the fact that Socrates' claim presupposes both sameness and difference between the subject and the predicate, Dionysodorus wants first to anchor Socrates on one side of this dilemma so that he can then engineer a sophistical refutation.

Socrates' immediate reaction to this wily question, a momentary pause to reflect on the overall justice of his desperate predicament, should not lead anyone to conclude that he is unfamiliar with the type of attack now under way. His carefully worded, carefully qualified response indicates that, far from being at a loss, he is all too familiar with the sophist's current strategy. Socrates' aporia arises not from the lack of an answer, but from the tragic situation itself. However much he might want to, he can't just leave, for that would be to abandon Kleinias to the clutches of these two monsters. But to stand his ground means that he must continue to have the fullness of his humanity eclipsed by the presence of this Crab, who wears the mask of a jovial colleague. Socrates' aporia, then, is not verbal but real, and highlights the fact that as the true bearer of the philosophical thyrsus he must on occasion suffer such painful encounters with his antipodes. But since he has been snookered into this trap, he now responds that the many beautifuls are "different from the beautiful itself, yet some beauty is present with each of them."[112] Beauty itself is neither the same as (absolutely identical to) nor different from (absolutely other than) the multiple instances of beautiful things. Neither sameness nor difference, conceived strictly, can account for the true relationship that holds between the many beauties and beauty, because this relationship demands that there be a third thing, a *tertium quid*, which mediates between the antinomous poles. For this third thing Socrates submits "beauty (κάλλος)", and suggests that the mediating relationship can be explained by "presence (πάρεστιν)".

Since beauty (κάλλος) is present with its instances, beauty itself is both qualifiedly the same as and qualifiedly different from the many beauties. At the very least, beauty itself and its instances have the same name, or that third thing which Socrates here represents by κάλλος, the visible form that is present with beautiful things and named after the characteristic beauty. Consequently, since beauty itself and the beautifuls share something, they cannot be absolutely different. Nor is the sameness so great as to swallow up the difference between the two and thereby to produce total identity. Beauty is *one*, the beautifuls *many*. In short, Socrates' answer to this eristic disjunction is "neither" and "both (οὐδέτερα καὶ ἀμφότερα)," the very answer that just caused Dionysodorus to perish at the hands of Ktesippus.[113] At any rate, the true sense of this solution, which Socrates has here offered to the eristic dilemma, cannot begin to emerge until we take into account the manifold senses of sameness and difference, and we need not anticipate that Dionysodorus is going to allow such an inquiry to arise in discourse.

Yet, by mediating between the two possibilities that were offered in the disjunctive question, Socrates has at least blocked the formation of the thesis that the sophist had hoped to foist upon him. So, to counterattack, Dionysodorus interprets that mediation in the worst possible light. By shifting the context of the argument and equivocating on presence, he delivers perhaps the most memorable joke of the dialogue: "If then, he said, an ox turns up beside you, are you an ox, and because I'm now present with you, are you Dionysodorus?"[114] In the mind of the sophist this clever piece of eristic chicanery produces a refutation, for the negative answer that the question demands reduces Socrates' solution to absurdity. Socrates can become neither an ox nor Dionysodorus by simply being present with or beside an adjacent object. Carefully ignoring the characteristic "oxness" or "manhood" as present with Socrates, as he should not have done if he were inclined to recognize the real distinction that Socrates submitted, Dionysodorus has instead deliberately and grossly materialized that mediating relationship so as to conceive "presence" as holding between two physical objects and, thus, as justifying an identity or absolute sameness between two obviously dissimilar entities.[115] Not, however, choosing to defend his solution at this juncture, Socrates simply bids him to refrain from such inauspicious speech, as if the sophist were uttering unholy words before the sacred. As a result, Dionysodorus is left without a cue for his next question, and he would have done well to complain about this fact. Instead, he moves to justify the seeming inappropriateness of his joke by reformulating it in such a way as to demonstrate, once and for all, that his attack is not only appropriate but inescapable. In a considerably more abstract way, he asks:

But just because something (ἕτερον) has turned up beside another entity (ἐτέρῳ), he said, how can that entity be the other (τὸ ἕτερον ἕτερον ἂν εἴη)?

(301 A 8–9)

When we apply this question to the exempla that it is most obviously intended to explain, it translates: how, because an ox has turned up beside Socrates, can Socrates be an ox; or how, because Dionysodorus is now present with Socrates, can Socrates be Dionysodorus? By forming his attack against presence in this way, Dionysodorus imagines that he has finally refuted his opponent. For there obviously cannot be the requisite identity or sameness between Socrates and the ox, or between Socrates and Dionysodorus, for *the one (different) entity to be the other (different entity)* (τὸ ἕτερον ἕτερον ἂν εἴη).[116] In this way, then, Dionysodorus imagines that he has demolished Socrates' solution to the relationship between beauty itself and the many beautifuls. But when we apply his attack to the original problem regarding the many instances of beauty, we see how much confusion he has allowed to creep into his argument by shifting from plural instances of beauty (τὰ καλά) to the singular entity (τὸ ἕτερον) and by refusing to acknowledge that third thing (κάλλος), which Socrates introduced to mediate between the poles. Had Dionysodorus retained Socrates' *tertium quid* and the plurality of beautiful things, the question would read: "How, because beauty has turned up beside beautiful things, can beautiful things be beautiful?" To this question Socrates could legitimately respond: "Because beauty itself (αὐτὸ τὸ καλόν) is present with beautiful things (τὰ καλά), beautiful things are beautiful (κάλλος)"; that is, beauty (κάλλος) can be predicated of or present with beautiful things (τὰ καλά), for the particular instances *have* what beauty *is* (ὅ ἔστιν) and so can have the eponym beautiful, which is named after beauty itself (αὐτὸ τὸ καλόν). Thus, Socrates could have saved such statements as "Many things are beautiful." But he does not allow any such development of his position to emerge. So why, we should ask ourselves, does Socrates suppress the substantive Idea at precisely this moment and begin, as he says, to imitate eristic wisdom?[117]

Are you troubled (ἀπορεῖς) by this? I said. (Finally I was trying my hand at imitating the wisdom of the pair, since I was eager to possess it.)

Of course I am (ἀπορῶ), he said, how can I and all other men not be troubled by what is not (ὃ μὴ ἔστι)?

What do you mean, Dionysodorus? Isn't the beautiful beautiful, and the ugly ugly (τὸ καλὸν καλόν ἐστιν καὶ τὸ αἰσχρὸν αἰσχρόν)?

Yes, if I think so, he said.

Then do you think so?

Yes, certainly, he said.

Then isn't both the same same and the different different (τὸ ταὐτὸν ταὐτὸν καὶ τὸ ἕτερον ἕτερον)? For surely the different is not (the) same (τό γε ἕτερον ταὐτόν), but I thought even a child couldn't be troubled by this, that the different is different (τὸ ἕτερον ἕτερόν ἐστιν). But, Dionysodorus, you deliberately passed over this sense, for in other respects, just like craftsmen, for whom it is fitting to ply their trade, both of you seem to me to polish off your dialectic with remarkable beauty.

(301 B 1–C 5)

In a display of good sense, Socrates did not answer Dionysodorus when he asked how the one (different) entity could be the other (different entity) by presence. Instead, he has now put a question to the questioner, seeking first to discover whether Dionysodorus himself is troubled by his own question. And when the sophist affirms that not only his but everyone's aporia can be traced to "what is not (ὃ μὴ ἔστι)," Socrates has his cue; for Dionysodorus has clearly revealed that his own difficulty is again rooted in the problem of "unreality" or "what is not." Since the particular beautiful thing is different from universal beauty or the idea beauty, it *is not* (beauty itself); and vice versa, since beauty itself, whether the universal or the idea, is different from a beautiful thing, it *is not* (the particular beauty). And since both are different from or other than each other, they cannot be the same.[118] Accordingly, one can say along with Antisthenes that "Man is man" or "Good is good," but not "Man is good," for the one entity "man" is different from the other entity "good," and vice versa (see *Sophist* 251 C). So now, having firmly tied Dionysodorus to the thesis that "the one (different) entity cannot be the other (different entity)" or, more literally, that "the different cannot be different," and, what is more, having uncovered the basis of this thesis in the dreaded "that which is not (ὃ μὴ ἔστι)," Socrates has clearly established his task. To refute the refuter, he must find a positive sense in which the different can be different (τὸ ἕτερον ἕτερόν ἐστιν).

Beginning with a question that preserves the same grammatical form as that of Dionysodorus' thesis, Socrates asks: "Is the beautiful beautiful and the ugly ugly?" At this point several commentators have grasped at straws in order to explain Dionysodorus' curious response: "Yes, if I think so." Here, attempting to fill an imagined lacuna in the text, they have supposed that the sophist might be temporarily torn between his Parmenidean and Protagorean loyalties.[119] But we need not travel so far back into the history of Greek philosophy to find a solution. The problem disappears once we recognize that Socrates has just reshaped his question in terms of that other limb of the inescapable question: "Are the many beautiful things the same as the beautiful ($\tau\alpha\dot\upsilon\tau\dot\alpha\ \tau\hat\omega\ \kappa\alpha\lambda\hat\omega$)?" Only now the subject is not the plural "many beautiful things," but the singular "the beautiful." Now obviously the ambiguity in the grammatical structure of Socrates' question "Is the beautiful beautiful" allows for the possibility that the subject, the beautiful ($\tau\dot o\ \kappa\alpha\lambda\dot o\nu$), refers to the particular beautiful thing ($\kappa\alpha\lambda\dot o\nu\ \pi\rho\hat\alpha\gamma\mu\alpha$), the class of beautiful things ($\tau\dot\alpha\ \kappa\alpha\lambda\dot\alpha$), or the idea itself ($\alpha\dot\upsilon\tau\dot o\ \tau\dot o\ \kappa\alpha\lambda\dot o\nu$).[120] But the nature of the subject is not the critical issue, for the refutation turns not on the subject, but on the predicate, "is beautiful ($\kappa\alpha\lambda\dot o\nu\ \dot\epsilon\sigma\tau\iota\nu$)." Dionysodorus, however, hedges at precisely this moment because he cannot determine on which side of his own dilemma Socrates is operating, whether the predicate "is beautiful" is different from or the same as the subject "the beautiful"; in short, whether this claim is predicative or tautological.

But when, under pressure, the sophist finally answers affirmatively, Socrates can spring his trap. He asks Dionysodorus whether he is also committed to the analogous proposition, that the same is same and the different different. Not, however, allowing him to respond, Socrates continues to explain why, in fact, he is committed to affirm this question as well. For obviously, he points out, the different cannot be [the] same, its opposite, any more than, say, the beautiful can be ugly. Only at this moment does it become clear that Socrates has shifted away from a predicative claim about a particular "beautiful thing ($\kappa\alpha\lambda\dot o\nu\ \pi\rho\hat\alpha\gamma\mu\alpha$)" or about a particular "one of two things ($\tau\dot o\ \dot\epsilon\tau\epsilon\rho\upsilon\nu$)" to a simple statement of identity, so simple, in fact, that not even a child could be troubled by it.[121] Dionysodorus treated "difference" or "otherness ($\tau\dot o\ \dot\epsilon\tau\epsilon\rho\upsilon\nu$)" as a relation holding between two individuals, for example, between a beautiful thing and beauty, between an ox and Socrates. Socrates, on the other hand, demolished that distinction by

altering "the different" in such a way that it became a relation referring to itself without any reference to individuals. He changed
"present with" to simply "is" and collapsed the predicative claim "the
different is different" into one of identity.[122] So, just as he set out to
do, Socrates has established a sense in which "the different is different
(τὸ ἕτερον ἕτερόν ἐστιν)."

To evaluate this argument properly, we must not forget that Socrates is consciously imitating eristic. Dodging Dionysodorus' questions in such a way as to entice him into exposing a thesis, Socrates
finally discovers a basis from which to launch an attack. Then, shifting
the context so as to allow only a partial grasp of his meaning, Socrates
forms a question on which the sophist has to hedge. When urged to
respond, he provides Socrates with "enough (ἀρκεῖ)" for a refutation.
Then, toying with ἕτερον, the key item of Dionysodorus' thesis, Socrates soundly defeats his opponent. Not attempting to direct him toward how things are, but remaining only on the level of words, Socrates pulls the chair out from underneath his adversary by differing
over terms. And though accomplishing precisely what he intends to
accomplish in this refutation, Socrates does not, in eristic fashion,
taunt his fallen victim, but ironically praises him for intentionally
passing over this sense in which the different is different. For, in other
respects, as Socrates says: "Both of you seem to me to polish off your
dialectic with remarkable beauty."

In conclusion, eristic wisdom does indeed prove to be "present
with" Socrates when he really desires it. Rather than elaborate upon
his mediating response to this real philosophical problem in which the
ideas would have come into view, Socrates adopts a defensive strategy.
Converting the eristic of the brothers into a weapon of his own for
warding off Dionysodorus' attack against presence, Socrates illustrates thereby how a dialectician can preserve eristic by sublating it
into a higher technique of argument.[123] And even though eristic cannot be a serious philosophical instrument for establishing truth, it can,
as Socrates has just clearly demonstrated, still have value as a means
for protecting higher wisdom from becoming the plaything of polemical buffoons. It is of some significance that Plato has chosen the Crab,
and not the Hydra, to launch this attack. The older and weaker of the
two is the ideal representative of a type with which Plato was all too
familiar: the enemies of the forms. These bottom feeders abstract his
thought from its context, juggle it about in a historical and philologi-

cal vacuum, bring against it a logical procedure that is foreign to its spirit, and then try to manufacture an illusory victory that they hope to cash out into profit and prestige for themselves.

IT IS FITTING TO COOK THE COOK (D19) (301 C 6–D 8)

It has been suggested that in (D18) the sophists "have come nearest to being philosophers," that here they show "an instinct for a genuine philosophical problem." [124] But just because Plato found the presence of the idea with its phenomenal instance to be worthy of his philosophical attention, we should not conclude that the brothers have a similar instinct. It has been said before, but it bears repeating: to eristics, all philosophical topics are of equal value, all are grist for their logical operation, and whether they grind that operation on the Idea itself or on the unfathered Socrates is a matter of indifference to them. The problem of presence sprang into prominence after the accidental surfacing of the trigger word *beautiful*, and it now passes away again with just as little fanfare, owing to the fact that Dionysodorus is about to secure another place from which to launch an attack:

> Then do you know, he said, what is fitting (προσήκει) for each craftsman? Do you know, first of all, for whom (τίνα) it is fitting (προσήκει) to forge?
> I do. The smith.
> And to work with clay?
> The potter.
> And to slaughter, to skin, and, after chopping up meat (τὰ κρέα) into small pieces, to boil and to roast it?
> The cook.
> Then if someone does what is fitting (τὰ προσήκοντα), he said, won't he act correctly (ὀρθῶς πράξει)?
> Most certainly.
>
> (301 C 6–D 2)

To soften the defeat of (D18), Socrates concluded his refutation by comparing the brothers to expert craftsmen for whom "it is fitting to ply their trade." With his unrivaled ability to bring the inessential into prominence, Dionysodorus discovers the trigger "it is fitting" in that subordinating clause of comparison which Socrates used to help illustrate the essential, and now returns to the attack: "Do you know what is fitting for each craftsman?" Not waiting for a response, he continues: "Do you know, first of all, for whom it is fitting to forge?" Socrates' answer "the smith," as well as his next two, "the potter" and "the cook," are programmable, requiring that he simply isolate and so name the agents who perform their respective activities. And once he performs his role properly and identifies three straight craftsmen, Dionysodorus leaps to a higher principle that is supposed to govern the particular cases in some way. He asks: "Then if someone does what is fitting, won't he act correctly?" Can we discern in this acrobatic leap another act of eristic folly? Clearly, the sophist has catapulted too far, too soon, without adding a qualification. At the very least, it would seem that the context requires him to ask first: "Then if someone does what is fitting *in his own particular craft,* won't he act correctly?" Furthermore, Dionysodorus has also left it quite unclear what relation he is trying to establish between "doing the fitting thing" and "acting correctly," whether he intends the two expressions to be synonymous or one to be a step on the ladder to the other. But since both correct action and what is fitting are required of the cook and the potter, no less than of the just and courageous man, Socrates can at least answer affirmatively. Already at this stage of (D19), Plato's purpose is not unclear. By depicting the enumeration of craftsmen and their crafts as premises or springboards to a superordinate generalization, he is obviously constructing a Dionysodorian parody of a type of argument familiar to all students of Socratic λόγοι. And now, to complete this farce, Plato is going to show us that Dionysodorus can descend from his higher principle just as gracelessly as he did when he ascended to it.[125]

> Fine, and (δέ γε) isn't the fitting thing for the cook (τὸν μάγειρον), as you say, chopping and skinning? Did you agree to this or not?
> I agreed, I said, but please forgive me.
> Well then, clearly, he said, if someone slaughters and cuts up the cook and then boils and roasts him, he will perform what is fitting. And what is more, if someone hammers the smith, and turns the potter into a pot, he, too, will do what is fitting.
>
> (301 D 2–8)

Assuming that he has cleverly concealed his eristic trick in the minor premise, Dionysodorus now commits what is usually regarded as the fallacy of the argument: "Isn't the fitting thing *for the cook,* as you say, chopping and skinning?" At a glance, we can tell that the cook can be either the subject or object of the chopping and skinning, but have we really solved this argument by uncovering this fact? Is this just another simple case of amphiboly, as some have assumed? [126] By limiting the noun *cook* (μάγειρον) with the article (τόν), Dionysodorus gives every indication that he wants Socrates to take the cook as the accusative subject of the impersonal verb. [127] In fact, he actually wants Socrates to take his words in their normal sense and to supply in thought the meat (τὰ κρέα) for the chopping and the skinning, so that in his final move he can transform the cook from the subject to the object. In this way Dionysodorus hopes to floor Socrates with a completely unexpected punch. Therefore, it is obvious that this instance of amphiboly in the minor premise becomes one only by hindsight, after the ear hears the sophist unambiguously convert "the cook" into the object of the skinning and chopping.

But to expose Dionysodorus' strategy in full, we need to reexamine his second question: "Do you know *for whom* (τίνα) it is fitting to forge?" From our present perspective, we can see that the interrogative τίνα is wholly ambiguous, and so the word can also be translated: "Do you know *what things* (τίνα) it is fitting to forge?" or "Do you know *whom* (τίνα) it is fitting to forge?" But earlier, when Dionysodorus asked this question, Socrates heard "for whom" and so answered "smith." He thus responded in the way he understood the question and, we should add, in the way Dionysodorus wanted him to respond. Consequently, the syntactical ambiguity was already present in (D19) as early as 301 C 7, and if this argument were just another simple case of amphiboly, Dionysodorus could have turned his trick immediately after Socrates answered "smith." More generally, the sophistical refutation or, if one prefers, the joke, doesn't consist in a simple amphiboly, but in the incongruity created by subsuming under the concept of fitting action, and so of correct action, the obviously incorrect and unfitting act of cooking the cook and potting the potter. In this ruse the sophist has indeed employed syntactical ambiguity to help establish that incongruity, but of course this trick is not his only trick. In fact, if we continue to focus on Plato's broader purpose, this argument too can be seen aright. By having Dionysodorus introduce three examples from the crafts, leap to and descend from a higher principle, unmistakably signal the transition to the minor premise with δέ γε, in short, by having him ply the eristic method in the manner of a bad butcher, Plato has again captured the essence of the satirical by having this clown manufacture another joke elenchus against the master of the elenchus himself.[128] To the doer it has been done, and Socrates has become the victim of just retribution, as only eristic can dish it out. Is this argument the witticism of a prankster or the perversion of a scavenger who delights in deconstructing the serious philosophical thought of others? Plato wants us to see that it can be both at the same moment.

SOCRATES CAN SELL OR SACRIFICE HIS ZEUS
(D20) (301 E 1–303 A 3)

We have observed the brothers crossing and recrossing now this path, now that, confronting us here with multiple choices and there with deceptive bifurcations. From one end of this seemingly endless maze to the other, we have been able to follow their routine, owing in large measure to the thread which Plato has left behind to guide us: the structural pattern of his work. And as we draw near to the end of our encounter with eristic, that artistic form is still discernible. Having allowed the eristic disputes to undergo a rapid deterioration from (D11) to (D19), Plato now reveals another dramatic function by bringing upon the stage a long, slowly developing λόγος that covers almost two pages of Burnet's text. The deliberate pace of (D20) is designed, therefore, to arrest the insane, downward movement to absurdity by building gradually to a crescendo so that (D21), ending as it does so abruptly in only six lines, not only provides the due sense of completion to the fifth episode, but also allows for a smooth yet quick transition to the dialogue's mock epinician ode.[129] But in addition to its proper place in the overall structure, this argument is of course a gem in its own right. From the beginning of the Greek tradition the Olympian gods occupied a favored position at the top of a hierarchical view of the world. Beneath them were a host of minor deities and heroes, then ordinary mortals, and still further below them the lower animals. Now, in the ultrasophisticated context of eristic, Plato shows how this vertical ordering of reality can be playfully transformed into pabulum for a joke-refutation. After all, what eristic would be worth his salt if he couldn't bring the battering ram of his method against popular lore?

Overwhelmed by the startling conclusion to (D19), Socrates exclaims in mockery: "Will this [wisdom of yours] ever turn up beside me so as to become my own (οἰκεία)?" Whatever else he may mean by wanting this eristic wisdom to become "his own," Socrates certainly doesn't intend his word οἰκεία to be taken in its literal sense; yet this is precisely what Dionysodorus is about to do. Concealing at first his real target, the sophist now manufactures a smooth series of slight equivocations in order to slide to his goal: (1) "Would you recognize it, Socrates, when it became your own (οἰκείαν)?" (2) "Do you suppose that you know your own things (τὰ σαυτοῦ)?"[130] (3) "Do you regard those things which you can rule and use as you please to be yours (σά)?"[131] And finally, concretizing Socrates' "things" with cows and sheep, he asks: (4) "Would you regard those things which you can sell, give away, and sacrifice to any god you please to be yours (σά)?" Growing impatient with the Crab, Socrates assents to each move.[132] So, continuing the attack, Dionysodorus places two more questions that exact from Socrates the required agreements: (5) "Do you call those creatures which have life (ψυχήν) living beings (ζῷα)?" And finally, (6) "Do you agree that of living beings only those over which you have the license to do everything I just now mentioned are yours (σά)?" Here, the most dazzling feature of the sophist's method is perhaps the remarkably skillful way he has used the example of cows and sheep to give force and meaning to this series of questions: Cows and sheep are living beings (ζῷα), which have a life force (ψυχή); they can be sold or sacrificed by their master, as he sees fit; their owner can know and recognize them as his own (τὰ οἰκεῖα); and they can in fact turn up beside and be present with Socrates. In just six steps Dionysodorus has driven Socrates from wanting wisdom to become "his own" to having license to sacrifice "his own things" to any god he pleases. Now, pleased with himself for having snared his victim, Dionysodorus halts momentarily and then springs his trap:

> Pausing quite ironically (εἰρωνικῶς) as if he were pondering something significant, he said: Tell me, Socrates, do you have an ancestral Zeus (Ζεὺς πατρῷος)?
> Because I suspected that the argument would arrive where in fact it ended, I began straightway to twist about desperately, trying to escape, as if I had already been caught in a net. But I said: No, Dionysodorus, I do not.
>
> (302 B 3–8)

We have reviewed numerous ways in which the brothers present a distorted image of the philosopher, and now we come upon another that calls for attention. Just imagine, the "ironical" eristic! Why not?

Everything else in this world has been turned ἄνω κάτω. Dionysodorus is now turning Socratic irony, a posture well suited for undercutting the bombast of sophists, into a mannerism by which he mocks Socrates.[133] Again, to the doer it has been done, and the result is another brilliant tour de force by which Plato contrasts the phantasm with the original. Whether this clown smiles, or blushes, or ponders ironically, we see, with unimpeded clarity, the outward characteristics of the imitator and can infer the inward emptiness of the charlatan. Clear, too, is the sophist's strategy; but how is Socrates to escape from this ἄφυκτος λόγος, once he has been lured into the net?[134] Foreseeing with the mere mention of "ancestral Zeus" that if he answers affirmatively, he gives enough for a refutation, Socrates tries desperately to wriggle out of the trap with a denial.[135] Dionysodorus then counters his recalcitrance by foisting upon him the extreme thesis. If Socrates doesn't have Zeus (πατρῷος), then he can't very well have the race of Olympians (θεοί πατρῷοι) fathered by Zeus. So the sophist immediately concludes that Socrates is an utter wretch and not even an Athenian, since he is without ancestral gods, shrines, or anything else beautiful and good. Now to a casual observer this conclusion might appear to be another cruel and shameless hoax; but in an eristic context it is simply an excellent move by which Dionysodorus attains his eristic purpose of forcing Socrates to clarify his stance and eventually to reveal a sense in which Zeus, Apollo, and Athena are "his." And that's enough (ἀρκεῖ) for the sophist. With that pettifoggery so characteristic of the eristician, Dionysodorus now forces Socrates to agree: (1) that these gods are his; (2) that since they have a life principle, they are living beings; and finally (3) that since they are "his" and "living beings," he can sell or even sacrifice his Zeus and the rest of his gods the same way he can his other possessions.

Dionysodorus has keenly observed that although we have never seen and cannot adequately conceive of God, in our representations we fashion him as a living being (ζῷον) that consists of a fusion of soul (ψυχή) and body (σῶμα) (see *Phaedrus* 246 C–D). So, taking advantage of this partial sense in which our household gods are like our household animals, Dionysodorus has manufactured a funny, yet irreverent refutation. As we should expect, this argument, too, can be easily reversed. If the gods of the higher order can be equated with the livestock of the lower and then sold in the open market or even butchered as their owner sees fit, then why not the other way around? Through a different act of jugglery, Dionysodorus could demonstrate, for example, that Socrates should honor and worship his ox the same way he does his Zeus. In this topsy-turvy world of eristic, the only standard that remains fixed is that all-too-sophistic animal, man, who has placed himself at the center of discourse.[136]

IS HERACLES PUPPAX? (D21) (303 A 4–9)

Once again Ktesippus, that distorted image of the helper, hastens to defend Socrates, who now lies speechless, almost as if he were beaten unconscious by the sheer force of this eristic λόγος.[137] Prefacing his reentry into the debate with the interjection "Puppax" and the vocative "Heracles," Ktesippus appears poised and ready to commence the offensive. But like a machine timed to react when the sensor is tripped, Dionysodorus plugs both items into the disjunctive formula and comes out with: "Is Heracles Puppax or Puppax Heracles?" How is Ktesippus to choose between these alternatives? At least his own utterance had a discernible meaning, even if it only expressed something like a confluence of surprise, pleasure, and mock admiration. But now Dionysodorus has managed to expunge even that thread of meaning. The result is another instance of sophistic jabberwocky. But one thing is certain: whichever alternative Ktesippus chooses to defend, Dionysodorus will try to contradict him, even as he attempts to flip him to the other limb of the disjunct.

In this ludicrous finale two points are worth stressing. By demonstrating, in such a brief exchange, so many features that we have come to identify with eristic—the quick attack, the smooth removal of trigger words from their context, the automatic release of the inescapable question, the sheer emptiness and stupefying effect of the question itself—Plato wants to suggest that Euthydemus and his brother plan a long stay in Athens during which they will continue to star in multiple performances of this charade.[138] Moreover, although eristic discourse is an intrusion into speech that is without beginning or end, Plato must nevertheless bring it to an end in order to complete his dialogue. Therefore, Ktesippus follows Socrates' withdrawal and stands aside.[139]

CONCLUSION

To concentrate our analysis upon the *Euthydemus* itself, we have mostly treated eristic in isolation from the historical process of which it played a part. So, to close our study of the fifth and final episode, we can perhaps profit by glancing briefly at a passage from Aristotle's *So-phistici Elenchi* of more than casual interest to historians of these matters:

> The training of those who have earned a salary from eristic ar-gumentation was something similar to that which emanated from Gorgias' school; for both camps handed over arguments for thor-ough memorization, the one rhetorical speeches, the other conver-sations in the form of question and answer, in which both sides imagined that they had for the most part included their rivals' con-tributions. Accordingly, the instruction of those who were studying with them was swift, but unscientific; for their instructors were as-suming that they could educate by imparting the goods of their craft, without having to trouble with science.
>
> (34.183 B 36–184 A 4)

Comparing the training of paid professors of eristic to that of Gorgias, Aristotle criticizes them for being under the delusion that they could impart a science of contentious argument by simply hand-ing over representative samples of it to their students for memoriza-tion; such training was swift, as he notes, but unsystematic. That sys-tematic basis for all argument he himself sought to establish in his own logical treatises, and he has combed the *Euthydemus* in particular for evidence for the final part of that logic, the systematic analysis of fallacy; and the *Sophistici Elenchi* is itself clear evidence that Aristotle, too, tried to prevent this pseudo-science of argument from insinuat-ing itself under the mantle of the genuine article. In fact, our tradi-tion generally and modern scholars in particular have consistently preferred his treatment of eristic to Plato's, owing, no doubt, to a prejudice in favor of his more systematic, more logically rigorous ap-proach. But Aristotle's achievement can no longer overshadow Plato's contribution to these matters, for the overall purpose and general fea-tures of his *Euthydemus* are no longer unclear.

Having surveyed the field of contentious debate, Plato in part dis-covered and in part invented twenty-one representative samples of eristic argument. Fully aware of the tediousness of these cavils, he sought to relieve it by arranging them in a most intricate, tripartite structure that, in its sum, forms a comprehensive unity. For the pos-sessors and users of this method he again surveyed the field and came up with the brother-pair to personify this two-edged sword of paradox. Slanting his portrayal of both the activity itself and its two-headed representative into an image of the ridiculous, Plato then incorporated that image within the ethical framework of the protreptic. Once having contained eristic in this fashion, he had Socrates recall from memory and deliver its wisdom in a definite order.

In the first eristic episode Plato showed what results the brothers could achieve after they had acquired a thorough grasp of their routine and encountered no resistance from Kleinias, who could not spoil their sport by injecting disruptive qualifications into their arguments. In the second display-piece he had the brothers parade before us, with varying degrees of success, six model disputes that revealed a tendency to come somewhat unraveled, owing partly to pressure from Ktesippus and Socrates and partly to their own incompetence and the inherent weakness of the method itself. Finally, in the third and longest exhibition, Plato treated us first to a grandiose satire on stand-up controversy by having Euthydemus ply the eristic method against Socrates himself in order to demonstrate that he is, was, and always will be omniscient. Then, transfiguring the brothers into the Hydra and the Crab, Plato permitted these two monsters to sweep Ktesippus into their vortex of words and complete his eristification. In the four concluding arguments he had the Crab regain the role of questioner and sidle his way to the finish.

In the course of unfolding this apotreptic discourse, Plato allowed the arrangement of the verbal disputes to become so haphazard and the philosophical content so absurd that in the end he revealed these fighters-in-words for what they are, the two-headed philosopher-comedian. At the same time he pursued this goal, so expertly causing the routine of the brothers to disintegrate and finally to turn disturbingly comic, Plato also worked out his hidden philosophical purpose by gradually unmasking this illogical logic for the very antithesis of his own method. That he was able to conceive of and to execute dramatically this model of otherness so contrary to his own logic should not be surprising; Plato gave no little thought to how not to proceed in philosophy. But what is surprising (and what must be credited to his inimitable powers of invention) is that all those grotesqueries which he has used to characterize the abuse of, and ultimately the antithesis to, his own dialectic—the misuse of verbal triggers, the devious employment of ambiguous words and syntax, incomprehensible talk, non sequiturs and sophisms, even radically abrupt transitions, insults and slanders of every description, eristical dodges, puns—are precisely the signs that point to the discourse of actors on the comic stage, except that our Tweedledum and Tweedledee are not practicing with a chorus of Aristophanes' but have the effrontery to strut about Athens alleging to be professors of conduct. The incongruity thus created by this masterly interpenetration of the serious and playful has produced a disconcerting yet extraordinary tragicomedy.

As for eristic itself, it is a one-dimensional procedure that treats all soul as the same, a point that Plato makes with some emphasis by displaying its use against three very different souls, Kleinias, Ktesippus, and Socrates. It posits bogus questions and expects other minds to recall predetermined answers, and we do not find in this method any attempt to redirect other minds toward the real or to assist them in the discovery of truth. It is a procedure, moreover, that picks over dry and stale topics that have exhibited the power to generate verbal controversy and then demonstrates no concern for consistent or coherent patterns of reasoning upon them, except insofar as each particular topic demands it. In fact, eristic assumes at the outset that a stable correspondence between word and object is impossible. It does help to promote eristic activity, however, if its opponent works on the unsophisticated assumption that λόγος has the power to articulate objective reality. What is more, since eristic is an agonistic, contentious, and adversarial form of argument in every sense, it cannot attain any meaningful agreement with its opposition. One is either on the side of eristic or against it, a member of the guild or an opponent: *non datur tertium.* So without subjective agreement or objective correspondence, eristic is left with a single criterion of success, victory over the opposition, and the longer it can sustain this victory the better. But even its victory is illusory because within the protreptic context this standard for measuring success becomes the cause of its undoing. Every time eristic succeeds in defeating the opposition, it loses in the serious game of exhorting others to pursue wisdom and to avoid ignorance. In effect, Plato has turned the tables on eristic by confining it in such a way that every illusory victory it attains is at the same time a real protreptic defeat.

As for eristics themselves, it is not right to call them "Eleatics," for they are not committed to "a metaphysics and a logic that is incompatible with change."[140] They are not committed to anything but themselves. If they produce Eleatic arguments, that is the result of historical accident, not philosophical commitment. They are not "eclectics" either, for they show no urge to paste together a workable philosophy from a judicious culling of opinions from the many and the wise. In terms of Plato's imagery, eristics are scavengers, who from time to time can be seen amid the mainstream of serious philosophical activity, if perchance some high tide impels them up and out of their familiar swamps where they normally delight in their dirty work. But to project the problem of eristic into a modern context, we can take a clue from Paul Shorey and others and conclude that eristics are *misologists* or *logical skeptics* in the special sense that they are haters of all λόγοι that strive to articulate objective truth.[141] Lovers of error, not wisdom, these skeptical controversialists are on a mission to destroy whatever they regard as weaknesses in the arguments of others. But in their ignorance of how to question and how to answer, they thrust to one side any consideration of the intention that informs the thought of others and are content with exercising a logical procedure that they hope will refute or at least derail any account that their opponents may offer. In this, their own proper work, eristics are aided by the fact that, on the surface at least, nothing serious appears to depend upon the outcome of their playful controversy, a fact that helps to defuse the hostility of their victims. A rowdy host of camp followers can also assist their cause. With their endless logomachies and badinage, eristics then and now produce a certain likeness to the philosopher, but in reality they are entirely different.

In Plato's vision, eristic and the brother-pair symbolize that measure of what philosophy and philosophers are in danger of becoming on those unfortunate occasions when they are at their worst. To Plato, the problem of eristic is not historical, nor is his treatment of it historical. In the *Euthydemus* he has treated the decline of philosophy itself, and his dialogue can be instructive any time, any place philosophy begins to resemble its opposite.

EPILOGUE

THE VICTORY CELEBRATION (303 B 1–304 B 5)

Plato is not about to break the sustained irony of this dialogue. So he crowns the final round of eristic foolery by picturing a disquieting scene in which the multitude of onlookers explode into deafening applause for the exemplary achievements of the brothers.[1] Even the columns of the Lyceum join in the festive atmosphere and are pleased by the victory. But in spite of this revelry, in spite of the clapping and the cheerful glee on the faces of all, that painful goad, so expertly applied by Plato, can be felt the moment we recall how often sham philosophy does indeed win the applause of the day, how often philosophical mannerists, by noting what prevails in the philosophical culture of their time, and by abstracting that and imitating it openly and with skill, can and do carry off a momentary victory. Although the affectations of such imitators can never impart the true, inner spirit to the philosophical life (since that can be done only by the genuine article), what better way is there for Plato to conclude this mighty conquest of appearance over reality than by having Socrates himself heap up praise upon his two antipodes for their noble accomplishments!

In the first part of his epilogue Plato distorts the serious tradition of praise poetry in which it is the custom for song to seek out merit.[2] In fact, a laudator's failure to eulogize the victors for their success, or his begrudging them their due encomium by stinting, is the mischievous work of immortal Φθόνος, something the generous and truly liberal poet must always try to avoid. So, pretending to concur in the spirit of the occasion, Socrates turns to praise the brothers for the unique qualities that have come to typify their natural talent and to counsel them on the future course of their activity.[3] But as in so much of the language of this dialogue, the surface denotations of Socrates' words carry a meaning contrary to their true intention.[4] In his mouth the praise turns disingenuous, spoken as it is by someone "absolutely

194

enslaved" to eristic wisdom (303 C 2). And his counsel, once stripped of its irony, is found to be a humorous strategy by which he seeks to eradicate the very existence of eristic from the public realm. The result is a superb parody of the epinician genre.

The Praise

(1) You show no concern for the many or even for the prominent and those who pretend to be something, but only for those who are like yourselves (ὁμοίων ὑμῖν); for I know that few would actually embrace these arguments of yours, men like yourselves (ὅμοιοι ὑμῖν), whereas the rest (οἱ δ᾽ ἄλλοι) are so ignorant of them that I'm sure they would be more ashamed (αἰσχυνθεῖεν) to refute others by their means than to suffer it themselves.

(303 C 8–D 5)

The fact that a philosopher doesn't attend to the many or even to the socially prominent may well be considered one of his virtues. Since he is neither excited by the illusory honors of politicians nor moved by the coercive pressures of an ochlocracy, the philosopher is free to pursue truth, wherever it may lead. Or so the apparent praise of this threadbare topic may suggest. The lofty tone of this sentiment, however, is undercut when Socrates pictures what in fact eristics actually do. In practice, they restrict their attention to a donnish clique of like-minded clowns who, though always remaining small in number, can nevertheless do extensive damage to the whole enterprise of philosophy. For above all they win over to their guild the young and gifted Ktesippuses by eliciting from them, and perfecting, all those impulses which distinguish the eristic. What brings like to like, according to Socrates, is the peculiar nature of eristic arguments themselves. Both master and pupil can warmly embrace ἐριστικοὶ λόγοι as their weapons for combat. At the same time, moreover, their affinity for such arguments acts to shield them from any direct contact with "the rest," who for the most part remain unconscious of these λόγοι, and even if they were, could not be lured into using them as instruments in a game of refutation: ordinary citizens have too much respect for others to do that.[5] And here we see something pertinent to eristic. In contrast to the rest, eristics are without any due sense of Respect (Αἰδώς) for the feelings of others. They are themselves heartless, and they wield a frigid argumentative procedure by which they refute their opponents without reflecting upon whether they may cause injury to the inner life of others.[6] Shame and its attendant blush or lapse into silence can be experienced by eristics only when they stumble and are defeated in their silly game of argument.[7]

> (2) Again, this, too, is another popular and courteous feature in your performance: When you affirm that nothing is either beautiful, or good, or white, or any such thing, or that one thing is not in any way different from others, although in fact you do simply stitch up the mouths of men, as you say, still, inasmuch as you not only stitch up the mouths of others, but your own as well, this feature turns out to be really elegant and helps to remove that ill will which can attach to your argumentation.
> (303 D 5–E 4)

Socrates' second piece of flattery has caused difficulty. If his words are taken to have a literal correspondence to some affirmation on the part of the brothers within the main body of the text, then only confusion will result.[8] For there is no such passage where the two have claimed anything of the sort. But if we do not overlook or forget that this portion of the epilogue is designed to evaluate eristic activity as a whole, then we have a way to control the interpretation of this passage. When, therefore, Socrates claims in mock praise that Euthydemus and his brother stitch up the mouths of men by affirming that nothing is either beautiful or good or white, he is in fact referring quite generally to an activity of argument that renders the combination of any predicate with any subject impossible, since this activity is the pseudo-demonstration that anything which can be said to be "white" can also be said to be "not-white" or "black."[9] The brothers are supposed to have accomplished such stitching up of men's mouths by a well-rehearsed argumentative routine in which they prove the contrary or contradictory of any affirmation made by an interlocutor. In this sense, then, Socrates has provided a general perspective on the related nature and value of all the arguments which they have used in the previous three episodes.

Now it might seem reasonable to expect that the brothers would encounter considerable hostility from their victims in the course of carrying out their work. But Socrates informs us that this is not the case. Since Euthydemus and Dionysodorus repeatedly suffer what they try to dish out, they not only muzzle others, but they muzzle themselves as well, a fact that carries important consequences. For although the brothers commit all the grotesqueries of argument that honest intellectuals deplore, their "self-refutation" actually shields them from the wrath of their victims, who naturally tend to feel sympathy for fellow sufferers (see 293 E 2–5); and in this matter, too, we can see how Plato is trying to guide our judgment. At the same time he reduces this trendy version of Eleatic formalism to absurdity by demonstrating that the brothers cannot prevent themselves from falling into the same snares as their victims, he is also using his satiric art both to attenuate the repulsive aspects of their character and to amplify all those qualities that distinguish them as comic buffoons. In this way he not only exposes the falseness of eristic method but even exhorts us to resist the urge to feel ill will and anger toward these two clowns. The proper way to confront the false philosopher, Plato wants us to see, is with ridicule, mockery, and laughter.

(3) But this is the greatest feature: By directing my full attention (τὸν νοῦν) to how quickly Ktesippus could imitate (μιμεῖσθαι) you right on the spot, I discovered that you have elaborated and arranged your system so skillfully (τεχνικῶς) that anyone at all can learn (μαθεῖν) it in almost no time.

(303 E 4–8)

By keeping his attention fixed on Ktesippus, Socrates discovered how quickly and how easily this young man could imitate the brothers. So, drawing his third and final piece of praise from this observation, he applauds them for the way they have skillfully invented and arranged their system of argument.[10] But here, too, Socrates' words picture the opposite of the true state of affairs. Without the power to unearth anything original in philosophy, eristics just scrounge around now here, now there, making it their goal to stylize what is old and stale in new and dazzling ways. Far from arranging a system of coherent arguments, they just leap from topic to topic, impelled by logical accident, not necessity. For, in truth, eristic is nothing more than an empirically derived knack of argument that has no scientific basis or internal consistency. Yet, since it does have "rules," this illogical logic can be imitated by all who are exposed to it and hence "learned."

That Socrates has returned for one final time to the topic of learning is significant. We have already seen that Kleinias exhibited both aspects of the equivocal act of learning by gathering knowledge about the nature of philosophical inquiry and by applying that knowledge with understanding in the search for the supreme science. Here Socrates reminds us that, like Kleinias, Ktesippus has also learned, albeit in a wildly distorted fashion. By imitating the brothers, he has "gathered partial knowledge" and applied it with "misunderstanding," so as to reveal how far he has advanced under the guiding influence of eristic. At the outset of the dialogue (275 B), Socrates expressed his fear that Kleinias might be turned away from the pursuit of philosophy and so corrupted. As it has turned out, Ktesippus is the one who has undergone this reversal. Yet the rapidity and ease with which he has been converted to the eristic way of life brings to light still another problem. The brothers must always fear that students may abscond with their pseudo-science without paying the gratuity. This fact now serves as the basis of Socrates' advice.

The Counsel

The best thing for you to do is to speak only to yourselves in private. But failing that, if you must speak before someone, then speak before that person who can pay cash. And if you are smart, you'll also repeat this same counsel to your disciples. Tell them never at any time to argue with anyone, except with you and with themselves; for what is scarce, Euthydemus, is valuable, but water commands the cheapest price, though, as Pindar says, it is best. But come, I said, please accept me and Kleinias here as your pupils.

(304 A 5–B 5)

Socrates voices what on the surface sounds like good financial counseling, namely that they refrain from discoursing before the public in favor of restricting their activity to themselves or to their followers. But the true and real force of this advice, its bitter criticism and caustic humor, comes to light when we recall that eristic activity must have interlocutors who willingly consent to answer questions. Thus Euthydemus originally undertook the protreptic address requested by Socrates only on the condition that Kleinias express a willingness to answer.[11] Accordingly, if the brothers were to follow the letter of Socrates' advice and were to restrict their discourse to themselves or to their students, they would not only cease to stalk the public realm for their victims, but they themselves and their disciples would stitch up their own mouths; for, aware of each other's tactics, they could at best only recreate the folly exhibited in the clash with Ktesippus or, more likely, never pass beyond quibbling over which of the two should ask and which should answer. Then, to cap the insincerity of this counsel, Socrates turns market analyst and explains to them how a free economy works. Since Ktesippus has without effort acquired this knack of argument in just that free demonstration intended to allure paying customers, Socrates reminds them that their wisdom, like any commodity, is subject to the law of supply and demand. If they continue to talk openly and often, they can expect the marketplace to become flooded with their product.[12] So he urges them to inflate the price of their goods by carefully attending to the principle of scarcity. Then, as if to illustrate the soundness of his economic theory, Socrates cites "water" as the very opposite of a scarce commodity, one that not unexpectedly commands a very low price. So don't, he advises, allow eristic to become as available as water. But then, almost as if it were an afterthought, he undercuts the value of his own *exemplum* by appealing to the authority of Pindar, the master encomiast himself, who reminds us that apart from its availability "water is best." Here, in one quick stroke, Socrates dashes to pieces the notion that price can be a guarantee of value. No matter how decked out in sophistic finery eristic wisdom may appear, it can never replace the real wisdom of Socrates. But aware that he has just advised them against accepting nonpaying customers, and that he himself has no cash, Socrates concludes by returning to that homoerotic theme on which he began (272 D 1–3). Dangling Kleinias before these inverted jokers as the bait, he asks them to admit two new pupils to their program.

SOCRATES' FINAL CONVERSATION WITH CRITO
(304 B 6–307 C 4)

For the shift from the narration to his final conversation Socrates returns to the exhortation that he has tailored for his longtime friend and companion: he bids Crito to join him in attending the school of the brothers. For just a moment we are allowed to imagine the unlikely prospect of a group of ancients, headed by Socrates and Crito, studying at the feet of the master eristicians and their clique. Although Crito is fond of listening and learning, as is evidenced by his for the most part patient auditing of Socrates' narration, it would be an unthinkable breach of *Αἰδώς* for him to partake in the brothers' activity. So just brushing aside this appeal by remarking upon the obvious, that he is "one of those not like Euthydemus," Crito stops short of issuing a direct warning to Socrates and instead begins to narrate a conversation that he had the day before with an anonymous critic of philosophy. Before examining the content of this conversation, however, we must digress briefly.

It is not infrequent in the history of Platonic scholarship that a problem only tangentially related to the interpretation of a text comes to assume a life of its own, and it is difficult to escape the impression that something of the sort has happened here, if we direct our attention to how much labor has been spent on the attempt to identify the anonymous critic introduced at the end of the *Euthydemus*.[13] Assuming that this final part of the epilogue offers access to a personal literary feud between Plato and one of his contemporaries, scholars have sought to leap outside the dialogue to that real historical target of this polemic by developing a case for now Isocrates, now Lysias, and then again Thrasymachus, Antiphon, and even Polycrates;[14] and each of these conjectures achieves a measure of probability precisely because all of these men are instances of the type represented by the critic. The simple fact remains, however, that Plato does not name him, and no amount of conjecture is going to overcome his silence on this point. But apart from where the truth may be found in these matters, we can isolate a common difficulty that continues to hamper any appreciation of this final section of the *Euthydemus*. In the various attempts to identify this unnamed critic, little effort has been made to demonstrate how this ending relates to the whole dialogue. To this consideration we now turn.

That this concluding conversation is not "a sort of appendix" (A. E. Taylor) or "so little in harmony with what has preceded, that we might almost imagine it to be an afterthought" (Grote), is clear from the work's formal structure.[15] Simply put, Plato has composed this final conversation between Socrates and Crito to balance their opening one. Moreover, when we join these two outer frames of discourse to the conversation they have in the fourth episode, we find another tripartite dialogue with its own unity and protreptic intention. But beyond this formal balance, the epilogue also exhibits essential thematic connections to the beginning. For example, the language of Crito's conversation with the anonymous critic closely corresponds to that which he used to initiate the very first action of the *Euthydemus:*

Crito, [the critic] said, you're not attempting to listen to these sages, are you? No, indeed, I said, for though I stood near by (προστάς), I was unable (οἶός τ' ἦ) to overhear (κατακούειν) because of the crowd (ὄχλον). Well it certainly was worth the hearing (ἀκοῦσαι), he said. Why? I said. Because you would have heard men talking (διαλεγομένων) who are currently the wisest of those engaged in this style of argument.

(304 D 7–E 2)

Who was he, Socrates, with whom you were talking (διελέγου) yesterday in the Lyceum? Quite a large crowd (ὄχλος) surrounded you (περιειστήκει), so that when I drew near (προσελθών), eager to hear (ἀκούειν), I was unable (οἶός τ' ἦ) to hear (ἀκοῦσαι) anything certain. Yet by peeking over and glancing down, I thought I saw you talking (διελέγου) to some stranger. Who was he?

(271 A 1–5)

What at first appeared to be a beginning *in medias res,* a question arising *ex nihilo,* we now discover to have been prompted by Crito's conversation with the anonymous critic.[16] The repetition in the language proves decisively that Plato is here employing the device of ring composition in order to link the epilogue to the prologue in both form and content, and that consequently the *Euthydemus* does not present a simple linear progression of events capped by a poorly constructed or inconsistent epilogue. If we still seek the beginning on the level of historical events, we must turn to the opening of Socrates' narration (272 E 1–4), where he informed Crito that he was dissuaded from leaving the undressing room of the Lyceum by the appearance of his familiar sign. Therefore, the first event in the plot of this dialogue is apotreptic, that is, a divine warning against turning away from an encounter with eristic wisdom; and such a sanction for this beginning should add to the discomfort of anyone who might want to dismiss the occasion of the *Euthydemus* as trivial. But this problem aside, Socrates preserves the beginning, middle, and end of his conversation with Crito throughout his narrative by addressing him, at judiciously spaced intervals, with the vocative, the overall effect of which is to bind this tripartite discourse with his longtime friend into a tight unity.[17] Hence to reduce this epilogue to an "afterthought" or to "sort of an appendix" or even to detach it from the whole for the sake of inquiring into the historical identity of the critic can seriously impede the attempt to evaluate this final conversation between Socrates and Crito.

Until Plato has Crito introduce this critic, the *Euthydemus* has presented for the most part a clear-cut antithesis between eristic and dialectic, between the brothers and Socrates. Now, finally, a third has
been given; but, as we shall see, this third turns out to be as antithetical to legitimate philosophy as eristic. Because the telling differences
between dialectic and eristic can easily become blurred in the minds of
undiscerning bystanders, opponents of philosophy can exploit this
situation for their own contentious purpose. In this particular case,
the critic is careful neither to distinguish philosophy itself from its
practitioners nor to make any effort to rank philosophers qualita-
tively. But simply stigmatizing their conversation by calling it "driveling," and charging them with a grotesque misapplication of their responsibility, the critic finally ends up rejecting the whole business as
base and ridiculous. Although perceptive enough to dismiss the critic's
outright condemnation of philosophy, Crito does make it clear to
Socrates that he, too, opposes the willingness to wrangle publicly
with such debaters.[18] In the incomprehensible talk and hairsplitting
quibbles of controversialists, decent citizens like Crito can see only an
uncalled-for disruption of proper behavior. And so indirectly (for it
would be impolite for him to act otherwise) Crito does succeed in issuing a warning to his friend about the danger of partaking in such public spectacles.[19]

The way Socrates responds to his anxious friend is most instructive.
Unconcerned for the personal identity of the critic, but just treating
him as a type, Socrates moves immediately to gain more information
about the class he represents:

> Such men are amazing, Crito, but I'm not sure what to say. Was
> the man who approached you and criticized philosophy a public
> speaker, one of those formidable at competing in courts of law, or
> someone who trains them, a composer of the speeches ($\pi o\iota\eta\tau\grave{\eta}s$
> $\tau\tilde{\omega}\nu$ $\lambda\acute{o}\gamma\omega\nu$) that public speakers use to do battle?
>
>   (305 B 4–9)

When Crito casually placed the critic "among those clever at forensic
oratory" (304 D 6), he failed to present Socrates with an adequate picture of the man. So with this query Socrates seeks to determine
whether he belongs to the guild of public speakers or to that of ghost-
writers. When Crito reports that the critic has never entered a courtroom but has earned a general reputation for being a specialist in the

art of speech composition, it certainly may appear that the target of Plato's attack is a speechwriter like Isocrates, who qualifies as a perfect instance of the type. But if we keep firmly before our minds some crucial passages of the fourth episode (289 B 4–290 A 5), it becomes immediately apparent that Socrates' question does not, in its primary intent, refer outside the dialogue itself. Rather, Socrates is here submitting the critic to that twofold criterion between the art of production and the art of use, between those who produce λόγοι and those who actually use them in the public realm. And inasmuch as this critic is a composer of speeches (ποιητὴς τῶν λόγων), that is, a mere speechwriter (λογοποιός) in the common sense of that term, he cannot be the possessor of the science that is going to solve the riddle of human happiness. So, having located the critic in his proper place, Socrates can now analyze the class represented by this individual:

> Now I understand, and I was just on the point of mentioning them. They are the ones, Crito, who, according to Prodicus, occupy the border region (μεθόρια) between the philosopher and the politician. They suppose that they are the wisest of all men, and that they actually appear so before the eyes of many, so that only those who pursue philosophy prevent them from being so esteemed by all. Accordingly, they believe that if they can eclipse the reputation of philosophers by causing them to appear good for nothing, then before all men they will finally and without challenge carry off the victory palm for first place in wisdom.
>
> (305 C 5–D 5)

Socrates' analysis is structured by an important antithesis between seeming (δοκεῖν) and being (εἶναι). The representatives of this group *are* those who occupy that no-man's-land between the philosopher and the politician. They imagine that they *are* the wisest of men, and that they actually *appear* so to the majority. In their view, philosophers alone *are* the only ones who can block what they really desire, universal *recognition* of their superiority in wisdom. Consequently, to attain this total victory, they scheme to undermine the *reputation* of philosophers by causing them to *appear* valueless.[20] In working out this strategy, however, they must avoid all direct contact with their antagonists, lest they appear to be defeated by those about Euthydemus (305 D 6–7). Thus, by manipulating the prejudices of those who have had their access to philosophy blocked by the crowd and so are dependent

upon others for an interpretation of its nature, these opponents of
philosophy seek to attain victory by producing a belief in their audience that they themselves, and not philosophers, are "the wise." The
critic of the *Euthydemus*, therefore, is not merely a critic but a rival,
another combatant in the contest for first place in wisdom. And we
conclude that by constructing his epilogue in such a way as to cast this
combat in wisdom against a still broader background, Plato is here
offering a concrete portrayal of that strategy by which these back-
fighters seek victory.

But this picture is still more complex. As we continue to learn from
Socrates, these rivals cannot avoid a glaring inconsistency in their polemical stance. Since they themselves are part-time students of philosophy and do in fact embrace a conception of the mean that sanctions
participation in both politics and philosophy to what they determine
to be just the right degree, they must be deceitful when they argue
that philosophy is base in itself:

> They partake moderately (μετρίως) in philosophy and moder-
> ately (μετρίως) in politics on the basis of what they regard to be a
> quite sound strategy; for they participate in both to the extent that
> is required (ὅσον ἔδει), and, while remaining aloof from the dan-
> gers of conflict, they continue to enjoy the fruits of their wisdom
> (τὴν σοφίαν).
>
> (305 D 8–E 2)

In these words we capture a glimpse of what our critic imagines his
wisdom to be. Working with the assumption that philosophy and politics are two distinct activities, he tries to extract from both what they
have to offer. From his study of politics, this semiphilosopher has
learned how to avoid the loss of reputation in the eyes of the many,
something that those who advance too far into the mysteries of philosophy will surely suffer; for the philosopher's obsessive quest for knowledge drives him outside the realm of the common understanding and
so ruins him for the serious political business of tracking down and
systematizing the opinions of the many. In short, the critic knows that
to pursue wisdom too far makes the lover of wisdom "unwise" for political action.[21] From his study of philosophy, on the other hand, this
semipolitician has culled the gist of his argumentative powers, together with the recognition that, to ensure his personal safety, he
must exercise them at some distance from the ever-present dangers of

the political arena. But since he has borrowed from philosophy only what he can use in his forensic art, that is, since he has not perfected his art of controversy by crowning it with the study of eristic, he remains no match for those about Euthydemus, if he should ever be so foolish as to become entangled in their weird arguments.[22] So firmly entrenched there where he perceives the middle to be, this part-philosopher, part-politician keeps his finger to the wind, trying to gauge how much he can profit from discrediting what appears to drift too far outside the vision of parents like Crito and Axiochus. To him, therefore, the brothers are not *the* distortion, but just another distortion, and Socrates is not *the* alternative, but just another Athenian in danger of being swept up into this verbal mania through his willingness to participate in it. Without any real standard, then, by which to determine good, better, and best, the critic of the *Euthydemus* has failed to read aright the antithesis between dialectic and eristic. Yet in his folly he imagines he has solved the riddle of human existence by exercising power behind the scenes of political action, even as he contrives to usurp the title "wise" from philosophers.

The plausibility of this argument has appealed to Crito, for whom moderation in all things is good. So Socrates must immediately subject it to analysis. But since Crito, like Kleinias before him, has failed to escape from the labyrinth by seeing that the philosopher and statesman are really one, that his knowledge is one, and that, strictly speaking, no compromise is possible, Socrates must demonstrate for him that this halfbacked theory, even on its own ground, fails to provide the correct reading of the antithesis between philosophy and political science. To do so, he simply points to the inherent weakness of the critic's position, namely that by dabbling in philosophy and politics on the assumption that they are two distinct activities, the critic, in truth a mere dilettante, ends up inferior to both philosophers and politicians in respect to their goodness (306 C 2–5). Yet impelled as he is by his desire to appear first in wisdom, this perennial type of compromiser cannot resist the temptation to seize what he imagines to be the mean, a plausible enough move all right, given that he has failed to recognize that by attaining this middle ground, he dwells in no-man's-land ($\mu\varepsilon\theta\acute{o}\rho\iota\alpha$).[23]

As if impatient with these abstract considerations, Crito does not respond to Socrates' analysis. Instead, his thoughts return to his persistent worry, his sons. Although he recognizes that it is his duty, as a father, to find teachers for Critobulus, Crito has thus far been unable to do anything more than bemoan the difficulty of finding anyone suitable to do the job.[24] And now, during his conversation with Socrates, he again realizes that it is sheer folly to attend to all manner of other things for the sake of his children, but to neglect their education. But even as he ponders these matters, it does not occur to him that the forces of corruption have already come to town and been engaged in their dirty work (275 B 4), and, what is more, that Socrates has already risked the danger of direct combat with them. Should we be surprised? What the Critos and Axiochuses cannot comprehend is that a persistent refusal to fight openly against the brothers (or, in the language of this dialogue, to refuse to go to their school) allows these self-seeking profiteers, without opposition, to usurp the role of genuine teachers; and that, unless they, as concerned parents, attend more carefully to what occupations are and are not legitimate in themselves and can determine on their own who are and are not the authentic practitioners of them, they will never be able to advance their children successfully, much less turn them to philosophy. For the *Euthydemus* shows that whether the tripartite eristic takes the form of military violence, legal chicanery, or contentious foolery, a force will always be present to corrupt youth in body, spirit, and mind—a force that, in its highest and purest form, can even come to reside within philosophy itself.

CONCLUSION

To appreciate more fully that in this final scene Socrates is not entangled in a predicament that is peculiar to the *Euthydemus*, but engaged in a far more serious and universal contest that may challenge anyone who loves wisdom correctly, it will be useful to place the second part of this epilogue against the wider context of the *Republic*. Although Plato continues to take up this contest throughout the central books, we can gather an adequate picture of the challenge it presents to Socrates from one key passage in book 6:

> By far the greatest and most severe slander comes against philosophy on account of those who profess to practice the activity, and they are the ones, as you [Adeimantus] say, whom our critic of philosophy can attack when he claims that most of those who court

her are utterly wicked, while the best are useless; and I admit that
you are right.

(*Republic* 489 D 1–5)

Here Socrates voices his general agreement with Adeimantus that
those charlatans who slip in under the mantle of philosophy and al-
lege to practice the discipline are precisely the ones responsible for
the slander that comes against it. For critics, themselves not indifferent, can pin the tag "utterly wicked" on the majority and "useless"
on the best.[25] Once serious philosophical activity, as practiced by Socrates, has been altered into its counterfeit image and marketed as a
commodity for public consumption, hostile rivals can, in their polemics, cause the whole activity to appear to the general public as nothing
but a socially irresponsible form of entertainment in which quar-
relsome "bastards," as Socrates calls them in the *Republic*,[26] just cling to
terms as if they were merely shifting counters in a game of draughts.[27]
The death of Socrates gives full testimony to the magnitude of the
public fury that this slander can and did unleash. Yet, caught in this
crossfire between wicked philosophers and self-seeking critics, Socrates chose to stand his ground. The *Euthydemus* recounts in detail
one such occasion when he did so, and although this dialogue concentrates primarily on the philosophical side of this challenge, Plato still
manages to embrace something of the larger context at the close of his
work. In this way, then, the *Euthydemus* refers beyond itself to what its
author has written in other works, especially to the central books of
the *Republic,* to which it, properly speaking, can be an appendix.
Minor only when compared to the total picture of life and community
that the *Republic* offers, the *Euthydemus* has presented, with much dramatic clarity, a concrete picture of a day in the life of Socrates.

For our final remarks we can now return to that quotation from
Paul Shorey with which we began:

> To the partisans of development the dialogue offers a dilemma.
> Either this mature logic must be assigned to an early work, or a late
> work may display comic verve of style and engage in a purely dra-
> matic, apparently unsuccessful, Socratic search for the political art.

This dilemma arises because the partisans of development, as Shorey
calls them, realign Plato's thought in accordance with a conjectural
chronology that pictures a trajectory from an out of which to an end,

making the individual dialogues moments or stages in the biography of their author. It has been the fate of the *Euthydemus* not to fit very well into this trajectory, and Shorey knew why: This method for controlling the meaning of the text, as it is usually understood and applied, cannot reconcile what he took for granted, namely that the *Euthydemus* combines both "early" and "late" characteristics. The prevailing tendency among moderns has been to ignore, or even to deny, its mature logic, leaving only the Socratic episodes to warrant treatment. Yet the treatment of these sections, when analyzed in isolation from their companion pieces, has only enhanced the general impression that this work is immature and misdirected, an occasional piece and minor dialogue. Militating against any successful interpretation of it as early, however, is the now undeniably mature logic that can no longer be ignored. But all of this, I take it, was obvious to Shorey when he wrote: "The *Euthydemus,* like the *Cratylus,* is a repertory of Platonic thoughts that link it to 'earlier' and 'later' dialogues." Shorey knew that this dichotomy between early and late, at least in the case of the *Euthydemus,* arises from a first falsehood, the sheer inappropriateness of trying to control the dialogue's meaning by a hypothesis that is contrary to its intention. For the *Euthydemus* itself is designed to prove that opposites can adhere in one and the same thing without contradiction. Eristic and dialectic, play and seriousness, appearance and reality, in fact the whole array of philosophical-pairs, find their way into this dialogue and receive their due share within the whole.[28] It is in this way, finally, that Plato refutes the then-emerging knack of sophistic antilogy, which has its source in Parmenides ("the most ἀντιλογικός of all," as Cherniss calls him),[29] but its trendy, momentary avatar in the brother-pair, that wildly disfigured yet hilarious personification of this reasoning dilemma. Further, to ensure that we have the proper perspective for interpreting this refutation, Plato also orchestrates a contrary movement in which he has used Socrates as a vehicle to articulate in what sense the world is truly antilogical.[30]

But nothing reveals Plato's purpose better than the artistic form of the work itself. The *Euthydemus* appears to offer a linear series of events, all of the same value, and unfolding in the manner of an Attic drama, with a prologue, an epilogue, and five episodes. But this horizontal dimension, an artistic illusion anyway, just disguises the fact that the *Euthydemus* is quite simply and quite literally a conversation between Socrates and Crito. But it is a conversation, moreover, whose major portion consists of Socrates' narration, and this narration, in turn, is a recollection or a culling of the gist of the phenomena which Socrates structures and projects upon an objective canvas. Once in this form, the details are rendered meaningful, the parts whole. Here, the eristic episodes do not balance the dialectical ones on the horizontal plane of history along which one creeps, for that would be to accept the devalued world of which the Hydra and the Crab are the measure. But through its conflict with eristic, dialectic emerges up and out of the horizontal antinomies of the brothers to establish that vertical dimension in respect of which we stand erect and can judge aright. By giving expression, on the one hand, to the extreme reaches of his satirical impulses in the caricature of the Tweedle brothers, and, on the other, by having Socrates advance Kleinias to the very threshold of the intelligible region, thus cutting a perfect path between the playful and the serious, Plato overcomes the apparently irreconcilable nature of opposites by allowing his readers to experience τὰ μεταξύ.

Each Platonic dialogue is an adequate account (ἱκανόν τι) of the subject matter that it treats; as such, it is complete and final, and so each work can be read as his last. To read Plato's dialogues in this way is to treat them as a plurality of entities, each possessing its own reality and identity. Viewed synoptically, on the other hand, these independent entities express a unity that can be and has been duly expressed in its simplicity and oneness. In the selfsame moment, then, Plato's corpus is a one over a many. To go too far in either direction, and so to converge upon the poles, can therefore distort what Plato has to teach. For to grasp that teaching requires the interpreter to establish himself in that place of perfect inbetweenness, a mean that only dialectic can establish. The *Euthydemus* has attained its unity and completeness in the fulfillment of its single purpose, the presentation of a conversation between Crito and Socrates, in which the latter told the tale of the clash between eristic and dialectic. And this dialogue, like a chord drawn to just the right tension, will strike a true response in that soul which aspires to the Good.

Appendix I

THE RHETORICAL
AND DRAMATIC DIVISIONS
OF THE *EUTHYDEMUS*

THE RHETORICAL DIVISIONS

Socrates' opening conversation with Crito (271 A 1–272 E 1)
Socrates' narration (272 E 1–290 D 8)
    Exordium (272 E 1–275 C 4)
    Part one (275 C 5–282 E 6)
Transitional interlude (283 A 1–283 B 3)
    Part two (283 B 4–290 D 8)
Socrates' central conversation with Crito (290 E 1–292 E 7)
Transitional interlude (292 E 8–293 A 9)
Socrates' narration (293 B 1–304 B 5)
    Part three (293 B 1–303 A 9)
    Peroration (303 B 1–304 B 5)
Socrates' final conversation with Crito (304 B 6–307 C 4)

THE DRAMATIC DIVISIONS

Prologue (271 A 1–275 D 2)
    Part one (271 A 1–272 E 1)
    Part two (272 E 1–275 D 2)
First episode (275 D 2–277 C 7)
    Transitional interlude (277 D 1–278 E 2)
Second episode (278 E 3–282 D 3)
    Transitional interlude (282 D 4–283 B 3)
Third episode (283 B 4–288 B 2)
    Transitional interlude (288 B 3–288 D 4)
Fourth episode (288 D 5–292 E 7)
    Transitional interlude (292 E 8–293 A 9)
Fifth episode (293 B 1–303 A 9)
Epilogue (303 B 1–307 C 4)
    Part one (303 B 1–304 B 5)
    Part two (304 B 6–307 C 4)

Appendix II
CATALOGUE OF
ERISTIC ARGUMENTS

FIRST ERISTIC DISPLAY

(E1) and (D1)	Are those who learn the wise or the ignorant? (275 D 2–276 C 7)
(E2) and (D2)	Do those who learn learn what they know or what they do not know? (276 D 7–277 C 7)

SECOND ERISTIC DISPLAY

(D3)	On becoming wise (283 B 4–D 8)
(E4) and (E5)	On the impossibility of falsehood (283 E 1– 284 C 8)
(D6)	On speaking badly of the bad (284 C 9–285 A 1)
(D7)	On the impossibility of contradiction (285 D 7– 286 B 6)
(D8)	On whether phrases have sense (287 D 7–E 4)

THIRD ERISTIC DISPLAY

(E9)	Socrates already possesses the sought-after knowledge (293 B 1–E 1)
(E10)	Socrates knows all things always (295 A 10– 296 D 4)
(D11)	On family relationships (297 D 3–298 B 3)
(K12)	A father is the father of all (298 B 4–D 6)
(D13)	Ktesippus beats his father, the dog (298 D 7– 299 A 5)
(E14)	On the need to possess many goods (299 A 6–C 7)
(D15)	On having gold "in" oneself (299 C 8–E 9)
(E16)	On things capable of sight (300 A 1–A 8)
(D17) and (E17)	Speaking of the silent and Silence of the speaking (300 B 1–D 2)

(D18)   Eristic in the treatment of the forms (300 E 1–
          301 C 5)
(D19)   It is fitting to cook the cook (301 C 6–D 8)
(D20)   Socrates can sell or sacrifice his Zeus (301 E 1–
          303 A 3)
(D21)   Is Heracles Puppax? (303 A 4–9)

Appendix III
ON ΜΑΘΗΣΙΣ

Plato approaches the topic of learning frequently and in a variety of contexts, but certainly one of the most celebrated passages in which he does so can be found in the *Meno,* where we confront the only argument in Plato explicitly designated as "eristic." Here, after several unsuccessful attempts at defining virtue, Meno tries to forestall the inquiry by dragging in an argument that Socrates immediately recognizes and reformulates as follows:

> I understand what you mean, Meno. Do you see that this is an eristic argument you are dragging in, that, forsooth, it is impossible for a man to search for either what he knows or what he doesn't know? For he can't search for what he knows—because he knows it, and so he has no need for the inquiry—or for what he doesn't know—because he doesn't even know what he will search for.
>
> (*Meno* 80 E 1–5)

Familiar now with the questioning procedure of the brothers, we can easily imagine how Euthydemus might reshape Meno's argument into an inescapable question similar to the one he used to trigger (E2). Consider the following question: "Which of the two, then, does he who searches search for—what he doesn't know or what he knows (πότερον οὖν ὁ ζητῶν ζητεῖ ὃ μὴ οἶδεν ἢ ὃ οἶδεν)?"; here Euthydemus simply replaces μανθάνειν with ζητεῖν and ἐπίστασθαι with εἰδέναι. Moreover, Socrates has also sketched out the two possible lines of attack by which Euthydemus might refute either thesis generated by his opponent's answer. For example, should an interlocutor formulate a thesis parallel to the one Kleinias did in (E2), it would take the following form: A man searches for what he doesn't know (ὁ ἄνθρωπος ζητεῖ ὃ μὴ οἶδε). Euthydemus could then preclude the possibility of inquiry, just as he did the possibility of learning, by arguing that there is no conceivable way for Kleinias or anybody else to begin searching into what is unknown, for "he doesn't even know what he will search for." Contrarily, were Kleinias to choose the other horn of the dilemma, the thesis would be: A man searches for what he knows (ὁ ἄνθρωπος ζητεῖ ὃ οἶδε). Euthydemus might then overthrow the thesis by arguing that Kleinias has no need to search for what is known, because, after all, "he knows it." Both lines of attack argue for the impossibility of either thesis (οὐδέτερα). On the other hand, Euthydemus could also support both theses (ἀμφότερα) by exploiting two senses of the pivotal term *search* in just the same way he did *learn* in (E1) and (E2). To argue that "a man searches for what he doesn't know," Euthydemus could construct an argument in which "search for" equals "begin to search for knowledge." Conversely, to argue that "a man searches for what he knows," he could shift to a stronger sense of ζητεῖν, to that of "research" or "critically reexamine" a subject matter already known. Thus, by juggling two senses of ζητεῖν, together with corresponding shifts in the linguistic environment operative in the entire context of inquiry, Euthydemus could easily transform Meno's paradox into the featured attraction of an eristic showpiece.

Plato solves this eristic argument by working between the horns of the dilemma. The very possibility of blank ignorance is inconceivable, because only those who have achieved a vision of reality can be incarnated into space/time, whereas complete knowledge is equally impossible, since somatic limitations prevent the human soul from attaining full access to the really real; but there exists an intermediate region for inquiry, the realm of opinion in which recollection can operate; on the object-side of this process, there are representations (δοξαστά) of the really real that can trigger subjective correlates or opinions that have remained latent in the soul. The process by which our opinions are tethered to their objective correlates is learning. To solve the subject-side of the dilemma, Plato also has recourse to the middle realm. In the *Symposium* he has Diotima note the peculiar psychological states of the wise and the ignorant vis-à-vis their subjective response to the pursuit of wisdom:

> No god philosophizes nor desires to become wise—for he already is; nor does anyone else who is wise philosophize. On the other hand, neither do the ignorant philosophize or desire to become wise, because ignorance has this cruel aspect to it: Those who have neither beauty and goodness nor intelligence turn out to be satisfied with themselves. Therefore, he who doesn't imagine himself to be deficient has no desire for what he doesn't fancy himself to lack.
>
> (*Symposium* 204 A 1–7)

Here, too, it is not difficult to imagine how Euthydemus might toy with the predicates "wise" and "ignorant" so as to formulate the following question: "Which of the two are those who search, the wise or the ignorant (πότεροί εἰσι τῶν ἀνθρώπων οἱ ζητοῦντες, οἱ σοφοὶ ἢ οἱ ἀμαθεῖς)?" Whichever way this alternative question is answered, we can be confident that Euthydemus would be prepared to argue "neither" and "both." When Socrates faces this dilemma in the *Symposium*, however, he quite reasonably asks Diotima: "Who, then, are lovers of wisdom, if they are neither the wise nor the ignorant?" (204 A 8–9). With her answer "those between the two" (οἱ μεταξὺ τούτων ἀμφο-τέρων: 204 B 1–2), she cuts a middle path between the antinomous dispositions. Human beings can never find themselves at either pole when the two psychological states refer, on the one hand, to the all-knowing (οἱ σοφοί) and, on the other, to the totally ignorant (οἱ ἀμαθεῖς). For, as Diotima explains, our psychological state is never one of complete ignorance; those whom we call ignorant are just self-satisfied and complacent, without any desire to become wise. Plato states the importance of this qualification in the *Lysis:*

> For this reason, then, we can claim that those who are already wise, whether they are gods or men, no longer philosophize. Nor, on the other hand, do those philosophize who are so ignorant as to be base; for no one who is base and ignorant can philosophize. There remain, then, those who, though they are handicapped by this evil, ignorance, have not yet been rendered stupid and igno-rant under its influence, but who can still recognize that they do not know what they do not know.
>
> (*Lysis* 218 A 2–B 1)

Here, too, both the wise and the ignorant are removed from the pursuit of wisdom. Between them, however, are those who can still recognize their own shortcomings because they have not yet been re-duced to a reprehensible state of folly by the cruel force of their own ignorance. Blessed in their *ars nesciendi*, these fortunate souls can be-gin the pursuit of wisdom.

NOTES

PROLOGUE

1. There are two helpful commentaries in English on the dialogue, Edwin Gifford's *The Euthydemus of Plato* (Oxford, 1905) and R. S. W. Hawtrey's *Commentary on Plato's Euthydemus* (Philadelphia, 1981); but neither work can be said to provide a systematic and coherent interpretation. Even in Germany, where little escapes the critical eye of scholarship, there is only one, Hermann Keulen's monograph *Untersuchungen zu Platons "Euthydem"* (Wiesbaden, 1971; hereafter *UPE*). We can expect this situation to change, for in France two works on the *Euthydemus* have recently appeared, Michel Narcy's *Le Philosophe et son double* (Paris, 1984) and Monique Canto's *L'Intrigue Philosophique* (Paris, 1987).

2. I. M. Crombie, *An Examination of Plato's Doctrines*, 2 vols. (London, 1963), 1: 223–224 and 2: 488–489. Crombie does, however, deny that the *Euthydemus* is "trivial;" he doubts "whether it belongs to Plato's youth;" and he opts instead for a "fairly late date" (1: 223).

3. One exception is the delightful discussion by Gerard Hinrichs, "The *Euthydemus* as a Locus of the Socratic Elenchus," *New Scholasticism* 25 (1951), 178–183.

4. Recently Vlastos has tackled a passage from Socrates' protreptic ("Happiness and Virtue in Socrates' Moral Theory," *Proceedings of the Cambridge Philological Society* 210 [1984], 199–201; or *Socrates, Ironist and Moral Philosopher* [Ithaca, 1991], pp. 227–231); see also "The Socratic Elenchus," *Oxford Studies in Ancient Philosophy* 1 (1983), 57–58; and "Elenchus and Mathematics: A Turning-Point in Plato's Philosophical Development," *American Journal of Philology* 109 (1988), 372–374 and 385–386; or *Socrates,* pp. 116–118 and 127–128. When, however, we compare his brief remarks on the *Euthydemus* with how much he has written, e.g., on the *Protagoras, Gorgias, Lysis,* and *Meno,* we cannot fail to see how consistently he has steered away from this dialogue. And most significant of all, Vlastos has not in any way engaged the eristic arguments of the *Euthydemus.*

5. An oversight that R. K. Sprague has corrected with the publication of *The Older Sophists* (Columbia, S.C., 1972), pp. 294–301, where we see how little is known about the brother-pair apart from Plato's dialogue.

6. C. J. Classen, *Sophistic* (Darmstadt, 1976), pp. 641–709.

7. W. K. C. Guthrie, *A History of Greek Philosophy*, vol. 3 (Cambridge, 1969), p. vii (hereafter *HGP*).

8. We know of their existence from two sources independent of Plato. Xenophon informs us that Dionysodorus was a military expert (*Memorabilia* III.1.1), and Aristotle twice associates Euthydemus with fallacies (*Sophistici Elenchi* 20.177 B 12 [hereafter *SE*]; and *Rhetoric* 2.24.1401 A 28). What we cannot prove with certainty is that Euthydemus and Dionysodorus were brothers, and so it has been argued that the coupling of the two is an example of Platonic roguery (*Schalkhaftigkeit*); see Keulen, *UPE*, pp. 8–9.

9. See Gregory Vlastos, "Socrates' Disavowal of Knowledge," *Philosophical Quarterly* 35 (1985), 1 n. 1, or *Socrates*, pp. 46–47. Charles Kahn has recently argued that the *Euthydemus* is to be classified as a "pre-middle" dialogue ("Did Plato Write Socratic Dialogues?" *Classical Quarterly* 31 [1981], 305–309) and to be read as a member of a group that includes the *Charmides, Laches,* and *Lysis* ("Plato's *Charmides* and the Proleptic Reading of Socratic Dialogues," *Journal of Philosophy* 85 [1988], 542).

10. For example, Edwin Gifford thinks the *Euthydemus* was composed after the *Phaedrus* (*The Euthydemus of Plato*, p. 32); Paul Natorp argues that it is an appendix to the *Theaetetus* (*Platos Ideenlehre* [Leipzig, 1921], pp. 119–122); Henry Sidgwick places the *Euthydemus* with the *Sophist* ("The Sophists," *Journal of Philology* 4 [1872], 306); and E. Pfleiderer puts it after (*Socrates und Plato* [1896], pp. 318–320, 330, 333, 342).

11. Paul Shorey, *The Unity of Plato's Thought* (Chicago, 1903), p. 76. To Shorey, this dilemma is false; his unity hypothesis allows him to bridge the gap between the two alternatives "early" and "late," which only appear to be mutually exclusive.

12. Sidgwick, "The Sophists," esp. pp. 298–307. A. E. Taylor successfully refutes Sidgwick's position; "Δισσοὶ Λόγοι," in *Varia Socratica* (Oxford, 1911), pp. 92–93.

13. So Vlastos can tell us that "in common with most scholars" he has been dating the *Euthydemus* before the *Meno* ("Socrates' Disavowal of Knowledge," p. 16 n. 37); but in fact he actually commits himself to a much stronger claim, that the *Euthydemus* "must precede the *Meno*" ("The Socratic Elenchus," p. 58).

14. One exception to this tendency is G. B. Kerferd, who has stressed the crucial importance of eristic and antilogic for Plato's thought (*The Sophistic Movement* [Cambridge, 1981], pp. 59–67). "The truth is," as Sprague notes, "Plato was much more interested in eristic

than most of his interpreters have been" ("Socrates' Safest Answer: *Phaedo* 100D," *Hermes* 96 [1968], 635).

15. Guthrie, *HGP* 4: 281.

16. See ibid., p. 279, and Harold Cherniss, *Selected Papers* (Leiden, 1977), p. 263.

17. In addition to Vlastos and Kahn, several others have embraced the "early" or "transitional" hypothesis without feeling any need to engage the eristic arguments: Marion Soreth ("Zur relativen Chronologie von *Menon* und *Euthydem*," *Hermes* 83 [1955], 377–379); E. R. Dodds (*Plato, Gorgias* [Oxford, 1959], pp. 22–23); R. S. Bluck (*Plato's Meno* [Cambridge, 1961], pp. 114–115); T. Irwin (*Plato's Moral Theory* [Oxford, 1977], pp. 291–292); Richard Kraut (*Socrates and the State* [Princeton, 1984], p. 4 n. 1); Michael Ferejohn ("Socratic Thought-Experiments and the Unity of Virtue Paradox," *Phronesis* 29 [1984], 109 n. 14); and Thomas C. Brickhouse and Nicholas D. Smith ("Socrates on Goods, Virtue, and Happiness," *Oxford Studies in Ancient Philosophy* 5 [1987], 1 n. 1). This short list could be significantly increased if it were to include those who do not address the dating issue but who proceed on the assumption that the *Euthydemus* is early. Among those who place the *Euthydemus* before the *Meno*, Paul Friedländer is an important exception. Though accepting the early hypothesis (*Plato,* vol. 2 [Princeton, 1969], p. 335 n. 3), he offers an excellent treatment of eristic. His analysis suggests that it is not the early hypothesis itself, but the way in which it is currently understood and applied that constitutes an obstacle to the study of the *Euthydemus*.

18. In addition to those already cited, there are a few scholars who have placed the *Euthydemus* with or after the *Meno;* see Wincenty Lutoslawski (*The Origin and Growth of Plato's Logic* [London, 1897], p. 211); E. S. Thompson (*The Meno of Plato* [London, 1901], p. 281); Theodor Gomperz (*Griechische Denker,* 4th ed., vol. 2 [Berlin/Leipzig, 1925], p. 425); Hans Raeder (*Platons Philosophische Entwicklung* [Leipzig, 1905], p. 146); Ulrich von Wilamowitz-Moellendorff (*Platon,* 5th ed., vol. 1 [Berlin, 1920], p. 308); Louis Méridier (*Euthydème,* vol. 5 [Paris, 1931], pp. 139–142); Kurt Hildebrandt (*Platon, Logos und Mythos,* 2d ed. [Berlin, 1959], p. 396); Constantin Ritter (*Hermes* 70 [1935], 30); Harold Cherniss (*Selected Papers,* p. 249); G. E. L. Owen ("The Place of the *Timaeus* in Plato's Dialogues," in *Studies in Plato's Metaphysics,* ed. R. E. Allen [New York, 1965], p. 329); and R. S. W. Hawtrey (*Commentary,* p. 10).

19. So, for example, A. C. Lloyd can write: "The *Sophist* is not the reply to the *Theaetetus* but to the *Euthydemus*" ("Falsehood and Significance according to Plato," *Proceedings of the Eleventh International Con-*

gress of Philosophy 12 [Amsterdam/Louvain, 1953], 69); Sprague has shown how the *Euthydemus* looks toward the *Parmenides* ("Parmenides' Sail and Dionysodorus' Ox," *Phronesis* 12 [1967], 91–98. The general picture that emerges from all seven attempts to define the sophist in the dialogue by that name fits the brother-pair more closely than any other sophist of antiquity, a point that J. L. Smith has made in his dissertation ("Plato and the Paradox of False Statements: A Study of the *Euthydemus* and the *Sophist*" [Virginia, 1975], p. 20); and Thomas Alexander Szlezák has explored the connection between the *Euthydemus* and the *Phaedrus* ("Sokrates' Spott über Geheimhaltung: Zum Bild des φιλόσοφος in Platons *Euthydemos*," *Antike und Abendland* 26 [1980], esp. 79–81).

20. Thus Owen: "And thereby the *Timaeus* at once ranks itself with the *Republic* and *Euthydemus*" ("The Place of the *Timaeus*," p. 329); cf. Cherniss, *Selected Papers*, pp. 340–342.

21. Thus R. S. W. Hawtrey, "How Do Dialecticians Use Diagrams—Plato, *Euthydemus* 290b–c," *Apeiron* 12 (1978), 16.

22. The attitude of scholars toward Plato's eristic appears to be similar to that of the Red King, after Alice tells him that the verses of the White Rabbit do not contain an atom of meaning: "If there's no meaning in it," said the King, "that saves a world of trouble, you know, as we needn't try to find any."

23. Lewis Campbell, *The Sophistes and Politicus of Plato* (Oxford, 1867), p. xii. An excellent place to begin inquiry into these problems is still Eduard Zeller, *Socrates and the Socratic School*, trans. O. J. Reichel, 3rd ed. (London, 1962), chap. 12, pp. 250–284.

24. For the Eleatic sources of eristic, see Keulen, *UPE*, p. 77 n. 68. A. E. Taylor has made a powerful case for the Zenonian origins of eristic ("Δισσοὶ Λόγοι," p. 92, and *Plato, the Man and His Work* [London, 1927], pp. 89–102; hereafter *PMW*).

25. Thus Keulen, *UPE*, pp. 84–90, though he acknowledges that eristic may be a "many-headed" phenomenon (p. 92). Sidgwick argues that both Protagoras and Zeno are the sources ("The Sophists," pp. 299–300).

26. See Wilamowitz, *Platon* 2: 155–156; and Karl Praechter, "Platon und Euthydemos," *Philologus* 87 (1932), 122–127.

27. Thus Taylor, "Δισσοὶ Λόγοι," p. 93.

28. Thus Sidgwick, "The Sophists," pp. 298–307; see also E. S. Thompson, *The Meno*, p. 278; and Hawtrey, *Commentary*, pp. 28–30.

29. For Isocrates, the most important texts are *Antidosis* (258–269), *Helen* (1–13), *Panathenaicus* (26–29), *Against the Sophists*, and *Letter to Alexander*. For a treatment of these problems, see Christoph Eucken,

Isokrates: Seine Positionen in der Auseinandersetzung mit den zeitgenössischen Philosophen (Berlin, 1983), esp. pp. 44–53.

30. And so Guthrie has remarked: "This word 'eristic' was so freely bandied about that it might be said that one man's philosophy was another man's eristic" (*HGP*, 4: 275).

31. Aristotle's critique of eristic was carried on by Theophrastus in his "Polemical Discussion on the Theory of Eristic Argument" (Diogenes Laertius 5.42; hereafter D.L.); the loss of Theophrastus' work has been lamented by Arthur Schopenhauer, who in his own *Eristische Dialektik* expresses a keen sensitivity to the power of eristic (*Parerga*, vol. 5, chap. 2).

32. See D.L., *Life of Arcesilaus*, 4.28.

33. Criticism of this type is especially prevalent among the older Germans; see Keulen, *UPE*, pp. 1–5. But we can still hear: "Our patience with the sophists is exhausted long before the end of the dialogue" (G. E. R. Lloyd, *Polarity and Analogy* [Cambridge, 1966], p. 137); "Why, we might ask, did Plato choose to show Socrates dealing with their elementary fallacies?" (Guthrie, *HGP*, 4: 266); and, after telling us that the eristic sections are "not very edifying" and delivered "by a pair of quite forgettable sophists," Ferejohn concludes: "To put the point delicately, these interlocutions are not exactly brimming with philosophical delights, which provokes one to wonder why Plato bothers to record or construct them in such fine detail" ("Socratic Thought-Experiments," p. 109).

34. These remarks are in no way intended to be a criticism of Aristotle's *Sophistici Elenchi*, on which I am currently preparing a monograph.

35. For the Greek of these two passages, see Keulen, *UPE*, pp. 19 and 17. All translations from the Greek are my own.

36. Our evidence indicates that it was not Plato but his younger associates, especially Aristotle and Xenocrates, who began the systematic study of solutions. Aristotle's treatment of them can be found in *SE* 16–33, and Diogenes credits Xenocrates with "solutions" in two books and "solutions to arguments" in ten (D.L. 4.13). Numerous post-Aristotelian treatises show that Hellenistic philosophers, especially the Stoics, carried on this interest in solving logical paradoxes.

37. M. J. Routh, *Platonis Euthydemus et Gorgias* (Oxford, 1784); Augustus Winckelmann, *Platonis Euthydemus* (Leipzig, 1833).

38. For Bonitz's list of eristic arguments, see *Platonische Studien*, 3rd ed. (Berlin, 1886), pp. 95–103. I have followed his catalogue with but two exceptions, duly noted at a later time. Prior to Bonitz, the best analysis of the *Euthydemus* is George Grote, *Plato and the Other Compan-*

ions of Socrates, vol. 1 (London, 1865), pp. 527–564, which is still a must for all students of the dialogue.

39. Two obvious exceptions are Taylor, "Δισσοὶ Λόγοι," pp. 91–128, and *PMW,* pp. 89–102; and Paul Shorey, *What Plato Said* (Chicago, 1933), pp. 160–168.

40. See esp. R. K. Sprague, *Plato's Use of Fallacy* (London, 1962), p. 7 n. 5. Sprague was not alone in detecting that Robinson's views could be harmful to the *Euthydemus.* Hinrichs wrote his article "*Euthydemus* as a Locus" to assess "the violence [Robinson had] done to Plato's conception of Socratic elenchus" (p. 178). Both Dennis Stuart ("An Interpretation of Plato's *Euthydemus*" [Ph.D. diss., Yale Univ., 1980], pp. 76–81) and J. L. Smith ("Plato and the Paradox of False Statements," pp. 51–56) have sharply criticized Robinson's views. And Narcy has recently attacked him for spawning "an exegesis of mistrust" ("une exégèse de la méfiance": *Le Philosophe,* p. 11).

41. Even as scholars apply Aristotle's critical apparatus to the *Euthydemus,* they clearly recognize that in a sense it is inappropriate to do so; see Sprague's remarks in "Logic and Literary Form in Plato," *Personalist* 48 (1967), 560–572, and in "Plato's Sophistry (II)," *Aristotelian Society Suppl.* 51 (1977), pp. 47–50.

42. C. L. Hamblin, *Fallacies* (London, 1970), p. 59. Hawtrey claims that "the twenty-one sophisms certainly constitute, in a sense, a 'handbook of fallacies,'" and that "the main purpose of the eristic sections is, then, gymnastic" (*Commentary,* p. 20); so too Gilbert Ryle, "Dialectic in the Academy," in *Aristotle on Dialectic,* ed. G. E. L. Owen (Oxford, 1968), p. 78; and J. L. Smith, "Plato and the Paradox of False Statements," pp. 15–17. These authors have attributed a gymnastic function to the eristic sections without reflecting on the difference between the public and private expressions of this "laborious game"; cf. *Euthydemus* 304 A–B and *Parmenides* 135 D–137 B. In the *Euthydemus* Plato is showing the disastrous consequences that eristic activity can have when it is given public expression, a point that did not escape George Grote (*Plato,* pp. 532–533).

43. See Richard Robinson, "Ambiguity," *Mind* 50 (1941), 141, and "Plato's Consciousness of Fallacy," *Mind* 51 (1942), 102–103, 107, 109, and 114.

44. Thus Narcy parodies the position of Robinson: "Il en reste donc à cette conclusion bizarre que Platon, piètre logicien, se fait l'adversaire des sophistes sans pouvoir établir clairement ce qu'est un sophisme!" (*Le Philosophe,* p. 11).

45. See Ryle, "Dialectic in the Academy," pp. 70 and 78. Ryle does not mention that, far from being stimulated, Kleinias is crushed by the first two arguments alone. Nor does he consider what effect eristic

stimulation has on Ktesippus, an altogether different young man. Ryle has really attributed to Plato an interest that is better suited not only to Aristotle and Xenocrates but especially to the Megarians, who were famous in antiquity for setting forth logical paradoxes for the purpose of training their students.

46. *SE* 34.183 B 36: οὐδὲν παντελῶς ὑπῆρχεν; see Sprague, "Logic and Literary Form," esp. pp. 560–561 and 567–568.

47. See Keulen, *UPE*, pp. 23–25, 35, and 40. But Keulen does express his preference for the Aristotelian treatment, owing to its greater clarity and logical rigor (p. 22).

48. See ibid., pp. 5, 34–39, and 58–60. Keulen also credits Bonitz and Friedländer with helping him to establish his thesis.

49. Importantly, Keulen's analysis does reveal how closely Plato has joined the two works; for, as he says, the *Euthydemus* awakens "den Eindruck geradezu einer Persiflage des *Menon*" (*UPE*, p. 51).

50. So, for example, in their immensely influential edition of Plato's corpus, Edith Hamilton and Huntington Cairns introduce the *Euthydemus* to their English readers thus: "This is perhaps of all the dialogues the one that makes the Athens of Socrates and Plato seem farthest removed from us" (*The Collected Dialogues of Plato* [Princeton, 1961], p. 385).

51. Natorp was one of the first to recognize that the *Euthydemus* could be compared to a satyr play ("wie eine Art Satyrspiel": *Platos Ideenlehre*, p. 119). We shall see that this genre, which permits an intermingling of the tragic and the comic, is ideally suited to the design of this dialogue.

52. For a formal analysis of the dramatic and rhetorical structure of the *Euthydemus*, see Appendix I.

53. For a quick review of the three branches of Greek oratory, see Aristotle's *Rhetoric* 1.3, and cf. *Phaedrus* 261 A–E. We should also remember that a deliberative oration can be delivered to a single individual (*Rhetoric* 2.18 1391 B 9), that it seeks to lead its listener to a judgment (κρίσις), and that the listener can best attain this judgment if the speaker distinguishes the alternatives as clearly and distinctly as possible (*Republic* 360 E).

54. For the references to this key term in the *Euthydemus*, see 275 A 1 (προτρέψαιτε), 278 C 5–6 (τὴν προτρεπτικὴν σοφίαν), 278 D 2 (προτρέποντε), 282 D 4–6 (τὸ ἐμὸν παράδειγμα . . . τῶν προτρεπτικῶν λόγων), and 307 A 2 (προτρέπω).

55. Two excellent works take up these issues of the protreptic genre: W. Gerson Rabinowitz, *Aristotle's Protrepticus and the Sources of Its Reconstruction* (Berkeley, 1957); and Ingemar Düring, *Aristotle's Protrepticus: An Attempt at Reconstruction* (Göteborg, 1961).

56. In the *Euthydemus*, ἀποτρέπειν is used only once, in Socrates' concluding admonition to Crito (307 C 1). In Aristotle (*Rhetoric* 1.3 1358 Bff.), the apotreptic and its counterpart, the protreptic, make up deliberative oratory. In the *Rhetorica ad Alexandrum* (1421 B 9), the apotreptic is a recognized genre in its own right.

57. As Leo Strauss notes, Crito's "Who is X" question belongs to the "sphere of gossip, of ordinary curiosity" ("On the *Euthydemus*," *Interpretation* 1 [1970], 1).

58. Cf. *Sophist* 218 C. Crito has the right name for the beast, but he is unfamiliar with its current manifestation as eristic.

59. Crito's three questions—"Who was he?" "Where are they from?" and "What's their wisdom?"—recall the Homeric formula for such greetings and add a charming epic touch that helps to prepare for the epiphany of the semidivine warriors of eristic (273 A).

60. See 272 A 8–B 1: ἐν τοῖς λόγοις μάχεσθαί τε καὶ ἐξελέγχειν τὸ ἀεὶ λεγόμενον, ὁμοίως ἐάντε ψεῦδος ἐάντε ἀληθὲς ᾖ. If there is any remark in the *Euthydemus* that is likely to be familiar, this is it.

61. To follow out the comparison between eristic and the pancration, see E. Norman Gardiner's *Athletics of the Ancient World* (Chicago, 1987), chaps. 14 and 16, and esp. his essay "Wrestling," *Journal of Hellenic Studies* 25 (1905), 14–31, in which he says: "The pankratiast, like the bully, sought by all means in his power to reduce his opponent to helplessness and to force him to acknowledge defeat, and the result in both cases was not infrequently fatal" (p. 27).

62. Nowhere in the *Euthydemus* does Plato state the obvious, that victory is the end of eristic argumentation. It is Aristotle who makes this connection (τῆς νίκης αὐτῆς χάριν); see *SE* 11.171 B 25–26.

63. Socrates' *narratio* is itself a sample of forensic oratory in which he produces a scathing indictment of eristic activity and a subtle defense of his own dialectic. Then, without actually saying so, he uses this indictment and defense for his deliberative purpose of calling for the rejection of eristic and the acceptance of dialectic. When we examine eristic apart from both its forensic and deliberative covering, it turns out to be a deviant form of epideictic oratory which exists merely to be observed as a playful form of argument for the sake of argument; see 286 D 11–13.

64. Cherniss, "Parmenides and the *Parmenides* of Plato," in *Selected Papers*, p. 286.

65. In *Plato's Earlier Dialectic* (Oxford, 1953), Richard Robinson provides a clear expression of this *consensus omnium:*

1. "Plato constantly has in mind a certain opposite of dialectic, something superficially like dialectic and yet as bad as dialectic is

good, something against which the would-be dialectician must always be on guard. He has two chief names for this shadow or reverse of dialectic, antilogic and eristic" (pp. 84–85).

2. "The reason why Plato constantly pillories eristic and distinguishes it from dialectic is that in truth his own dialectic very closely resembled eristic" (p. 85).

3. "In spite of Plato's care to keep the word 'dialectic' for a good method distinct from the prevalent 'eristic', it often came near to being confounded therewith" (p. 88).

Nearly everyone who has commented on the *Euthydemus* has made similar remarks. Consider, for example:

4. Theodor Gomperz: "His [Socrates'] friendly exhortation, his fatherly way of encouraging and guiding his listener to the acquisition of positive results, stand in absolute opposition [*steht in schroffem Gegensatze*] to the barren and intimidating paradoxes of the two eristics. This far-reaching, carefully calculated contrast-effect [*Kontrastwirkung*] may be regarded as the goal [*Ziel*] and purpose [*Zweck*] of the whole dialogue" (*Griechische Denker,* p. 425; my translation).

5. F. M. Cornford: "But in fundamental motive controversy, which neglects truth to gain victory, is diametrically opposed to the philosophic art of conversation" (*Plato's Theory of Knowledge* [London, 1935], p. 190).

6. Paul Friedländer: "Eristics has emerged as the very opposite of "philosophy" and has collapsed as far as any careful observer is concerned" (*Plato,* 2: 189).

7. Alexander Nehamas: "Socrates' practice is in stark contrast with the method of Euthydemus, despite their apparent similarity" ("Meno's Paradox and Socrates as a Teacher," *Oxford Studies in Ancient Philosophy* 3 [1985], 19).

See also Grote (*Plato,* p. 530); Sidgwick ("The Sophists," pp. 296, 299, and 305); Thompson (*The Meno,* p. 272); Campbell (*Sophistes,* pp. xi–xii); Gifford (*Euthydemus,* pp. 10–13); Guthrie (*HGP,* 4: 275–276); Szlezák ("Sokrates' Spott über Geheimhaltung," p. 81); Henry Teloh (*Socratic Education in Plato's Early Dialogues* [Indiana, 1986], pp. 195–196); and Robin Waterfield (*Early Socratic Dialogues* [Harmondsworth, 1987], pp. 300–303).

66. At the end of the dialogue Plato introduces the critic of philosophy as a vehicle for showing that the brothers are popularly regarded as philosophers (305 A 5).

67. The one exception to this trend in scholarship is Szlezák, who has argued forcefully for this thesis in the best article on the dialogue: "Euthydemos und Dionysodoros sind in allem das genaue Gegenbild des wahren Philosophen" ("Sokrates' Spott über Geheimhaltung," p. 81).

68. Since he is unfamiliar with the pair (271 B 9), Crito can have no knowledge of this measure. Since knowledge of opposites is the same, he can have no knowledge of the opposing measure in all philosophy, Socrates. Consequently, to the end of the work Crito remains and must remain unable to see that Socrates is the one who can turn his boy to philosophy.

69. It will be demonstrated by numerous examples how Plato uses ironical inversion, the rhetorical figure of enantiosis, as a structuring device by which he has the characters of his dialogue mean the *opposite* of what they say.

70. In his essay "Laughter," Henri Bergson argues that the comic character per se wears Gyges' ring with reverse effect (in *Comedy*, ed. Wylie Sypher [Baltimore, 1986], p. 71). His analysis of the comic grimace (pp. 74–79) applies with precision to Dionysodorus' smile (275 E 4) and reveals how carefully, in just this one detail, Plato has stigmatized Dionysodorus as a comic buffoon. For the serious smile of the true dialectician, see *Phaedo* 86 D 6.

71. Plato does this, in part, by rigging the eristic refutations of the brothers in such a way that every time they turn the tables on their opponent, they reinforce a still clearer knowledge of what is not proper philosophical behavior. This negative knowledge of what to avoid and to reject can be viewed as an advance in knowledge.

72. As Woody Allen puts it in *Crimes and Misdemeanors:* "What is comedy? Comedy is tragedy plus time." It is now clear why Vlastos does not prove his case when he argues that the *Euthydemus* "must precede the *Meno*," for it does not "anticipate its metaphysical, epistemological, and methodological novelties" ("The Socratic Elenchus," p. 58); he is, presumably, referring to their apparent absence from the Socratic episodes. Our analysis will show, however, that it is precisely these "novelties," already presupposed, that impart to the eristic sections their full satiric force. Thus Cherniss is more likely to be correct when he calls the *Euthydemus* "a dialogue earlier than the *Republic* and roughly contemporary with the *Meno*" (*Selected Papers*, p. 249).

ONE. THE FIRST ERISTIC DISPLAY

1. The throng following Kleinias forms a group that corresponds to the eristic clique, and Ktesippus, in particular, becomes the person-

ification of that vast reservoir of talented young men who are to be corrupted by this eristic phase of sophistry.

2. To this encounter, we should contrast the machinations by which the brothers plot to flank Socrates and Kleinias (273 B 3–7).

3. Thus Kleinias is on the opposite end of the social ladder from Meno's slave boy. Unlike Hippocrates, who longed to study with Protagoras before having met the man, Kleinias shows no enthusiasm for foreign wisdom; and, like Aristoteles in the *Parmenides,* he cannot spoil the sport of the brothers by suggesting the kind of distinctions and qualifications that Socrates and Ktesippus will in the fifth episode.

4. Thus Gerard Hinrichs, "The *Euthydemus* as a Locus of the Socratic Elenchus," *New Scholasticism* 25 (1951), 179.

5. We must say "indirectly" because eristic will not allow the problems of human psychology to arise in discourse; see 295 B–E, where Euthydemus quashes Socrates' attempt to introduce the soul.

6. This fact makes the *Phaedrus* relevant to our dialogue, the import of which has been treated by Thomas Alexander Szlezák, "Socrates' Spott über Geheimhaltung: Zum Bild des φιλόσοφος in Platons *Euthydemos*," *Antike und Abendland* 26 (1980), esp. 79–81.

7. The brothers twist their twofold arguments around the same topic (περὶ τοῦ αὐτοῦ); here αὐτοῦ refers to μάθησις (276 D 6–7). One characteristic, then, of an eristic display is the power to place disjunctive questions on the same topic, thus creating the illusion of exhausting it; see *Parmenides* 128 A–B and *Phaedrus* 235 A.

8. As we can gather from *Theaetetus* 197 A–B and 199 A, controversialists at the time were delighting in dragging about the concepts of learning and knowing.

9. Euthydemus is here illustrating how asking a question, as if he were seeking to learn, can prepare the way for an eristic attack; see *SE* 12.172 B 23–24.

10. Thus Kleinias becomes he who upholds the argument (ὁ ὑπέχων τὸν λόγον) and is expected to be able to sustain it against his attacker; see 285 E 7.

11. Since Euthydemus leads the questioning in the first attack, I have used the symbol (E1) as a handy way of referring to this fact. So, for example, (D3) would indicate that Dionysodorus is the questioner in the third eristic argument. For the system used to refer to each eristic argument, see Appendix II. All translations of the *Euthydemus* follow Burnet, *Platonis Opera,* vol. 3 (Oxford, 1974).

12. Even here there is irony in Euthydemus' use of καλεῖν; for the question formula "Do you call something (X) by something else (Y)?" asks whether an interlocutor will acknowledge a real correspondence between word and object (E. S. Thompson, ed., *The Meno of Plato*

[London, 1901], p. 91 n. 12). Eristics neither acknowledge nor are concerned about such a correspondence (Keulen, *UPE*, pp. 64–65). For the properly Socratic use of καλεῖν in the *Euthydemus*, see 277 E 6 and 278 A 1–4.

13. That the lyre master and grammarian are topical exempla in discussions on learning is clear from Δισσοὶ Λόγοι (VI.7), Aristophanes' *Clouds* (961 ff.), and *Lysis* (209 A–C); see also *Euthydemus* 279 E 1–4.

14. Since there is no middle ground between learning and knowing, "not to know" becomes the identical of "to learn," in the sense of "to be gathering knowledge;" cf. Dionysodorus' remarks at 277 B 6–C 1. So the third question could also read as follows: "Is it the case that, when you were learning, you were learning (scil. ἐμανθάνετε for οὔπω ἠπίστασθε) what you were learning?" Needless to say, Euthydemus doesn't tell us anything (nor, for that matter, does he intend to tell us anything about the world by juggling such synonyms.

15. It is easy for translators of this argument to obscure one of Euthydemus' more clever acts of jugglery. Here, learners (μαθηταί) are by definition "unlearned (ἀμαθεῖς)," in the sense that they are just beginning to gather knowledge. The alpha privative in (ἀ)μαθεῖς may disguise the fact that μαθηταί and ἀμαθεῖς are synonyms. Corresponding to this move is the synonymous relation between "was learning" and "did not yet know."

16. Consider *Symposium* 202 A 2–3, where Diotima asks: "Is it also the case that whatever is not wise is ignorant? Or are you not aware that there exists something between wisdom and ignorance (ἔστιν τι μεταξὺ σοφίας καὶ ἀμαθίας)?"

17. In particular, *wise* (σοφοί), *ignorant* (ἀμαθεῖς), *learn* (μανθάνειν), *know* (ἐπίστασθαι), and *objects* (ταῦτα). But, as we shall see, the key linguistic items of all twenty-one eristic arguments are never intended to be clarified.

18. Thus Plato is consciously having the brothers exemplify what Richard Robinson has called "sliding amibiguity" ("Ambiguity," *Mind* 50 [1941], 142).

19. See A. E. Taylor (*PMW*, pp. 91–93), Paul Friedländer (*Plato*, trans. Hans Meyerhoff, 2d ed., 3 vols. [Princeton, 1969], 2: 184) and R. K. Sprague ("Plato's Sophistry [II]," *Aristotelian Society suppl.* vol. 51 [1977], 51).

20. That is, Euthydemus is not arguing *ad rem*, to how matters stand (a point that Socrates will make at 278 B), but *ad puerum*; cf. *SE* 8.170 A 12–19.

21. Ἐκδεξάμενος, used twice in this episode for taking over the ar-

gument (276 C 2 and 277 B 4), can almost carry the technical sense of seizing the second half of an argument-pair. Note its use again at 298 B 4, where it signals the return of Ktesippus, who similarly seizes upon the limb of an eristic argument.

22. This second reminder that eristic refutations are *ad hominem*, not *ad rem*, is a fact to which Socrates will allude when he justifies why he can call eristic "play," and not a technique of argument that seeks to discover how things are (278 B). The brothers are so unconcerned about "how things are" that they will actually use this expression as grist for an attack *ad Ktesippum;* see 284 C 7–E 5.

23. That eristic intentionally toys with "both" and "neither" (οὐδέτεροι ἢ ἀμφότεροι) receives unambiguous confirmation at 300 D 1. See also George Grote (*Plato and the Other Companions of Socrates*, vol. 1 [London, 1865], p. 545) and Leo Strauss ("On the *Euthydemus*," *Interpretation* 1 [1970], 6).

24. The longest piece of continuous discourse that the brothers offer is only eight lines (296 C 8–D 4). Whereas Plato frequently touts the superiority of dialectic over other forms of discourse on the basis of its brevity, here he is demonstrating the perversity of what normally constitutes a virtue.

25. For the connection between (E2) and Meno's paradox, the only argument in Plato explicitly labeled an ἐριστικὸς λόγος, see Appendix III.

26. So at 276 A 7–8, Kleinias could respond: Ναί, ἐμανθάνομεν γράμματα ἃ ἤδη ἠπιστάμεθα. Σοφοὶ ἄρα ἦμεν.

27. See, in particular, where Socrates uses the Zenonian dilemma to turn the tables on the brothers themselves (287 E 2–288 A 2).

28. That is, οἱ ἀμαθεῖς [ἢ οἱ μὴ ἐπιστάμενοι] ἄρα μανθάνουσιν, ὧ Κλεινία, ἀλλ᾽ οὐχ οἱ σοφοί [ἢ οἱ ἐπιστάμενοι].

29. A point that Bonitz has noted: "Bestreitet Euthydemos in der zweiten Argumentation das, was er selbst in der ersten erwiesen hatte, und ebenso Dionysodoros" (*Platonische Studien*, 3rd ed. [Berlin, 1886], p. 96 n. 3).

30. See R. K. Sprague, trans. and ed., *Plato, Euthydemus* (Indianapolis, 1965), p. 13 n. 20; hereafter *Translation*.

31. Now that we have seen how this eristic showpiece operates, we can hazard a guess at the shape of the next disjunctive question that might have triggered the third fall: Πότεροί εἰσι τῶν ἀνθρώπων οἱ μανθάνοντες, οἱ εἰδότες ἢ οἱ μὴ εἰδότες; This question would require only that the brothers introduce the participle from εἰδέναι for the subject term of the disjunction. That the word can function in this way is indicated clearly by Socrates at 278 A 7 (τῷ τε εἰδότι καὶ ἐπὶ τῷ μή).

In this line of questioning, λαμβάνειν could gloss μανθάνειν and ἔχειν could gloss ἐπίστασθαι, as they do in (D2). The possibilities for this kind of eristic sport seem almost endless.

32. Since we are now aware that the ambiguous term *students* (μαθηταί) can refer to either the wise or the ignorant, we can easily grasp the undertone of Socrates' remark at 276 E 6–7. These eristic students, to whom (παρὰ τοῖς μαθηταῖς) the brothers appear wise, are the *ignorant* (οἱ ἀμαθεῖς) in the pejorative sense of that term.

33. It is possible that both "wise" and "ignorant" or "neither" can be correct answers to Euthydemus' first question. It depends on the twist in meaning that one gives to the other terms in the question. Aristotle has described this trick for us: "Of questions some require an answer that is paradoxical whichever way they are answered" (*SE* 12.173 A 19–20); see also *SE* 30.181 B 1–8.

34. Richard Robinson thought that Plato's insight into the fallacious question did "not amount to much" ("Plato's Consciousness of Fallacy," *Mind* 51 [1942], 104). But it will become obvious that the eristic portions of the *Euthydemus* are from beginning to end a study in bogus questioning procedures.

35. Once the thesis has been inserted, the next trick is to stitch the mouth shut (303 E 1). Throughout the *Topics* Aristotle suggests numerous techniques for defeating an answerer, yet he usually assumes that the answerer is at least aware that he is defending a position. What we have here is the trick of concealment (κρύψις), a technique used by those who argue for contentious purposes (*Topics* 8.1.155 B 23–26 and *SE* 15.174 A 27–29).

36. Aristotle provides evidence that practicing controversialists were advised to memorize a vast number of arguments based on primary theses and first principles (*Topics* 8.14.163 B 17–33), and to classify them according to a system (*Topics* 1.14.105 B 12–14). It will become clear, as we work our way through the dialogue, that the brothers have done something very similar to what Aristotle recommends.

37. In two specific passages (*Topics* 2.5.111 B 32–33 and *SE* 12.172 B 25–28), Aristotle refers in a disparaging way to this very procedure by which eristics so manipulate their opponents.

38. We should not allow the extremity to which Plato goes in his parody of this fantasy to disguise the fact that philosophers can fall under its spell at any time. In fact, an obsession of this sort is discernible in the persistent attempt of moderns to construct a systematically coherent and unassailable ontology and epistemology for their own sakes.

39. There are not only triggers for initiating argument-chains, but sign-off formulae as well. Both Euthydemus (293 B 8) and Dionysodorus (302 D 3) use "enough (ἀρκεῖ)" as a sign-off formula to indicate that they have received from their interlocutor all the concessions necessary for their argument. Here we meet another disease of the philosophical soul to which eristics are prone, that of listening to their interlocutor for only that "hinge" upon which their argument turns. Notice also in this regard Euthydemus' use of οὐδὲν διαφέρει (293 C 3).

40. Here Euthydemus well illustrates Aristotle's remark that a controversialist must first discover a basis from which to launch his attack (*Topics* 8.1.155 B 4–5). That the brothers have seized upon the problem of falsehood should not surprise us, for sophists are wont to lurk about this vague region of unreality; see *Sophist* 236 DE and 239 C.

41. That Scythians have become a topical exemplum in argumentation is clear from Δισσοὶ Λόγοι II.13.

42. See 303 C 2: παντάπασι καταδουλωθείς.

43. The one exception is (K12), where Socrates and Dionysodorus provide the triggers for Ktesippus to crank out an eristic argument against Euthydemus; see 297 E–298 A–B.

44. Aristotle's logical works confirm the existence of the questioning procedure here attributed to the brothers. In the *Topics* (2.5.111 B 32–112 A 11), he speaks of a sophistical method of argument by which a questioner steers his opponent toward a topic on which he is well supplied with attacks (cf. *Topics* 8.1.155 B 4–5). After listing several occasions on which this method is both useful and necessary, Aristotle rejects its use when it becomes merely a tactic for leading an opponent toward an area which is unnecessary to the immediate discussion, but which allows the questioner to achieve an easy victory. In the *SE* (12.172 B 25–28), Aristotle makes an obvious cross-reference to this same argumentative method and again criticizes its improper use. This latter reference confirms that the method is linked to eristics.

45. Thus the thesis of W. B. Stanford's *Ambiguity in Greek Literature* (Oxford, 1939). He just assumes (and Sprague supports him: "Plato's Sophistry," p. 61) that Plato fully understood and consciously employed ambiguity.

46. According to Paul Shorey, it was not the logical problems about learning and knowing that most occupied Plato's attention, but subtler, psychological ones: "Quaestio autem subtilior, cuius gratia doctrina ἀναμνήσεως profertur, eadem est, quam Aristoteles per totam Metaphysicen se ipsum et lectores misere torquens numquam ad liquidum perducere potuit" (*Selected Papers* [New York, 1980], 1: 270).

Shorey's position is defended and argued at greater length by Harold Cherniss (*Aristotle's Criticism of Plato and the Academy* [Baltimore, 1944], 1: 69–72).

47. Long before Robinson called into question Plato's consciousness of fallacy, R. G. Bury had written: "Consequently we ought to regard the fallacies unearthed by Grote, Apelt and others—the confusion between a thought and a thing, between the absolute and the relative, between the ambiguous senses of ὄν and μὴ ὄν, of ἕν and τἄλλα and ἐν and πρός—as all intentionally introduced to show the logical inaccuracy or dishonesty of the sophistic method of reasoning, and the consequent need on the part of tiros in philosophy of a cathartic process which should guard them from being misled by the dangerous arts of the eristic" ("The Later Platonism," *Journal of Philology* 23 [1895], 185).

48. Socrates interrupts the first eristic display before the brothers can do enough damage to instill misology in Kleinias. But this scene is designed to typify the kind of activity in which misology is nurtured; see *Phaedo* 89 D–90 C. The influence of these eristic disputes upon Ktesippus will lead within the dialogue itself to his complete eristification.

49. With this remark Socrates notes that eristic produces the wrong kind of wonder in its interlocutor (μὴ θαύμαζε). In fact, Euthydemus wants wonder directed toward himself in admiration for his power (276 D 4–5). In his protreptic address Socrates will counter the unfamiliar arguments (ἀήθεις) of eristic with familiar ones which evoke in Kleinias the true sense of philosophical wonder; see 279 D 7–8.

50. That Corybantic initiates were induced to yield to some force outside themselves is the important discovery of Ivan Linforth (*The Corybantic Rites in Plato,* University of California Publications in Classical Philology, vol. 13 [1946], esp. 133–134 and 156).

51. See ibid., pp. 134 and 156.

52. R. S. W. Hawtrey has noted that Socrates will conduct this initiation ("Plato, Socrates, and the Mysteries: A Note," *Antichthon* 10 [1976], 23, and *Commentary on Plato's Euthydemus* [Philadelphia, 1981], p. 71); cf. also A. W. H. Adkins ("Clouds, Mysteries, Socrates and Plato," *Antichthon* 4 [1970], 23) and Szlezák ("Socrates' Spott über Geheimhaltung," p. 79).

53. Yet Socrates does make it clear that he didn't want to hear Prodicus' wisdom. He wanted a protreptic discourse, which could have proceeded without sophistic rites. Shorey (*Selected Papers,* 1: 482), not Keulen (*UPE,* pp. 22–23), draws the correct conclusion regarding the role of Prodicus in this passage.

54. Aristotle obviously has this passage in mind when he uses μανθάνειν as his model for equivocation (*SE* 4.165 B 30–34). But, as Shorey has noted (*Selected Papers*, 1: 482), credit for distinguishing τὸ δισσόν, or the double meanings of words, falls to Plato.

55. We can speak of "occasions when" because of the pervasiveness of temporal indicators in this passage (ὅταν, ἐξ ἀρχῆς, ὕστερον, ἐπειδάν, ἤδη, ὅτε). Note that Plato must put his solution to the first eristic display in a context where it too becomes just one of Socrates' many techniques for exhorting Kleinias to pursue philosophy. If Aristotle's classifications and technical terms are mechanically applied to a subject matter, they can appear to be, in the words of Sprague, "a collection of dead butterflies" ("Logic and Literary Form in Plato," *Personalist* 48 [1967], 567–568).

56. Just as e.g., "figure" can apply to both the straight and to the round; see *Meno* 74 D–E. Once this lesson has been established for the first argument-pair, Socrates need only refer casually to the similarity of the second in order to secure his point. The disputed καὶ τὸ [ὄνομα] refers to the word in question, i.e., μανθάνειν, indicating that it too can be applied to objects (and not just subjects) in opposite states; see Keulen (*UPE*, pp. 22–25) and D. G. Stuart ("An Interpretation of Plato's *Euthydemus*" [Ph.D. diss., Yale University, 1980], pp. 62–65).

57. See Robinson, "Plato's Consciousness of Fallacy," pp. 102–103. Robinson treats Socrates' solution as if it were an example of ambiguity in Aristotle's sense, though it could not be appreciated as such "until Aristotle had done his work" (p. 109). Far from revealing Plato's awareness of the fallacy of equivocation, this use of μανθάνειν is "one of those crass ambiguities out of which puns are made" (p. 107). In his view, Socrates' solution is paradigmatic for Plato's "naive state of human beliefs about ambiguity" ("Ambiguity," p. 141), and, on the basis of this passage, he concludes that for Plato, "ambiguity is of no importance to the philosopher" ("Plato's Consciousness of Fallacy," p. 114).

58. In Stanford's terms, Plato is here using the type of ambiguity most closely associated with Sophocles, who makes his "characters use unconscious rather than deliberate ambiguities" (*Ambiguity*, p. 164). This type of ambiguity forms the basis for Keulen's thesis (from Shorey), that the *Euthydemus* is a repertory of early and late in which Plato reveals his own thought amid the antics of the brother-pair (*UPE*, p. 5).

59. Sprague has explained why it is not enough merely to note the equivocation in μανθάνειν: "The detection of a fallacy at one particular point in a dialogue is not of much value without an analysis of the role which that fallacy has to play in the development of the whole

argument in which it appears" ("Logic and Literary Form," p. 571). We will continue to examine the role of μανθάνειν throughout the dialogue.

60. Thus Kleinias himself becomes the perfect example of how one and the same subject can take on the contrary predicates wise and ignorant.

61. The use of the plural ὀνομάτων indicates that Socrates' analysis has a general and particular application: particular in that it applies specifically to the equivocation on μανθάνειν, general in that it applies to all equivocal terms which eristic uses.

62. Socrates does not allow us to forget that eristic is a form of παιδιά. In 278 B 2–D 1, he uses words for play seven times to characterize this eristic performance. Rather than play, Socrates wants serious instruction; see 278 C 3 (τὰ σπουδαῖα [μαθήματα]) and compare 283 B–C and 288 B–D. Throughout his writings Plato stigmatizes the activity of arguing theses as a self-indulgent form of play; see, e.g., *Apology* 27 A, *Theaetetus* 167 E and 169 C 9, and *Sophist* 237 BC.

TWO. SOCRATES' PROTREPTIC MODEL

1. See 278 C 7 and 282 D 5; for still earlier and later vocative addresses showing that the conversation between Socrates and the brothers is maintained throughout, see 273 C 3, 274 A 2, 274 D 4, 288 A 2–3, and 303 C 6–7.

2. See 275 C 5 and 283 A 1.

3. For what can happen when a critic separates the second episode from the rest of the *Euthydemus* and then uses this part to pronounce upon the meaning and significance of the whole, see Michael Ferejohn, "Socratic Thought-Experiments and the Unity of Virtue Paradox," *Phronesis* 29 (1984), 109, 115, and 117–118.

4. See 278 D 5–7: ἀπαντοσχεδιάσαι and ἰδιωτικῶς; see also 282 D 6.

5. See 288 A 6–7: ἀκρίβειαν λόγων.

6. Kleinias takes control of the λόγος at 289 D 2 and guides it until 290 D 8, where Crito challenges the verisimilitude of Socrates' narration.

7. For an outline of the argumentation that informs Socrates' protreptic address, see A. J. Festugière (*Les Trois "Protreptiques" de Platon: Euthydème, Phédon, Epinomis* [Paris, 1973], pp. 25–31) and R. K. Sprague (*Plato's Philosopher-King* [Columbia, S.C., 1976], pp. 48–51).

8. See 278 E 4–5: καταγέλαστον καὶ ἀνόητον.

9. Gregory Vlastos uses Socrates' inescapable question as an occa-

sion to catapult outside the dialogue frame and to establish a biographical fact in the development of Plato's thought, which proves, according to him, that the *Euthydemus* "breaks with the modalities of elenctic argument" ("The Socratic Elenchus," *Oxford Studies in Ancient Philosophy*, 1 [1983], 58). In another context, Vlastos again uses this passage in the *Euthydemus* to leap from the effect to the cause and to posit "a profound change in Plato himself," which requires, in his view, that our dialogue postdate the *Gorgias* and antedate the *Meno* (*Socrates, Ironist and Moral Philosopher* [Ithaca, 1991], pp. 116–118). But it should be clear by now that the evidence he advances does not prove his case. There is no need to go to the extreme of hypothesizing "a profound change in Plato himself," when there is a much more obvious reason why Plato uses this occasion to set forth this universal proposition: he wants to distinguish, as sharply as possible, this Socratic beginning from that of the brothers. We must resist treating the *Euthydemus* as nothing more than a steppingstone from here to there, from this to that. In the *Euthydemus* our author has arrived.

10. We are not to suppose that the task of recollecting eristic wisdom is really difficult. The surface denotation of "so immense (ἀμήχανον ὅσην)" has beneath it the real meaning of "without means" or "resource." Socrates' ironical remark is just one of the many indications that the logical problems of eristic never presented Plato with significant difficulties.

11. In this regard we should also note that Socrates cannot establish with certainty either the *origin* of the eristic masters themselves (271 C 2–3), or *when* they began to study eristic (272 B 9–10).

12. All artists must establish a necessary or probable order for the action of their work. Whenever it becomes difficult to achieve this for some reason, Greek authors frequently circumvented the problem by invoking the Muses. By its conventional signification, then, this invocation informs us that Socrates faces a random collection of details, haphazard in their nature, but one that he will order for the unity of his narration.

13. Surely Socrates means that this question offers greater room for foolishness and naivete (εὐηθέστερον). The many, for example, would affirm it immediately, since they tend to identify happiness with good things, and especially with good fortune (279 C 7–8).

14. Socrates' emphasis falls on whether the classification of psychic goods will be done *correctly*. His use of ὀρθῶς adds a significant nuance, for it looks forward to the correctness component in knowledge. Consider the similar nuance given by ὀρθῶς in ὀρθῶς πράττειν (280 A 8) and by the six uses of ὀρθῶς or μὴ ὀρθῶς with χρῆσθαι

(280 E 3–281 A 8, 282 A 4). The adverb appears in participial form in κατορθοῦσα at 281 B 1 and finally in the noun ὀρθότητα 282 A 4; cf. 288 D 9.

15. οἱ σοφοί has been used eight times, σοφώ three, and σοφισταί and πάσσοφοι once each.

16. See 305 D 4–5 (σοφίας πέρι); for more combat over wisdom, see *Philebus* 49 A ff. That the attainment of wisdom is a crucial issue of the *Euthydemus* is the original intuition behind Vanhoutte's dissertation ("La Notion de la Σοφία d'après l'*Euthydème* de Platon" [Ph.D. diss., Louvain, 1942]).

17. The *locus classicus* for the discussion of this passage is to be found in Hermann Bonitz (*Platonische Studien* [Berlin, 1886], pp. 96–97 and esp. n. 4). He quite rightly, I think, has pointed to the ambiguity in εὐτυχία by suggesting that it means "das gute Glück" at 279 C 7, and then shifts toward "das richtige Treffen" at 279 D 6, and finally, when Socrates introduces τυγχάνειν at 280 A 8, it has come to mean "die Fähigkeit das Richtige zu treffen" because "Einsicht" governs it.

18. As such, it can allow them to fare well without having to strive for wisdom, so long as the events of which it is the cause turn out "well" for the individual. Socrates may then be hinting at the hypocrisy in the wholly subjective response to fortune on the part of the φαῦλοι.

19. Cf. Bonitz (*Platonische Studien*, p. 97 n. 4); "In dem gewöhnlichen Sprachgebrauche bezeichnet εὐτυχία das günstige Zusammentreffen von Umständen, die von dem handelnden Subjecte nicht abhängig sind"; cf. *Meno* 99 A and Aristotle's *Rhetoric* 1.5.1361 B 39 ff.

20. For a host of contemporary thinkers, chance and wisdom (and their various synonyms) formed a standard opposition. If this opposition is not overcome, then pure chance, as a cause of goods, can seriously endanger the success of a protreptic. For, without effort, one can imagine that he has attained our universal goal by just being lucky.

21. Similarly, what would make it bad is whether the events turn out "badly (δυστυχῶς)" for someone.

22. Cf. 276 D 6–7. Here Socrates' remark shows how his paradigm works on two levels; his questioning guides Kleinias, even as it qualifies the action of the brothers.

23. It is easy to miss the import of γνούς (279 D 8), which has a clearly defined, dialectical significance. It reveals Socrates' awareness of Kleinias' true needs, that he has been quickened for the inquiry and is ready to move on. Of similar significance are the uses of γνούς at 275 D 7 and 277 D 2; see also ἔγνων at 295 D 1 and 303 E 7. For the

eristic perversion of the "awareness" signified by γνούς, see 276 D 3 and 287 D 2.

24. Cf. 276 A 5.

25. This is Socrates' way of encouraging us not to go chasing after counterexamples.

26. Cf. 277 B 1 (ἐπίστασαι and μανθάνεις) with 280 A 1–3 (μετέχοις and κινδυνεύοις).

27. It is of some historical interest to note that not only does Aristotle use an argument of this type to illustrate induction (*Topics* 1.12.105 A 10–19), but that the argument itself is as old as Homer (*Iliad* 23, 315–325).

28. Cf. *Republic* 340 E. A wisdom that never errs is precisely what eristic pretends to be.

29. This is the first mention of error, a concept that will reappear toward the end of this protreptic (281 C 1) and become quite significant in the third episode (287 A and E).

30. Nor does Socrates probe any possible connection between error and good fortune's antonym, bad fortune (δυστυχία); but see 281 C 1–2.

31. This break in Socrates' questioning and one other (281 D 1–2) help to give the protreptic its unprofessional, unsystematic tone.

32. Συνωμολογησάμεθα stresses the cooperative effort involved in achieving this final agreement. Socrates' success is linked to Kleinias'.

33. In this regard, see Aristotle's *Topics* 1.2.101 A 30–34.

34. The focusing device that Plato has here roughly imitated has come to be called *priamel;* its importance for the choral poetry of Pindar has been demonstrated by Elroy Bundy (*Studia Pindarica* [Berkeley, 1986], p. 5.). Because this device selects one object for special attention, it is perfectly suited to elevate σοφία to its place of primary significance. That the priamel is a poetic form of inductive argument has been shown by John Kirby (*Classical Journal* 80 [1985], 142–144), and how extensively it is used by classical authors has been treated by William Race (*The Classical Priamel from Homer to Boethius* [Leiden, 1982]).

35. The ἄν with εὐδαιμονεῖν is not a new addition; it was present in Socrates' second question (279 A 2). In fact, all hypotheses of this protreptic, except three (280 E 3–6, 281 D 6–8, and 282 C 1), are in the optative mood, and Socrates will continue to use ideal conditions in the fourth episode. Note too that Socrates has expanded εἴη (279 A 3) to παρείη (280 B 6); he can do so under the influence of παρούσης and παρῇ at 280 B 2.

36. This fact does not preclude the possibility that εὖ πράττειν at

278 E 3 can still retain its active sense of "to succeed." For example, Waterfield has recently used "success," "successful," and "to be successful" to translate the uses of εὖ πράττειν in Socrates' protreptic (*Early Socratic Dialogues* [Harmondsworth, 1987], pp. 327–330). It is part of Plato's purpose here to hold together both senses of this pivotal term.

37. The ambiguity in ἔργον might pass unnoticed. The word refers both to the activity and to the result of the activity of craftsmen. As such, it corresponds nicely to the two senses of εὖ πράττειν.

38. Soon we shall find Socrates performing a similar operation on κακῶς πράττειν (281 C 2), a point that Sprague has made with much clarity (Sprague, *Translation*, p. 19 n. 26).

39. Πλοῦτος again has the emphatic position, as it does at 279 A 7 and 281 A 7. It is replaced by χρήματα at 282 A 8 and by χρυσίον at 288 E 3.

40. Even the similarity in the sentence structure reinforces this close relationship between εὖ πράττειν and εὐδαιμονεῖν; cf. ἆρ' ἂν οὗτοι εὖ πράττοιεν διὰ τὴν κτῆσιν (280 C 6) with ἆρ' ἂν εὐδαιμονοῖ διὰ τὴν τούτων κτῆσιν (280 D 3–4).

41. Socrates also reveals his excitement at having reached this plane by shifting from the ideal to the anticipatory condition and by using the neutral term πράγματι for what were formerly called goods.

42. I have translated the participles of this question into the form of the ideal condition in order to indicate that for the downward path Socrates is continuing to use the hypothetical method.

43. Socrates is obviously indifferent to what term he uses (whether ἐπιστήμη, σοφία, φρόνησις, or νοῦς), provided his meaning is clear.

44. To see how Aristotle would analyze Socrates' protreptic, consider *Topics* 1.11.104 B 1-20. By making so-called goods good accidentally, while predicating good essentially of wisdom, Socrates, a man famous in philosophy, has formed a thesis, or a conception contrary to general opinion, and is now using it to guide his interlocutor to make a choice that will entail both pursuit and avoidance.

45. This exhortation "to become wise (σοφὸν γενέσθαι)", which Socrates and Kleinias have arrived at through patient inquiry, will provide "by accident" the trigger for (D3).

46. After having spent no little effort in picturing how wisdom can be taught, Plato presents the acceptance of the hypothesis on its teachability as if it had suddenly welled up in the consciousness of the young Kleinias, a flash of insight that causes our protreptic master to feel pleasure (ἡσθείς: 282 C 5).

47. See *Symposium* 204 A–B.

48. See *Phaedrus* 276 E 6: ψυχὴν προσήκουσαν.

49. See *Republic* 521 C 5–8; for the περιαγωγή, see *Republic* 518 B–519 B.

THREE. THE SECOND ERISTIC DISPLAY

1. R. S. W. Hawtrey (*Commentary on Plato's Euthydemus* [Philadelphia, 1981], p. 94) and R. K. Sprague (*Plato's Use of Fallacy* [London, 1962], p. 13).

2. Sprague, *Plato's Use of Fallacy*, pp. 13–14.

3. The structuring principle is thus: ὁμοίωσις τοῖν ξένοιν. Socrates notes that the brothers only care for those who are like (ὁμοίων) themselves and that only men like (ὅμοιοι) the brothers would approve of their eristic arguments (303 D 1–3).

4. See *Phaedo* 90 C and G. B. Kerferd, *The Sophistic Movement* (Cambridge, 1981), p. 66.

5. It is now clear why Ferejohn is wrong to assert that "the *Euthydemus* reveals no interest on Socrates' part in metaphysical issues" and to complain about Socrates' "almost willful indifference to metaphysics and epistemology" ("Socratic Thought-Experiments and the Unity of Virtue Paradox," *Phronesis* 29 [1984], 115 and 117). Unlike the brothers, Socrates shows his good sense in avoiding such problems in his protreptic address, which he has tailored to fit the needs of the young Kleinias.

6. The phrase "conversion to logic" simply labels the process by which the brothers abstract responses from their given context, juggle them about as mere terms or linguistic items, and finally reshape them into weapons for verbal combat; cf. Aristotle's notion of transference (μετενεγκεῖν: *SE* 11.172 A 4).

7. To Dionysodorus' trigger question Socrates could have responded simply "Yes, we are serious." But Plato allows us to penetrate into Socrates' thought where we find him pondering the possibility of error in his own understanding (283 B 8–10). This little scene points forward to where the possibility of error in thought is ruled out of existence (287 A) and to where the problem of misunderstanding between interlocutors finally surfaces (295 C).

8. Socrates frequently repeats his interlocutor's position at the beginning of an elenchus in order to eliminate any confusion (e.g., *Gorgias* 474 B–C). Dionysodorus has made an apparently similar move for an eristic purpose.

9. Edwin H. Gifford, *The Euthydemus of Plato*, rev. ed. (Oxford, 1905), p. 28 nn.

10. To clarify this matter further, we can analyze Dionysodorus' statement at 283 D 2–3 in the following way:

    a. You want him, who does not exist, to come into being.
    b. You want him to become (a person) that he is not.
    c. You want him, who now exists, no longer to be.
    d. You want him no longer to be (the person) that he is now.

Dionysodorus wants Socrates to "hear" and therefore agree with (b) and (d) so that in his fourth question he can slide to (c) and then cap "no longer to be" with "to perish."

11. See R. K. Sprague, "Logic and Literary Form in Plato," *Personalist* 48 [1967], 565–566, and "Plato's Sophistry (II)," *Aristotelian Society Suppl.* vol. 51 [1977], pp. 49–50, for how Plato could illustrate such solutions.

12. Notice the rhetorical force of the optatives (εἶεν and ποιήσαιντο) by which he coyly feigns embarrassment over the impact of his capping term.

13. By reaching out with his claws and seizing upon numerous bits from Socrates' protreptic, Dionysodorus illustrates how he will later earn the epithet "Crab" (297 C 4); for φίλοι τε καὶ ἐρασταί, cf. 282 B 1–2; for πολλοῦ ἄξιοι and περὶ παντὸς ποιήσαιντο, see 282 E 5 and 275 A 9. With the mention of "beloved," we may imagine that Dionysodorus grins from ear to ear at Ktesippus; see 275 E 4.

14. Here we have a standard eristic trick. Dionysodorus has reduced the important topic of wisdom and its acquisition to something trivial; cf. *Phaedrus* 267 A–B.

15. Ktesippus passes by the injustice of the remark and goes directly to the impiety done to the deity Eros. His expression "same to you" looks forward to ἀπόλωλε (300 D 5) where Ktesippus playfully destroys Dionysodorus in argument. Here, however, he is deadly serious; note the personal language: μου . . . ἐγὼ οἶμαι . . . ὡς ἐγὼ . . . βουλοίμην; he uses personal references again at 284 E 7–9.

16. Thus, the first move in the eristification process is to separate the subject from its attachment to its object.

17. In studying these two arguments we should remember that behind them stands the very real problem of falsehood, which Plato takes up in duly constituted contexts in other works; see, e.g., *Sophist* 236 E. But here in the *Euthydemus* Plato is satirizing the use of this topic in an improper context.

18. With this quick turn on the part of Euthydemus to club Ktesippus with the λόγος, we see that the brothers were all along intending to pounce upon anyone who came to Kleinias' defense; cf. *Lysis* 216

A – B and *Theaetetus* 165 B – E. The use of δοκεῖ in the trigger question is significant. Euthydemus is asking, in effect, whether Ktesippus holds as *true* the opinion (δόξα) that falsehood is true and real. Later in this episode (286 D), eristic will rule out of existence not only false opinion but opinion as such.

19. Euthydemus is aided in this move by the habit of the Greek language to drop prefixes from compound verbs when they are repeated after their first occurrence. So to drop κατά from ψεύδεσθαι can appear quite natural.

20. Aristotle notes that this trick, which Euthydemus has used for injecting the falsehood topic into the debate, has recently come under attack because eristics are now asked: "What does this have to do with the original point (τί τοῦτο πρὸς τὸ ἐν ἀρχῇ)?" (*SE* 12.172 B 21). Had Ktesippus asked Euthydemus what his question on falsehood has to do with Dionysodorus' rude accusation, he would have disrupted the transition from the inescapable question to the inescapable argument. But it is too early in the dramatic action for Ktesippus to employ such a strategy.

21. Λέγειν τι contains a crucial ambiguity; "to speak a thing" can mean (1) to speak about the subject matter of a λόγος or (2) simply to speak a verbal utterance or sentence; see *Sophist* 237 D and F. M. Cornford (*Plato's Theory of Knowledge* [London, 1935], p. 205). As (E4) and (E5) develop, Ktesippus will adhere to (1), and Euthydemus to (2).

22. By replacing αὐτό with ἐκεῖνο, Euthydemus gains a distinct advantage. Since ἐκεῖνο refers to a more remote object, he can more easily slide away from the concrete context (πρᾶγμα), which limits Ktesippus' indictment, to the notion of the real embedded in τὸ ὄν.

23. For this trick, see the *Topics* 8.2.158 A 7–13; *SE* 15.174 B 8–11, 38–40; and *Rhetoric* 3.18.1419 B 1. By putting the conclusion in the form of a statement, Euthydemus creates the illusion that the reasoning has been completed.

24. The labels predicative, existential, veridical, and factual are used for the sake of convenience; see C. H. Kahn's important article "The Greek Verb 'To Be' and the Concept of Being," *Foundations of Language* 2 (1966), 245–65.

25. G. J. De Vries is certainly right to point out that οὐδαμοῦ can carry the sense of "in no way" ("Notes on Some Passages in the *Euthydemus*," *Mnemosyne* 25 [1972], 47). But here its primary sense is "nowhere," as we discover when Euthydemus caps it by submitting a locus before the people (ἐν τῷ δήμῳ). The "modal tinge," as De Vries calls it, is first introduced with ὅπως at 284 B 5.

26. The translation of this difficult line (284 B 6) and the one below (284 C 4) follows Gifford (*Euthydemus*, pp. 30–31 nn.).

27. With the introduction of κατὰ τὸν σὸν λόγον, Euthydemus tries to create the illusion that, out of his own mouth, Ktesippus has established the antithesis of (E4), that it is impossible to falsify.

28. We must not underrate the significance of Ktesippus' response; not only has he given a quasi-existence to saying things which are not (τὰ ὄντα μὲν τρόπον τινὰ λέγει), but here (and later, at 284 D 1–2) he has also articulated the equivalent to the definition of a true and false λόγος in the *Cratylus* (385 B–C); see Harold Cherniss, *Selected Papers* (Leiden, 1977), p. 341.

29. In other words, eristic can be viewed as just another species of rhetoric, as indeed is suggested by *Phaedrus* 261 D.

30. Ktesippus first introduced the modal requirement with two expressions τρόπον τινά and ὡς. Now Dionysodorus has capped them by stating it interrogatively with πῶς.

31. Τὸ κακῶς λέγειν is a highly ambiguous expression; cf., e.g., *Meno* 95 A, where Socrates points out that Anytus is ignorant of what *speaking ill* means. Κακῶς in this expression can be translated "critically," "poorly," "maliciously," "untruthfully," and "ignorantly."

32. See the *Gorgias* 473 E 2–3 and Aristotle's *Rhetoric* 3.18.1419 B 5.

33. The force of this response has not been appreciated. At the very least Plato has put it into Ktesippus' mouth in order to stigmatize eristics as heartless and insensitive debaters and to label their pseudological arguments as the distasteful jokes of second-rate comedians.

34. From the moment he entered the debate, Ktesippus has spoken the truth, as he sees it. But his remarks, true though they be, can also be inappropriate or even rude and abusive, if they overstate "how" things are. To illustrate this problem, how Ktesippus' personal commitment to the content of the debate has distorted his judgement, Plato finally has him burst forth with repeated uses of the first person pronoun (ἔγωγε . . . ἐμοῦ . . . ἐγώ) and first person verbs (φιλῶ . . . νουθετῶ . . . πειρῶμαι . . . βούλομαι . . . ποιοῦμαι); cf. these remarks with those of his earlier outburst (283 E 1–6).

35. This intervention continues the theme already established (277 D) that a dialectician must know when to break off a discussion; cf. 288 B. Finally, it is Socrates who tells us how things really hold; the disputants are behaving "more rudely (ἀγριωτέρως . . . ἔχειν)." He must use the comparative here, for they began acting rudely at 283 E 2; cf. *Meno* 75 D for the unfriendly nature of eristic discourse.

36. Thus Socrates counters eristic play by demonstrating a proper use of play. There may be good reasons to differ over words if they

are real indices to things. But here Socrates' point is simply not to differ over "mere" words; cf. *Meno* 87 B–C and *Charmides* 163 D. Eristic, however, is a form of argumentation that attacks mere words (κατὰ ὀνόματα); see *Republic* 454 A.

37. On the pseudo-problem of whether the brothers found or learned their skill, this passage cannot be used to suggest that Protagoras is the founder of eristic (Gifford, *Euthydemus,* p. 31 nn; and Hawtrey, *Commentary,* p. 105). At 285 A 8–B 1, Socrates is simply using a formula; see *Theaetetus* 150 D, *Laches* 186 E, and *Phaedo* 85 C and 99 C.

38. Thus, παραδίδωμι (285 C 3) prepares the way for Socrates' re-entry into the debate before Ktesippus' silence, together with wonder, brings him in officially (286 B 7–8). With the introduction of Medea, we find the first allusion to the sophist as mythic figure.

39. See 283 E 1: ἠγανάκτησεν.

40. See, e.g., Demosthenes 40. 32: ἐξ ἀντιλογίας καὶ λοιδορίας. It is also possible that Ktesippus is guilty of both; he can be delivering "abusive contradiction."

41. The introduction of ποιῇ τοὺς λόγους should cause us to reflect back upon 284 B 5–C 6. Dionysodorus is going to reject the possibility of contradiction on the ground that one cannot "make" what is not actually exist (τὸ μὴ ὂν μὴ οἷόν τ᾽ εἶναι μηδένα ποιεῖν); cf. 286 A 2 (μηδένα λέγοντα ὡς οὐκ ἔστι).

42. Ἀντιλέγω πρὸς ταῦτα ἅ μοι δοκεῖ πρός με μὴ καλῶς λέγειν.

43. (E4) and (E5) illustrated how easily an interlocutor can become entangled unawares in eristic controversy. Now (D7) reveals how difficult it is for an interlocutor to avoid eristic, even after he has been warned "not to differ over a mere word"; cf. *Republic* 454 A.

44. According to *Phaedrus* (261 C–E), ἀντιλογικοί have the ability, by science, to make the same thing appear to the same people, now just, now unjust, now good, now bad. So too our two-headed Palamedes can make one and the same affair appear to one and the same group, now a contradiction and now not a contradiction.

45. Cf. 274 D 2–3: ἐπιδείξασθαι τὴν δύναμιν τῆς σοφίας.

46. See 284 C 2–3. Although the status of the "thing" is never clarified, we can ascertain from (E4) that it is one distinct thing, apart from others (284 A). So too is the λόγος that corresponds to it.

47. Ktesippus can still be thinking that contradiction arises between one person asserting X, another Y; X states how or that the thing is, Y how or that it *is not* (i.e., how or that it is *other than* or *different from* X). Ktesippus need not be thinking that Y attempts to assert the existence of the absolutely unreal.

48. This very narrow sense of the impossibility of contradiction does not allow for the soul to be in contradiction with itself (a favorite theme of Plato's) or for two souls to be contradicting each other without articulating in words the sense in which they are opposed. As experience teaches, this form of contradiction often leads to very bitter hostility; cf., e.g., Ktesippus' silence at 286 B 7 with his eruption at 288 A 8–B 2.

49. The denial of the possibility of contradiction is for Aristotle the star example of a dialectical thesis (*Topics* 1.11.104 B 19–21). Here Plato undermines the seriousness of its defense by putting it in the mouth of someone who is not famous as a philosopher. For a delightful modern parody that captures the spirit of (D7), see "The Argument Clinic" (*The Second Monty Python's Flying Circus,* Paramount Home Video, 1970).

50. The undertone of ἐχρῶντο (286 C 2) suggests that those about Protagoras have misused this argument by doing violence (σφόδρα) to it.

51. Again, we should not be surprised to find Dionysodorus lurking about this vague region of unreality; cf. *Sophist* 236 D–E (εἰς ἄπορον εἶδος).

52. See *Cratylus* 430 A. Euthydemus will treat Socrates' παραφθέγματα (296 A–B) as mere noise.

53. So whatever can pass through one's mind and receive formulation in speech is true and real. A more sophisticated disputant might want to add the Protagorean qualification, "at least, to the person who so formulates it," but Dionysodorus does not fortify his position with this addition.

54. To capture the full force of λόγος and λέγειν in Socrates' question, we can translate it literally as follows: "For the sake of *argument,* Dionysodorus, do you *argue* your *argument* in order *to argue* an outlandish *argument,* or truly in your opinion is no one ignorant?"

55. Socrates must consider this possibility, for there is a sense in which no one is ignorant, if by "ignorant" one means absolutely ignorant.

56. Plato has the brothers construct their "epideictic context" beyond good and evil so that they can argue merely for the sake of argument in much the same way that modern artists present art merely for the sake of art; see Keulen (*UPE,* pp. 64–65).

57. Plato will give us the complete picture of this "epideictic context," in which the eristic pseudo-science of argument finally attains its τέλος, in the fifth episode (298 B 4–300 D 9).

58. This activity of arguing for the sake of argument should not be

confused with the serious, approbative sense that Plato occasionally gives to ἀδολεσχία; see *Phaedrus* 270 A and *Parmenides* 135 D.

59. Cf. *Meno* 75 D for the unfriendly eristic challenge to refute.

60. If refutation is impossible, then the chief activity of eristic is abolished. As Heinz Neitzel has noted, an elenchus is impossible unless we assume the existence of not-being; see "Platon, Euthydemos 286e," *Hermes* 112 (1984), 373.

61. We should not miss the ironical inversion intended by this remark. Socrates fails to understand (μανθάνω) their arguments because they are so stupid and poorly established (τὰ ἀμαθῆ καὶ κακῶς ἔχοντα); they are, quite simply, bad arguments, nothing more than words for the sake of words which Socrates can only roughly conceive in his mind (παχέως πως ἐννοῶ).

62. At 287 A 8, τίνος refers on the one hand to the student of instruction (τῷ ἐθέλοντι μανθάνειν) and on the other to the subject matter (ἀρετήν). Here we see a still clearer sense in which the brothers betray virtue (ἀρετὴν παραδοῦναι). Their conception of "philosophy" leaves them no excellence to impart and no one to impart it to.

63. This attack may be called Socrates' existential elenchus, aimed at calling into question the very existence of the brothers in Athens. But aware of its personal features, Socrates apologizes before introducing it by suggesting that it has arisen from his rough (παχέως) grasp of their positions.

64. Here Plato is considering time and its relevance to discourse. Expressions such as "now," "just now," "at first," "last year," and "at the present moment" should lead us to ponder the connection between "time" and the "significance" of a speaker's statements; cf. *Meno* 89 C and *Theaetetus* 158 D 11–12. For Socrates, because the claim to teach virtue is so significant, it remains and has remained present to his mind ever since Euthydemus first uttered it (273 D 8). To Dionysodorus, on the other hand, that boast was said "at first" and is no longer relevant to what is being said "at the present moment."

65. In his book *Toward the Soul* (Yale University Press, 1981) David Claus has remarked: "There is, obviously, in this exchange a decisive pun on the division of animative and cognitive aspects of ψυχή" (p. 174). The eristic trick Dionysodorus has used to pull off this pun is most illuminating. By positioning the equivocal ψυχή in such a way as to balance ἄψυχα, he has forced "soul" to slide to its animative aspect.

66. Cf. 275 E 5–6: ὁπότερ᾽ ἂν ἀποκρίνηται ὁ Διονυσόδωρος, ἐξελεγχθήσεται. Contrary to Gregory Vlastos, who denies that the *Euthydemus* contains the "methodological novelties" of the *Meno* ("The Socratic Elenchus," *Oxford Studies in Ancient Philosophy* 1 [1983], 58),

Wincenty Lutoslawski sees in Socrates' refutation "the hypothetical method taught in the *Meno*" (*The Origin and Growth of Plato's Logic* [London, 1897], p. 211).

67. The habit of inquiring with too much precision, unless required for some specific purpose, is a sign of illiberality (*Theaetetus* 184 C). In this detail, too, Plato continues to stigmatize the brothers with a quality undesirable in philosophers; see *Republic* 486 A and Aristotle's *Metaphysics* 995 A 9–15.

68. Comic inversion, analogous to comic repetition, is, according to Henri Bergson, one of the universal structuring principles in all comic action. As he says: "We meet with hundreds of variations on the theme of the robber robbed. In every case the root idea involves an inversion of roles, and a situation which recoils on the head of its author ("Laughter," in *Comedy*, ed. Wylie Sypher [Baltimore, [1986], p. 122).

69. Here is one of Plato's masterly touches. It may have escaped even the most careful reader that Ktesippus, who now insults these two "Thurians" or "Chians" (288 B 1), was never told about the origins of the brothers (cf. also 283 E 2). Socrates informed Crito of this fact at 271 C 3, but no such information has been given to Ktesippus. Rather, as Plato frequently does, he allows young men to have such information by rumor; cf. *Charmides* 156 A and *Theaetetus* 148 E–149 A.

70. This is one way for eristic dueling to end, in abuse and quarreling, with the disputants unable to part as friends; cf. *Gorgias* 457 D.

71. In portraying the brothers in this manner, Plato has given to eristic a quasi-existence (εἶναί πως). As Charles Bigger notes (*Participation: A Platonic Inquiry* [Baton Rouge, 1968]), "*Euthydemus* . . . is very much like the fantasy of Lewis Carroll, an imaginative representation of the look of a world devoid of logical laws, especially contradiction and identity, and expresses the thesis, at least by inference, that logic must have its foundation in ontology" (pp. 58–59). "Philosophers such as Wittgenstein are very much mistaken, as both Carroll and Plato demonstrate, when they claim one cannot talk about an illogical world; they very much underestimate the power of the human imagination" (p. 58 n. 34).

FOUR. THE PROTREPTIC CONTINUES

1. For the first two interruptions, see 277 D and 285 A. This act of "calming down" (κατεπράυνον: 288 B 3) refers back to 285 A 3 (προσέπαιζον) and continues the theme that the serious dialectician must know how to use play correctly.

2. With μιμεῖσθον and γοητεύοντε (288 B 8), cf. *Sophist* 235 A 8, where the beast is called γόης καὶ μιμητής. Γοητεύοντε is important because it replaces παίζοντε and so further defines the antithesis between play and seriousness.

3. Ktesippus, however, will imitate not Menelaus, but the brothers themselves; see μιμεῖσθαι, 303 E 8.

4. Thomas Alexander Szlezák's thesis is thus confirmed: "Der wahre Esoteriker nennt die falschen Philosophen höhnisch 'Esoteriker.' Die Handlung des Dialogs erweist schrittweise, dass Euthydemos und Dionysodoros nichts im Hintergrund haben, womit sie ihren λόγοι 'zu Hilfe kommen' (sie 'retten') könnten" ("Sokrates' Spott über Geheimhaltung: Zum Bild des φιλόσοφος in Platons *Euthydemos*," *Antike und Abendland* 26 [1980], 84–85).

5. To confirm this observation, cf. 288 C 6–D 1 (ὅθεν and τὸ ἐξῆς) with 282 E 1. It should also be noted that Socrates will continue to guide (ὑφηγήσασθαι) the brothers by presenting them with a model for imitation (288 C 5–6).

6. By κτῆσις, Socrates does not mean some concrete thing that can be handed over or inherited, but an activity or process by which the possessor continually puts his acquired knowledge to use. He who does so correctly (ὀρθῶς) must therefore benefit from its use.

7. The topic of music has already surfaced several times; see 279 E 1–2, 276 A 5, 272 C 2–5. At 289 C 1–4, Socrates not only provides Kleinias with the linguistic tools to reject the logic-art (289 D 4–7) but also foreshadows his own use of logical division (289 E 5–290 A 4).

8. Ὑπολαβών (289 C 9) signals that Kleinias is about to take control of the argument for the first time; cf. 294 B 11. Socrates' call for evidence has an antecedent; see 289 B 3.

9. Thus, in this serious protreptic context Plato portrays how easily an answerer may respond on the basis of only a partial grasp of the question before this problem is treated explicitly in an eristic context; see 295 B–C, esp. C 4–6.

10. Kleinias caps this use of ζητοῦμεν with ζητητέον at 290 D 8, and then the notion of inquiry quickly surfaces several times; see 291 A 8, A 9, C 1, C 2, C 10; and 293 D 4. Eristic, by contrast, is not a ζήτησις at all.

11. Although the full articulation of this science would require extensive references to other dialogues, especially to the *Phaedrus* and *Republic*, we have here a concealed reference to the true rhetoric; see Paul Friedländer (*Plato*, 2d ed. [Princeton, 1969], 2: pp. 190–191) and Szlezák ("Sokrates' Spott über Geheimhaltung," p. 83).

12. This passage also provides a unifying link that refers forward

to the more extensive treatment of this problem in the epilogue; see esp. 305 B 4–9. Here, in the midst of a work that primarily treats the clash between eristic and dialectic, Plato reminds us of another hostile clique, just as deadly to philosophy as eristic.

13. Thus Hans Von Arnim: "absolut überflüssig" (*Platos Jugenddialoge* [Leipzig, 1914], p. 130). He does see, however, that we are to join this passage with the one at the end (305 B) where Crito introduces the semi-philosopher.

14. At 289 E 5, ὑποδεεστέρα may also suggest that logic-production does not extend as far as wizardry. In this list a key item is ὄχλων. Both at the beginning and at the end (271 A 2 and 304 D 9), Crito tells Socrates that his access to philosophy was blocked by the "crowd."

15. Logic-production as a branch of the science of wizards, with its ends of "enchantment" and "consolation," is an ironical reference to conventional rhetoric, with its goal of persuasion.

16. The playful use of this rhetorical device, which can be found throughout tragedy and oratory (e.g., *Medea* 502 and Lysias 29.2), is another indication that Socrates is not ignorant of the solution to the riddle. The charm of Socrates' remark will cease, however, the moment we recall how often rhetoricians do turn to the military for a solution to their problems. At this point we should remember that before they perfected eristic the brothers were military and forensic masters (271 D 1–272 B 1).

17. Plato allows the science of hunting to come forth from Kleinias' mind as if he had suddenly grasped the superordinate genus; cf. 282 C 4–5. The boy can intuit the art of hunting because he is not just exploring the intricacies of language but tracking down and searching for something real, exterior to his mind.

18. Plato will contrast Kleinias' behavior in this regard by having Ktesippus employ the brothers' moves as fast as they can generate them; see 298 B 4–300 D 9.

19. These cooks are users, not producers as the -ποιοί termination may suggest. Plato has exercised great care in putting ὀψοποιοῖς in Kleinias' mouth, thereby prompting us to reflect back upon the λογοποιοί to consider whether they, too, may be users.

20. The translation of this passage is difficult. Beginning with the first γάρ at 290 C 2, I take the Greek to mean: "Since they too are hunters [and not just producers, as one might suspect], for they are not engaged in producing figures and proofs, but in discovering realities (τὰ ὄντα)"; see Harold Cherniss, *Selected Papers* (Leiden, 1977), p. 249.

21. Kleinias' use of ἀνευρίσκουσιν caps Socrates' use of ηὑρηκέναι at 290 A 9.

22. Thus Cherniss: "the *Euthydemus* says not that the geometer should refrain from constructing figures but that in doing so his purpose is not to create the figures that he constructs but to hunt down those that already and truly exist" (*Selected Papers*, p. 251).

23. See *Republic* 527 B 7–8: "Geometry is the knowledge of the eternally existent (τοῦ γὰρ ἀεὶ ὄντος ἡ γεωμετρικὴ γνῶσίς ἐστιν)"; cf. *Republic* 510 D–E.

24. Who are these διαλεκτικοί or "masters of philosophical argument," as Gregory Vlastos calls them ("Elenchus and Mathematics: A Turning-Point in Plato's Philosophical Development," *American Journal of Philology* 109 [1988], 385; or *Socrates, Ironist and Moral Philosopher* [Ithaca, 1991], pp. 127–128)? Our analysis indicates that they are the opposite of the ἐριστικοί. But at the very least, it would seem to be incumbent upon the partisans of developmentalism to explain what sense "dialecticians" can possibly have in this passage before the *Meno* exists. Until they offer such an explanation consistent with the whole of the *Euthydemus* and not just with its Socratic portions, we hold to our position that this reference to "dialecticians" is a sphragis that unquestionably marks the *Euthydemus* as mature.

25. Richard Robinson (*Plato's Earlier Dialectic*, 2d ed. [Oxford, 1953], p. 74) and R. K. Sprague (*Translation*, p. 35 n. 56). But see R. S. W. Hawtrey ("How Do Dialecticians Use Diagrams—Plato, *Euthydemus* 290b–c," *Apeiron* 12 [1978], 14–18) and esp. A. E. Taylor (*PMW*, p. 98 n. 1).

26. On this point, Cherniss has remarked: "This view of the nature of mathematical reasoning and its objects, the doctrine that the meaning of the entities which the mathematician discovers is not his province but that of the dialectician, and the concomitant distinction between mathematician and dialectician remained firm and unaltered convictions of Plato's at least from the period during which he wrote the *Euthydemus* to that of the last of his writings, the *Philebus* and the *Laws*" (*Selected Papers*, p. 252).

27. Thus C. H. Kahn: "it is hard to see how this mystery could be unravelled by anyone who had not read the account of dialectic in *Republic* 6 and 7, or heard Plato give some comparable explanation" ("Did Plato Write Socratic Dialogues?" *Classical Quarterly* 31 [1981], 317); cf. Hawtrey ("How Do Dialecticians Use Diagrams," p. 15).

28. See *Meno* 85 C–86 B and *Phaedo* 73 A–B. Socrates has brought Kleinias to the point where philosophical discoveries are vir-

tually exploding from his mind, as he reaches out toward the real. In this way Plato presents the kernel of his own ideas in the soul of the noble Kleinias, just as we can find a debauched view of them in the arguments of the brothers.

29. See *Republic* 518 C–D, 521 C 1–3, and 533 C 7–D 4.

30. It is part of Plato's joke to undermine speech writers by comparing them to wizards, generals to game hunters, and politicians to restaurateurs and quail-keepers. In this analysis the dialecticians remain untainted by such an ironical point of comparison.

31. Here Kleinias' eagerness to continue the ζήτησις should be contrasted with the lazy counsel of eristic; see *Meno* 81 D–E and 86 B.

32. See 283 A 1 and 283 B 1. This break into the outermost frame of the dialogue is also a highly stylized device by which Plato portrays the immediacy and naturalness of discourse, two qualities lacking in eristic. Yet never flustered in discussion, Socrates uses Crito's interruption as an occasion to walk him (and so us) through that labyrinth of discourse into which he and Kleinias fell in their search for the supreme science.

33. We are not, however, to doubt Socrates' retelling of events. Twice he assured us that he was giving his full attention to what happened (272 D 7–9 and 273 B 5–6), and he even invoked the Muses and Memory to assist his recollection (275 D 1–2).

34. See 291 A 1–7. Crito takes this answer to be an unambiguous reference to Socrates himself as the source.

35. By referring to the object of the search with ἐκείνην and using the aorist verbs ἐζητήσατε and ηὕρετε to capture the action (291 A 8), Crito shows how distant he is from the process that has constituted the inquiry.

36. The image of the two pursuing crested larks is important. It not only carries on Kleinias' reference to quail hunters but also confirms that the art of hunting is a metaphor for the dialectical search for an object exterior to the mind. In fact, hunting is the perfect symbol for that philosophical inquiry in which dialecticians seek to capture τὰ ὄντα, which exist in their own right and are not produced in the way that sophistry manufactures bogus images of its own wisdom. The perversion of this dialectical hunt is of course eristic; see 302 B 6–7 and esp. 295 D 2, where Euthydemus tries to hunt down and capture (θηρεῦσαι) his quarry in a net of mere words (τὰ ὀνόματα περιστήσας); cf. *Theaetetus* 165 C–E and 166 C 1.

37. Socrates must qualify his return to the beginning with ὥσπερ (291 B 8), for he doesn't want to deny how much they have gained

even in their failed attempt; see R. K. Sprague, *Plato's Philosopher-King* (Columbia, S.C., 1976), p. 53.

38. Cf. 301 E 8–9, where Socrates mocks the arbitrary beginning and end of eristic, and *Phaedo* 101 E.

39. For a helpful analysis of the significance of the Greek labyrinth, see Philippe Borgeaud's important article, "The Open Entrance to the Closed Palace of the King: The Greek Labyrinth in Context," *History of Religions* 14 (1974), esp. pp. 21–27.

40. See 291 E 5–292 A 2. Medicine has already been introduced at 289 A 5, but agriculture is a new exemplum, showing how Socrates tries to tailor the argument to suit his interlocutor.

41. See 292 B 5–C 1. Just as Kleinias' benefactor was to share knowledge with him (282 B 3), so the royal art is supposed to share (μεταδιδόναι) its knowledge with the citizenry. At 292 D 3, Socrates caps μεταδιδόναι with παραδιδόναι.

42. Here the language σοφοὺς ποιεῖ τοὺς ἀνθρώπους καὶ ἀγαθούς certainly suggests that we have found the ἔργον of political science; cf. 280 A 6 and 282 C 9. In connection with this passage, C. J. Rowe has remarked (*Plato* [Brighton, 1984]): "The function of politics as properly understood, whether in the *Euthydemus* or any other dialogue, is the production of virtue among the citizens; all other supposed ends are to be subordinated to that" (p. 134). Further, we can see that this function of the statesman has been present in the *Euthydemus* from the start, if we look back to 274 D 8, where Socrates asked the brothers whether they could produce a good man (ἀγαθὸν ποιῆσαι ἄνδρα).

43. The ambiguity in τί (292 D 8) and ὅτι (292 E 1) is important for this argument. The "at what" can refer to an immanent activity— what Sprague has called the first-order arts and their first-order products (*Plato's Philosopher-King*, pp. 48–56)—or to the outer objective standard "at which" we look when we assign the good and the useful (*Republic* 505 A–B).

44. As if Crito, too, were not in trouble (292 E 6–7). Crito's aporia is over his sons; he can produce them, but he doesn't know how to cope with what he has produced (306 D 3–4). Socrates, on the other hand, removes Kleinias from any blame by taking full responsibility for the failure (ἐνεπεπτώκη: 293 A 1). Plato does not permit Socrates to solve the regress because he wants to reserve that honor for the brother-pair.

45. We can now see that the transition from medicine and agriculture to kingship (291 E 5–292 A 5) is intentionally misleading; it is

what Sprague has called the leap from "the first-order arts" to the "atypical case" (*Plato's Philosopher-King*, p. 52). As the identical to πολιτική (291 C 4–5), kingship differs from medicine (and the like) by the fact that it governs the soul and not the body; cf. *Gorgias* 464 A–B (τὴν ἐπὶ τῇ ψυχῇ πολιτικήν). Here, in the context of the *Euthydemus*, "governing the soul" means "making the citizens wise and good."

46. See *Republic* 505 A–B. This standard will appear in a grotesque, eristic form at 294 A 4–B 5, where the brothers solve the regress by becoming its solution.

47. Paul Shorey, *What Plato Said* (Chicago, 1933), p. 164.

48. Paul Shorey, "The Idea of Good in Plato's *Republic*," in *Selected Papers* (New York, 1980), 2: 45.

49. As Szlezák says ("Sokrates' Spott über Geheimhaltung," p. 87), Plato can keep his ideas "in his pocket" ("in der Tasche behalten").

50. The fiction that the brothers are blessed for the acquisition of their knowledge is maintained throughout the dialogue; see 293 B 3 and 303 C 4. Moreover, we can now see why Socrates said they were more to be blessed than was the Great King for his empire (ἀρχῆς: 274 A 6–7): their knowledge would make them philosophic rulers. But as the opposite of dialectic, eristic is really the acquisition of ignorance (κτῆσις τῆς ἀμαθίας).

51. See 280 A 6–8, 281 B 2–4 and D 6–E 5, and 292 A 7–C 1.

52. Here we glimpse the "esoteric" doctrine of the *Euthydemus*. Insofar as the context has permitted, Socrates has argued his position openly and honestly, but he cannot simply hand over the answer. Instead, he leaves it "here somewhere (ἐνταῦθά που)" for anyone who wants to track it down.

53. In connection with this point, Borgeaud has remarked: "Nothing indicates whether the labyrinth of the dialogue surrounds a center toward which one strives, or rather, on the contrary, the center is outside, which would indicate that the definition sought is beyond the discourse which seeks it: the discourse in which the seeker is enclosed and which reveals itself as a barrier to the truth" ("The Open Entrance," p. 26).

54. Borgeaud has shown that the iconography of the labyrinth reveals two opposing representations, which correspond perfectly to eristic and dialectic: "According to one it is a place of the most extreme confusion with crossing and recrossing corridors in which the wanderer finds himself at every turn confronted by multiple choices and deceptive bifurcations. According to the other, however, there is

simultaneously a complete iconographic tradition (the major tradition which proceeds from Mycenean Crete through the labyrinths of medieval churches) in which the labyrinth is indeed a long and complex passage, but one without ambiguities or traps, leading necessarily after many twists and detours to the center" ("The Open Entrance," p. 22).

FIVE. THE THIRD ERISTIC DISPLAY

1. For the sense in which it is real, see *Meno* 82 A–B, where Socrates can prove (ἐπιδείξωμαι), but cannot teach (διδάξαι) that learning is recollection; his exhibition will consist of an operation performed upon the slave boy, who will achieve the right answer not by learning (μανθάνων), but by recollecting (ἀναμιμνῃσκόμενος). Here Euthydemus' distinction is empty, for, whichever alternative Socrates selects, he will perform the same operation; see 274 A 10–B 1, where teaching and proving are not in opposition.

2. Here Socrates would be ἀμαθής or ἀνεπιστήμων, and learning would be bridging the gap between ignorance and knowledge by gathering knowledge of what he is learning or doesn't know; cf. 277 B 6–7 and 277 E 7–278 A 1.

3. By proof or ἐπίδειξις, Euthydemus simply means to display the "fact" that Socrates has the knowledge, not to cause him to recollect what it is. The joke on the sophist will be that he cannot even prove the "that," much less the "what."

4. In this case, Socrates is σοφός or ἐπιστήμων; cf. 277 B 8–9, where knowing is ἔχειν ἐπιστήμην ἤδη, and 278 A 2–5, where it is ἔχων ἤδη τὴν ἐπιστήμην ἢ συνιέναι.

5. Many have felt these echoes from the first eristic; see Paul Friedländer (*Plato*, 2d ed. [Princeton, 1969], 2: 191), Hermann Keulen (*UPE*, p. 49), and Michel Narcy (*Le Philosophe et son double* [Paris, 1984], pp. 81–82). Thus again we encounter one of the favorite tricks of these modern philosophers, the constant display of what is old and stale in new and tantalizing guises.

6. But as we can tell from 288 A 2–3, Socrates views his refutation as holding for both sophists, although he argues directly only against Dionysodorus.

7. His answer "many, but small" puts quantity and quality back to back. What Socrates knows is many small things, but what he wants to know is one great science that can determine the relative value of all things in the universe.

8. In the language of the first eristic Euthydemus has moved from

Socrates is "wise" to Socrates is "ignorant" and from "having knowledge already" to "not yet having knowledge"; see 276 A 7–B 2 and 277 B 8–C 1.

9. Note the adroit use of ἄρτι, again illustrating how the eristic copes with the immediate point at issue. Euthydemus can take Socrates' two claims, to be a knower and a not-knower, as if they were uttered without intervening qualifications because he regards Socrates' additions as mere noise, or what he will soon call παραφθέγματα; see 296 A 8 and B7.

10. Here we have a hilarious parody of what may be called the "Euthydemian law of noncontradiction." His introduction of κατὰ ταὐτὰ ἅμα, almost as if it were an afterthought, is an amusing touch. The ἅμα caps ἄρτι, continuing the illusion that Socrates' remarks were spoken without qualifications, and κατὰ ταὐτὰ does not, as one might expect, refer to the objects of knowledge but to Socrates himself, *qua* knower. In connec.ion with this passage Charlotte Stough has remarked ("Forms and Explanations in the *Phaedo*," *Phronesis* 21 [1976], 19 n. 25): "There is no evidence that Plato ever took seriously the sophistries based on failure to indicate the varying times, relations, and respects in which a subject might be said to 'suffer, be, or do opposites.'"

11. At *Philebus* 17 A, Socrates tells us that eristic differs from dialectic in that its practitioners pass from the one to the many (and vice versa) too quickly and in haphazard fashion and consequently disregard what lies in between (τὰ μέσα); see R. Hackforth ("On Some Passages of Plato's *Philebus*," *Classical Quarterly* 83 [1939], 23–24). Here (and in what follows, esp. 293 E 5–294 D 3), Plato presents a comic burlesque of this flight from the μεταξύ.

12. Socrates is thus doing precisely what he did earlier; see 286 C 3–6 and 288 A 2–7, as well as 298 B 4–5, where Ktesippus imitates the method.

13. Behind this startling revelation stands the serious presentation of its possibility in the *Meno* (81 C–D), where it is said that we can pass from one to all though the exercise of *anamnesis*; see Keulen (*UPE*, p. 53). But this possibility (and here is the joke) requires the existence of the soul, which eristic cannot and will not allow to arise in discourse; see 295 B and E.

14. The flip side of this thesis is: All men know nothing, if (and because) they do not know a single thing. If a subject knows one thing, he is a knower (ἐπιστήμων), and hence, omniscient (σοφός); if he fails to know something, then he is a not-knower (ἀνεπιστήμων), and hence, utterly ignorant (ἀμαθής). Thus, this eristic trick is just an-

other way of reworking the exclusive antinomy between οἱ σοφοί and οἱ ἀμαθεῖς.

15. Here Keulen is correct to point out that Dionysodorus' ἕν is devoid of any content (*UPE*, pp. 54–55). But this fact does not exclude Friedländer's interpretation that the "Good" stands behind the one as its fulfillment. In the *Euthydemus* it is Plato's intention to hold together opposing perspectives at one and the same moment.

16. Friedländer, *Plato*, 2: 192.

17. Here we, too, can say with Socrates (294 A 4–5):ʾΩ Ζεῦ . . . ὡς θαυμαστὸν λέγεις καὶ ἀγαθὸν μέγα πεφάνθαι.

18. At 294 B 10, εἶτ᾽ expresses Dionysodorus' impatience with Socrates and so invites the change in speakers. As it did for Kleinias at 289 C 9, ὑπολαβών now signals that Ktesippus is about to take charge of the λόγος.

19. Contrast his behavior here with 283 E 1–6, 284 E, and 288 A 8–B 3.

20. From this question George Grote humorously concluded that they were "almost toothless" (*Plato and the Other Companions of Socrates* [London, 1865], 1: 528).

21. Here Ktesippus again displays how quickly he can learn. Taking over Socrates' example of uncountables, he has just now called for an answer to something that can be counted.

22. The brothers are exhibiting an obsessive urge to avoid contradiction by conforming their thought to their version of the law of noncontradiction. The outcome of this rigid conformity has required them to reject "partial knowing" and to embrace "omniscience." Meanwhile Socrates and Ktesippus have tested their claim by applying it to excessively minute and even disgusting particulars. In this way the brothers are shown to be completely out of touch with real experience. The discrepancy thus created illustrates to perfection how pedantry becomes ludicrous; cf. *Theaetetus* 174 A 4–B 1. For the comic theory, see Schopenhauer (*Die Welt als Wille und Vorstellung*, vol. 1, chap. 13), and for its practice, see Pangloss in Voltaire's *Candide* and Pancrace the Aristotelian and Marphurius the Pyrrhonian in Molière's *Le Mariage forcé*.

23. Keulen (*UPE*, p. 52) has compared the language of 294 E with *Phaedo* 75 C–D. Here Plato is depicting the brothers' glee, as they anticipate the discussion's moving into the region of "their" doctrine of recollection. On this point it is worth quoting Narcy (*Le Philosophe*, p. 82): "En leur bouche le platonisme lui-même est rendu sophistique."

24. The demand that Socrates answer reminds us that this is an inviolable "rule" of eristic; see 275 C 1 and 287 C 4–D 6. For his part,

Socrates is most pleased to respond, for he views his upcoming "refutation (ἐξελέγχομαι)" as an opportunity to be refuted out of his false notions.

25. If the eristician puts his question correctly, the answerer is supposed to respond with a simple yes or no; see *SE* 17.175 B 8–14. Here and in his next three questions (295 E 4–5, 296 A 5–7, 296 B 4–5), Euthydemus fails in his role as questioner, each time allowing Socrates to spike his gun with παραφθέγματα.

26. Keulen sees Socrates' counterquestion as an instance of the σμικρόν τι motif by which Socrates attempts to force the essential factor into the argument and thereby deflect the line of questioning in a significant way (*UPE*, pp. 48–50); cf. Friedländer (*Plato,* 2: 191–92). We should also recall that Dionysodorus has repeatedly dodged questions from his opponents by submitting counterquestions; see 285 E 1–4, 286 A 3–6, 287 A 4–B 5, 294 B 8–C 6.

27. Eristicians experience shame for failure to adhere to their rules of questioning and answering. For them, the proper response to such misbehavior is to blush or to fall silent; see 286 B 7, 297 A 8, and 299 C 8.

28. See 284 E 6, where Ktesippus violated eristic decorum with verbal abuse; 286 D 11–E 9, where Socrates foolishly asked whether they were merely arguing theses; 287 B 2–5, where Dionysodorus criticized Socrates for not responding to the point at issue; and esp. 287 C–D, where for the first time Socrates challenged Dionysodorus directly on his method.

29. The sudden and unexpected appearance of "soul" in this passage offers startling evidence of how and why Plato keeps his ideas in his pocket. In the *Euthydemus* he has carefully excluded the word ψυχή from the prologue, epilogue, transitional passages, and even from the two protreptic episodes, where we might reasonably expect to find it. He has thus far allowed ψυχή to surface only once (287 D 7–10), in an eristic context where it has its traditional animative sense of "life force"; there he put the word into Dionysodorus' mouth in order to demonstrate how the sophist could use "soul" as just one item among many, for his purpose of attaining a verbal victory; cf. 302 A 8 and E 1–2. But Plato has kept his own "cognitive" sense of ψυχή in reserve until this very moment, when he has Socrates innocently release it in such a way as to jar Euthydemus' expectations and to produce the maximum comic effect. David Claus has called attention to this "quite extraordinary" use of ψυχή in the *Euthydemus* and has also noted, with precision, what its presence in this passage entails: that given the

movement of the argument thus far (294 E 5–295 B 5), "Socrates can be said to have knowledge based on prior existence and to have such knowledge through the agency of his ψυχή, an argument he will himself demonstrate for the slave boy in *Meno*" (*Toward the Soul* [Yale University Press, 1981], pp. 173–174). Predictably, however, Claus slips into the orthodoxy in these matters and concludes that this use of ψυχή anticipates "the epistemology of *Meno*." But far from anticipating the *Meno*, the *Euthydemus* has become Plato's vehicle for parodying "philosophers" who produce arguments on the topics of learning and knowing without any, much less his own cognitive, sense of ψυχή. In this way Plato provides a negative defense for his psychology, the positive aspects of which he works out in the *Meno*, *Phaedo*, and elsewhere. So this appearance of ψυχή must constitute another irrefutable proof of the "maturity" of the *Euthydemus*. And as if Plato doesn't want us to forget this fact, a few lines later he has Socrates again inform Euthydemus that he knows what he knows "by the soul" (295 E 5).

30. Plato is here making a joke on φλυαρία. Socrates, who always tries to avoid φλυαρία in favor of philosophical discussion, is now being charged with "driveling"; but, of course, through the rhetorical figure of enantiosis, it is eristic that is φλυαρία. Further, although ἀρχαιότερος does carry the sense of "overly simple and silly" (Liddell-Scott-Jones; hereafter LSJ), here it also indicates that Socrates is old-fashioned and completely out of step with the way these "moderns" are doing philosophy.

31. The sophist is angry at Socrates for taking apart or poking holes in his speech. Διαστέλλειν is not "to define precisely" (LSJ), but to expand assertions through qualifications in order to counter the tight-fisted argumentation of this pseudo-logician.

32. At the same time the boys can be the bait that lures these predators out into the open so that Socrates can trap them; see 272 D 2–3 and 304 B 5.

33. Socrates used ὅτε at 294 E 9 to refer to an instance of everlasting time, whereas Euthydemus is now using it to refer to discrete moments in which the act of knowing occurs.

34. Robin Waterfield, *Early Socratic Dialogues* (Harmondsworth, 1987), p. 355.

35. Even as Socrates withdraws his addition, he manages to call attention to it again. The open way in which he subtracts ὅταν should be contrasted with the covert way Euthydemus is about to remove τούτῳ.

36. Among English translators, W. H. D. Rouse appears to be the only one who recognizes that the two uses of ἀεί at 296 B 2–3 are to

be taken more closely with τούτῳ than with ἐπίστασαι (*Euthydemus*, trans. W. H. D. Rouse, in *The Collected Dialogues of Plato*, ed. Edith Hamilton and Huntington Cairns [Princeton, 1961], p. 409).

37. Aristotle, too, is aware of how Socratic qualifications can disrupt question-chains; see *SE* 17.175 B 8–14 and 176 A 15.

38. Thus Edwin H. Gifford (*The Euthydemus of Plato*, rev. ed. [Oxford, 1905], pp. 49–50) in his analysis of this obscure argument. My only quibble with him is on the possibility that "all" and "all things" are synonyms; otherwise his interpretation is correct.

39. Socrates has already used the two terms indifferently at 293 D 5–6, and Euthydemus will do so at 296 C 10 and D 3–4.

40. Here "all (ἄπαντα)" is either a harmless gloss on "all things (πάντα)" or, as Gifford notes (*Euthydemus*, pp. 49–50), a reference to 296 B 5.

41. But in spite of his efforts to the contrary, Euthydemus has been unable to prevent this true thesis from shining through the eristic elenchus: *By the soul, always, whenever he knows, Socrates knows all things, at least what he knows.* What is more, Socrates has been able to generate this thesis while abiding by the eristic rule to respond to what he understands on each occasion.

42. With his use of ἔοικα, Socrates indicates (as he will again at 298 A 9) that the conclusion is only apparent. Here, too, he harmlessly glosses ἄπαντα with πάντα. Since both terms are empty, it doesn't matter which of the two he uses.

43. In this respect Euthydemus' behavior in argument contrasts most sharply with the spirit of inquiry expressed at *Phaedo* 95 E.

44. On this special talent of eristics, Lewis Campbell has remarked: "From the want of any true command of ideas, they distinguished in the wrong place and failed to distinguish in the right," (*The Sophistes and Politicus of Plato* [Oxford, 1867], p. xii).

45. At 296 C 8, ἀεί is again most naturally taken with τούτῳ (see Rouse in *The Collected Dialogues of Plato*, p. 410). Then, in the γάρ clause (296 C 9–10), which doesn't explain or justify the preceding sentence but confirms the "truth" of what Socrates is imagined to have stated, Euthydemus again drops out τούτῳ, leaving ἀεί to go with ἐπίστασθαι. At 296 C 10, Euthydemus is using ἄμα the same way he did at 293 D 1, as a (near) synonym for ἄρτι, carrying on the fiction that Socrates' qualifications are mere noise; but cf. R. S. W. Hawtrey's emendation ("Plato, *Euthydemus* 296 C 8–10," *Liverpool Classical Monthly* 4 [1979], 41) and J. N. O'Sullivan's revised punctuation ("Plato, *Euthydemus* 296 C 8–10 (Burnet)," ibid., pp. 61–62).

46. At 296 D 3, Euthydemus uses an oath for the first and only time.

47. On this final act of "megalomania," as Friedländer calls it (*Plato*, 2: 192), see Keulen's most perceptive remarks (*UPE*, pp. 71–72).

48. Those who have analyzed these portions of the *Euthydemus* cannot avoid seeing what Hermann Keulen calls "den Eindruck geradezu einer Persiflage des *Menon*" (*UPE*, p. 51). See Friedländer (*Plato*, 2:192), Keulen (*UPE*, pp. 25–40, 49–56, and 26 n. 56), Leo Strauss ("On the *Euthydemus*," *Interpretation* 1 [1970], 17), Hawtrey (*Commentary on Plato's Euthydemus* [Philadelphia, 1981], pp. 141, 149, and 155–56), Thomas Alexander Szlezák ("Sokrates' Spott über Geheimhaltung: Zum Bild des φιλόσοφος in Platons *Euthydemus*," *Antike und Abendland* 26 [1980], 82), and Narcy (*Le Philosophe*, p. 82).

49. Cf. *Meno* 81 E 1 (ἐργατικούς τε καὶ ζητητικούς) and 86 B 6ff., where Socrates opposes the "lazy counsel" of Meno's question.

50. For Euthydemus' words, see 296 A 2. Ktesippus will also parody the sophist's language at 300 C 6–7.

51. Dionysodorus thus interprets Socrates' proposition to be an example of τὰ μηδαμοῦ ὄντα; cf. 284 B 4–7. Plato has carefully prepared the way for the sophist to reenter the debate by having Socrates mention his name at 296 D 8. But the last time he actually spoke in the work was some time ago, at 294 E 11. Thus we should imagine that though very eager to do so, Dionysodorus has been unable to join the fray for some time, so that now, when the opportunity comes, he just blurts out "Nowhere"; cf. 300 D 1, where he behaves in a similar way.

52. This blush, a comic touch similar to his smile (275 E 4), causes Dionysodorus to appear, in Henri Bergson's words: "Immersed and absorbed in the materiality of some mechanical occupation, instead of ceaselessly renewing his vitality by keeping in touch with a living ideal" ("Laughter," in *Comedy*, ed. Wylie Sypher, 4th ed. [Baltimore, 1986], p. 79).

53. Thus the point of Socrates' prediction (296 D 7–8), that Dionysodorus would have to join with Euthydemus in order to secure Socrates' omniscience.

54. At 297 B 2, ταχύ foreshadows the quickening pace of the second half of the fifth episode. We are already familiar with Dionysodorus' artless moves to commandeer the λόγος; see 287 C–D.

55. Flight (φυγή) is an attempt to escape the inescapable question (ἄφυκτον).

56. See F. M. Cornford, *Plato's Theory of Knowledge* (London, 1935), pp. 208 and 256.

57. Twice, at 297 B 4–5 and 297 D 8–9, Socrates refers to this problem as something he wants Euthydemus to teach him.

58. Thus Cornford: "any statement (true or false) which conveys meaning cannot refer to 'absolute nonentity'" (*Plato's Theory of Knowledge,* p. 205).

59. For the sources of and variations on this combat myth, see Joseph Fontenrose, *Python* (Berkeley, 1959), p. 356. Plato has carefully prepared for the introduction of these grisly monsters, first with τέρας (296 C 3), and then with τερατώδεσιν (296 E 2).

60. We are accustomed to Socrates comparing the sophist to mythical figures, but here he renders the mythic figure intelligible by its likeness to sophistry; cf. 285 C 4 and 288 B 8.

61. One head of the Hydra was said to be immortal and to extend all the way to Hades.

62. E. S. Thompson (*The Meno of Plato* [London, 1901], p. 273) and Gifford (*Euthydemus,* p. 52) interpreted the allusion to refer to Ktesippus, but R. K. Sprague (*Translation,* p. 47 n. 75), G. J. De Vries ("Notes on Some Passages in the *Euthydemus,*" *Mnemosyne* 25 [1972], 51), Hawtrey (*Commentary,* p. 159), and Waterfield (*Early Socratic Dialogues,* p. 358 n. 1) have denied it.

63. At 293 A 2–3, Socrates first introduced the theme of coming to the aid of the λόγος (ἐπικαλούμενος σῶσαι ἡμᾶς), when he asked the brothers to rescue him and Kleinias. Now he returns to this theme at 297 C 7 with an allusion to Ktesippus as his helper (βοηθὸν ἐπεκαλέσατο). This reference in turn looks forward to 303 A 5, where Ktesippus again comes to rescue Socrates (ὡς βοηθήσων) for (D21), the final eristic argument.

64. In electing to convert the items that he does, Dionysodorus carefully avoids the primary objects of the simile: Socrates' allusion to sophists, heads of argument, adequate help in defense of the λόγος, and especially the Hydra and the Crab. The evidence of the *Euthydemus* indicates that eristics direct their attention toward the inessential, the decentered.

65. Of course, Socrates has just submitted a figurative sense in which Iolaus is his nephew; but since Dionysodorus has dragged him back into the eristic universe, he responds in the way he understands the question.

66. The emphatic position of "yours (σός)," both here and in the trigger question, may suggest that Dionysodorus wants to turn (D11) on the possessive adjective. Perhaps he plans to argue, as he will in (D20), that since Patrocles is "yours," that is, belongs to Socrates, Socrates can sell or sacrifice his brother to anyone he wants, just as he

can the rest of his possessions (τὰ σά). But since Socrates doesn't allow this ruse to get off the ground, we can only speculate.

67. Thus it is Socrates who introduces the problem of "is the same" and "is not the same," which Dionysodorus will cap with "is" and "is not" (297 E 5–6) and then with "different from" and "same as" (298 A 3).

68. Here Plato shows how blindly Dionysodorus is committed to the Euthydemian law of noncontradiction by having him fancy that he can secure a refutation by simply tricking Socrates into asserting contrary predicates of one and the same subject; cf. *SE* 5.167 A 7–20. It now appears that the conclusion Dionysodorus has here established may be something like the one he was hoping to attain when at 297 B 2 he introduced the term *brother*.

69. At 298 A 2, the ambiguous τοῦ, here rendered by "a" father, cannot be satisfactorily translated into English. Dionysodorus is hoping that Socrates will take it for the possessive "yours" and so answer simply "yes," thus giving him the opportunity to shift from "different from" to "is not." But Socrates derails the trick by adding ἐμοῦ to τοῦ in order to make perfectly clear that Chaeredemus is different from his father Sophroniscus, who is another father; cf. J. L. Smith, "Plato and the Paradox of False Statements: A Study of the *Euthydemus* and the *Sophist*" (Ph.D. diss., University of Virginia, 1975), pp. 36–48.

70. So at 298 A 3, Dionysodorus is not referring to the proverbial stone (Gifford, *Euthydemus,* p. 52; Sprague, *Translation,* p. 48 n. 77; De Vries, "Notes," p. 52; Hawtrey, *Commentary,* p. 162; and Waterfield, *Early Socratic Dialogues,* p. 359), but simply to a rock that is not the same as Socrates. At 298 A 4, it is Socrates who comes back with the figurative or qualified sense of being rendered dull and stupid as a stone.

71. At 298 A 8–9, read οὐκοῦν with manuscripts B and T and οὐ with W. Inasmuch as he has already stipulated in what sense the two men are and are not fathers, Socrates feels no urge to contest the conclusion and so answers "apparently (ἔοικεν)." Since Dionysodorus is imparting force and meaning to words as he sees fit, Socrates responds to him the same way he did to Euthydemus at 296 C 6.

72. Euthydemus' sudden return and automatic urge to finish off the attack is reminiscent of his sally against Ktesippus at 284 E 2–3. To assist our understanding of (D11), Charles P. Bigger has provided this helpful analysis: "Schematically, we can exhibit the Megaric character of this language game as follows: Assume X is P and Y is P. Here 'X is P' is understood as 'X is same (identity) as P.' Thus if Y is other than X, it cannot be P. If both X and Y are P, then X = Y, by Leibniz's

law" (*Participation: A Platonic Inquiry* [Baton Rouge, 1968], p. 62); cf. *SE* 5.166 B 32–36.

73. Having already designated eristic arguments as "knockdowns" at 277 D 1 and at 288 A 4, Plato need not refer to them here as such; cf. also 286 C 4: ἀνατρέπων.

74. Thus a familiar feature of Plato's art of transition; cf. how Polemarchus takes over for Cephalus (*Republic* 331 D) and Polus for Gorgias (*Gorgias* 461 B–462 B). It is no accident that Plato has expressed this transition with ἐκδεξάμενος. He has already used this word twice (276 C 2 and 277 B 4) to describe Dionysodorus taking over the eristic argument from Euthydemus.

75. This argument, (K12), is attributed to Ktesippus because he performs the role of questioner in the dispute.

76. Cf. ταὐτὰ ταῦτα πέπονθεν at 298 B 5 with πέπονθας τοῦτο τὸ αὐτὸ πάθος at 293 E 2–3.

77. Here again we come across the universal πάθος that eristic arguments suffer; see 286 C 4, 288 A 5, 293 E 2–3, and 303 E 1–4. Since eristic cannot stand its ground against its own attacks, it proves useless as a serious philosophical method for attaining truth. But in suffering what it dishes out, eristic becomes comical and is thus able to deflect any anger and hostility that its victims might otherwise feel; cf. 293 E 4–5 and 303 E 2–4.

78. Both here (298 C 1) and below (298 C 8–9), Plato has Ktesippus use the disjunctive formula (πότερον . . . ἤ) in order to show how eagerly he is embracing this feature of eristic method.

79. Richard Robinson clearly underestimates the force of Ktesippus' remark when he cites it as evidence for Plato's unconsciousness of faulty analogy ("Plato's Consciousness of Fallacy," *Mind* 51 [1942], 104); cf. Waterfield (*Early Socratic Dialogues*, p. 360 n. 1). If one views the line "not sewing like to like" in isolation from everything else Ktesippus says in the dialogue, then Robinson's judgment may seem plausible. But when we consider the young man's contribution to the falsehood problem (284 B 1–2, C 7–8), his detection of the equivocal κακῶς λέγειν (284 E 1), his use of the evidentiary criterion (294 C), his exposure of the tricky "yours" (299 E 6), of the Euthydemian law of noncontradiction (300 A 6–8), of the fallacious question (300 C 4–D 5), and so on, we are justified in concluding that these illustrations are too numerous, too precise, and too consistent to be accidental and thus "Plato knew what he was doing" (Paul Shorey, *What Plato Said* [Chicago, 1933], pp. 289–290).

80. Here, with Ktesippus' two uses of πάντων (298 C 7–9), Plato shows how eagerly he is imitating the eristic urge to drive one's oppo-

nent to the unqualified universal position without having to pass through the middle (τὰ μέσα).

81. Here Bigger has remarked: "The condition of being a father will constitute an immanent nexus of paternal relations; but such nexus can be everywhere throughout nature, provided of course that there are beings who can exhibit this relation scattered about also. The only way out of the internal relatedness envisaged by the Sophist is to recognize that form has the status of a possible, that it functions as a limit (*peras*) of a Dedekind *Schnitt* and is of recurrent character" (*Participation*, p. 63); cf. Szlezák ("Sokrates' Spott über Geheimhaltung," pp. 82–83), who sees in (K12) "eine burleske Variation" of *Meno* 81 C 9–D 1: τῆς φύσεως ἁπάσης συγγενοῦς οὔσης.

82. Ktesippus signals his conclusions, in eristic fashion, with three straight uses of ἄρα. Although Hoeffer's conjecture κάπρος (298 D 5) is remarkably clever and accepted by Burnet, it is better to trust B T and W, especially since all three manuscripts agree on καὶ πρός.

83. Here we see a parody of the ridiculous sense in which two eristic debaters can reach agreement; see 286 A 4–7.

84. In a recent article ("Aristotle, the Fallacy of Accident and the Nature of Predication: A Historical Inquiry," *Journal of the History of Philosophy* [1988], 5–24), Aníbal Bueno has provided the Aristotelian analysis: "'the dog' is the subject, 'father' the accident and 'yours' the attribute. The fallacy consists in asserting that the attribute 'yours', which is true of the subject 'dog', is also true of the accident 'father'. What is true of the dog *qua* individual is not true of it *qua* father." "Of course, some of Aristotle's examples can also be explained in terms of other logical mistakes. Thus the famous dog argument exploits the ambiguity of the possessive pronoun 'yours'. 'The dog is yours' is an incomplete expression that can, if completed in different ways, convey a number of different relations. In the argument, it is an elliptic way of saying 'The dog is your property'. If the premiss is fully stated, we get a valid argument with the truistic conclusion, 'The father is your property'" (pp. 10–11). One can also explain (D13) as a fallacy of composition by calling attention to the fact that Dionysodorus has deviously subtracted ὤν from the ὥστε clause and thus left "yours" positioned beside "father"; cf. Sprague (*Translation*, p. 50 n. 81) and Hawtrey (*Commentary*, p. 164).

85. It is difficult to imagine why, without manuscript authority, Hawtrey would want to attribute 298 E 6–10 to Euthydemus (*Commentary*, p. 165). "This little argument" is not, in his words, "a mere elaboration of what precedes it" (p. 165); but Dionysodorus is now using the conclusion "the dog is your father" as a way to attain the

coup de grâce, the "proof" that Ktesippus is a father-beater. It is better (with Benjamin Jowett, *The Dialogues of Plato*, vol. 1, 4th ed. [Oxford, 1953], p. 238; and Rouse, in *The Collected Dialogues of Plato*, p. 412) to read οὐκοῦν at 298 E 4 as introducing a statement with ὥστε giving the conclusion. In this way the sophist completes his joke without inviting Ktesippus to respond. At 298 E 9, he again uses inferential οὐκοῦν for his concluding statement.

86. His playful behavior here should be contrasted with how angry he was at 283 E 1–6. With the first mention of "laughter (γελάσας)," Plato not only undercuts Ktesippus' heretofore serious demeanor; he is also beginning to prepare us for his loud outburst (ἀνακαγχάσας) at 300 D 3.

87. Even as he imitates the pair, Ktesippus can mock them as σοφούς and their science as σοφία; cf. 300 B 7. As the emphatic position of κυνιδίων indicates (299 A 5), Ktesippus does in fact reverse (D13) by indicating that the brothers, too, are puppies and their father a dog.

88. For his trigger Euthydemus converts Ktesippus' reference to "enjoyment (ἀπολέλαυκεν)" to "need (δεῖται)." He then restricts need to that opportune moment (ὅταν δέηται and ὅταν ἴῃ) when in fact (good) drugs and (good) weapons are needed; cf. 299 B 6 (ὅταν δέῃ) and C 1–2 (ἐν τῷ πολέμῳ). Then he tries to reduce both occasions to absurdity by swinging the trigger term *many* (πόλλα) to the extreme with ὡς πλεῖστον and ὡς πλεῖστα.

89. Euthydemus first slips "men (ἀνθρώπων)" into the argument at 299 A 9. Then, after introducing a sick man (ἀσθενοῦντι) and a soldier (ὅπλα ἔχοντα), he comes back with "man (ἀνθρώπῳ)" at 299 B 6 to reinforce the standard against which the need for many goods will appear excessive. That Ktesippus knows his opponent is playing on the man / measure principle is indicated both by his reference to Delphi and to ὁ ἀνδριάς.

90. Cf. 286 B 7 and 303 E 1–3. (E14) is the first defeat for which Euthydemus is solely and unambiguously responsible. From here he will go down to defeat in (E16) and (E17) and thus depart from the dialogue with three straight losses.

91. Although (E14) and (D15) share the same topic (299 D 1), they do not form an argument-pair; so I have altered Bonitz's catalogue to reflect that difference.

92. With his use of "always" and "everywhere," Dionysodorus again exhibits that eristic impulse to swing the argument to the extreme limit. Familiar as we are with the move to attain the sense of "time everlasting" from "always" (see 294 E), we might suspect that

the sophist is preparing to turn this trick on ἀεί. But as we shall see, he is here concentrating his attention on πανταχοῦ.

93. Aristotle has observed that a sophistical refutation can also be a joke; see his remarks on γελοῖοι λόγοι at *SE* 33.182 B 15.

94. This apparent refutation affords us the opportunity to contrast the eristic paradox with the Socratic. Both undermine the *consensus omnium*, that many goods and, in particular, gold are necessary and sufficient for the happy life. But for Socrates, the opinions of the many are a foil for the true account of the one good, wisdom. For the brothers, on the other hand, the eristic paradox is a tool by which they undermine any confidence in the power of λόγος to articulate the truth of ὄντα. The eristic paradox leads to skepticism and misology; the Socratic inspires the listener to pursue wisdom.

95. Like inept boxers who telegraph their punches, the brothers are now revealing their strategy by calling for "agreement" at the very moment they fancy they have their opponent on the ropes; cf. ὡμολόγεις at 299 B 5; in this regard, cf. also 298 D 8 and 296 C 5–9. Here, at 299 D 5–6, Dionysodorus has alerted Ktesippus with ὁμολογεῖς, which the young man caps with Ὡμολόγηκα μὲν οὖν; cf. 301 D 3–4. It is no accident that, after picturing the brothers "differing" with their opponents in the first and third episodes, Plato now has them seeking "agreement"; cf. also 294 B 10 and D 1–2; 295 A 5; and 302 B 1, D 7, E 1–7. Plato wants to show, in the words of Campbell, that "the devotees of this 'illogical logic' of disputation . . . confused verbal agreement with real agreement and difference" (*Sophistes*, p. xii); cf. *Theaetetus* 164 C 7–D 2.

96. In this way Ktesippus again returns tit for tat for what he suffered in (D13). But his youthful enthusiasm for eristic, together with his desire to display his skill openly for Kleinias (300 C 1), has led him to expose the fallacy once again. He will have to learn to conceal these devious tricks before he can become a full professor of eristic.

97. Here we should pause for a moment to note the remarkable way Ktesippus has countered every move of his adversary; he defends the commonsense attitude toward wealth, which Dionysodorus has tried to reduce to absurdity, by submitting "what they say (φασί)"; he caps Dionysodorus' four uses of ἔχειν with ἔχουσιν and ἔχοντες; he picks up the reference to the happiest man with εὐδαιμονεστάτους and then caps it with ἀρίστους; he matches the reference to "in the skull" with "in the skulls" of Scythians and returns to the desirability of having much (πολύ) gold (cf. 299 D 3); he overturns the θαυμαστὸν λόγον of eristic (cf. 288 A 8) by submitting something even more amazing (θαυμασιώτερον) and then goes on to balance his opponent's

reference to "in the belly" and "in each eye socket" with "drinking out of" and "looking down inside"; and finally, he caps the whole by adding his own contribution with "in the hands."

98. *Contra* Burnet, I read this line (with Hawtrey, *Commentary*, p. 169) as a question.

99. Hawtrey is certainly right to puzzle over this strange use of τί δέ (*Commentary*, pp. 169–170). But on the assumption that the text is sound, I read τί δέ (with Jowett, *Dialogues*, p. 240; and Rouse, in *The Collected Dialogues of Plato*, p. 413) to be elliptical for "But what [can they see quite clearly]?"

100. Ktesippus' remark at 300 A 6 has produced some confusion, with Jowett (*Dialogues*, p. 240; cf. also the third edition, p. 163) and Rouse (in *The Collected Dialogues of Plato*, pp. 413–414) reading B and W, and Sprague (*Translation*, p. 53) reading T. If we follow Jowett and Rouse and translate "Perhaps you don't think that they see (αὐτὰ ὁρᾶν)," then Euthydemus is being criticized for trying to uphold (2c), that their cloaks are things which cannot see. If we follow Sprague and read "You perhaps don't suppose you see them (ὁρᾶν αὐτά)," then Euthydemus is being mocked for supporting (2d), that their cloaks are things which cannot be seen. However, to appreciate the full force of the joke, we must see that here Ktesippus, too, is consciously employing the syntactic ambiguity embedded in the neuter accusative and infinitive construction so as to hold together both readings at the same time. Louis Méridier's translation, "Toi, tu leur refuses peut-être la vue," captures the Greek nicely (*Euthydème*, vol. 5 [Paris, 1931], p. 186); cf. Hawtrey, *Commentary*, p. 170.

101. With λέγοντα μηδὲν λέγειν . . . ποιεῖν, Ktesippus recalls 284 C 1–4 and 286 A 2, B 6, and C 6–8. With his reference to falling asleep, he goads Euthydemus for having become as dull and ignorant as a rock.

102. Having cut off the head of (D17), Ktesippus cauterizes it by taunting his opponent: "And so, because of your wisdom, you failed to realize that you said nothing on this point." Here, too, Ktesippus has provided a perceptive analysis of error: Dionysodorus has spoken falsely because of "ignorance."

103. As τὸ ἕτερον at 300 B 8 indicates, (E17) is the second limb of an argument-pair, thus requiring a correction of Bonitz's catalogue. Ktesippus is now so confident in his ability to play the game that he even invites his opponent to launch the next attack. Speculating on the cause of his aggressiveness, Socrates suggests that he is motivated by his παιδικά. As the brothers play to their clique, so Ktesippus competes for his beloved.

104. Euthydemus' use of γε at 300 C 6 should recall Socrates' use of limiting γ' at 296 B 5.

105. Cf. 275 E 5–6 and 287 E: ὁπότερ' ἂν ἀποκρίνηται ὁ Εὐθύδημος, ἐξελεγχθήσεται.

106. Plato shows how carefully he has designed this finale to mirror the first eristic display by having Kleinias laugh at the moment of defeat and by having Ktesippus demonstrate his potential for orchestrating the eristic θόρυβος, so disruptive of serious philosophical discussion; cf. 276 B 7 and D 1, and 303 B 4–6.

107. In this way Plato shows how a young man who is generously endowed with the outstanding qualities that one must have to be a candidate for philosophy (*Republic* 484 A–487 A) can have those very qualities warped by his "educators" in such a way that he is turned toward and finally comes to embrace the opposing measure.

108. In *Lysis* 211 B–C, Plato shows how eristic is spreading among Athenian youth by introducing Ktesippus as a teacher of eristic and Menexenus as his student; see Shorey, *What Plato Said*, p. 115. But Socrates never breaks off his association with him; see *Phaedo* 59 B 9.

109. For more on this pathology, see esp. *Republic* 489 D ff.

110. Cf. *Republic* 539 B. In presenting this clash between Ktesippus and the brothers, Plato has given a vivid picture of the "distorted lawlessness (παρανομία)" that had currently infiltrated the practice of dialectic and rendered it base (κακόν); see *Republic* 537 E. As Socrates tells us (300 D 7–9), Ktesippus has been able to pick up eristic through his "distorted auditing (παρηκηκόει)" of their method, for wisdom of this kind (τοιαύτη σοφία) does not belong to any other "moderns" (τῶν νῦν ἀνθρώπων). In *Philebus* 16 C–17 A, Plato unambiguously stigmatizes eristics as "moderns" (οἱ δὲ νῦν τῶν ἀνθρώπων σοφοί) and contrasts them with the "ancients" (οἱ μὲν παλαιοί), who, because they lived closer to the gods, practiced dialectic properly. As is now clear, when Plato calls these eristics wise (σοφοί), he does not mean what he says. They are again the ignorant (ἀμαθεῖς), who always seem to be too much with us; cf. *Phaedo* 101 E 5 (ὑπὸ σοφίας) and 90 C 2 (σοφώτατοι), *Lysis* 216 A 7 (πάσσοφοι), and *Meno* 75 C 8 (τῶν σοφῶν).

111. By having Dionysodorus once again employ the antinomy between sameness and difference against Socrates (cf. 298 A 2–9), Plato not only provides a structural device by which he links (D18) to (D11); he also shows how easily and mechanically this concept juggler can slip into a familiar line of attack.

112. We have in this argument, as Friedländer puts it, "an undeniable reference to what is called Plato's 'theory of forms'" (*Plato,*

2 : 192); and Shorey adds: "The joke about παρουσία in the *Euthydemus* is a distinct and familiar allusion to the Platonic idea of beauty" (*The Unity of Plato's Thought* [Chicago, 1903], p. 31). For others who see the Idea in this passage, see Harold Cherniss (*Selected Papers* [Leiden, 1977], p. 263); R. K. Sprague (*Plato's Use of Fallacy* [London, 1962], pp. 25–30; *Translation*, pp. 55–57; and "Parmenides' Sail and Dionysodorus' Ox," *Phronesis* 12 [1967], 91–98); Strauss ("On the *Euthydemus*," p. 18); R. E. Allen (*Plato's "Euthyphro" and the Earlier Theory of Forms* [New York, 1970], p. 122); Keulen (*UPE*, pp. 56–58 and esp. n. 66, where he surveys German scholarship on this problem); Hawtrey (*Commentary*, p. 175); Richard Mohr ("Forms in Plato's *Euthydemus*," *Hermes* 112 [1984], 296–300); Szlezák ("Sokrates' Spott über Geheimhaltung," p. 83), D. G. Stuart ("An Interpretation of Plato's *Euthydemus*" [Ph.D. diss., Yale University, 1980], pp. 254–263); and Narcy (*Le Philosophe*, pp. 87–91). Gregory Vlastos (*Socrates, Ironist and Moral Philosopher* [Ithaca, 1991], p. 74) passes over the significance of αὐτοῦ γε τοῦ καλοῦ; cf. Shorey (*Unity*, p. 31 n. 199).

113. It has not gone unnoticed that the antinomy between sameness and difference is one of the best devices that eristic has for generating controversy; see *Republic* 454 A–C. But it has not been appreciated how brilliantly Plato has satirized this very antinomy by employing it in his dramatic portrayal of the brothers themselves. Are they one or two? We might feel an inclination to say that the Tweedle-pair are so much alike that it doesn't matter which of the two performs the lead role in the questioning; that, in short, the two are the same (ταὐτόν), or what geometers call "enantiomorphs," mirror-image forms of each other. As such, Dionysodorus does not differ from Euthydemus, and so any merely apparent differences between the two may be swept aside. And yet Plato has left a word here, a word there, to indicate that the one (τὸ ἕτερον) is different from the other (ἕτερον). After all, Euthydemus and Dionysodorus are not one but two (271 A 6–7), and besides, they have different names. So are the brothers the same or different? Neither and both.

114. We are doubtless to imagine that Dionysodorus delivers this joke with a grin from ear to ear; cf. 275 E 4. To be funny, the joke requires that both sameness and difference exist between the objects compared. That Socrates is not unlike an ox in appearance is obvious. But the possibility that he could be Dionysodorus forces him to say εὐφήμει.

115. Thus Sprague ("Parmenides' Sail," p. 93).

116. The question τίνα τρόπον . . . τὸ ἕτερον ἕτερον ἂν εἴη, which Dionysodorus uses to express his attack against presence, is a simple,

idiomatic way of asking "How can one thing (Socrates) be another (an ox)?" But the task of rendering these words into English has overwhelmed translators; see Sprague (*Plato's Use of Fallacy,* pp. 26–27, and *Translation,* pp. 56–57), W. K. C. Guthrie (*HGP,* 4: 278 and esp. n. 2), and Hawtrey (*Commentary,* pp. 176–177). Dionysodorus is not trying to speak "cryptically" (Sprague), nor is he trying "to confuse" Socrates and reduce him to "meaningless repetition" (Hawtrey). The problem is how to capture the Greek in such a way as to be "lucid" and "to make sense" (Guthrie), without at the same time obscuring the rest of the argument. For Socrates will come back with *the same words* (τὸ ἕτερον ἕτερόν ἐστιν) at 301 B 8 and C 1–2, but in *a different sense.* And again to capture this transition from the one to the other requires us to use the same English words for both passages. Sprague's translation "How can the different be different?" achieves this goal but leaves her open to attack from Guthrie for "making no sense." His translation, on the other hand, "How can one thing be made different?" is lucid but then he undervalues the rest of the argument.

117. "Plato, of course," as Shorey says, "is not going to discuss the theory of ideas in this connection. So Socrates attacks the Sophists with their own weapons" (*What Plato Said,* p. 166). And Szlezák adds: "Wir sehen Sokrates seine Kenntnis der Anamnesis- und Ideenlehre . . . in der Tasche behalten" ("Sokrates' Spott über Geheimhaltung," p. 87).

118. The importance of (D11) for (D18) is now clearly evident. Just as

1. Chaeredemus, who is different from a father, *is not* (a father); and
2. Socrates, who is different from a stone, *is not* (a stone); so too
3. The Idea itself, which is different from its instance, *is not* (its instance).

119. See Gifford (*Euthydemus,* p. 60), Hawtrey (*Commentary,* p. 178), and Waterfield (*Early Socratic Dialogues,* p. 367 n. 1).

120. It is not important what the subject is, for identity holds on all three levels. What we need to observe here is that Socrates is just juggling words eristically. We need not fear that in deflecting one eristic quibble Socrates may be undone by another, the self-predicating fallacy; see Cherniss (*Selected Papers,* pp. 330–336), R. E. Allen (*Studies in Plato's Metaphysics* [New York, 1965], pp. 43–47), Sprague (*Plato's Use of Fallacy,* p. 27 n. 15), and Stuart ("An Interpretation," p. 273 n. 27).

121. Thus Benson Mates ("Identity and Predication in Plato," *Phronesis* 24 [1979], 222): "It is striking that in the dialogues no inter-

locutor ever hesitates a moment before agreeing to τὸ καλὸν καλόν
ἐστι ('the beautiful is beautiful'), τὸ δίκαιον δίκαιόν ἐστι ('the just is
just'), and the like; nobody ever says 'Wait a minute; that doesn't make
sense' or even 'I don't quite follow you, Socrates.' The reason, I think,
is that for any Greek such a sentence would be a logical truth, in the
Quinean sense that (a) it is true, and (b) every result of substituting
another adjective for its only non-logical constant is equally true. In
short, such a sentence would be felt as obviously and trivially true."

122. Here Socrates is hoisting Dionysodorus on Euthydemus'
lemma (cf. 293 B 8–C 1 and 298 C 4–5). Just as

1. He, who is a father, is a father; and
2. He, who is a man, is a man; and
3. Gold, which is gold, is gold; so too
4. The different, which is different, is different.

Therefore, Socrates has indeed established a positive sense in which
the different can be different, one that is the *same as* Dionysodorus'
thesis in *word,* but *different* in *meaning.*

123. Plato has shown how being "present with" eristics forces Socrates to imitate their wisdom. In fact, (D18) is ideally suited to serve
as a model for how eristic, under the guidance of wisdom, can be used
for a good end. Therefore, Socrates can argue "eristically" if he so
chooses, as Bonitz noted in his polemic with Susemihl (*Platonische Studien,* 3rd ed. [Berlin, 1886], p. 117 n. 13).

124. Thus Sprague (*Plato's Use of Fallacy,* p. 29) and Narcy (*Le Philosophe,* p. 91).

125. In this argument Dionysodorus' ascent and descent are reminiscent of his brother's in (E9) and illustrate the problem of generalizing "too hastily both in the way of induction and deduction" (Campbell, *Sophistes,* p. xii); cf. 279 E–280 A for the properly Socratic way to
conduct these leaps.

126. Hawtrey (*Commentary,* p. 179) and Waterfield (*Early Socratic
Dialogues,* p. 367).

127. A Greek writer normally uses the article to avoid any confusion that may arise in an ambiguous construction of this type. By contrast, Dionysodorus made no effort to avoid this ambiguity at 300 B
1–3 by limiting σιγῶντα and λέγοντα with the article. That Socrates is
not fooled by this amphiboly is clearly indicated through his plea for
"forgiveness" (301 D 4).

128. For the serious counterpart to this parody, consider the testi-
monial of Alcibiades from the *Symposium* (221 E 1–222 A 6): "If anyone consents to listen to the arguments of Socrates, they will at first

appear quite ridiculous (γελοῖοι); with such words and phrases are they wrapped on the outside . . . for he speaks of pack-asses, smiths, cobblers and tanners. . . . But when someone opens them up and, crawling inside as it were, obtains a fresh view, then he will find that they alone have intelligence (νοῦν) . . . they alone pertain to what is fitting (προσήκει) for a good man to consider."

129. So we should not be put off by critics who find here "Plato somewhat below his best" in this "verbose" argument (Hawtrey, *Commentary*, pp. 180–181). No one knew better than Plato how tedious eristic cavils can be; yet that fact did not prevent him from seeing the need to critique them. Plato can, of course, dismiss eristic disputes if the occasion warrants it; see *Republic* 436 C–437 A.

130. In just this second move Dionysodorus has already converted the term οἰκείαν into what he wants, for τὰ σαυτοῦ [οἰκεῖα] most naturally refers to Socrates' household goods or property.

131. After (D11) and (D13), this verbal machine returns to the possessive adjective "yours" for a third time. Thus Plato continues to parody the eristic mind for the way it automatically falls into familiar grooves and habitually retraces decayed ground.

132. Moreover, the role played by the three verbs (ἐπιγνοίης, γιγνώσκειν, and ἡγῇ/ἡγοῖο) in assisting these slight equivocations should not be underestimated. Dionysodorus begins the questioning as if he wanted to know whether Socrates has some way of "recognizing" and "knowing" what is his own, and then finishes by establishing a criterion for what Socrates "regards" or "holds" to be the conditions for the ownership of cows and sheep.

133. For the serious counterpart to this ironical pondering, see *Phaedo* 95 E 7–8.

134. Socrates of course does not want to suspect (ὑποπτεύσας) where the λόγος will end; see *Gorgias* 454 B 8–C 5.

135. As he explains below (302 D 1–2), Socrates can answer "no" to this question because the epithet πατρῷος is not properly applied to "his" Zeus. At 302 C 4–D 3, Socrates responds to Dionysodorus the way he did at 297 E 1–298 A 2, by detailing the facts of his family history as if the sophist were again asking for real information.

136. See *Phaedo* 62 B–D for a text that pictures the proper ordering of God, man, and beast.

137. This is not the silence that supervenes upon the defeated in eristic controversy, but that of the dialectician who can no longer endure contact with his antipode. Throughout (D20), Plato has carefully prepared the way for Socrates' withdrawal by picturing his growing impatience with the Crab; see 302 A 5–6, C 2–3, D 8, and E 6.

138. By bringing back Ktesippus as βοηθός and showing Dionyso-dorus operating on Heracles again (303 A 5–8), Plato carries us back to 297 C–D in order to leave us with the eerie feeling "Here they go again."

139. Familiar as ἀφίσταμαι is from *Olympian* 1.52, the term is par-ticularly apt for signaling Ktesippus' withdrawal and for prefiguring the epinician ode with its concluding reference to "water is best." For the evidence that a philosopher never "stands aside" from real dia-lectical encounters, see *Theaetetus* 169 B 6–8. Socrates brings his nar-ration to a close with a stylish use of asyndeton (303 A 9); cf. Aristotle, *Rhetoric* 3.19.1420 A 7.

140. See Sprague (*Plato's Use of Fallacy*, p. 17), Friedländer (*Plato*, 2: 336 n. 9), and Waterfield (*Early Socratic Dialogues*, p. 300).

141. Shorey (*Selected Papers*, 2: 131); also A. E. Taylor ("it is pre-cisely those who have been most occupied in the construction of anti-nomies who are most in danger of ending as sceptics and misologists"; "Διссοὶ Λόγοι," in *Varia Socratica* [Oxford, 1911], p. 91) and Camp-bell ("a vain-glorious scepticism"; *Sophistes*, p. xii).

EPILOGUE

1. Here the eristic θόρυβος is directly contrary to the atmosphere that Plato wants to prevail in philosophical discussion; cf. *Republic* 492 C.

2. Behind this part of the epilogue stands the Olympic event of the pancration, in which the athlete who first brings his opponent to the ground for three falls wins the victory. On the surface of the work's structure, the brothers are assumed to have achieved these three falls in episodes one, three, and five. Thus, the mock epinician ode, imme-diately following the fifth, is not an accident of literary arrangement.

3. Socrates signals the transition to his encomium with τὸ ἐπαινεῖν τε καὶ ἐγκωμιάζειν (303 C 3).

4. For example, when Socrates says that he has seen "no men so wise" (303 C 1), he means, by ironic inversion, that the brothers are the very paradigm of the "not-wise" or "ignorant"; in his remarks at 303 C 4–5, μακάριοι continues the fiction that they are "blessed" gods for their acquisition of virtue; τῆς θαυμαστῆς φύσεως refers to their baseborn talent to pervert philosophical wonder; ταχύ has the under-tone of "rashly" or "too quickly"; and ἐξείργασθον hints at the fact that they have destroyed dialectic.

5. As the primary instance of this type, we have Crito (304 C 8).

6. Cf. 284 E for the coldhearted nature of eristic discourse.

7. See 286 B 7, 297 A 8, and 299 C 8. For the critic of philosophy, shame attaches to Crito for simply being the friend of someone who partakes in this wordplay (305 A 2).

8. See R. K. Sprague (*Translation*, p. 62 n. 106) and R. S. W. Hawtrey (*Commentary on Plato's Euthydemus* [Philadelphia, 1981], pp. 186–187).

9. We can see the broader application of this passage (303 D 6–E 1) if we note that τόδε points forward to the upcoming general claim; that the use of the topical exemplum "white (λευκόν)," which has no direct point of contact with any previous passage, clearly indicates that Socrates is moving away from the immediate text to a general overview; that ἄλλο τῶν τοιούτων expands the entire focus so as to include the whole array of philosophical-pairs (τὰ ἐναντία); and that the denial that one thing is different from other things (ἑτέρων ἕτερον) refers quite generally to the power of eristic to wipe out all distinctions.

10. For earlier parodies of this theme, see 286 E 8–9, 288 A 5–6, and 301 C 3–5.

11. See 275 C 1 and 295 A 4.

12. But if they only talk to each other, then of course they cannot create an artificial demand in the marketplace for what the public doesn't need.

13. W. H. Thompson still provides the best analysis of the difficulties involved in trying to identify this critic; *The Phaedrus of Plato* (London, 1868), app. II, pp. 170–183.

14. For Lysias and Antiphon, see Jowett (*The Dialogues of Plato*, vol. 1, 4th ed. [Oxford, 1953], pp. 202–203); for Polycrates, see Hermann (*Geschichte und System* [Heidelberg, 1839], p. 629); for Thrasymachus, see A. G. Winckelmann (*Platonis Euthydemus* [Leipzig, 1833], xxxiv); and for Antiphon, see A. E. Taylor (*Plato, the Man and His Work* [London, 1927], p. 101). The best case for Isocrates is given by W. H. Thompson (*The Phaedrus of Plato*, pp. 179–182), who is supported in this by George Grote (*Plato and the other Companions of Socrates* [London, 1865], 1: 561), Paul Shorey (*What Plato Said* [Chicago, 1933], pp. 167–168), G. C. Field (*Plato and His Contemporaries* [London, 1930], p. 193), and I. M. Crombie (*An Examination of Plato's Doctrines* [London, 1963], 1: 224). The best case against Isocrates can be found in Ulrich von Wilamowitz-Moellendorff (*Platon*, 5th ed. [Berlin, 1959], 1: 304 and 2: 165–167) and Paul Friedländer (*Plato*, 2d ed. [Princeton, 1969], 1: 194), who both argue that the critic is a *type*, not a specifiable individual.

15. In addition to calling the epilogue an "afterthought" (*Plato*,

p. 556), Grote thinks that Plato wrote it "without reflecting whether it is consistent or not with what had preceded" (p. 559). Grote does suggest that up until this point where the epilogue is introduced the *Euthydemus* was "among the most popular of all the Platonic dialogues: not merely because of its dramatic vivacity and charm of expression, but because it would be heartily welcomed by the numerous enemies of Dialectic at Athens" (p. 555). For Taylor, the epilogue is a "sort of an appendix" to a "minor" dialogue (*Plato, the Man and His Work*, p. 100).

16. We should imagine that after a night's sleep, Crito awoke and went searching for Socrates to question him about what took place in the Lyceum.

17. For these vocative addresses, see 275 C 5, 283 A 1 and B 1, 292 E 8, 294 D 7, and, finally, 303 A 4 and 303 B 1.

18. Neither Crito nor the critic acknowledges that Socrates advised the brothers to keep their argument-game out of the public realm (304 A–B). One of Plato's strongest objections to eristic is precisely the hostility that it engenders when it is given public expression; see *Parmenides* 135 C–137 B and Grote (*Plato*, pp. 532–534).

19. Since the critic knows that Crito and Socrates are friends (305 A 2), he can assume that Crito will pass along this warning.

20. The antithesis between seeming and being continues throughout this final section; the goal of this class is *to appear* first (πρῶτοι δοκεῖν), whereas in reality they *are* third (τρίτοι ὄντες), and we are to judge them *to be* such as they *are* (τοιούτους εἶναι οἷοί εἰσι: 305 C 5–7). Crito, too, confirms that the critic imagines himself to be wise (εἶναι σοφός: 304 D 5).

21. Cf. *Republic* 494 A and *Gorgias* 487 C–D 2. These critics are lovers of opinion, not wisdom.

22. Grote (*Plato*, p. 559) and Leo Strauss ("On the *Euthydemus*," *Interpretation* 1 [1970], 20) have misunderstood this point. Both assume that Socrates is here citing Euthydemus as the true representative of philosophy. But since κολούεσθαι (305 D 7) depends upon ἡγοῦνται (305 D 2), Socrates is clearly presenting the view of the class that takes "those about Euthydemus" to represent philosophy.

23. Since the critic travels upon the horizontal axis of contentious debaters, he has attained the middle ground (μεθόρια) that is the distortion of the true middle (τὰ μεταξύ). Socrates and Kleinias also find themselves in the middle between the poles (271 A 8–B 8), but their orientation is directed upward, toward what is good, better, and best, and ultimately toward the divine, where God, not man, is the measure.

24. The use of ἡλικίαν here (306 D 5) should cast light on the disputed meaning of ἡλικίαν at 271 B 3. What prompts Crito to recall

Critobulus is the critical moment of his son's age, not his size; see G. J. De Vries, "Notes on Some Passages in the *Euthydemus*," *Mnemosyne* 25 (1972), 42.

25. Plato's account of the origin, generation, and full force of this slander continues until 497 A. The critics of philosophy turn out to be those φιλόδοξοι (480 A) whose refutation requires that Socrates unfold the true philosophical nature, as lover of wisdom (484 A–487 A).

26. Besides "utterly wicked (παμπόνηροι)," "useless (ἄχρηστοι)," and "bastards (νόθοι)," Socrates also calls these perverse philosophers κακοί, ἀνθρωπίσκοι, χαλκέως φαλακροῦ καὶ σμικροῦ, and ἀλλόκοτοι (with ἀλλόκοτοι, cf. ἀλλόκοτος, 306 E 5). These sham artists give birth to "sophisms" (σοφίσματα: 496 A 8), the only use of this term in Plato that approaches the sense given to it by Aristotle (see *Topics* 8.162 A 16–17).

27. Cf. *Republic* 487 B–D with *Euthydemus* 305 A 4.

28. We have at last uncovered why the *Euthydemus* has always been a goldmine for unitarians. It is difficult to escape the impression that the "fixing" of the *Euthydemus* before the *Meno* has not been carried out by scholars who were entirely motivated by disinterested curiosity. Rather, there seems to be at work here a desire to identify the Socratic episodes of the dialogue as evidence for the Plato who speaks for Socrates in the early dialogues and, therefore, as evidence for "Socratic" as opposed to "Platonic" philosophy. In this project the dating hypothesis has functioned as a convenient tool for expanding the evidence of that Socratic philosophy. The inadequacy of this method, however, has been glaringly revealed in its inability to account thus far for more than twenty pages of Burnet's text. If the partisans of development are still satisfied with their pre-*Meno* date, then our analysis has shown that even in an "early" or "transitional" dialogue, Plato can consciously and deliberately treat problems that he usually reserves for middle or late works, and so the *Euthydemus* provides irrefutable evidence for the essential unity of its author's thought. Or if, as is more likely, they now want to place the *Euthydemus* with or after the *Meno*, then it is "Platonic" philosophy that must undergo the expansion of the evidence, and as a result they are now required to admit that the *Euthydemus* constitutes a significant contribution to the mature, fully developed phase of its author's thought. Either way, the current trend in Euthydemian criticism is refuted, and Paul Shorey is again proven to be correct.

29. Harold Cherniss, *Selected Papers* (Leiden, 1977), p. 284.

30. By fusing the twofold λόγοι, eristic and dialectic, in his single dialogue, Plato instantiates what G. B. Kerferd has identified as the

art of antilogic. "It consists," he tells us, "in opposing one logos to another logos, or in discovering or drawing attention to the presence of such an opposition in an argument or in a thing or state of affairs" (*The Sophistic Movement* [Cambridge, 1981], p. 63); cf. Cherniss (*Selected Papers*, p. 28). It is fair to say then that the *Euthydemus* constitutes not only Plato's grandiose satire (ὁ γελοῖος λόγος) on sophistic antilogy but also his correction (ὁ ἐπανορθωτικὸς λόγος) of its defects. As such, this dialogue not only deserves to be considered by scholars who analyze the problems of antilogy in Euripides, Aristophanes, Thucydides, and others; it also should figure prominently in discussions on the *Parmenides, Theaetetus,* and, above all, the *Sophist,* where the name that most especially identifies the beast is ἀντιλογικός (*Sophist* 232 B).

SELECT BIBLIOGRAPHY

Allen, R. E. *Plato's "Euthyphro" and the Earlier Theory of Forms.* New York: 1970.

——, ed. *Studies in Plato's Metaphysics.* New York: 1965.

Bergson, Henri. "Laughter." In *Comedy,* ed. Wylie Sypher. 4th ed. Baltimore: 1986.

Bigger, Charles P. *Participation: A Platonic Inquiry.* Baton Rouge: 1968.

Bonitz, Hermann. *Platonische Studien.* 3rd ed. Berlin: 1886.

Borgeaud, Philippe. "The Open Entrance to the Closed Palace of the King: The Greek Labyrinth in Context." *History of Religions* 14 (1974), 1–27.

Bueno, Aníbal A. "Aristotle, the Fallacy of Accident, and the Nature of Predication: A Historical Inquiry." *Journal of the History of Philosophy* 26 (1988), 5–24.

Bundy, Elroy L. *Studia Pindarica.* Berkeley: 1986.

Bury, R. G. "The Later Platonism." *Journal of Philology* 23 (1895), 161–201.

Canto, Monique. *L'Intrigue Philosophique. Essai sur l'Euthydème de Platon* Paris: 1987.

Cherniss, Harold. *Selected Papers.* Leiden: 1977.

Cornford, F. M. *Plato's Theory of Knowledge.* London: 1935.

Crombie, I. M. *An Examination of Plato's Doctrines.* Vols. 1 and 2. London: 1963.

De Vries, G. J. "Notes on Some Passages in the *Euthydemus.*" *Mnemosyne* 25 (1972), 42–55.

Festugière, A. J. *Les Trois "Protreptiques" de Platon. Euthydème, Phédon, Epinomis.* Paris: 1973.

Fontenrose, Joseph. *Python.* Berkeley: 1959.

Friedländer, Paul, *Plato.* Trans. Hans Meyerhoff. Vol. 2. 2d ed. Princeton: 1969.

Gifford, Edwin H., ed. *The Euthydemus of Plato.* Rev. ed. Oxford: 1905.

Grote, George. *Plato and the Other Companions of Socrates.* Vol. 1. London: 1865. Pp. 527–564.

Guthrie, W. K. C. *A History of Greek Philosophy.* Vols. 3 and 4. Cambridge: 1969–1975.

Hackforth, R. "On Some Passages of Plato's *Philebus.*" *Classical Quarterly* 83 (1939), 23–29.

Hawtrey, R. S. W. *Commentary on Plato's Euthydemus.* Philadelphia: 1981.

———. "How Do Dialecticians Use Diagrams—Plato, *Euthydemus* 290b–c." *Apeiron* 12 (1978), 14–18.

———. "Plato, *Euthydemus* 296 C 8–10." *Liverpool Classical Monthly* 4 (1979), 41.

———. "Plato, Socrates, and the Mysteries: A Note." *Antichthon* 10 (1976), 22–24.

Hinrichs, Gerard. "The *Euthydemus* as a Locus of the Socratic Elenchus." *New Scholasticism* 25 (1951), 178–183.

Jowett, Benjamin. *The Dialogues of Plato.* Vol. 1. 4th ed. Oxford: 1953.

Kahn, C. H. "Did Plato Write Socratic Dialogues?" *Classical Quarterly* 31 (1981), 305–320.

———. "The Greek Verb 'To Be' and the Concept of Being." *Foundations of Language* 2 (1966), 245–265.

———. "Plato's *Charmides* and the Proleptic Reading of Socratic Dialogues." *Journal of Philosophy* 85 (1988), 541–549.

Kerferd, G. B. *The Sophistic Movement.* Cambridge: 1981.

Keulen, Hermann. *Untersuchungen zu Platons "Euthydem."* Wiesbaden: 1971.

Klosko, George. "Thrasymachos' *Eristikos:* The *Agon Logon* in *Republic* I." *Polity* 17 (1984), 5–29.

Linforth, I. M. *The Corybantic Rites in Plato.* University of California Publications in Classical Philology, vol. 13 (1946), 121–172.

Mates, Benson. "Identity and Predication in Plato." *Phronesis* 24 (1979), 211–229.

Mohr, Richard. "Forms in Plato's *Euthydemus.*" *Hermes* 112 (1984), 296–300.

Narcy, Michel. *Le Philosophe et son double.* Paris: 1984.

Neitzel, Heinz. "Platon, Euthydemos 286e." *Hermes* 112 (1984), 372–377.

O'Sullivan, J. N. "Plato, *Euthydemus* 296c8–10 (Burnet)." *Liverpool Classical Monthly* 4 (1979), 61–62.

Praechter, Karl. "Platon und *Euthydemos.*" *Philologus* 87 (1932), 121–135.

Rabinowitz, W. Gerson. *Aristotle's Protrepticus and the Sources of Its Reconstruction.* University of California Publications in Classical Philology (1957).

Robinson, Richard. "Ambiguity." *Mind* 50 (1941), 140–155.

———. "Plato's Consciousness of Fallacy." *Mind* 51 (1942), 97–114.

———. *Plato's Earlier Dialectic.* 2d ed. Oxford: 1953.

Rouse, W. H. D., trans. *Euthydemus.* In *The Collected Dialogues of Plato,* ed. Edith Hamilton and Huntington Cairns. Princeton: 1961.

Routh, M. J. *Platonis Euthydemus et Gorgias.* Oxford: 1784.

Ryle, Gilbert. "Dialectic in the Academy." In *Aristotle on Dialectic,* ed. G. E. L. Owen. Oxford, 1968. Pp. 69–79.

Scolnicov, Samuel. "Plato's *Euthydemus:* A Study on the Relations between Logic and Education." *Scripta Classica Israelica* 8 (1981), 19–29.

Shorey, Paul. *Selected Papers.* Vols. 1 and 2. New York: 1980.

———. *The Unity of Plato's Thought.* Chicago: 1903.

———. *What Plato Said.* Chicago: 1933.

Sidgwick, Henry. "The Sophists." *Journal of Philology* 4 (1872), 288–307.

Smith, J. L. "Plato and the Paradox of False Statements: A Study of the *Euthydemus* and the *Sophist.*" Ph.D. diss., University of Virginia, 1975.

Soreth, Marion. "Zur relativen Chronologie von *Menon* und *Euthydem.*" *Hermes* 83 (1955), 377–379.

Sprague, R. K. "Logic and Literary Form in Plato." *Personalist* 48 (1967), 560–572.

———. *The Older Sophists.* Columbia, S.C.: 1972.

———. "Parmenides' Sail and Dionysodorus' Ox." *Phronesis* 12 (1967), 91–98.

———. "Platonic Unitarianism, or What Shorey Said." *Classical Philology* 71 (1976), 109–112.

———. *Plato's Philosopher-King.* Columbia, S.C.: 1976.

———. "Plato's Sophistry (II)." *Aristotelian Society Suppl.* Vol. 51 (1977), 45–61.

———. *Plato's Use of Fallacy.* London: 1962.

———. "Socrates' Safest Answer: *Phaedo* 100D." *Hermes* 96 (1968), 632–635.

———, trans. and ed. *Plato, Euthydemus.* Indianapolis: 1965.

Stanford, W. B. *Ambiguity in Greek Literature.* Oxford: 1939.

Stough, Charlotte. "Forms and Explanations in the *Phaedo.*" *Phronesis* 21 (1976), 1–30.

Strauss, Leo. "On the *Euthydemus.*" *Interpretation* 1 (1970), 1–20.

Stuart, D. G. "An Interpretation of Plato's *Euthydemus.*" Ph.D. diss., Yale University, 1980.

Szlezák, Thomas Alexander. "Sokrates' Spott über Geheimhaltung: Zum Bild des φιλόσοφος in Platons *Euthydemos.*" *Antike und Abendland* 26 (1980), 75–89.

Taylor, A. E. "Δισσοὶ Λόγοι." In *Varia Socratica*. Oxford: 1911. Pp. 91–128.

———. *Plato, the Man and His Work*. London: 1927.

Thompson, E. S., ed. *The Meno of Plato*. London: 1901.

Thompson, W. H., ed. *The Phaedrus of Plato*. London: 1868.

Vanhoutte, M. "La Notion de la Σοφία d'après l' *Euthydème* de Platon." Ph.D. diss. Louvain, 1942.

Vlastos, Gregory. "Elenchus and Mathematics: A Turning-Point in Plato's Philosophical Development." *American Journal of Philology* 109 (1988), 362–396.

———. "Happiness and Virtue in Socrates' Moral Theory." *Proceedings of the Cambridge Philological Society* (1984), 181–213.

———. "Socrates' Disavowal of Knowledge." *Philosophical Quarterly* 35 (1985), 1–31.

———. *Socrates, Ironist and Moral Philosopher*. Ithaca, N.Y.: 1991.

———. "The Socratic Elenchus." *Oxford Studies in Ancient Philosophy* 1 (1983), 27–58.

Von Arnim, Hans. *Platos Jugenddialoge*. Leipzig: 1914.

Waterfield, Robin. *Early Socratic Dialogues*. Harmondsworth: 1987.

Wilamowitz-Moellendorff, Ulrich von. *Platon*. 5th ed. Berlin: 1959.

Winckelmann, A. G. *Platonis Euthydemus*. Leipzig: 1833.

Designer: Ina Clausen
Compositor: G&S Typesetters
Text: Baskerville
Display: Baskerville
Printer: Thomson-Shore, Inc.
Binder: Thomson-Shore, Inc.